More praise for *Point of Purchase*:

"It's easy to condemn shopping, but it's more difficult—and more important—to understand it. If you've noticed that shopping is becoming ever more inescapable and ever less satisfying, Sharon Zukin's intimate yet authoritative exploration of the retail experience will tell you why."
—Thomas Hine, author of *I Want That! How We All Became Shoppers*

"Over the last two decades, Sharon Zukin has expertly guided us through urban spaces and what she inventively called 'landscapes of power.' Now, in *Point of Purchase*, she steers us through today's 'landscapes of consumption'—the department stores, discount chains, consumer guides, and Internet websites where Americans are daily redefining themselves. With Zukin as our intrepid navigator, the familiar waters of commerce suddenly become the cutting edge of contemporary American culture."
—Lizabeth Cohen, author of *A Consumers' Republic*

"A fascinating story…Zukin is very good at exploring the deeper cosmologies that lie behind ordinary acts [and] she has produced a mature work of analysis."
—Daniel Miller, *Contexts*

point of purchase

of

purchase

HOW SHOPPING CHANGED

AMERICAN CULTURE

SHARON ZUKIN

Routledge
Taylor & Francis Group

NEW YORK AND LONDON

Published in 2005 by
Routledge
270 Madison Avenue
New York, NY 10016
www.routledge-ny.com

Published in Great Britain by
Routledge
2 Park Square, Milton Park
Abingdon, Oxon OX14 4RN
www.routledge.co.uk

First Routledge hardback edition, 2004
First Routledge paperback edition, 2005

Routledge is an imprint of the Taylor & Francis Group.
Printed in the United States of America on acid-free paper.

Library of Congress Cataloging-in-Publication Data

Zukin, Sharon.
    Point of purchase: how shopping changed American culture / Sharon Zukin.
        p. cm.
ISBN 0-415-94597-6 (hbk) – ISBN 0-415-95043-0 (pbk)
Includes bibliographical references and index.
        1. Consumption (Economics)—Social aspects—United States. 2. Shopping—Social aspects—United States—History. 3. Consumer behavior—United States—History.
I. Title.
        HC110.C6Z84 2003
        306.3'0973—dc21   2003009421

For Frances A. Zukin
and in memory of Vincent D'Attolico

One knew of places in ancient Greece where the way led down into the underworld. Our waking existence likewise is a land which, at certain hidden points, leads down into the underworld—a land full of inconspicuous places from which dreams arise.

—Walter Benjamin, "The Arcades of Paris"

contents

prologue
what shopping is

Take a day off. . . . Go shopping.
> —Mayor Rudolph Giuliani, asking New Yorkers
> not to go to their jobs in the Wall Street area
> on the day after terrorists destroyed the
> World Trade Center, September 11, 2001

When terrorists struck the World Trade Center, in Lower Manhattan, on September 11, 2001, Mayor Rudolph Giuliani rapidly took command. With three hundred thousand stockbrokers, office workers, security guards, and food vendors seeking refuge in other parts of the city, emergency workers painstakingly began to clear the debris. Thousands had died, and many police officers and fire fighters also lost their lives when the towers came down. Not only the downtown financial district but most of the city—and the nation as a whole—was emotionally drained. But the mayor tried to establish a sense of normalcy. New Yorkers could find comfort, he said, if they thought of this terrible time as a day off from work. Watching the mayor on TV, I expected him to counsel us to stay at home with our families, to relax and play a game of softball, or to pray. Instead, he urged us to go shopping.

The underground shopping mall at the World Trade Center lay in ruins: plate-glass windows shattered at The Gap, lights darkened at Borders Books, bottles of Tylenol and bars of Dial soap buried under rubble at Duane Reade drugs. Farmers from upstate New York, who had brought the tart, green apples of early fall to the regional Greenmarket at Church and Liberty Streets, which was held every Tuesday and Thursday in the Twin Towers' shadow, ran for their lives.

But uptown, at Thirty-fourth Street, shoppers were just getting ready to enter Macy's, where they would hunt for bargains between the back-to-school sales and the weeklong promotions that honor Columbus Day. On the East Side, Bloomingdale's was opening its doors to customers who were looking for the latest fashions from Ralph Lauren, Calvin Klein, and DKNY. Over on Madison Avenue, black-clad sales clerks were dusting off showcases of bright-colored silk scarves, sleek cashmere sweaters, and solid gold watches at the same designers' flagship stores, as well as at the boutiques of Hermès, Prada, Max Mara, and Bulgari. Meanwhile, out in the suburbs of Long Island and New Jersey, shoppers were driving into mammoth parking lots surrounding the "big box" stores; alighting from their cars, they would push giant metal carts into Wal-Mart, Kmart, and Home Depot, and stream through the broad, familiar aisles.

It was all, in a way, very normal. You see people shopping every day. Yet Mayor Giuliani understood just how closely shopping is keyed to our expectations of normalcy—and also defines the spiritual territory of our lives.

Think about it. Do you ever daydream of finding the perfect pair of pants? How much time do you spend doing "research" before buying a new computer? Can you remember the first time you went shopping for yourself—probably with your older sister? For nearly all of us, shopping shapes our daily paths through space and time; major purchases—a computer, a car, a house—mark ritual stages in our lives. We separate ourselves from others by deciding where to shop and what to buy—yet in no other activity are we so immediately in the presence of others. In normal and abnormal times, shopping is both a tedious chore and a moral preoccupation. Love it or hate it, shopping is our life.

But everyone has their own approach to shopping.

When my friend Kathy has nothing to do on a Saturday afternoon, she calls her mom and suggests that they go shopping. They meet for lunch, and then spend the afternoon going from store to store. They browse through the racks, fingering the silk and denim and microfiber, trying on a sweater or a pair of pants, especially if it's on sale, and making mental notes about items that might be useful at another time, or for one of their friends, or for Kathy's father.

"My husband laughs at us," Kathy says, with a chuckle of her own. "He says we're 'vapid.'"

Paul, Kathy's husband, hates to go to stores. He gets bored after twenty minutes of pawing through sweaters heaped on counters, he can never spot a salesperson, and he swears he never finds khakis in his size among the choices at The Gap. When Paul logs onto the Internet, however, he's a happy shopper. He spends hours checking the prices of computers and comparing new models, and he enters his measurements at Lands' End with the greatest satisfaction.

And then there's me. Unlike Kathy, I don't consider myself a shopper. And unlike Paul, I haven't found happiness shopping on the Internet. But at some point during the 1990s, it became clear that for me, too, shopping was taking over my world.

It wasn't that I was shopping more, myself. Except for the birth of my daughter, in 1990, which temporarily bonded me to the 100 percent-cotton infants' outfits at Macy's and the plastic playthings at Toys "R" Us, my shopping habits have remained unchanged for years.

I take weekly strolls to East Village Cheese, for prewrapped sections of Brie and H&H bagels at cut-rate prices.

I take occasional longer walks to Dean & Deluca for artisanal goat cheese made by small farmers in France and Oregon, seasonal wild salmon jetted in from Alaska, and a dazzling array of wild mushrooms, breads, and pastries. Half the fun of shopping at Dean & Deluca is just looking at this richness and feeling like a "regular" when I hear the comments of tourists and suburbanites who come to marvel at the bounty.

I am also a frequent customer at the small, storefront dairy where Joe makes the best smoked mozzarella in Manhattan and at the nearby pasta shop where the owner sits behind the cash register and occasionally shares her recipes with me. Working in a warehouse nearby, other family members make the sheets of green and white dough that are sliced into strips of fettucine and lasagne on an ancient black machine in the back of the store.

Every few days, I walk in another direction, to the Jefferson Market, an old-style grocery store and meat market whose plate-glass windows display, year in and year out, rows of uniformly round, brightly colored apples and grapefruit. Inside, behind a high, refrigerated showcase of white enamel and glass, the last remaining Irish butchers in New York City ply their knives and chat with customers, never forgetting to ask whether they should trim one more layer of fat from a sirloin steak.

Every few weeks, I visit the coffee bean store, where Peter, the grandson of the original owner, who is around my age, used to wax philosophical about the weather in Brazil and its effect on coffee prices, and about the old days on Bleecker Street in his parents' generation, before he got busy with the wholesale side of the business, mail orders, and Internet sales, and disappeared from the shop. Peter sold me my espresso machine, and taught me how to wiggle my coffee cup under the steamer spout to foam milk for cappuccino.

And, as often as I can, I make a pilgrimage to the Greenmarket at Union Square, where Vincent D'Attolico, an electrician from Brooklyn who moved to the country to grow organic vegetables, taught me how to choose the deep-colored squash for their sweetness, and Elizabeth sells blackberry jam and offers tastes of apple, and tells me about the Central American farm workers she has brought to the Hudson Valley to pick these apples and mill them for sweet, thick cider, and the usually quiet Keith talks with great passion, if you ask him, about the risks in genetically engineered food. In summer, the melons and tomatoes at the farmers' market are of such exceptional lushness and ripeness that I stuff my canvas bag and strain my arms to carry home too many peaches, zucchini, and ears of corn. Later in the year, I fill my bag with leeks, cabbages, Winesap apples, and golden new potatoes.

My farmers' market on the cusp of a new season—between the apples of fall and the herbs of spring. Photo by Richard Rosen.

Underneath these grand themes that punctuate the rhythms and seasons of my life, my shopping routines are bounded by a small supermarket, pharmacy, and dry cleaner, all of them around the corner from my house. Making my rounds to these local shops helps me to feel both serene and secure. The variety of goods, the scale of the stores, the easy conversations with farmers and shopkeepers: these are things I love about New York; they make the city's huge size and fast pace bearable.

But most Americans, and many people around the world, no longer live like this. Unlike me, they don't walk home from the market with organically grown heads of lettuce stuffed into their canvas bag. They don't get to chat with the local egg seller or book dealer.

Instead, most women—and growing numbers of men—drive to the Super Stop 'N Shop, where they cruise the aisles with shopping carts the size of sport utility vehicles, stalking frozen vegetables and dough-wrapped snacks. When they come to the checkout line, a bored cashier shifts each package from the conveyor belt to the scanner so a computerized cash register can read a bar code that cannot be deciphered by the human eye. Then shoppers wheel their carts, now overflowing with giant brown paper

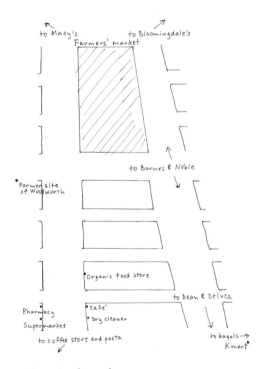

My shopping routes. Drawing by author.

bags, to an enormous parking lot, and drive away with a week's supply of Hamburger Helper, Skim Milk Plus, jam-filled granola bars, and diet soda.

I admit to a perverse envy. We New Yorkers complain about the narrow selection of brands in our small supermarkets, and I feel defeated when the store around the corner runs out of vanilla ice cream during a heat wave. When I visit a friend in Williamstown, Massachusetts—a college town whose two blocks of Main Street and small stretch of state highway do not provide much scope for shopping—she kindly takes my daughter and me on a field trip to the local Super Stop 'N Shop, so we, too, can cruise the aisles as wide as boulevards and marvel at gallon-size containers of mayonnaise, while we gape at the miraculously low prices, which are always cheaper than in the city.

And our visits to Wal-Mart and Kmart! Racks of shirts and pants as far as the eye can see, followed by basketballs and tennis rackets, bicycles and toaster ovens, toys and toiletries, all organized in a functionalism more severe than Le Corbusier's. White fluorescent lighting floods metal shelves and bare vinyl or cement floors, in a supersize box of a windowless building surrounded by parking lots. Signs of prices promise heaven will come when you buy two, three, or even four items for the price of one. There are too many savings and too much temptation: the superstores reverse Mies van der Rohe's modernist credo, in the devout belief that More Is Less.

In the last few years, however, the gap has narrowed between my New York way of shopping and Super Stop 'N Shop. Kmart opened a branch a few blocks away, on the site of the old John Wanamaker department store, from which Wanamaker's had decamped before my time, replaced by back offices of American Express. By the mid-nineties, the building was vacant once again, until Kmart rented the ground floor and basement, installed an entrance leading directly into the store's basement from the adjacent subway station, and attempted to attract the area's jaded, and hip, young shoppers. At Kmart I now buy six-packs of paper towels, giant boxes of dishwashing detergent, and rolls of toilet paper by the dozen.

Since the nineties, my neighborhood has changed. New York City has changed. And it has something to do with shopping. I've seen more stores—and bigger stores—opening all around me. The number of consumer magazines has doubled. Each time I log onto the Internet, the screen is covered by pop-up advertisements for retail websites. And every place I travel, from the gift shop in the art museum to the mail-order catalog in a hotel bedroom, urges me to buy.

The American way: customers waiting in line at Costco, Astoria, Queens. Photo courtesy www.hellskitchen.net.

Shopping is consuming our lives—but bringing us less satisfaction. More goods are for sale—but we can never find exactly what we want. Each store promises happiness, every label guarantees high quality—but we're still dreaming of the virtuous ideal: Truth. Beauty. Value.

Everyone knows that shopping is no longer a simple matter of buying a can of beans at the corner store. The activity of shopping keeps modern economies afloat, links the family looking for jeans at Wal-Mart in California to factories in China and Bangladesh, and enables us—if we buy and sell on eBay—to turn our shopping into an entrepreneurial investment. But shopping is also a cultural activity. Because it is usually what we do when we "go out," shopping is how we satisfy our need to socialize—to feel we are a part of public life. Moreover, we often feel that shopping is our most available means of creative expression. We forget that our purchasing patterns are anxiously scrutinized by market researchers, stock analysts, and politicians; we put aside the nasty thought that our choices are determined by product designers, advertisements, and stores. In fact, whether we shop at the Super Stop 'N Shop or the farmers' market, shopping is both our most creative and our most controlled behavior.

Shopping is our means of pursuing value. It has become an arena of struggle, in recent years, precisely because it is one of the few means we have left of creating value. Deprived as we are of direct contact with nature or with making goods ourselves, shopping gives us a way to satisfy our drive for beauty, to get what we think is "the best," and to hone our ability to make judgments, shape time, and use money. We shop because we long for value—for a virtuous ideal of value that we no longer get from religion, work, or politics.

Since the nineties, however, shopping has become our *principal* strategy for creating value. With the shift of the economy toward consumption, and our weaker attachment to traditional art forms, religions, and politics, shopping has come to define who we, as individuals, are and what we, as a society, want to become. The social spaces and cultural labels of shopping offer us hope of achieving the American Dream: Low prices define our conception of democracy. Brand names represent our search for a better life. Designer boutiques embody the promise of an ever-improving self.

I started believing that I was born to write about shopping when I realized that it defines the way we think about society. I don't accept the idea that we're all shopaholics, or even that the main purpose of shopping—despite the impact of consumption on our economy—is to buy more things. Neither am I overly impressed by the impact of advertising, despite the way it creeps into our consciousness and surrounds us with things to buy. No, I am fascinated by the everyday normalcy of shopping—the way it has taken over the way we think about getting everything we need to survive. The normalcy of shopping makes us accept as natural the idea that humans exist to sell and buy. Shopping teaches us how to live in a market society.

Just because I feel I was born to write about shopping doesn't mean I was born to shop. I don't own a car, and I haven't moved in years, so I don't have to do the kind of shopping—for a house and car—that most Americans are automatically plugged into. And if we're talking about my personality, I would never describe myself as "a shopper." (My worst nightmare would be to be locked up overnight in Bloomingdale's.) I don't even enter a store unless I have something specific in mind. (I looked for months to find just the right watch, but since I bought my Ole Matthiesson wristwatch fifteen years ago, I have worn it every day.) I don't go to outlet stores. (But I love Macy's sales on underwear: Buy Three—if you can find your size—and Get One Free.) If I have a free afternoon, it doesn't occur to me to spend it in a store. (Don't ask me to meet you at the mall.) And I never—well, hardly ever—buy anything on the Internet.

I've always liked being surrounded by stores. To me they say: Big City. In Philadelphia, where I grew up, I happily ran errands for my mother at the butcher store, bakery, and delicatessen on the shopping street in our neighborhood. I walked to the movies nearby, on Broad Street, where I had a student savings account at the local bank and shopped for school supplies and toys at Woolworth's. Twice a month, I went downtown, to Center City, with my mom to visit the department stores. I loved the way Broad Street, which bisects the city, stretched for miles with store after store on every block. I never realized how narrow the streets are, by design, in Philadelphia because there were so many shop windows filled with dresses, or cakes, or jewelry, or books: endless possibilities of reinvention.

When I moved to New York, as a college freshman, I was fascinated by the stores. Compared to Philadelphia, all of Manhattan was a "downtown" shopping district, and Broadway, with its endlessly repeating commercial clusters, stretched even farther than Broad Street. It wasn't that I spent a lot of time inside stores, or buying things. I just liked the crowds, the big glass windows, and the variety of experiences that they suggested.

Maybe I do have shopping in my blood. My grandparents on both sides, at some point in their lives, owned stores. Like many Jews who came to the United States around 1900, they found it fairly easy to save money, open a shop, and sell things. My family didn't get rich as shopkeepers— no story of Macy's or Sears, Roebuck here—but the idea of having a store, even if it disappeared many years before my birth, was a kind of heritage within the family. My husband's grandparents also owned a store. They came here from Russia and somehow made their way to Kansas City— maybe as peddlers, or maybe they just took a train—and opened a corner grocery. Though that store also failed to make a fortune, it deepened my interest in, and my connection to, what goes on, on both sides of the counter.

For most of my adult years, I have lived near Broadway, in Lower Manhattan, where I am in touch with the ghosts of famous stores of the past. Walking on Broadway, I am constantly reminded by the old, cast-iron buildings, with their big, plate-glass windows, of the crowds that must have shopped there a hundred years ago. Brooks Brothers. Lord & Taylor. Tiffany. B. Altman. If I walk from Bond Street up to Nineteenth Street, then over to Sixth Avenue and back down to Union Square, I can cover the whole history of mass consumption in New York City. Fortunately, this is still a vibrant shopping area, and I can feel the pulsating rhythm of the late-afternoon crowd striding past store windows up and down Broadway, the hum of bargain hunting, often in different languages, along Fourteenth Street, and the thrill of discovery when I notice an old hardware store that is still hanging on despite the steady advance of chain stores and boutiques. And, best of all, though I live in the heart of New York City, I can go to the farmers' market.

It's not enough—and not even right—to trace the pervasiveness of shopping in our time to an excess of greed, "luxury fever," or the "urge to splurge." To understand where, and why, I shop, you have to look at both big structures of the economy and culture and little structures of feeling and desire. You have to look at the institutions that form the supply side of consumption: business organizations dedicated to selling us things, financial consultants with an appetite for corporate growth, and repeated demonstrations that, in a market economy, social status and distinction can be bought. You also have to read the magazines and consumer guides that create the very idea of lifestyle. And you will only understand what the public has become if you examine the branded stores, boutiques, discount chains, and websites where we shop. For this is where we form our dreams about a perfect society . . . and about a perfect self.

1

a brief history
of shopping

Cash or charge?
—Barbie "Shop With Me" cash register, 2001

Some years ago, when I lived in Belgrade, capital of the former Yugoslavia, I liked to shop at the farmers' market. On weekend mornings in the spring, I would get up early, before the sun grew hot and the streets became dusty and airless, and walk to the local *pijaca* (pi´-ah-tza) to buy the few supplies I needed for the week.

Older men, and women of every age, milled around thirty or forty outdoor stands, fingering tomatoes, apples, heads of lettuce, eggplant, beans—whatever fruit and vegetables were in season. (During the long winter months, when the weather was cold, there were only piles of cabbages.) A few stands, enclosed by windows, sold loaves of white bread, most of which was made at large, worker-owned bakeries, and several sold thin leaves of homemade dough for pita or strudel. Older women, their gray hair covered with scarves, stood at tables selling whole chickens, loose eggs, and cheese, the way farm women always do at markets. "*Beli sir,*" they called out. "White cheese. Taste it, Miss! Taste it!"

If you came close, and knew the routine, you asked the woman what kind of cheese she had. There are only two kinds of fresh cheese in this area of the world—dry and saline, like feta cheese, and moister, younger cheese, like ricotta, that only hints at salt. "Not too salty!" I always said.

The cheese seller would immediately spear a new ball of cheese from her barrel or, if one was already on the table, deftly cut a swath with her knife. I can't remember whether I took the piece directly from the knife blade or picked it up from the table with my fingers, but I enjoyed the subtle taste of fresh cheese in my mouth and the feeling that I was about to make an important decision.

If I liked the cheese, I asked how much it cost. But when the woman named a price, I usually tried to bargain. It's not that the cheese was so expensive—certainly not for someone who came from New York City—but trying to bargain was part of the experience. Bargaining showed I knew the routine and used the language as well—or almost as well—as a native. Though I wasn't Yugoslav by blood, and had only a few close friends in Belgrade, shopping at the *pijaca* every week made me feel I belonged.

This to me is the origin, the ur-experience, of shopping. A true marketplace brings buyers face to face with sellers; the resulting exchange begins in rough equality and ends in mutual benefit. The best exchange, I think, is when the seller is also the producer—the baker who made the bread, or the farmer who made the cheese, that you buy. But if you can't get this close to the producer, the next-best thing is getting close to the goods—close enough to touch and taste them—and to talk to a knowledgeable seller.

Even in ancient cities, sellers were often merchants rather than producers. They bought oil and cheese from farmers, or brokered long-distance trade; their stores dotted the streets, setting the tone of each quarter and gathering their own frequent customers. Around the Roman Forum, there were streets that specialized in selling books, or spices, or bronzes. The Via dell'Abbondanza, in Pompeii, ran the whole length of the city—like Broad Street, in Philadelphia—and had as many shops and workshops as Fifth Avenue. Customers were as likely to buy from artisans or slaves as they were to meet the merchant himself. But in these small shops, they had a direct relation with both the goods and sellers. Merchants undoubtedly set different prices and offered different qualities of goods, yet buyers decided what to buy directly—not on the basis of brand names or advertisements.

Shopping from local merchants is the other ur-experience of shopping. Every developing society goes through the process of moving trade indoors, from public markets and bazaars to specialized stores. And these stores eventually become bigger, more complicated collections of articles for sale. Like a bureaucracy, department stores lose the ancient merchant's immediacy and special relations with customers—in order to bring shoppers the world.

Olive oil shop, Pompeii, buried by volcanic lava in the year 79. Photo by Richard Rosen, 2002.

In basic economic terms, shopping is a complex system for integrating people into worlds of goods. Trading in a simple village marketplace gets goods to circulate from one group of people to another, and not only satisfies, but also stimulates desires that can't be satisfied at home. Likewise, shopping in the supermarket or shopping mall distributes the bread, frozen orange juice, jeans, and compact discs that are produced by some of us, to others who use them. These days, even more than in Pompeii or colonial America, most consumers are located far from where their products are made. Our orange juice comes from Brazil as well as Florida; the jeans we buy at Target and The Gap are made in the Northern Mariana Islands or in Bahrain. We shop in corporate-owned chain stores where we don't know the salespeople, cashiers, security guards, or owners. Just as in a simple marketplace, however, the very activity of coming into immediate contact with goods—smelling the strong aroma of coffee or fresh bread, squeezing the tomatoes, or even, with less sensual gratification, reading the labels on the frozen food or compact disc—excites us. We want to be around these things; often, we want to have them on our bodies and in our homes.

The bustling crowd contributes to our excitement—to the point of frenzy, when you have to climb over other people to get items from a sale rack, or irritation, when you have to wait in a long line at the checkout counter. But regardless of how processed the goods may be, or how processed by the routines we, ourselves, feel, shopping is the zero point where the whole economy of people, products, and money comes together.

This is not just a matter of exchanging money for goods. As the sociologist Georg Simmel had already pointed out by 1910, all exchanges in a money economy involve the "objectification" of value.[1] The things I buy have to be worth something to me—and this worth may be social, as when I buy something to earn the respect of my peers, cultural, as when I feel a sense of appropriateness or fit, or economic, in terms of a reasonable balance between price and quality. But this value is both abstract, when it is expressed in terms of price or popularity, and personal, when it has a specific quality just for me.

Moreover, judgments of value are usually social, cultural, *and* economic. Not only is it hard—and maybe even useless—to try to separate the different sources of influence, they often influence us in contradictory ways. I try on a pair of jeans in a designer shop in an outlet mall. The jeans fit me perfectly, but they are too tight for me, a middle-aged college professor, to wear in public. They were made, probably under frightful conditions, in a sweatshop. But because they were made in a sweatshop, I can afford to buy two pairs instead of one. The "objectification" of the value of these jeans is made by the price, by my social position, by what I read about sweatshops—and by a mass culture of value that links the public life of marketable commodities to my private dreams.

Our mass culture is based on the belief that shopping is a patriotic duty. I'm not thinking of the punning slogan "Go 4th and Shop" that Old Navy painted on its billboard advertisements around Independence Day, July 4, several years ago, or of Mayor Giuliani's and President George W. Bush's encouragement of shopping to fight both an economic recession and the mood of despair after September 11. I'm thinking of the importance economists and politicians have assigned to shopping—to consumption, in general—since John Maynard Keynes's time.

In the 1930s, governments around the world, beginning with President Franklin D. Roosevelt in the United States, adopted the Keynesian view that spending, rather than saving, would help fight the industrial economies from the Great Depression. The supply of goods, swollen rapidly and enormously by the uncoordinated competition of mass production, could most efficiently be absorbed by increasing demand for them by any possible means. In the forties, that means was found—efficiently but cruelly—in the giant war machines with which the industrial economies fought World War II. Since the war ended, in 1945, a kinder but not always more efficient means of increasing demand for goods has transferred the responsibility from government's hands to those of consumers. Much of the postwar economic boom was based on consumers buying the washing machines, TV sets, and automobiles they could never afford before. Our nostalgic memories of the fifties and early sixties recall the public, and especially the private, spaces created for mass consumption: drive-in restaurants and movie theaters, shopping centers, and the family den.

Shopping became more important—and important in different ways—in the sixties, as some economies, again beginning with the United States, started to depend on services and global integration. With fewer Americans making things in factories and workshops, more of us were shuffling papers, waiting on tables, and selling things to other consumers.

In the next few years, as American manufacturers reshaped or abandoned their traditional role, shopping took on greater weight in the economy. Companies began to shut down plants in the United States and move production overseas, where labor was cheap and government restrictions were lax. They often remained in business by marketing products they bought or imported. While the number of American factory workers dramatically decreased, the number of shoppers remained the same. Indeed, as we in the baby boom generation bought homes, started families, and explored facets of the good life, shopping grew more intense. In the aftermath of the presidential election of 1984, most of the political battles over job loss due to overseas production were swept away by a new feeling of entrepreneurial freedom and a rising stock market. Political leaders now encouraged us to buy imports in order to keep American companies afloat and maintain the country's leading role in the world economy.

While consumption fueled the economy, new entrepreneurs kept us shopping. From the late sixties, even the most trivial items of clothing—including jeans—sprouted designer labels. Between the sixties and the eighties, stores, manufacturers, and journalists promoted a vast array of branded products, including sneakers and toys, to satisfy our cravings for individual identity, social status, and a sense of membership in a national culture. At the same time, our fascination with countercultural rebellion sparked the metamorphosis of an underground retail sector of granola, acid rock, and "head shops" into the corporate economy of Whole Foods, Tower Records, and The Gap.

In the eighties, Wal-Mart shifted from selling American-made products to imports, and grew into a multibillion-dollar-a-year discount store. Designer labels, led by Ralph Lauren, created multinational chains of designer boutiques. Credit card companies issued more than one billion credit cards, and L. L. Bean joined more than six thousand specialty mail-order merchants who mailed out five billion catalogs a year. Much of the software produced in our "information economy" tried to persuade us to buy more things, while also making it necessary for us to shop for the hardware.[2]

Since the eighties, shopping has commanded more serious attention by economic analysts. Annual retail sales in the United States add up to more than $3 trillion a year. Consumer spending is thought to account for two-thirds of national economic growth. Elected officials quote the Consumer Confidence Index, which is based on a household survey of consumer spending, as if it were the new gospel of prosperity. Newspapers, business magazines, and television news programs report holiday retail sales figures as a drama of boom or bust, complete with a Greek chorus of comments by investment analysts. These analysts look for a company's growth, in terms of increased sales volume, to raise its stock price: they want us to keep shopping.[3]

Responding to these cues, America has become, more than ever, a nation of shoppers. In 1987, the country had more shopping malls than high schools. More Americans shopped while they traveled—and took trips in order to shop—than relaxed in outdoor recreation or visited historical sites, museums, and beaches. Airlines offered special excursion rates for one-day trips to the Mall of America in Bloomington, Minnesota, and the Potomac Mills outlet mall near Washington, D.C. By 1997, sales at Wal-Mart exceeded $100 billion a year, a hundred times greater than the chain's record-breaking sales volume of 1979. Though the amount of retail space per person has quadrupled over the past thirty years, big retail chains like Wal-Mart, Target, Home Depot, and The Gap are building ever bigger stores—up to 200,000 and even 300,000 square feet.[4]

Around the end of the twentieth century, shopping became a critical metaphor for excess and for an alienation from life itself. The size of the retail industry, the ubiquity of stores, the obsession with brand names from

Main Street to Wall Street: you couldn't fail to be struck by the pervasiveness of shopping—especially if you didn't look at yourself, but at other people.

In the nineties, the conceptual artist Barbara Kruger made an artwork of the slogan "I shop, therefore I am." Off-Broadway theater pieces offered the audience a familiar "supermarket of popular cultural references" and asked them to choose between alternative props and narratives. The economist Robert Frank wrote a book condemning the status-seeking consumption or "luxury fever" that he saw replacing a concern for social equality. Another economist, Juliet Schor, described "the overspent American," who maxes out credit cards after hearing coworkers talk about their own recent purchases. Rap musicians sang about Adidas shoes, gold jewelry, and the girl who "look[s] as though [she] shops at Abercrombie & Fitch." And a mixed-media installation by the artist Vera Frenkel juxtaposed photographs of a shopping mall with an ironic narration that began, "This is your messiah speaking, instructing you to shop."[5]

There is no central authority compelling us to shop. Nevertheless, the cultural critic Walter Benjamin was right to see in the arcades—those mid-nineteenth-century shopping malls of European and American city centers—archeological traces of social power.[6] Though my most intimate experiences of shopping, in recent years, are limited to New York City, New York's intense commercial vitality, and the enormous variety of its stores, allow me, as I walk around the city, to trace a larger cultural history of social power. The ebb and flow of fortunes, as specific stores rise and fall; the abstraction of markets, as the "dream palace" of department stores is replaced by the faceless discount chain; and the rebirth of the ethnic marketplace, as new immigrants and new money fill gaps in older neighborhoods—you see all this as you walk around New York City.

When I walk down Broadway to Dean & Deluca today, I can imagine the crowds of fancy dressers and window shoppers that used to throng these streets 150 years ago. Fashionable ladies and working women, dandies and factory hands, all strolled past elegant temples of commerce. A. T. Stewart's Marble Palace, with its Ladies' Parlor on the second floor, the old stores of Tiffany and Brooks Brothers, and scores of clothing, china, and book shops created a dense traffic of pleasure and leisure, making this street one of the Empire City's great attractions. While the cast-iron buildings remain in place today, those stores are gone. Many moved uptown before the nineteenth century ended; most have disappeared. When I first began walking on lower Broadway, back in the seventies, the only stores were wholesale fabric shops, which were an outgrowth of the nearby rag and remnant dealers and of the small manufacturers who remained in darkened loft buildings on the surrounding blocks.[7]

At that time, artists began a trend of living downtown, and opened galleries and performance spaces around Broadway. Dean & Deluca started a small cheese and sandwich shop on a side street, some artists opened an informal restaurant called Food, and a discount store for young people—Canal Jeans—began to lure a different retail trade from all over the city. Gradually, as more art buyers, students, and tourists visited the area, now called SoHo, the surrounding neighborhood supported more art galleries, restaurants, and crafts shops. The New Museum for Contemporary Art and a branch of the Guggenheim Museum opened on Broadway. Foot traffic increased, rents rose, and fancy clothing, jewelry, and design shops replaced many of the original galleries. In the nineties, Dean & Deluca moved to a 4,000-square-foot corner store on Broadway. During the next decade, it was joined by Banana Republic, Pottery Barn, Armani A/X, and H&M. Broadway, again, was crowded with shoppers.

New York has always been a crucial meeting point for shipments of goods and a critical mass of eager consumers. In the nineteenth century, the city's economy was enriched by great building projects that furthered trade and travel: the Erie Canal, in the 1820s; the gradual expansion of the port, in the following years; and the construction of railroads from the 1830s on, especially during the 1880s. The extraordinary concentration of wealth these projects brought to New York City established a large group of people who could, and would, buy luxury goods, and artisans migrated to New York from all over the country and from Europe to make and sell them.

The city also occupied a privileged position in the flow of information from European centers of style and innovation. Eyewitness reports by travelers, fabric samples, scale models, printed sewing patterns, fashion magazines: in every medium, new goods reached New York first. From the city, they were shipped by boat or train around the country. New York merchants and manufacturers competed to introduce the latest trends. This competition led to the economies of scale and lavish displays of department stores, while ambitious entrepreneurs with less access to capital opened the many small shops that catered to different ethnic groups, to the very rich, and to the very poor.

"Shopping in Broadway," originally published in *Harper's Weekly*, March 19, 1870. Despite the columned floor, male sales clerks selling fabrics, and stools provided for customers at the counter, several elements of the shopping experience are still the same today: young women customers looking closely at fashionable merchandise, the long-suffering mother waiting nearby, and the father fingering money in his wallet before paying the bill. Museum of the City of New York.

During the golden age of department stores, from the 1880s to the 1920s, a growing number of men, women, and materials both dramatized the shopping experience and tied it to the city's rapidly changing physical fabric. Plate glass, electric lights, and atrium construction made stores seem bigger and more spectacular. Elevators and escalators expanded shoppers' perceptions of moving rapidly through space and time. A profusion of goods, brought from everywhere and piled in luxurious displays, made "just looking" at merchandise a popular pastime, both within the store and on the streets, even when stores weren't open for business. In the evening, and during the seasonal promotion of new goods, when a store changed its window displays and turned on the lights, window shopping became a special attraction. If department stores were the new theaters of consumption, men and women shoppers and even passersby became an audience for, and performers in, the drama.

The provision of safe spaces like rest rooms and tearooms made shopping more convenient for women who didn't feel comfortable going about in public by themselves. Charge accounts made shopping especially convenient for those women who had a fair amount of leisure and money at their disposal, although still under their husband's or father's control. Department stores also drew on the work of a growing number of "stylists" and "brokers"—display designers, marketing executives, event coordinators, psychologists, and advertising copywriters—who invented ways to embed the physical presence of the stores, and evoke their spectral images, in the daily lives of millions of people. A rapidly growing population, combined with aggressive real estate development, led to an ideal, modern marketplace. Standing at the intersection of standardized mass production and different group identities, New York stores like Macy's, B. Altman, Brooks Brothers, and Tiffany helped to make shopping one of the city's major activities, as well as an early tourist attraction.[8]

Yet big stores like these represent only one layer in the shopping experience. Over time, the social spaces of shopping—and of the city itself—have been made and remade by political reformers, shifting patterns of investment, and social class power.

From the 1830s to the 1930s, housewives, working women, and grocery store owners in New York City all procured their daily provisions at outdoor public markets. The markets were a constant target for city authorities, who tried to regularize their operations and control their resistance to municipal tax collectors and health inspectors. Mayors wanted to root out corruption in the wholesale food trade; they were also pressed to eliminate the peddlers who crowded the streets, made a mess with their garbage and debris, and took business away from store owners who paid taxes and were an important political constituency. Social reformers and local merchants continually urged the city government to regulate both markets and peddlers. But when Mayor Fiorello La Guardia finally shut down the outdoor public markets in the 1930s and moved street peddlers into indoor markets built at the city's expense, he changed shopping as a social experience as well as an economic transaction.[9]

Moving food shopping indoors helped to end informal haggling over prices, and limited the opportunity for poor women to buy unsold fruit and vegetables at lower prices late in the afternoon. Although it reduced exposure to insects and dirt, indoor shopping also diluted the sensuality of food display. Shoppers ran less of a risk of smelling fetid fruit, but developed a more antiseptic approach to food in general. Shopping also grew quieter and more sedate. Shoppers no longer had to compete with food sellers' raucous shouts; the sellers, themselves, did not have to be, or hire, barkers. By this time, moreover, grocery store chains like A&P were poised for a great expansion.[10] Replacing public food markets with indoor stores, including branches of grocery chains, created a different kind of shopping experience. If it was more predictable in terms of cleanliness and pricing, it was also less directly social.

Food shopping was thus opened to influence by a more upscale decor, by a hierarchy of sales clerks and managers, and, from the 1880s, by standardized packaging and brand names like Quaker Oats and Uneeda Biscuits. Gradually, as all clothing and furniture began to be mass-produced rather than custom-made, and chain stores added branches, people had a more routinized experience—in the sense of both more "rational" and less "human"—when they did their daily shopping.

There were also more stores than ever before. Reflecting enormous increases in the volume of long-distance trade throughout the nineteenth and early twentieth centuries, shopping districts expanded, changing residential neighborhoods and creating dynamic new commercial zones. From the 1840s, street corners sprouted butcher shops, bakeries, and grocery stores, while more expensive shops for luxury goods clustered in the center.[11] All these shops, grouped according to the social status of their clientele, formed a hierarchy of shopping spaces that, in turn, ordered New Yorkers' mental maps.

As Manhattan's commercial core moved steadily northward, wealthy merchants' houses were converted to shop fronts and then razed to build the palatial stores of dry goods merchants. New York's first department store, A. T. Stewart's Marble Palace, opened in lower Manhattan, near City Hall, in 1848. Within twenty years, Stewart expanded, moving the store two miles north to a big, new building at Ninth Street and Broadway. When Manhattan's most elegant shops moved even farther north, to the Ladies' Mile on Broadway, between Fourteenth and Twenty-third Streets, in the 1870s, Stewart's was left behind. The Ninth Street building was eventually bought by another department store, John Wanamaker, and the

Grocery store interior, Belleville, New Jersey, 1905. Grocers already combined fresh produce and meat with canned goods and packages.

site was inherited, in my time, by Kmart, the discount chain. After 1900, B. Altman and Macy's department stores, as well as elite specialty shops like Tiffany, Brooks Brothers, and Lord & Taylor, moved farther uptown, to Fifth Avenue north of Thirty-fourth Street. By 1930, elegant stores like Saks Fifth Avenue and Bonwit Teller, following their richest shoppers, established beachheads north of Fiftieth Street.[12]

The growth of different shopping districts for rich and poor proved to be a fluid barometer of a New Yorker's social position, as well as of the city's general prosperity. Where women shopped reflected their wealth and social class, but it also determined who they were. If you shopped north of Fiftieth Street, you were rich; if you shopped south of Fourteenth Street, you worked in a factory. Department stores on Fulton Street, in downtown Brooklyn, and on the Grand Concourse, in the Bronx, catered to upwardly mobile shoppers who wanted to transcend their immigrant origins and arrive in the middle class.

After World War II, the major department stores continued to pursue more affluent shoppers—this time, to the suburbs. Families who moved from Brooklyn or the Bronx, and had shopped at Alexander's in the Bronx or at Macy's on Thirty-fourth Street, soon felt at home in the malls on Route 4 in Paramus, New Jersey, and at Roosevelt Mall on Long Island. On Long Island, rich suburban shoppers went to B. Altman and Bonwit Teller in Manhasset; in Westchester, they shopped at Saks Fifth Avenue in White Plains. The branches of big downtown stores were followed by many small specialty shops that moved out of the neighborhoods. Building suburban shopping malls was a piecemeal process, and families moving out of the city often traveled back for the larger selections of downtown department stores and the personal relations and ethnic foods of shops in their old neighborhoods. But they gradually got used to the new convenience of traveling by car to shop, especially after department stores opened suburban branches and they no longer had to carry packages on foot or in a crowded train. Malls also provided them with a semblance of the city's crowds and variety. Developers' huge economic investment required malls to attract a large number of shoppers from all over the region, which meant they had to mix high-status and low-status stores. Yet malls maintained the social pecking order by separating groups of shoppers by income and social class. In large malls, the lowest-status shops and restaurants were placed on the bottom level, with the more exclusive stores on top. And a small number of malls containing only expensive stores were built in the most affluent suburbs.[13]

By the sixties, the movement of stores out of both central business districts and neighborhood shopping streets created serious gaps in the city's economy. The changing ethnic composition of the city's population was reflected in a different, and poorer, customer base for department stores downtown, which continued to drive more affluent shoppers away. In New York, Philadelphia, Baltimore, Chicago, and Los Angeles, white shoppers were replaced by blacks and Latinos and many neighborhood stores simply disappeared. Residents who remained in "bad" areas of the city were underserved by too few stores and shoddy goods—and often had to pay higher prices for them.[14]

Shopping in the poor neighborhoods only worsened over time. When riots broke out during the sixties and African American residents targeted local, white-owned stores, those merchants felt their lives were too short and their profit margins were too slim to keep the business going. Most of them either left or shut down. Bank branches disappeared, their white marble pillars marking the new site of evangelical churches. Vacant storefronts were boarded up. Windows of cheap clothing stores and small bodegas were covered by heavy steel gates. Although I lived through the gradual disappearance of stores from New York's ethnic ghettos in the seventies, the most graphic example of alienated shopping I have ever seen was in Frederick Wiseman's documentary film *Public Housing* (1997) that was shot at the Ida B. Wells Houses in Chicago. In one scene, black children line up to buy snacks at a grocery store whose owner guards against crime by not permitting shoppers to enter the store after dusk. Where the front door would be, the owner installed a revolving window. The children put their money into the window and announce they want to buy potato chips, the owner or a clerk turns the window around, takes the children's coins, and sends out a bag of chips.[15]

Department stores that were located in the center of the city were buffered from the most extreme changes. Yet they were at risk economically, since their wealthier customers began to shop exclusively at suburban branches. Although most owners remained committed to the survival of their flagship stores for their symbolic value, they starved them of fresh inventory, cut the unionized workforce, and waited for the city to fall down around them. Outside of Manhattan, some chains abandoned their flagship stores, with the shuttering of Hudson's in Detroit and Namm's in downtown Brooklyn among the most flagrant examples.

By the eighties, investors viewed the surviving center-city department stores much as they viewed businesses in other declining economic sectors: the stores were bundles of financial assets waiting to be plucked. A tsunami wave of mergers and leveraged buyouts swept through the biggest stores, including Macy's and Bloomingdale's, leaving in its wake managers who had too many debts to rebuild the stores and outside investors who had no experience as merchants.

Only in the nineties was the suburbs' drain on the city's shopping spaces partly reversed. Immigrant entrepreneurs, who came to the United States after the immigration laws were changed in 1985, opened stores in low-rent commercial streets that had long since fallen off the shopping maps. Many small merchants catered to specific groups of ethnic shoppers. Brooklyn, in particular, thrived with this new retail trade. New Russian immigrants set up delicatessens in Brighton Beach to sell caviar and smoked sturgeon, and dress shops in Bensonhurst, started years before by Jews or Italians, the children of a previous immigrant generation, hired Russian-speaking saleswomen and stocked larger sizes for Russian shoppers. Chinese herbalists and groceries opened for business along Eighth Avenue in Sunset

Main Street in trouble: empty 19th century storefronts, North Adams, Massachusetts. Photo by Richard Rosen, 1995.

Park, creating the newest of New York's three Chinatowns. Music stores on Utica Avenue sold reggae as well as rap tapes, and greengrocers on Church Avenue offered mangos and cassavas from the Caribbean.

Immigrant merchants also filled niches in markets that had been abandoned by other ethnic groups. Koreans opened small fruit and vegetable stores in ghetto neighborhoods throughout the city, moved into the dry cleaning business, and almost single-handedly, by opening inexpensive "nail salons," brought manicures back in style. Dominicans followed Puerto Rican *bodegueros*, but, before long, they in turn were bought out by Mexicans. Albanians ran Italian pizzerias. Syrians took over newsstands and opened stores where they sold magazines. Still other immigrant merchants catered to bargain hunters of every ethnic group, especially along Fourteenth Street and Canal Street and on Fulton Mall, in downtown Brooklyn.

Shop window, Home Boys, Brooklyn. Photo by Alex Vitale, 1997.

Out on the sidewalks, immigrant peddlers, licensed or not, did a thriving business—to the dismay, once again, of city officials, store owners, and the police.

Immigrant shoppers not only shopped for themselves, they sent shipments of goods back to relatives in the home country. For this reason, teenagers in the back country of Haiti were as likely to wear Nikes and Yankees T-shirts as their cousins in East Flatbush. Home Boys, a beauty products store in Flatbush, sold cosmetic preparations made in Africa as well as in the United States, and some customers sent these products back to Africa because they were cheaper and more readily available in Brooklyn. Mainly because of immigrant shoppers, the Queens Center shopping mall, in the borough of Queens, enjoyed one of the highest sales volumes per square foot of malls throughout the entire country.[16]

In addition to neighborhood shopping streets reinvigorated by new immigrants, new luxury trade and mass-market stores were built by "foreign" money—at least, by corporations located outside New York City. Kmart, Bradlees, Toys "R" Us, Circuit City, Staples, and the British-owned Virgin Megastore moved into the Union Square neighborhood near my home. Midtown and uptown shopping districts were brought to new life, and higher rents, by Disney Stores, Warner Brothers Studio Stores, Nike Town, Hermès, Sephora, The Gap, and all the Armanis—Giorgio, Emporio, and A/X Exchange. "Family-oriented" stores and entertainment anchored the redevelopment of Times Square, where the theming of cartoon characters and professional sports activities not only drove out raunchy movie theaters and pornographic bookshops, but provided a populist storefront for the new headquarters of media and financial corporations.[17]

From the Lower East Side to Tribeca, shopping also revitalized Lower Manhattan. Lofts and tenement storefronts were gradually turned into design boutiques and trendy restaurants. Clothing and shoe stores drove most of the art galleries out of SoHo, with a branch of DKNY moving into a building at 420 West Broadway that had been the headquarters of four famous art dealers in the early seventies. During the nineties, NoLIta, a previously unremarkable, Italian working-class neighborhood north of Little Italy and east of SoHo, became a hot location. In the nineteenth century, immigrants who lived in tenements on Elizabeth Street might have done piece work in their apartments, labored as carpenters or metal workers in workshops on the same block, or walked to work in the garment factories of SoHo. In the 1990s, however, in counterpoint to the bustling pan-Asian shopping streets of Flushing, in Queens, and the mainly Caribbean stores on Church Avenue, in Brooklyn, Elizabeth Street shed its old ethnic image. The large plate glass windows of new European and Asian design shops opened to the street, replacing small, dark, Italian American social clubs where crime bosses and their cronies had hung out, local butcher shops whose interiors were covered in tiny, white tiles, and dusty hardware stores. *Vogue*, *W*, and the *New York Times* touted the area for dynamic new fashions. Elizabeth Street was becoming part of a recharged, transnational shopping economy.

Much of the street-level revitalization in all big cities since the 1980s is due to these kinds of changes. Both products and stores have become more individualized by name and more standardized by type, and shopping districts are widely recognized as both a force and a symbol of economic development. The wealth and variety of new shops in New York enable the media to present shopping as one of the city's cultural attractions—an alternative to the suburbanization and standardization that have engulfed the rest of the country, if not also the rest of the world. After September 11, 2001, these distinctions were even more important to maintaining the city's image and economy.[18]

New shops in old tenements, Elizabeth Street. Photo by Richard Rosen, 2000.

Places where we shop are landscapes of power. Over time, because of changes of scale and ownership, and of geography and technology, these landscapes change. Department stores, which once imposed a centralized control over fashions and prices, have been overshadowed by discount chains and branded boutiques. The hulking glass boxes of superstores reflect the ghosts of a thousand corner groceries. The human "beehives" of the mail-order pioneers have been swallowed whole by multimillion-dollar "order fulfillment centers," and individually owned brick-and-mortar stores have been swept aside by regional and virtual malls.[19]

Shopping spaces not only delineate a corporate landscape of power. They also discipline our bodies and our minds. Whether virtual or real, stores are a "totalizing institution." We are bound by their constraints, from limited inventories to self-service, and immobilized by their rewards, from electronic gift cards to discounts for "frequent buyers." A store is gentler than the prison, school, and army Michel Foucault describes in his classic studies of totalizing power, and more comfortable than the mental hospital immortalized by Erving Goffman. But once we accept its values, we are its captives.[20]

Our bodies internalize the discipline of stores from the time we are first taken shopping in strollers, and placed carefully in the top seat of a shopping cart, to our old age. My mother, who, at eighty-nine, has trouble seeing and walks with the help of a metal walker, revs up to speed when we enter a supermarket and wants to push the cart herself toward where she remembers the bananas are. The colors, shapes, and symbols of the packages, the layout of the gondolas or shelving units, the routine of pushing our cart through the aisles past the fresh produce at the entry, to the milk and yogurt on the back wall, and alongside the frozen foods in the last aisle before the checkout: we know this order, it is in our very bones.

Shopping is one of those disciplines of the body by which we find our places in society.[21] Neither as raucous a carnival as the early modern market-place, where pickpockets mingled with aristocrats and fishmongers,[22] nor as closed a community as the general store, where folk traditions and rural isolation enforced conformity,[23] modern shopping spaces keep us in our place. Yet we mobile shoppers get the effect of constantly moving through times and spaces—as long as we keep pushing our carts through the aisles or keep clicking our selections into the "shopping cart."[24]

Like the character Julia Roberts plays in the movie *Pretty Woman*, our bodies internalize the price and status differences of stores and the snooti-ness or friendliness of the sales staff. As the historian William Leach points out, the plate-glass windows that began to be widely used in storefronts after 1880 placed a wide variety of goods on continuous, public display, but they also separated people from the goods they desired.[25] We bear the responsibility for reading the hierarchical signs and sales clerks' attitude, and adjusting our behavior. If we dare to enter a store whose facade we read with foreboding, we are primed for arrogance, rejection, and rebuke: "the life-crushing disenfranchisement of an entirely owned world."[26] If we are homeless, young, or dark-skinned, the discipline of shopping in down-town stores or upscale malls is strictly enforced by curfews, locked doors, products chained to racks, and the refusal of sales clerks to serve us. Prices, both immanent in visual displays and explicit on printed labels, are a less contentious means of enforcing status exclusions. Most of us wouldn't even try to go into a shop that doesn't hang price tags on its goods—and, if we do try to go in, we dress differently for the encounter.

Shopping forces us both to take account of our place in society and to imagine what it would be like to rise above it. When shopping is a social encounter, when it is done in the supposedly democratic air of a public space, this imagined upward mobility gives us a sharp experience of being on the edge between freedom and inequality. If a man goes unaccompa-nied into Victoria's Secret, or a McDonald's worker enters a Giorgio Armani store, they feel the thrill and pain of an unavailable yet all-too-visible world, with its own code of difference, style, and value.[27]

Shopping is, most intensely, a learning process. This lifelong learning begins in childhood, when our parents first take us shopping. They dress us up for an excursion, take us where they want to go, buy us what they think we need, and all too seldom indulge us with a really terrific toy. From the parent's point of view, however, shopping is an opportunity to teach children a moral lesson. While we shop, we talk to our children about how to discern the differences between products, how to respond to the sales clerks' deference or disdain, how to weigh alternative choices, and how to live with a decision. For the parent, therefore, a shopping excursion with children is a narrative of responsibility, contrasting with the easy, selfish days of their young adulthood, and limiting their opportunities for both leisure and pleasure. But children also see the possibility of freedom as well as the burden of responsibility in shopping. In our society, teenagers begin to break free of their parents when they start to shop for themselves. Even preteens are savvy about learning to shop in age-branded stores; "Claire's is where you shop before you're old enough to shop at Ricky's," my eleven-year-old daughter tells me, as she discusses the relative merits of the stores near our house that sell cosmetics and fashion accessories. Chatting with friends, handling both goods and money, dealing with the outside world without parents to run interference: teenagers' shopping experiences are both exhilarating and scary, centered only on themselves, their friends, and the few stores where they can afford to go—with Canal Jeans, The Gap, or Claire's sketchily representing adult society. We learn to be adults by learning to shop.

When we are adults—especially if we are women—we learn to shop for other people: for our children, our spouses, and, eventually, our aging parents. And when we shop, we think about using shopping to fulfill moral obligations. We think about buying our child organic oatmeal instead of sugary Fruit Loops. We think our spouses should buy a present for us instead of our buying a present for them. We think we should be shopping for a Lexus, not a Honda.[28]

Our grocery list is an everyday lesson in learning to cope with pressure. The things we need to buy are framed by our love for the significant others we buy for,[29] by cultural measures like schedules and budgets, and by social norms of appropriate equipment for going to work, going out, and keeping house. Our shopping routines are also pretty well determined by the things we already own: we seek to maintain a consistent moral and aesthetic quality, according to the "Diderot effect" Grant McCracken describes, in an amusing story about the eighteenth-century French philosopher, who kept striving to upgrade his possessions after someone gave him a luxurious dressing gown that was out of keeping with his shabby apartment.[30]

As we grow older, our shopping experiences—especially for women—are often dramatic lessons in how to deal with our bodies. The truth we see by the harsh light of the dressing-room mirror, the search for the perfect fit, the dress or bathing suit—*especially* the bathing suit—that "got away" because it didn't fit right: learning to shop is all about enduring mortifications of the flesh, not feeling comfortable in our skin, or, occasionally, and much more happily, feeling good because we have found something that makes us look good. Shopping for clothes is a process of learning to accept—as well as to deny—our imperfection.[31]

Women and teenage shoppers are often accused of succumbing to the seduction of the brand name or the designer product. But men are just as likely to seek out the Armani suit, the Tommy Hilfiger shirt, and the Nike shoes. At any rate, we often consciously struggle against the manipulation we know the designer name implies, and we learn how to rationalize our choices. Why pay more for an Armani suit—unless it's really made of better material? Why go out of your way for Nikes—unless your friends will mock you for wearing Payless sneakers? We are free to reject the meanings foisted on us by brand names and designer labels; but, through peer pressure and our sense of entitlement about getting "the best," we *learn* to want the designer name.

The critical language of consumer guides sets up a dialogue between the use value we learn from our parents and the exchange value we learn from advertising, merchandising, and marketing. On a middle ground between our parents' lessons of thriftiness and producers' desires to sell us goods, the authors of shopping guides—the "honest brokers" of consumer society—teach us to be smarter shoppers. They are paid to do the comparison shopping that we lack time and money to do: they try out five brands of washing machines, they overload the hard drive on the computer, they eat the lousy as well as the wonderful restaurant meals. Then they tell us which products are worth our time and money; they objectify our values for us. From the earnest, scientific product reviews of *Consumer Reports* in the 1930s to the ecstatic, hedonistic restaurant reviews of *New York* magazine in the sixties and the pseudodemocracy of *Zagat* surveys in the eighties, these honest brokers of consumption guide us toward a general theory of value. They create a rhetoric of "best buys," "stars," and ratings that naturalizes consumer choice. Yet this important part of the culture of shopping—consumer guides—did not exist, in the United States, until 1936, and it only took the form we use today during the sixties.

In recent years, we have developed an extraordinary trust in the honest brokers of consumption. Not only do we depend on them to show us the right way to shop, we have also come to depend on them to guide our public debates about value. They are a popular version of the rational choice theory that, at least theoretically, informs business and politics. Regardless of how rational we think we are, or how often we actually consult shopping guides, we incorporate this language into the way we make both small and large decisions. And why not? The honest brokers' values reflect our own. Their skepticism about producers' claims cuts close to the roots of our unspeakable anxiety about getting the best value. They give us a *critical* language—a means of both demystifying and challenging the power of manufacturers and retail stores. This language of shopping objectifies the value of commodities in ways that favor *us*.[32]

Looking at the birth of the department store at the turn of the twentieth century, the historian William Leach shows that cultures of mass consumption depend on "strategies of enticement" and "circuits of power." But since the thirties, and especially since the sixties, honest brokers of consumption have sought to limit the lures of merchants and the power of producers. Consumer activists and writers who draw attention to fraud, monopoly, environmental harm, and sweatshop production widen the public discourse of consumption. They hold commodities, and those who sell them, accountable to the law, to morality, and to social justice. To the extent that they influence laws, social movements, and our individual behavior, these honest brokers enlarge the public space of shopping into a modern public sphere for debating the social responsibility of both business and government. They struggle to create value for us.

The writings of philosophers like Jurgen Habermas have accustomed us to think of the public sphere as an elite but democratic space between civil society and the state.[33] But the revolutionary achievement of mass consumption has been to construct another space between the self and civil society—and by shopping, we place ourselves in this space. Neither completely free nor completely democratic, the public sphere of shopping is a space of discussion and debate. It is a space of manipulation and control, but also of discretion and fulfillment. It is, in fact, an ambiguous or a heterotopic space, where we struggle to combine principles of equality and hierarchy, and pleasure and rationality, to create an experience we value. This experience contrasts with—and often contradicts—the totally constructed shopping of "the experience economy."[34]

Through our struggles over value, this space of shopping has created its own discourse of democratic rights—partly borrowed from labor struggles, partly from a crude self-interest, and partly, too, from a keen sense of fairness and market equity. If royal authority was the moral keystone of premodern society, and reason played the same role in parliamentary democracy, then the source of morality in today's public sphere is the self—implying, at best, our right to both selfish satisfaction and human equality.

It is worth noting that, in contrast to the modern public sphere based in politics and production, the public sphere of consumption has mainly been constructed by, and for, women.[35] Some people might interpret this as compensation for women's historical exclusion from the other public sphere, or even as a special (or "surplus") manipulation of women, who bore the brunt of mass consumption in the early twentieth century by getting arrested for shoplifting and being accused of a morally deficient kleptomania.[36] But women have also played key productive roles in mass consumption. Held back, for many years, from promotion to responsible positions in retail and financial corporations, women worked as stylists and managers, advertising copywriters, and entrepreneurs of fashion. Their decisions, not only as shoppers but as shop owners and sales clerks, determined forms and expressions of social status.[37] Women sellers, and selling to women, often cleared the way to admitting the self into public discussion through a franker acknowledgment of weakness and desire. Public confessions of self-doubt, conflict between self-sacrifice and gratification, autonomy, sensuality, and community: these are all attempts to infuse public life with the complicated etiquette of both intimate relations and self-examination. At best—and, sometimes, at worst—this focus on the self is what shopping is all about.

But shopping is not just about the self. Despite the many forms of self-expression by which the past century has been enthralled, shopping is a public realm in which we struggle to create an objective ideal of value. This realm has always been dominated by merchants and manufacturers, and their advertising people, display directors, and marketing consultants. Since the sixties, and even more so since the nineties, the competition among these groups to sell us more goods has led to a vast expansion of shopping in our lives. Whether they lure us to superstores or designer boutiques, or through branding, the Internet, and lifestyle stores, they are asking us to believe we can find true value by entering their world. For over a hundred years, we have been lulled by the sprawl of abundance they have placed before us, and placated by their cheap prices and brand names. Yet during the past few years, we have also become more critical shoppers. Then why do we still believe?

We still believe because shopping is the one area of our lives where we think we can balance creativity and control. While we know we can't really "have it our way," as the television commercials tell us, we persist in believing that shopping is a realm of freedom from work and politics, a form of democracy open to all, and an exercise of skill to get the cheapest and the best. But we also still believe because we can't escape from shopping. About that we have no choice at all.

Though like my friend Paul, many people say they hate to shop, they do spend a lot of time shopping. We all spend a significant portion of our lives going to stores or on the Internet to look at products, check prices and ratings, buy things, and then complain about them. Like me making my rounds to neighborhood stores, we derive emotional support from our shopping experiences. Yet most of the time, we shop alone. With significant exceptions—Kathy and her mom, courting couples, girlfriends, and teens—shopping fuels our individualism. As both a public and a private search for value, it feeds the dominant culture of our time.

We rarely pause to examine what all this shopping means. Yet only by peeling away the layers of social spaces, cultural labels, and critical guides that have accumulated around shopping can we understand the power this activity wields over our imagination. Peel away these layers, and we will understand the shoppers we have learned to be.

2

julia learns
to shop

Just Divorced. Gone Shopping.
—Headline on feature story, *New York Times*, 2001

Learning to shop is more demanding than figuring out what things to buy. The most important part of shopping is learning to steer your way between what you desire and what you know is right. In New York, where the display of status items is inescapable, just thinking about these things creates a bond among strangers—and is a constant source of guilt and frustration.

I'm sitting in the hallway of my daughter's music school in Greenwich Village one Saturday morning, when the voice of Julia, a piano teacher, breaks into my thoughts. *"I know that bag,"* I hear her say.

I raise my head. Could Julia be speaking to me? I look around and see that she is, in fact, staring at my purse.

But why? Julia has never spoken to me before. My purse is one of those subtle Italian handbags, whose manufacturer expanded the business from a little leather shop in Vicenza to an international chain of luxury goods boutiques. Until recently, when they were bought by a multinational conglomerate of luxury brands, the company refused to put a logo on their products. They said their work was so distinctive, it didn't need a logo. This makes them, in short, a noteworthy unbrand—unlike, say, Louis Vuitton, whose logo has been replicated so often by factories in Hong Kong and Taiwan that, several years ago, to the dismay of the LVMH company, almost every New York City schoolgirl carried a knockoff, light brown backpack, with those initials printed in dark brown, on her shoulders.

What Julia knows: my no-logo brown leather purse. Photo by Richard Rosen.

But why would Julia, of all people, be interested in my plain brown purse? For years I have seen her around the music school, always wearing a T-shirt and jeans. She's sharp and funny and serious about music. She should be talking about Mozart, not about Italian leather bags.

Yet Julia has interrupted her conversation with a violin student's father because she does want to talk about Italian handbags. She doesn't want to tell me she *likes* my bag; she wants to tell me she *recognizes* it. She wants to tell me she knows how much it costs and where you can buy it and *what it is*: an expensive Italian purse that deliberately, self-consciously, carries no brand logo. She wants to have a conversation—the first real conversation

I have ever had with her—about this bag. Julia wants to tell me she appreciates my purse because she is a shopper.

She begins by lecturing the boy's father about my bag—although he shows only the mildest trace of interest. She tells him the bag is expensive and explains how the company's branding strategy plays up the absence of a logo; she mentions the company's boutique on Madison Avenue.

I manage to stammer that I got the purse as a gift.

But Julia is on a roll. Despite her casual outfits, she is a connoisseur of bags and shoes. Though she cannot afford to buy from Prada or Fendi, she knows what their products look like and describes how they feel when you hold their buttery soft leather in your hands. She knows which of their styles fit her and which don't. She knows the differences between the straps on their backpacks.

Julia tells us she also knows a lot about gemstone earrings. She knows how they are made and recognizes little differences in their design. "I know these things," she says, and smiles at us both shyly and proudly.

Despite my interest in shopping, I don't really know what a Prada bag looks like, and I don't pay much attention to jewelry. Since Julia doesn't earn a lot of money as a music teacher and usually runs around in a T-shirt and jeans, I wonder how she knows about these things. Maybe she reads *Vogue* or watches fashion shows on cable television.

No, Julia knows about these things because she shops. "When I travel," she says, "I always check out the expensive jewelry stores." She doesn't buy anything in these stores, she says; this is a different kind of shopping. Like many of us, she shops because she wants to do "research" on the products.

Julia will go into a store and look carefully at the array of merchandise, noting the styles, craftsmanship, and prices, and then file that information in the back of her mind for future use. Maybe she'll find a cheaper version of one of these products in another shop or an outlet store. Maybe she'll find a knockoff or a slightly different style. At least, she'll have a reference point for comparison shopping—for judging whether a cheaper product in another store is truly a bargain.

Even if she doesn't use this information for buying something, the research is useful for sizing up strangers or people whom she meets; she can categorize them by the products they wear. This woman's a Fendi, that one's a JanSport. This one paid more for a Kipling backpack so she could have the little stuffed animal on the key chain; that one paid more for the chic dark colors of a Tumi. Julia can also use the information to fuel a conversation—the kind of conversation about goods and stores that has become commonplace these days, among both friends and strangers.

The first time I realized these conversations were becoming so common was back in the eighties. Russell Baker, an op-ed page columnist for the *New York Times*, wrote a humorous essay about dinner party conversations that focused on the food rather than on political topics. Not only did people compliment the food, they talked at length about the origins of the dishes, the quality of the ingredients, and the stores where you could buy them. As they ate a dish, they reminisced about where they had eaten such a dish before, how much it had cost them, and where you could procure the best version of that dish—which often happened to be in Provence or Tuscany. Baker poked fun of these conversations because they allowed people to avoid serious political discussion. Since then, however, writers from Tom Wolfe to Robert Frank and David Brooks have ridiculed these concerns as a new form of status consumption—a rebirth of the drive to display luxury goods that Thorstein Veblen criticized at the turn of the twentieth century. Brooks and other writers blame the middle-aged hedonism of baby boomers, especially those of liberal political views, as well as the youthful narcissism of yuppies. But neither age nor political beliefs can explain the cultural sea change to an aesthetic pleasure in consumer goods that Americans had never acknowledged so frankly. Since I was writing about cuisine at the time, I thought that changing attitudes toward food consumption reflected the growing influence of food writers and chefs. Listening to Julia, however, I realized that this shift really reflects the growing influence of shopping.[1]

Shopping isn't just a process of *acquiring* goods and services—it's a lifelong process of *learning* about them. And the faster these products change, the more we have to keep up with the changes by shopping. What we know about products, their prices, and where to get them provides us with news and conversation when we run out of things to say about work or school, and when political events are too depressing to consider. Shopping also gives us a common frame of reference for checking each other out: look at the way middle-class parents ask where your children go to school, or teenagers ask each other where they bought their jeans. Since we often shop, we always know something about shopping; and when we talk about shopping—in contrast to talking about work or politics—our opinions seem to count. We're not just complaining, although we do plenty of that, too. By talking about our responses to goods, we're explaining the topic that ultimately interests us most: ourselves.

Or is it only in the status-conscious big city that conversation turns to shopping? "It's New York," Julia says. "In Syracuse, they don't care whether you're carrying a Prada bag or JanSport or anything else."

But I wonder whether this is true. *Vogue* publishes articles about where celebrities of the fashion world shop, complete with the stores' addresses and phone numbers. Celebrity endorsements by athletes are big news. Almost every website carries information about products, in addition to advertisements, throughout the world.

"I think we all pay attention to those things these days," I say.

Then the boy's father enters the conversation. "I pay attention," he says. I look into his face to see whether he is joking.

"I see whether someone looks like an 'L. L. Bean person,'" he explains, "not whether they're cool, but whether I'd like to be friends with them."

He isn't joking. He actually believes in the sociologists' idea of a "taste community": you're not only what you eat, you're what your friends eat, too. The French sociologist Pierre Bourdieu developed this idea in the eighties, around the same time that Russell Baker noticed his friends in New York talking about different types of olive oil. Bourdieu had seen that Parisians, who have always waxed philosophical about cuisine and fashion, were making new distinctions between people based on whether they showed different preferences, or tastes, for goods. Unlike the usual explanation of individual tastes, Bourdieu theorized that tastes are clustered together by social class—or, more precisely, by social status. High-status people are likely to eat thin slices of whole-grain bread, while peasants buy baguettes. The main exception is the distinctive, "high-end" tastes of people who are highly educated but not enormously wealthy—in other words, the very people who want to talk about the olive oil would likely be Pierre Bourdieu's and Russell Baker's friends. Like Baker, Bourdieu was curious about the new visibility of these people—the more affluent professionals and intellectuals. He was interested in how they used the quirkiness of their tastes to set new fashions, offsetting the power of the upper class and traditional elites. These issues became important to both consumer culture and the economy as the upper middle class and their pundits grew more affluent, and also more influential, during the eighties, in Europe as well as in the United States.[2]

With Julia, however, we're not dealing with affluent tastes defined by *acquiring* goods. We're dealing with affluent tastes acquired by merely *shopping* for goods. By going into stores, reading about goods, and talking about them, shoppers like Julia accumulate cultural capital. Like economic capital, cultural capital is a resource of privileged social groups. As Bourdieu describes it, people derive cultural capital from education and from experience within a privileged milieu. Yet Julia's cultural capital—not her musical knowledge but her familiarity with expensive consumer goods—comes from the seemingly democratic process of shopping.

Though very few people can afford to buy real Prada bags, anyone can acquire familiarity with them by shopping—by the vicarious consumption that we do when we flip through the fashion magazines, and by the direct participation we do by visiting stores, examining the merchandise, and feeling the goods. Shopping through a store's displays permits us to develop knowledge about goods without acquiring the goods themselves. We can even become fans of some goods and critics of others without committing ourselves to spending any money. Shopping gives us the proximate experience with goods we need to make true distinctions. We can tell whether someone is carrying a real Prada bag or only a fake. We don't do this because we're snobs . . . but because we're truly interested in the aesthetic quality of the things themselves.

Indeed, just then Julia says there are "snobs" who pay attention to such matters. She has a friend who doesn't like a certain store "where they sell Mandarina Duck bags"—another Italian brand—because the salesman in there was nice to her only when she wore Ralph Lauren sunglasses. "It's not the people who can buy the most expensive bags who care whether someone is wearing a real Gucci bag," she says. "It's the others, who shouldn't be spending money on it, who care." So Julia thinks of herself as a moralist. Just because she shops doesn't mean she's a snob.

"You know, I come from a totally different background," she says, "where these things weren't important. My family were immigrants and socialists. When I was growing up, T-shirts didn't have designers' names on them. I don't really like all this." And she smiles again—this time, more shyly than proudly.

Julia experiences a conflict many shoppers feel—a conflict between shopping to supply her needs, as her parents brought her up, and shopping to acquire social status and cultural capital, which is the kind of shopping that has become more popular since the eighties. Though Thorstein Veblen pointed out the prevalence of status shopping in the early 1900s, it was limited, at that time, to the small segment of the population that had financial security and lived in some degree of comfort. Status shopping began to be more widespread with the growth of the middle class after World War II. It became more influential in the sixties when the spending habits of rich people and celebrities began to be widely publicized in the print media and on television. At the same time, the large numbers of women who began to work outside the home and pursue their own careers anxiously sought badges of their new distinction. A broad public for status shopping formed, consisting of the traditional upper-class matrons whom Veblen had depicted as status shoppers, the nonworking, suburban house-wives who tried to "keep up with the Joneses," and the working women who wanted to keep up with their peers at work and had more financial leeway in making spending decisions.[3]

Women are not the only status shoppers. Men have always considered their social status when shopping for the big purchases—cars and houses. In the sixties, however, men, especially unmarried men and gay men, took a bigger role in making decisions about the clothes they wore and the food they ate—decisions that used to be left to wives and mothers. As many men became more interested in style, shopping provided them with new cultural capital. These social changes did not necessarily persuade consumers to buy more. But they did encourage people to approach shopping with more interest—and with more anxiety about making the right choices.[4]

Beginning in the late sixties, a mass public of consumers was surrounded by the new social space of designer boutiques and discount stores, the cultural labels of branded goods, and a booming literature of product reviews and shopping guides. The influx of products, stores, and texts created a complex, and occasionally overwhelming, culture. Shoppers responded by neither rejecting the whole idea of consumption nor becoming, as many authors would have it, baby-boomer snobs. Instead, shoppers learned to use shopping as an opportunity to do research on goods—and gain cultural capital.

Like Julia, many of us can't afford to buy the things we would like to have. Through magazines, television, and books, we gain cultural capital by vicarious consumption. Looking at goods in stores or on the Internet, reading reviews, and talking about them train us, as they have trained Julia, to appreciate their subtle differences. And once we have developed a fine eye for differences among the goods, we can make distinctions among the people who use them. This is a different approach to shopping from the early years of mass consumption, when most mass market products were homogeneous and most people didn't spend so much time thinking about them. If we're over forty, or if we learned to shop *before* the sixties, we sense a change in ourselves—a contradiction, if you will—with which we're not completely at ease.

"My mother was a good shopper," says Catherine, a woman in her late fifties who lives in Toronto, one of a number of middle-class shoppers I have talked to recently about shopping.[5] "But shopping was different in those days. I grew up in an affluent family, but even so, you shopped for essentials. You probably got one good outfit a year, or maybe two, if you grew. In those days [the fifties], we wore skirts to school, and a skirt would last you four years. You just kept letting the hem down. You might get a new blouse if you got bigger on top. So you'd have three outfits and one for the weekends—jeans and maybe a flannel shirt. It was right after the War, but my parents had come through the Depression, and it affects their mentality—and yours."

Marian, a New Yorker of Catherine's age, has similar memories of shopping. She grew up in a small town in Maine. "My favorite store as a child was the five-and-dime," she says. "I still like five-and-dimes. They're junky places that have everything, and there's always one or two neat things you can find. There were comic books, penny candy . . . so it was all affordable." Like many men and women over forty, Marian remembers an older bargain culture that predates the discount superstore. She remembers when a bargain was about buying less rather than buying more.

"My mother never shopped for me," Marian continues. "I always wore hand-me-downs from my older sister. I wore hand-me-downs until the eighth grade when, thank God, my sister went away. My mother wasn't into shopping for clothes, period. But I remember once she bought us matching dresses. She brought them all the way from Boston. Mine was blue, and my sister's was yellow, and I thought that was pretty neat! I wore my new dress, and when I grew up, I wore my sister's."

Now, however, Marian lives in Manhattan, and she likes the social diversity of her neighborhood. "I like the fact that you have brownstones and projects in the same block," she says, "with a bodega in between." She appreciates that the Korean grocers who have bought most of the bodegas stay open all night: "the neighborhood is safer." But she also likes "the big, suburban grocery stores," especially on Long Island, where she has a vacation home, and the new superstores in Manhattan—"The Gap, Bed Bath & Beyond, T. J. Maxx. . . . I don't have to go more than three blocks to buy anything."

Marian straddles two worlds: those of the more affluent and the less affluent shopper. She has moved from wearing hand-me-down dresses and shopping in the five-and-dime to owning a second home near the ocean on Long Island. Despite being upwardly mobile, however, she doesn't feel comfortable in exclusive stores. Once, when Marian and a friend went into Tiffany, on Fifth Avenue, the two women felt awkward and out of place, especially since they "were only wearing trenchcoats." Marian prefers shopping at K-Mart, a big discount store on Long Island, where rich home-owners shop alongside working-class local people, and you can buy both soda and garden supplies: "I'm more comfortable there than in those exclusive places where you have to spend a lot of money."

Marian, Catherine, and Julia are not shopaholics. They were raised in plain, middle-class families. But shopping is important to them: it provides them with pleasure, variety, convenience, and a taste of living beyond their financial means. Yet shopping also plunges them into a state of conflict. They're not sure they should like having a lot of things, and they feel under pressure because they can't afford to buy everything anyway.

If upper-middle-class women often feel ambivalent about the contrast between their modest shopping past and the broader options they have today, working-class women have fewer choices. They develop strategies for stretching their money—by using deferred payment plans, buying from mail-order firms with ironclad guarantees on merchandise and a generous returns policy, and traveling around the city and driving to the suburbs in search of bargains. Or they buy every member of their family socks for Christmas when they find a huge supply in a "99-cents" store. Since jobs and children don't leave them much time to shop, they take a bargain where and when they find it.

When I ask a group of women whom I meet at a community center in East New York, one of the lowest-income areas in Brooklyn, where they shop, several of them immediately answer, "Sales!"

"I go to New Jersey," says Olivia, who owns a car. "Jersey, Connecticut, Pennsylvania. The quality is better outside New York."

"Some people have the bus trips to malls in Pennsylvania," says Dolores. "I'll go there and just pick up anything—"

"I go to the Pathmark supermarket right here on Flatlands Avenue," says Linda, who also drives. "I go to Green Acres shopping mall [on Long Island] when I got to go to Macy's, J. C. Penney. It's all in one place. If

Pathmark is having a sale and I see Key Food has a better price on one item, I go get that item at Key Food. I travel all over."

I don't expect to find this much geographical mobility among low-income black and Latino women, but most of these women are employed.[6] Yet some are in the last stages of AFDC, the federal welfare program of Aid to Families with Dependent Children, and they are constantly juggling their salaries and their benefits to see what they can afford to buy. While one woman mentions shopping for house plants as a pleasurable shopping activity, and another tells me quietly she likes to shop for furniture for her house, Diane says she relishes food shopping.

"To me it is pleasurable," she says, "because if I can pick up an item that maybe I haven't eaten in months because I am on a budget, to me that is pleasurable. Like lasagna. To make a lasagna, you have to get so many ingredients, by the time you finish buying them, it costs $20 or $25. That's not something you can just go ahead and make every month or every week."

Yet, despite their common economic situation, these women make different decisions about what to buy and how to shop for it. Olivia, the woman who drives around to shop for bargains, is one of fifteen children. She sits at the table fingering a heavy gold chain. "I tell you," she says, "when you wanted something with that brand name, you could ask everyone in your whole house, and someone would get it for you. I think that's one of the reasons that everything I see, I want."

Priscilla, a plainly dressed, younger woman who was born in the Caribbean, disagrees. "I come from a family with ten kids. You never saw my mother go to the store to buy clothes for us. She would buy material and make the clothes herself. Or the panties—they'd come from the same material as the dress. And you had one pair of shoes to wear, and they had to last you the whole year. Food comes first, and then clothes," she says. "I think it comes from my upbringing."

Her decision not to buy things unless they're needed may reflect her Caribbean upbringing; being an immigrant also affects her goals in life. "I look at where I want to be five to ten years from now," Priscilla says. "I can go to the salon and do the nails, but if I have a priority to make a home in my country, then that is my priority. Everybody has a different priority. When I'm sixty, am I going to end up in a nursing home? I shop for my kids, but not for me. I need food, transportation, money for whatever medication the kids need, emergency money. That's all I can afford."

"But we get up and go to work every day," Olivia says. "There has to be something you're working *for*. When my kids get grown, I'm going to be inside these four walls—OK?!"

Diane suggests there are severe limits on what a white-collar salary, even a decent salary, will buy. "I worked for over sixteen years," she says. "I started as a secretary and I ended as an administrator at Episcopal Hospital, making $16.50 an hour. When I saw that after the rent and the food was taken care of, I had only $50 [a week]—that's disgusting. Out of all that money, I had only $50—and I got to use that for transportation till the next payday. So one day I said to myself, When does *my* turn come? It's really hurting—you get up every morning . . . and sometimes you have to borrow money until that next paycheck."

"So how does this affect the way you shop?" I ask her.

"If I can get that good meal that maybe I haven't had in a month, I'll treat myself that way," Diane says. "Maybe have breakfast out—whatever it is."

For these women, treating themselves to something special is the most delightful part of shopping—maybe more so than for more affluent shoppers. Since the middle-class shoppers never talk to me about the "treats," I think the special treat, for them, is buying something they don't really need. Maybe, for Julia, it's a treat just to be surrounded by good things she can't afford to buy.[7]

"I like the part where I go for lunch when I go shopping," Dolores says.

"What about the hair and the nails?" Linda adds.

"That's every two weeks!" says someone else.

"If you're working and you can't afford to do something for yourself," Dolores continues, "you're working for nothing. You have to do for yourself."

"Financially, it's not a necessity," Olivia explains. "But emotionally it is. I need something in this world that says everybody loves me, too. What I do for my kids and my husband shows I love them. But at some point in the day, I have to say I love myself." And the women break into empathetic laughter.

"When you work," Olivia goes on, and I later find out she holds two jobs, "those are the things you have to do for yourself. I have three kids and a home to take care of. This treating yourself is something you work for. If you don't do it, no one else is going to do it for you. It gives you that boost, to want to do more for your family."

Plainly dressed Priscilla says she saves money by doing her own hair, but Rita, a vivacious young mother of three children, has a different approach.

"I used to do what you do," Rita says. "I used to say I'm buying a $9.99 perm and $10 of goop to fix it up. But I started noticing, if I can spend $16 for both my boys to get haircuts and buy grease and barrettes to fix my daughter's hair, why can't I go sit down and relax? I can do my own hair, give myself a perm or wrap it up. But I started feeling that somebody needs to treat *me*—to say, 'Ooh, your hair looks nice, what do *you* want?'"

Rita has a reason to spend money on her appearance. Not only does she have a job, she also has a fiancé, and she wants to look good for him. Yet like the other women sitting around the table, she faces a constant conflict of values between shopping for herself and shopping for her children.

"I'm getting married in June," Rita says, "and I want a tiara. But food has to come into my house first. I can wait to buy the tiara till June—or I'll be walking down the aisle without it! On the other hand, my mom says, 'You have to have it!' But I say, 'Mom, *you* taught me the food comes first!' That's just the way I am."

For Rita and all the women, having children was the crucial turning point in their shopping lives—the beginning of the neverending conflict between shopping for what they want and shopping for what they need. Once they have kids, they are perennially short of time and money. And going to stores is no longer a source of pleasure when moms are accompanied by young children.[8]

"Before having children," Rita says, "I would shop for whatever I liked, I didn't care what the price was—as long as I felt good about getting it, and I knew I had the money, and I had no one to answer to but me. But once the kids began to come, then it was budget, budget, budget. Timing, scheduling, putting their needs first before my needs."

"Sometimes you do go out to buy something for yourself," adds Dolores. "And then you walk by Young World and you see something on sale that they need . . . so you buy it instead of something for yourself."

"I'm not going to lie," Rita says. "Where I work, if you're sellin', and I like it, I want it. I'm going to buy it." But then she thinks about her children. "With three kids, I was getting paid only $103 every two weeks. I was like, Now I know what my mother was talking about! To get my kids what they needed, I had to make a budget."

I ask what sort of lessons she has learned.

"I don't get my son"—who is ten and a half—"Michael Jordan sneakers," Rita says. "The 'hang-out crowd'—they had to have it, so he had to have it. But I explained to him, 'You can't have it because I can't afford it.' I remember, that's how my mother was."

Rita also describes how she tries to teach her younger son, at age four, to discriminate between the allure of a brand name and rational shopping. "I hold up a Nike shirt, and I say to him, 'If I take the name Nike off this shirt, what'll it be? Just a shirt. So which one do you want?'

" 'All right, mommy,' he says. 'I don't want that one.'

"I'm teaching him, 'You just like it because you've heard of Nike, and Michael Jordan wears it.' "

"I don't go into that stuff," Linda says. "If it's strong"—she means durable—"I buy it. I go into The Gap when they have sales, I go to Old Navy when they have sales, I buy from Lands' End. I know it's not what they're wearing, but I don't go into that name-brand stuff. I work hard for my money. All these name brands—they got millions!

"God forbid when you don't have the money to buy for your kids. My daughter may not look like the other kids, but I know she's clean, no holes in her clothes. I'm not going into this Hilfiger and all of that."

Sometimes there is a conflict on this point in the family—a conflict not just between mothers and children, but between mothers and fathers. Rita's fiancé likes to buy her sons expensive sneakers. And Olivia's husband "would always say, 'He's got to have those sneakers,' even if they cost $100—that's not cheap!

"But me, I talk to the children," Olivia says. "I say, 'Why do you want that?' I went through the whole scenario with my son, so then he started realizing, 'My mother's right.'

"When he got old enough to buy his own clothes"—which was at the age of twenty—"he went my way. He called me up and said, 'Mommy, guess what, I found two dress shirts up in the Bronx for $35!' "

None of these mothers talks about brands as a connoisseur, the way Julia does, but, after all, Julia is a single woman with no kids and a different kind of cultural capital. The main comparison these women make isn't between Prada and JanSport, it's between The Gap, Lands' End, Spiegel catalogs, and the outlet stores, and between Nikes and Payless sneakers. With the exception of Julia, the middle-class shoppers I have spoken with never mention shopping for brand names. In total contrast, these working-class mothers are either more open to talking about them or are more moralistic about the dilemmas. Shopping for brand names—rather than by price or quality—creates one of the biggest conflicts of values in their lives.

The teenagers I meet at the same community center in East New York are savvy shoppers. Fifteen-year-old Arthur makes a list before he goes shopping for clothes, and he never spends more than $45 on a pair of pants.

Chris, a slightly younger boy, says, "Sometimes, before I go shopping, I browse the stores. That way, I know exactly what I want—I go get it, get on line, and get out quick."

But fifteen-year-old Jeffrey is less organized. "Me, I be watching a music video, and I say, 'Man, look at that brother's pants. That looks hot. I got to get something like that.'"

Kwame agrees. "You see something on TV, you say, 'I like that. I'm gonna see whether this store has that.'"

"You see something on TV, that's expensive," says one of the other boys.

"How do you know which store has the clothes?" I ask.

"You don't," Kwame says. "I went to Jimmy Jazz," an urban-wear store with branches in New York, "and got it—the one in Long Island."

So Kwame is mobile, too. But he is also keen on bargains. "Everything's cheaper at the outlets," he says. "That's, like, not in New York. At this bargain store, they sell name-brand stuff like a real Tommy Hilfiger shirt for $20. Out on Pennsylvania Avenue, across the street from Modell's. They got Pelle-Pelle too."

Chris furrows his brow. "You've got to look at the tag," he says, speaking about the label. "Half the time the tag'll be saying 'Food of the Loom' and stuff like that."

Kwame nods his head. "If you're gonna buy something like that and it be that cheap, you've really got to look at it."

"You really don't want to get caught with something fake around your friends," Arthur chimes in. "It's better to get something without the name than to get a name brand that's fake."

Lower-class kids have the option of shopping for brand names on the "gray market," from guys who sell clothes, bootleg cassettes, and surplus goods of all kinds on the street. But the boys know that it's risky to buy from these guys. They all have friends who were burned by showing off a logo that turned out to be a fake.

"One of my friends has this Tommy Hilfiger shirt. It was funny because we knew he bought it on the street, and he kept insisting that it was real. He was, like, 'Look at the tag!' And when we looked, all it said was '100 per cent cotton.' He got really crushed.

"From that day on, everyone called him Cool Joe."

But it's hard to resist the temptation of buying a brand name cheap. Arthur says he bought a shirt on the street that turned out to be fake, and he wears it underneath another shirt.

"I don't buy name-brand pants because most of the time people don't see [a logo]," says Chris. "I buy name-brand shirts."

"Why?" I ask.

"Because it's the style and *I'm* not paying for it . . . till I get a job."

"The way I look at it," says Kwame, "if I see something I like, I'll get it. And if it's a name brand, that's even better."

Like their fathers, these boys prefer to shop for brand names. The logos are an assurance of quality—not an assurance of the durability of goods their mothers seek, but an assurance of the personal quality their fathers value. When they look for name-brand shirts, the boys are shopping for the respect of other males—their peers. Unlike some of the more self-assured girls, the boys rely on brand names because they doubt their ability to make good choices.[9]

"I had the [Air] Jordans that said G," Jeffrey says, "but then I saw the Jordans with a J in a window. When I wore mine, they was looking like Ronald McDonald shoes, and my friends was dissing on me."

The girls are not so dependent on brand names. Fifteen-year-old Maria and her sixteen-year-old sister Anna like to window-shop. They'll consider buying any clothing, Maria says, "as long as it's cute." They go into stores, try on clothes, and decide what they like. "Then we go home and tell our parents, and our parents give us the money. Then we go back to the store and get it."

"I *love* going shopping!" their friend Alicia says. "Especially when I've got more than $200. I know my mother don't be making a lot of money, but I don't care!" Later Alicia shows me her photo album, with snapshots of her family and friends . . . and of Nike's Air Jordan sneakers, which she tells me she's crazy about. Generally, however, the girls say they would buy generic sneakers at Payless as long as they looked "cute." Whether the styles are "cute" or "cool," it's the judgment of one's peers that determines whether the teens' choices are acceptable.

Like older men, the boys claim they don't like to shop. Worse yet, going shopping with a girl would be like "committing suicide," Chris says, "because they're never satisfied. They see a dress or shoes in this store for, say, $15. Then they say, 'Let me go off to these other stores and get something cheaper.' Then they go to three other stores and find out it's more expensive, so they got to walk right back to the first store, and, after they get this, they see something else, and it starts all over again. . . . I can't handle it."

Of course, the way the girls shop gives them the opportunity for plenty of research. They know the styles and prices, and which store has the goods they want: this research enables them to choose without the security blanket of the logo. While they don't need the logo to feel they are smart shoppers, however, the girls do need to invest a lot of time.

What all the teens like is shopping for clothes without their moms. Shopping alone, or with their friends, makes them feel independent. To be a teenager today means going through the rite of passage of learning to shop for yourself—which begins, for these kids, around the age of thirteen or fourteen, for girls, and fifteen, for boys—the same age when lower-class children, in the past, became apprentices or went to work in factories. These teens receive money from their mothers for shopping; other relatives, not knowing what to give as a birthday present, give them money, too. Though many teenagers have part-time jobs, these teens didn't mention this.

"My mom sometimes picks out good clothes, and I like them," Kwame says. "But sometimes she goes. . . . " his voice trails off. "The clothes store is far from where we live, so she drives me."

Shopping, however distant the interaction with others, is still a social experience—and teenagers are painfully aware of that. "There are other teenagers in the store," says Kwame, "and they look at you, like, who's that lady over there? You can't associate with other teenagers when your mom's with you."

"I don't like going shopping with my mom all the time," Arthur says. "Because if I pick up something that I like, she makes this facial expression, like, 'I don't like that!'"

"My mother acts, like, 'OK, you can have it,' but she don't like it," adds Chris. "She says, 'You can get it,' but now she's got me feeling guilty. So I tell my mother, 'Fine, but you don't like it,' and then we say to each other, when I get older, when I got the money, I can go shopping by myself."

Teenagers shopping: a rite of passage. Photo by Richard Rosen.

Boys sometimes prefer to go shopping, especially sneaker shopping, with their fathers because the men are more excited by brand names. "I like to go with my father," Kwame says, "because he don't care how much the sneaker costs, he just get it for me. My mom, she's like $80 maximum, and some sneakers under $80 is so cheap."

The moms, of course, have a different interpretation of their own behavior. "I have a fourteen-year-old," says Linda, who happens to be Chris's mother. "I shop for him whether he likes it or not. It doesn't make a difference what it says on the label. My son's the kind of person who knows how to carry himself. The other teenagers see him, and they don't think he can afford his clothes, because he looks so nice!"

Though mothers draw a firm line on the teenagers' clothing purchases, they enjoy dressing up the younger children to go shopping. All the teens I spoke with remember how their moms loved to buy them fancy outfits, especially for holidays—though these memories contrast with the mothers' emphasis on bargain hunting.

"My mother always liked polka dots and stripes," Arthur grins. "She always used to get the whole outfit."

"Yeah, you looked like a prisoner," Kwame teases him.

Anna and Maria's mother used to dress them up in matching outfits. She "would always look for the cutest little outfit, like the skirt with the fishnet stockings and little socks with bows and shoes with little heels." Alicia's mother arranged her hair in ponytails and dressed her in a smaller version of her own outfit. Michelle says her mother bought her "a hat with a little turkey on the side" for Thanksgiving. "I just couldn't stand that, but my mother thought it was cute."

The downside of teenagers' shopping without their parents is that they are shadowed by sales clerks and security guards in stores. Sometimes this happens because they're dark-skinned, but usually it's just because they're teens. This isn't a topic that they bring up themselves, but they tell me about it when I ask.

"For my junior high school prom," Chris says, "I got a suit with a cummerbund and everything. I put the cummerbund in my bag, but I was thinking, 'I better remember to put that out when I leave.' So the guard started looking through my bag and said, 'What's this?'

"I said, 'I took that,' but my friend said, 'Wait a minute, don't buy that,' and he started cursing them out. We walked out."

"I hate going to an expensive store by myself," Arthur says.

"You be puttin' your hand in your pocket, and they think. . . . " Kwame begins.

"You know you have the money for it, but *they* think you don't," Arthur continues. "They ask you, 'Are you going to pay for all of that?' "

Alicia, who is darker-skinned than the other Latinas in the group, had an especially frustrating experience while shopping. "We went, four or five friends, to a 99-cents store—it had all kinds of stuff. The people working there didn't know I speak Spanish, and they said, 'Watch the one in the black hood,' and that was me!"

The middle-class shoppers I spoke with also remember learning to shop for themselves as a teenage rite of passage. As children, they all shopped with their moms; then, in their early teens, they began to go shopping with older siblings—usually sisters; and, finally, in their late teens, they went shopping with their friends. The tension they used to feel with their moms—over buying toys, in the early years, and, later, over differences of taste in clothes—evaporated when they shopped for themselves.

Michael, a reporter in his early thirties, stopped shopping with his mother when he entered his first or second year of high school. "Up until then," he says, "it's always mom who has the money or the car."

Michael grew up in a small town on the Jersey shore where there weren't many stores to choose from. "We would go to the same stores—Steinbeck's, Sears, Bill's Work Clothes—and I remember switching to another store in high school—Brave New World. It was like a surf shop and an upscale clothing store. When I started shopping on my own, I would only go to Brave New World and Bill's Work Clothes."

Changing stores is symbolic of changing identities, and Michael is conscious of the importance of this shift. "Steinbeck's and Sears were more my mother's stores. They were more her style. The clothes were a little less expensive and more conservative. I needed a more hip look." Not only was Brave New World a youth-oriented store, it was also leisure-oriented. "I was into skateboarding, so Brave New World met all my needs. I could identify with every aspect of the store."

The social space of Sears and Steinbeck's was too diverse for the teenage Michael. In those early years of niche marketing, he was eager to differentiate himself from the older fuddy-duds who shopped at Sears by shopping with his peers. "In Steinbeck's, you had clothes not just for young people but also ladies' clothes, men's clothes, clothes for elderly ladies. As a kid, you don't want to have to deal with those other sections. It's like going to Banana Republic or The Gap nowadays. You have clothes for young people, you don't have a section for elderly ladies."

Betsy, a woman in her thirties who works in marketing for Ralph Lauren, remembers shopping with her younger brother at Jeans Wearhouse when she was a teenager in New York City. "It was the coolest place," she says. "It was in the seventies, when designer jeans were becoming big. The jeans were all hung up on the wall, and it was the coolest. Everybody went there. It was an end-of-summer rite."

These specialty shops geared to teens—a new space developed by retailers in the seventies—made shopping easy and mass-produced the idea that shopping was fun. "Brave New World simplified the whole shopping experience," Michael recalls. "That was very important to me. It still is."

Michael didn't want to spend much time shopping for clothes, and he didn't feel as pressured to economize on money as Chris, Arthur, Kwame, and their friends do. The Brooklyn teens may spend more time and energy shopping because they can't afford to buy all their clothes in one "cool" shop, like Jimmy Jazz; they go to discount and outlet stores and even shop on the street.

Nevertheless, no matter where they shop or what they buy, teenagers use shopping to learn how to be autonomous. Alex, a Manhattan architect in his late twenties, grew up in western Canada. He remembers the first time he went shopping without his mom as a wonderful experience:

"I was maybe twelve or thirteen, and my sister and I were going to go shopping. I had no needs, and no idea of what I might want, but we were going to go downtown and go shopping. There are a series of stores in downtown Calgary, with The Bay and Eaton's—the big department stores—at either end of the street, about four blocks apart.

"I actually bought a couple of things. It felt really good, like it was mature. I had an allowance, but I didn't know what I wanted to buy. I remember browsing, looking for something I might want. I bought a tin trash can and a couple of other things. It was for my room, for my own space." The steps toward autonomy are measured by exercising a consumer's choice.

The middle-class women I talked to also learned to shop with their older sisters. Shopping with a sister not only provides you with a ready-made mentor; it also creates a special form of intimacy. This is especially important for girls: an older sister acts as a surrogate mom, while the younger sister is her apprentice. These roles enact a bond between the girls of a family, and between material goods and the desire to be grown up. They also enable girls to come to a tacit agreement on standards of value.

Sarah, an editor in her late twenties who lives on the Upper West Side of Manhattan, grew up in Ohio. "I'm the fourth of five daughters," she says. "I learned to shop by going with my sisters and with my friends— mostly with my sisters. My middle sister is an 'aesthete,' truly a shopaholic. She used to go visit clothes that she really wanted but couldn't afford. She'd go to the shop," Sarah laughs, "and say, 'These are mine!'"

These shopping trips with her sisters taught Sarah how to shop. "We all had to shop very carefully," she says, "because we didn't have a lot of money. Even when I was a teenager, and I was shopping with my own money. So we would just look a lot."

"Just looking," in this case, is not a tired tactic to evade a salesperson's attention. "Just looking" means doing research on goods, as Julia does, to determine a product's quality and general characteristics, as well as to compare different styles.

"We would see this is made of silk, this one is linen, and this is wool," Sarah says. "We'd look at the patterns and the cuts, and touch all the fabrics. It wasn't a formal education, but it was about figuring out what we liked. Because we did this mostly in department stores, it was nice that we were ignored by salespeople. We could just run around and really look at things."

So Sarah's sister—the "shopaholic," as she calls her—is more of a practical aesthete than a hedonist. The time spent looking at goods as a teen has given Sarah some of her sister's cultural capital, and has also made her a more practiced shopper. Her experience "just looking" gives her a rational basis for choosing goods.

Cindy, a woman in her twenties who grew up in San Jose, California, also learned how to shop from her older sister.

"There's a certain way she shops," Cindy says. "I was the little sister, so of course I wanted to shop the way she shopped. If she has a particular thing in mind, she'll run through the store, zeroing in on that one thing. She does the 'Highlander charge.'" She pauses to laugh. "An important thing for her is the feel of things. If it doesn't feel right, she won't get it.

"I'm like that, too. You're wearing it, right? So you want it to feel good."

This tendency to touch goods—to run your fingers down a rack of trousers or through a pile of sweaters—is often ridiculed by the men who accompany women while they shop. But, like the teenage boy's description of the girls who run around to several stores looking for the cheapest prices, the tactile strategy is vital to learning to shop. It provides a knowledge of different fabrics and finishes, suggests density and durability, and gives grounds for predicting whether a product will satisfy. Not only does touching give some of the sensual pleasure of shopping, it makes women more expert shoppers.

Men acknowledge women's expertise when they delegate clothes shopping to the women in their lives. André, a website designer in his twenties who grew up in Montreal, admits he always goes shopping "with a girl" because "I'm not very good at it." André is color-blind, but more than this, he says, "I think they know how to choose. Everything I've ever bought these last few years, girls have chosen for me. I let them choose, and then I buy."

Yet if many men allow women to buy their clothes, they delight in being expert shoppers themselves for *some* things. They often spend a lot of time shopping—but they call it "serious" research, especially when they're shopping for an important item. In that case, men consider the time they spend shopping justified by the cost—or "financial investment"—of the purchase. The bigger the purchase, the more shopping—or "research"—is required.

Though André relies on women to choose his clothes, he takes pride—like many men—in doing research for his music purchases. "When I actually started shopping for myself," he says, "I was a teenager. I'd shop for used CDs and records every weekend. I'd shop with my best friend, and we'd blow our entire allowance. It was a competition, trying to see who could get the best deal. We have so many good memories from that! That was important."

This kind of research led to André's purchase of a guitar when he was an older teen. "Shopping for my first-ever guitar was the ultimate shopping adventure," he says, "because it was a huge investment. It's a financial investment. To research that, I went to different stores. You have to search out where the stores are, which are the best stores, and which stores have what you want. All that comes after deciding what you need. A lot of it is by word of mouth."

Yet men still claim they shop differently from women. Michael, the reporter who shopped at Brave New World when he was younger, says he is "one of the fastest shoppers in the world. I enjoy shopping, but I don't make a big production out of it." Like Chris in East New York, he boasts of deciding on what he wants to buy in advance, then zeroing in on the merchandise. "I go in, I see what I want, and I get it. I don't even like the process of trying things on."

But like André, Michael invests a great deal of time in choosing certain products. "I'll take my time looking at shoes," he says. "In Manhattan, there are so many good shoe stores, especially in the Village, along Broadway. I like buying shoes more than any other piece of clothing.

"I enjoyed buying the three suits I own, too. It's a really important purchase, so you have to take your time. It's enjoyable to spend time differentiating between the higher-priced Italian designers because the differences are so subtle. Like, you're looking at workmanship. It's not like looking for casual shirts. You're buying a suit for important purposes, so it forces you to focus on the purchase.

"I have two Armani suits, and when you get to that level, it's important to take your time and educate yourself."

So Michael justifies shopping for *Armani* suits as an exercise in connoisseurship. Like Sarah's sister the "shopaholic," who has an "aesthetic" approach to clothes shopping, he uses shopping to learn to appreciate "subtle differences" in fabric and craftsmanship. While shopping for the suits, Michael probably felt all the jackets on the rack.

But the typical, brusque male attitude toward shopping is repeated by Jacques, a business strategist in his midthirties who has recently moved to New York from Paris. "Shopping to me is a waste of time," he says, "especially when it's for clothes." Lacking an older sister, he goes shopping with his younger sister. "She knows what goes with what and has very good taste. And she knows my taste." Jacques doesn't like to spend time on routine shopping, which is what he considers clothes shopping to be. He wants to be "efficient": "I'm very efficient when I go grocery shopping, too. I know what I want and where it is."

"In France," he says, "if I need something I go to Galeries Lafayette, where they have everything I need. I only go to one store. It's organized like Macy's, by brand, so it's easier for me." Jacques regards branding with approval, as a mapping strategy that eases his passage through the chaotic world of goods. He is unconscious of how deeply rooted his dependence on branding is. He does not know—or care—that many older women prefer the old organization of department stores' merchandise by functional categories to the postseventies organization by designer boutiques. It was easier and quicker to find a blue, long-sleeved shirt in the "Blouses" department than to look in separate boutiques divided according to the different price categories of various designers.

When Jacques moved to New York, he asked friends to show him where to shop. "Over three days, my friends took me to different stores—to Macy's, to Century 21," a discount store in lower Manhattan. Though "Century 21 is a mess," he complains, compared to the organization-by-boutiques at Macy's, "now I know where to go next year when I need to go shopping."

Bookstores, however, represent a different, more desirable kind of shopping. "I like books," Jacques says. "I could go to Barnes & Noble and look for an hour and not buy anything. But then, it's a pleasure; it's not shopping."

The middle-class shoppers take a more aesthetic approach to shopping than the working-class women I spoke with. Most of the middle-class shoppers make negative comments about large, discount stores, even though they shop there. Many praise small, neighborhood stores, where they see the same clerks whenever they go—shops that, for this reason, have a "small town" feeling. The working-class women don't talk about interacting with the people who work in stores. They are more likely to praise discount stores for their low prices than to criticize the impersonal atmosphere. Perhaps this reflects different kinds of cultural capital, which in turn reflects the broader economic options of the middle class. Looking for atmosphere or intimacy in a store is a form of luxury. Even though I share this preference, it reminds me of the opposition to superstores in more affluent towns and the support for them in areas where residents are poor.

Sarah's husband, Dave, describes warehouse clubs as a source of entertainment. Though the couple wants to save money, and actually belongs to a "wholesale club" outside the city, Dave presents himself as a detached observer of the store's displays and atmosphere.

"We have a good time there," he says. "It's hysterical. The aesthetic in there . . . ," and he stops because he doesn't quite know what to say. "Shopping in a warehouse is fun," he continues. "There's stuff in there you'd never buy, but it's funny to see, like those huge cans of refried beans."

"But at the same time," Sarah says, "they manage to display most of the stuff at eye level, so you can actually see everything—"

"And get at it!" Dave exclaims. "There's certainly an entertainment value."

Though it sounds as though Dave may be in denial about saving money, he and Sarah—a middle-class couple with no children—like to talk about stores that provide a personal quality of service. "Sometimes you want the homey feeling," Dave says. "There's this one store that's run by a couple, and they're always there. The hours are never certain, because they only open when they want to. So you go by and just hope it's open, but it's great. They're really nice. If you get something, they'll engage you in conversation, tell you about where they found it, what market they went to to find it."

"And that's very genuine," Sarah adds.

Dave's favorite store is in Jersey City, where the couple used to live. "The store seems almost untouched by time," he says. "That's so unusual. It takes time to find these places. There's this Salvation Army store in the worst part of the city, and there's this guy, Willie, who works there. He's so nice. My friend took me there, and I got a bowling shirt, another shirt, and a stack of old LPs that are worth quite a bit. All that for four dollars. You're not going to find that anywhere in Manhattan. People are just too savvy; they know what things are worth."

Like most middle-class shoppers, Dave likes to have a range of options.

"I don't want to buy my underwear [in the Salvation Army store]," he laughs. "For that, I'll go to J. C. Penney."

This attitude is echoed by Terry, a receptionist in a doctor's office in upstate New York. Though she can afford to shop at Ann Taylor, she prefers to shop for bargains at Kmart. "I'll spend $120 on some item, then I'll spend $4 on a pair of shoes. There's no limit upward to what I'll spend . . . well, there's always a limit. But there's no limit down, either. I have no shame!" Terry pauses to laugh heartily.

"Part of me loves bargain hunting," she says. "I would much rather spend $20 on a used suit in a consignment store and get loads of compliments than buy something for $120. I bought a pair of $16 shoes, and people would run over to me and say how much they liked them. You know those big, clunky shoes with the chunky heel and buckle? I found them before they were 'in.'"

Terry thrills to bargain hunting because it establishes that, even if she isn't rich, she has cultural capital. Especially when she wore a cheap, navy suit she bought at Kmart to a wedding shower, and told the hostess's "millionaire friends" she "got it at a boutique in New York City. . . . There was no way I was going to tell them that I got it at 'Le Kmart!'"

But she also aggressively pursues the "thrill" of shopping in dollar stores and discount stores: "I was a Price Club member, but now I'm a member of Sam's." She once was ecstatic to find $3 sweat pants for her young son, decorated with an action figure he liked, in a bin in the basement of an odd-lots store in Manhattan. Nonetheless, Terry has the option of going to Ann Taylor or Talbot's "when I want to feel pampered." She has enough money to choose the "atmosphere" in these stores over bargains.

Betsy, with her marketing job at Ralph Lauren, has been transformed by the aesthetic experience of shopping in the company's flagship store on Madison Avenue.

"It's an old mansion," she says about the store. "It's incredible. You walk in there, and you understand how [Ralph Lauren] can sell clothes like that, that cost that much. There's beautiful mahogany, chandeliers, carpets on the floors. Everyone is super nice.

"In the mansion, you feel like what you're buying is really worth something. You know it's good, that it won't fall apart on you. It really conjures up an image.

"It's very hard to shop elsewhere now, to look at things when your eye has been trained by such beauty. You get jaded."

Before she worked for Ralph Lauren, Betsy was a bargain shopper. "I'd go to Loehmann's, or Filene's Basement, or Century 21," she says. "I'd never just walk into any store and buy something. Now I do almost all my shopping at Ralph Lauren. . . . It's a whole lifestyle."

Though Ralph Lauren is not an option for the mothers in East New York, they wrestle with the demons of desire, too. Their children's desires for Nike shoes, the trips to the discount stores outside the city, the running around to different supermarkets to buy items on sale: for these women, every shopping experience is a struggle for value. They know they should take the rational approach, but still, shopping creates a greater conflict than they are willing to admit.

Rita, who tries to teach her four-year-old son not to want a Michael Jordan shirt, finally admits to a conflict of values. "I buy my kids the name brands because *I* didn't have them," she says. "It's not a necessity, but if I can afford to give it to them, I'll buy it.

"With my mother, it was always, 'No!' It was never, 'If you'll be good, you'll get it.' My grandmother was like that, so my mother was like that too. But I'm not. If I can afford it, I'll give it to them. If I can't afford it, I'll tell them so."

Even Linda, who shops for fourteen-year-old Chris, admits she buys her children brand-name sneakers. "I never had name brands myself," she says. "I used to go with my parents to a store on Williams Avenue—Sunnydale Farms." ("Oh, yeah," several of the other women exclaim.) "I used to come out with new sneakers and everybody would go like, 'Oh, my god!' That was very embarrassing. In those days, those sneakers would cost you $1.99!"

These women have learned to subdue their desires. Olivia, who says she "used to be a shopaholic," stopped using her credit cards after her family bought a house. Joleen, who uses the deferred-payment plan from the Spiegel and Lands' End mail-order catalogs, says she "had credit cards, but I got rid of them." Linda says, "I put mine in the drawer. I use it for emergencies."

"This is reality," Olivia says. "You sit down and say, 'Ninety-nine cents, that's fine for me.' "

But the memory of desire lies deep. When Joleen tells how, as a teenager, she learned to sew her own clothes to make special outfits for parties, she recalls that "the name Gloria Vanderbilt was big when I was coming up." Just the mention of the old designer name makes all the women chuckle fondly.

"Gloria Vanderbilt!!" they exclaim in unison, betraying more than a passing interest in the brand labels on designer jeans. "Sergio Valente!!!"

Our memories show that shopping is a lifelong learning process: learning about goods, learning about stores, and learning how to be "a choosing subject." Shopping is not only—nor primarily—an activity of acquiring *goods*; it is a social encounter, a research operation, and both a moral and an aesthetic experience of acquiring *values*.

The mothers of East New York reveal many of the conflicts experienced by shoppers—especially women. Their major conflict comes from balancing the need to adhere to a strict budget with their children's desires for brand-name clothes and shoes. But these women also feel conflict within themselves. Dolores says you have to buy things for yourself—which I think reflects both the philosophy of the women's movement and the L'Oréal ads of recent years (". . . because I'm worth it!")—but she can't pass a children's store without buying something for her kids instead of going shopping for herself.

Women shoppers also feel conflict about their bodies. When I ask the East New York mothers why shopping is sometimes an unpleasant experience, they don't talk about price; they respond with one voice: "Size!" When Sarah, the editor, mentions a bad shopping day, she tells me about "a small boutique in Chelsea where I saw the perfect dress in the window. All the people who work there are these thin models who care more about what they look like than anything else. I tried on a size 10 and it was a little bit tight, but when I asked for a size 12, one of them looked at me and said"—she mimics her condescending voice—" 'We don't carry anything in size 12!' "

Neither Sarah nor Dolores is a status shopper. None of the women I spoke with lust after designer names, though they often lust after bargains. Olivia is a self-confessed, reformed shopaholic, and Priscilla denies herself little treats so she can build a house in her country. Terry flaunts her cultural capital by wearing an outfit from Kmart to a party where the guests are in Ralph Lauren. Yet while older women who grew up in the fifties remember shopping modestly and wearing hand-me-downs, women who grew up in recent decades don't have this experience. Even Olivia says that no one wants to buy secondhand clothes these days. The common point is: Regardless of income, everyone wants to buy something new, something good, and something that gives them pleasure. But how do you know what's really good? Do you buy what your mother taught you, or do you go for the brand name?

Our desire to shop derives from the biological drive of hunting for food, the modern ideology of individual choice, and the social drive—which has accelerated since the sixties—to get "the best." But we are thwarted by subjective factors like our bodies, by objective factors like price, and by simply not knowing where, at a specific moment, to find the bargains.

No wonder shopping isn't easy.

3

from woolworth's to wal-mart

They did nothing different than almost any other person who visits the state of Maine. . . . They went to eat, they gassed up their car and they visited Wal-Mart.

—A spokesman for the Maine Department of Public Safety, describing the activities of two terrorists on the evening before they crashed a jet plane into the World Trade Center in Manhattan (*New York Times*, 2001)

Shopping is one of the few activities that still bring all classes of people together in a public, or somewhat public, space. I'm talking about the discount stores, of course, the places where you don't shop for something special that you can't find anywhere else: you shop for the lowest prices. These are our public squares, our contemporary marketplace; they give us the opportunity to be surrounded by the shiny, tawdry, giant-size, and most standardized products of mass society. Everyone can find a bargain here, and we love it.

Just look at me, standing on Astor Place in front of Kmart, at 8:55 one morning, waiting for the store to open. There's no special sale today, but I'm waiting patiently with ten other people for an employee to unlock Kmart's revolving door.

We're all kinds of shoppers: college students from NYU in jeans and sneakers or black leather jackets, at least one of them with blue-streaked hair; middle-aged women who have climbed out of the nearby subway station on their way to work in offices; some men who might be clerks at the post office on Fourth Avenue, and others who look like new media producers from the East Village—and me, in my red Patagonia windbreaker and black Mephisto tie-shoes, stopping by for a six-pack of Bounty paper towels after dropping my daughter off at school.

I'm actually surprised that we're so hot to shop at Kmart. When the store opened, in the late nineties, I was pretty sure that it would fail. My neighborhood, Greenwich Village, has a bohemian reputation; we're known for vintage clothing stores, coffeehouses, and off-Broadway theaters, and local organizations raise a constant war against tall buildings, chain stores, and all kinds of schlock. I wondered how Kmart's racks of cheap socks and polyester slacks, displays of plastic storage bins, and meager grocery department, specializing in snacks and convenience foods, would play downtown. Despite the store's location astride two subway lines, at a heavily trafficked intersection, people don't shop much on that side of the neighborhood. Kmart is isolated from the bargain stores of Fourteenth Street, and hidden from passersby with giant photographic blowups of smiling models in the windows instead of enticing displays of merchandise.[1]

Yet those of us who do the household shopping are drawn to the low prices on big cartons of name-brand paper towels and laundry detergent that are so much costlier at the small, neighborhood supermarkets. We know these purchases would be even cheaper at a warehouse club like Costco, on the Brooklyn waterfront, if we could get there easily by bus or subway.

Like the warehouse clubs, Kmart has a minimalist decor. It looks like any other Kmart and like most of the Wal-Marts I have seen. Fluorescent lighting, beige vinyl tile floors, steel and plastic shelving, open racks. There's an abundance of goods, but it all looks improvised—as though the store could pack up overnight and move away. The security guards and cashiers wear red jackets or vests over their street clothes; the cashiers have printed name labels pinned to their chests. The only sales clerk I have ever seen stands behind the cosmetics counter. If you're not interested in perfume and want to ask a question about anything else in the store, you have to try a cashier or hunt for the manager. I have glimpsed the manager only once, when she came to a checkout line in the grocery department to speak to the cashier.

The first floor, with the usual jewelry and cosmetics displays, gardening supplies, and women's sportswear, is fairly cheerful, and so is the grocery department in the basement. But if you shop at Kmart on a weekday morning, you could get lonely cruising the wide, empty aisles of the upper floor, with its random assortment of suitcases, picture frames, Martha Stewart sheets and towels, and a few racks of children's clothing. It's sad up there. Although you can sit on plastic chairs in the Kmart café and gaze through a large, plate-glass window onto the bustling street below, you can't escape the feeling of emptiness. The lack of character in the store's design helps you to focus on the merchandise.

To my surprise, however, the store is often crowded, especially on the weekends. Shoppers scurry around carrying mops, drying racks, and vacuum cleaners they're buying because they have recently moved or they're setting up their first apartment. Kmart has almost everything they need, including starter sets of Rubbermaid storage bins. These shoppers tend to be younger than most of the other customers and to shop in pairs. Many of them are students at nearby universities and art schools. In terms of age, the shoppers are a microcosm of the neighborhood.

They are even more a microcosm of the city's ethnic diversity. While I wait in line at the grocery checkout on a Sunday afternoon, a young couple speaks Chinese behind me, a father talks to his young son in Korean, and another woman customer jokes with the cashier in the soft, slightly southern accent of an African American New Yorker. A thin woman with short white hair, shoulders slightly stooped from age, slowly counts out seven one-dollar bills and laughs. "This means I don't buy nothin' else," she says, in a gnarly voice I connect with Irish Americans who live in Brooklyn.

Everyone comes to Kmart. Even my neighbor, who paid a million dollars for his apartment several years ago, smiles when he sees my Kmart plastic shopping bag and I tell him about the paper towels. "Sure," he says, "and they're even cheaper at Costco."

Most shoppers come to Kmart because it's the kind of store they're used to—if they grew up anywhere outside New York City. Before the 1990s, New York was an exception to the rest of the United States: we didn't have discount superstores.

Until that time, shopping in the city's residential neighborhoods was an intensely personal experience. You shopped for each item in a small, special-ized, independently owned store, whose owner usually had a story, and hearing that story was part of the experience of both living in the neigh-borhood and shopping there.[2]

Shopping for bargains was also a personal experience. In an older gener-ation, many New Yorkers had a relative or a neighbor in the garment industry who would get them an item much cheaper than in the stores. "I can get it for you wholesale" even became the title of a Broadway musical in 1962. If you didn't have these connections, bargain hunting required you to travel outside your neighborhood—to the stores on Orchard Street, on the Lower East Side, to Fourteenth Street, or to Brooklyn. In that case, you had to mobilize all your skills for hunting and gathering. You would ask your cheap friends who always brag about paying the lowest prices, and you would look carefully for announcements of sales. When you did decide to buy something, you haggled with the shopkeeper to see if you could get a better deal. It's like buying a car—no one wants to pay the sticker price—but New Yorkers make the refusal to pay list price on anything a point of local pride.

Many people think this kind of bargain shopping, and the psychic wear and tear it causes, are all too typical of New York City—and they are right. But the city has only been able to maintain these traces of the past, and resist discount superstores, because of its peculiar mix of geography, economics, and local politics.

The key factor is real estate. Land has always been expensive in New York, so it is costly for a store like Wal-Mart to assemble the four to six acres the chain requires for a store and parking lot. Superstores also depend on getting frequent deliveries by supersize trucks; New York City's crowded streets are infamous for causing traffic jams. Moreover, unlike in small towns and rural areas, most elected officials in New York City continue to favor local merchants. Since 1974, the city's zoning laws have supported the mix of department stores, small supermarkets, and independently owned shops the city is known for. These laws ban superstores that sell carpets, clothing, and food, with the exception of those large stores that were "grandfathered" because they were already here when the laws were passed. Although most stores have grown bigger over the years, the zoning laws freeze the size of stores permitted to be built "as of right" at standards set at the turn of the twentieth century. While stores larger than 10,000 square feet are banned, a typical superstore is twenty to thirty times that size.

The zoning laws limit a superstore like Costco's warehouse club, which is willing to pay the high land prices and operating costs typical of New York City, to a location in the half-vacant manufacturing districts along the waterfront. Such a site is not very convenient for a walk-in trade, but a retail chain can build there at the scale they want without seeking special zoning approvals. As late as the nineties, the largest supermarket in New York City had only 66,500 square feet, and that was in a middle-income apartment complex built in the "green fields" of the Bronx.[3]

New Yorkers are well aware of the advantages of shopping in big stores. Like shoppers in Philadelphia, Washington, D.C., and Chicago, we complain about the narrow selection of goods, high prices, and untidiness of local supermarket chains. We use extraordinary means to search for bargains—borrowing a yarmulke and shopping on Sundays in stores owned by Hasidic and Orthodox Jews,[4] or making weekend excursions to shopping malls in the suburbs. Bus companies run routes to outlet malls outside the city, and inner-city churches charter buses to take members to these malls.

But when Home Depot or Costco announces plans to open branches in New York City, lots of New Yorkers react angrily rather than with delight. Strong community opposition forced the IKEA chain, which operates a superstore in Elizabeth, New Jersey, to give up after making several attempts to build another store in or near the city—first, in the northern suburb of New Rochelle, and then, near the Gowanus Canal, in Brooklyn. Like the residents of small towns who become activists by joining Sprawlbusters, a nationwide coalition of community groups opposing superstores, these New Yorkers fear that the blank outer walls, absentee corporate ownership, and heavy car traffic of "big box" stores will ruin their community.[5]

The debate over superstores turns partly on aesthetics and a sense of place: these stores are ugly, they turn their backs to the street, they buffer themselves with acres of asphalt parking lots, and they look the same no matter where they are. They attract too many shoppers, whose automobiles clog the streets and pollute the air. But the argument against them also reflects economic self-interest. Local merchants oppose superstores because they know they cannot compete with their low prices, range of merchandise, and ability to pay high rents. The merchants' fears are not put to rest when business experts advise them to focus on personal service and "niche" merchandise, or to forget about the physical store and sell their wares on the Internet. Among shoppers, it's usually the more affluent people who oppose superstores because they want to maintain the physical scale and social diversity of their local community. They can afford to pay the higher prices in small shops, or they can get into their cars and drive to a warehouse club. On the other hand, less mobile and less affluent people support superstores because they want to improve their shopping opportunities. They know these stores will bring them a wider variety of merchandise. And they hear the discounters' siren song: "Low prices, always."[6]

It's difficult to win an argument against the bargain culture in which superstores wrap the shopping experience. When a Wal-Mart, Costco, or Barnes & Noble opens, we compare the prices, hours, and variety of goods they offer with those of local stores, and the big box wins us over. The superstore's lure is practically unbeatable if we are poor and our town is economically depressed.[7]

But according to an anti-Wal-Mart activist in east Texas, the arrival of a superstore sets a disastrous chain of events into motion. Independent stores shut down, the town loses jobs and property taxes, local newspapers earn less advertising revenue, and the superstore's profits are sent out of the local community—and often out of state—to the corporate headquarters and the business services it deals with. When Wal-Mart is faced with opposition, however, it threatens a town council to get its way. If the council won't allow it to buy the land, or grant it the building permits, that it wants, the chain will never open a store in that town. But after it gets what it wants, and opens the store, Wal-Mart doesn't do anybody any favors. Once everybody shops at the new Wal-Mart, local stores close and the downtown is dead. At that point, the chain is free to consolidate. It closes the superstore and shifts operations to a new and even larger supercenter in another town. From the point of view of a community that doesn't want them, or one that they abandon, these superstores are today's "satanic mills."[8]

Yet to most shoppers, discount superstores are sublime. By 2000, all the major discount chains—Wal-Mart, Kmart, Target, and Home Depot—were among the top ten retailers in the country, and the other six were supermarket chains. Moreover, as superstores have sprouted in the suburbs of New York, people who live in the city have flocked to them. These stores offer us larger selections at lower prices than we pay in the city, and—because they are located in small towns with smaller budgets than New York's—the sales tax we pay there is only half the city's rate. In 1994, Mayor Rudolph Giuliani announced his intention of recapturing some of our fleeing tax revenues by changing the zoning laws to permit superstores to build in the city. The City Planning Department supported the mayor on this issue. They cited a Gallup Poll of a thousand New York City residents showing that 32 percent of them regularly shop in large retail stores in the suburbs. Each resident, on the average, makes twenty-two out-of-town shopping trips a year. And these trips cost the city government $3 *billion*.[9]

Losing tax revenue is no small matter for New York City, where large budget gaps have been endemic for years. To make matters worse, in the early nineties, the city was still suffering from the stock market crash of 1987. Many people were unemployed. Investment bankers and stockbrokers—the big spenders of the eighties—no longer had the large bonuses with which they bought oil paintings, Rolex watches, and rare Bordeaux wines—all of which are subject to the city's sales tax. Real estate developers had ceased, temporarily, to build, because cutbacks in the labor force left offices vacant. Desperate to encourage new economic development, city officials cast a calculating eye at the large retail-and-entertainment complexes being built elsewhere. Compared with shopping venues in other cities, the director of the City Planning Department, Joseph Rose, declared, New York's retail economy was "anemic." If only the City Council would legalize superstores, Rose said, New York could "take advantage of the next generation of retail investment."[10]

But the City Council wouldn't change the zoning laws. Council Democrats, anticipating a fierce campaign for Giuliani's reelection, were furious with the Republican mayor for trying to impose his will and sway public opinion. Neighborhood merchants' associations feared annihilation by superstores' competition. Local community boards were angry because the mayor had not consulted them. For my neighborhood to get a Kmart, I thought mistakenly, there would have to be a shopping revolution.

What is truly revolutionary about the superstore, I have come to realize, is not its place in the city, but the space inside the store. This space is "universal": it's the same for everyone. The emphasis on low prices tends to minimize social class distinctions and nurtures the illusion that shopping is the same for everyone—because all of us love a bargain. The heterogeneous assortment of goods in a universal store recalls the open market squares of medieval towns and the Middle Eastern bazaar. But modern universal stores are big, enclosed, fronted by plate-glass windows, and adroitly divided by wide aisles where everyone cruises between packages of things to buy. We can never forget that money determines how much we buy. But *what* we buy in a universal store is the same for everyone.[11]

Unlike the early twentieth-century department store's hierarchical arrangement of floors, beginning on the bottom with the bargain basement, the universal store brings rich and poor shoppers together in a uniform, one-level space. Goods are displayed together regardless of price, and every item wears a price tag. Here there are neither secrets nor privacy—nor even fitting rooms or a place to sit down and try on shoes.

Moving beyond the department store's use of glass and light, the universal store makes the shopping experience totally transparent. Whether we're in the supermarket or the discount store, fluorescent light floods every corner. Bottles of extra-virgin olive oil from Italy stand shoulder-to-shoulder with store-brand vegetable oil and Mazola. Filet mignon and ground chuck are equally exposed in their plastic wrapping. Designer jeans are just another rack of goods. If the display windows of department stores, in William Leach's words, "democratized desire," the universal store moves the practice of democracy right into the aisles of the supermarket and the five-and-dime.[12]

During the 1870s, around the same time that B. Altman and R. H. Macy were transforming the fancy dry goods shop of the city into the department store, enterprising young managers like F. W. Woolworth were changing the traditional general store of country towns into the modern "variety store." Woolworth opened the first of his five-and-dimes in Lancaster, Pennsylvania, and Utica, New York; like the mail-order companies that also began around that time, they reduced the cultural gap between consumers in the big city and everywhere else. Variety stores assembled a selection of small consumer goods that were newly produced in factories, and offered them to customers in a single, well-lighted space. Tools, paper goods, fabrics, thimbles, thread, cookware, decorative objects

Bargain paradise: F. W. Woolworth Co. five-and-ten-cent store, Brooklyn, around 1930. Museum of the City of New York.

for the home: everything you needed every day was available, and it was cheap. Many items were so new to be manufactured in standard form, especially for household use, they were seen as revolutionary. But in an even more radical innovation, Woolworth did away with bargaining: he openly set the same low prices for all shoppers, regardless of who they were. By limiting the price ceiling to five cents, and allowing people to browse as long as they liked, Woolworth invited everyone to be a shopper.[13]

Unlike department stores, which were known to cater to different social classes, the five-and-dime welcomed everyone. "Nor does even the aristo-cratic shopper feel any sense of shame at being found in a Woolworth," says a lengthy profile of the legendary five-and-dime stores that was published in *Fortune* magazine in the 1930s, "although she would not like to be found in Woolworth stockings, bloomers, or brassiere." This is a remarkable taboo—this taboo against buying cheap underwear—in the early years of the Great Depression, but it also signals, for the first time, that women of different social backgrounds shop in the same store. Rich or poor, they can always find something they like at Woolworth's—and something they can afford. "On Fifth Avenue the debutantes come in for glass reindeer or beer mugs or ivy plants or 'guest-size' toothpaste. On First Avenue the lower classes arrive for perfume and underwear and bedbug destroyer." Woolworth's merchandising has the knack of appealing to every-body. It has "a remarkable capacity *for being all things to all women.*"[14]

But this sense of equality never extended to the workforce. Like the more expensive department stores, five-and-dimes minimized and ratio-nalized the sales clerks' role. By 1909, Woolworth's stopped building storage shelves behind the counters, and moved all items to counter tops where shoppers could reach them without asking a sales clerk for help. Four years later, when A&P, the earliest grocery chain, reorganized itself as an "economy store," that company also rearranged the merchandise, placing most of it within shoppers' reach and reducing the number of clerks. Within five years, nearly all grocery stores followed this example. Self-service meant lower labor costs, and lower costs suggested bargains.[15]

If self-service permitted stores to offer shoppers lower prices, it also subjected them to the store's control. When they first instituted self-service in the 1910s, grocery stores required shoppers to enter through a turn-stile. Managers believed shoplifting would increase now that women shop-pers could freely handle the goods, and they hoped turnstiles would curb the shoppers' sense of freedom.[16] With a turnstile, shoppers had to enter the store one by one rather than in a crowd; once they got into the store, the turnstile guided them toward the first aisle. From that point, the layout of gondolas, or shelving units, required shoppers to go up and down all the aisles, following a mazelike route past every type of merchandise, before wending their way to the fresh meat and milk at the back of the store, and then to the cashiers. It's astonishing that, with the exception of wider aisles and more checkout lines, this is the same route we travel through super-markets today.

Entering the grocery store, shoppers pick up a basket—or, since the 1930s, a shopping cart—and select what they want without a clerk's assis-tance. The only exception, until recent years, was the fresh meat, fruit, and vegetable counters, where clerks stood ready to select, cut, weigh, and wrap shoppers' choices. The combination of packaging, open shelves, and limited service made it easier in many ways for women to shop, but it also encour-aged a new reticence, or self-discipline, on the shoppers' part. You couldn't poke the packaged bread or smell the shrink-wrapped meat to see whether it was fresh, and you were less likely to scold a clerk in the store for including a rotten peach in the bag than you would scold Sam the local greengrocer.

Instead of waiting for clerks to add up their purchases and pack them, customers carried their baskets, or wheeled their carts, to centralized cashiers. They placed their choices on the conveyor belt and, after paying the cashier, brought their purchases home themselves, in their own shop-ping carts or automobiles. As early as the 1920s, many grocery stores elim-inated amenities like free deliveries and charge accounts. Yet at Woolworth's, the policy had always been "cash and carry." Shoppers accepted a lack of amenities as a part of the new bargain culture.

Self-service depended on earlier innovations in packaging as well as on new technology and store design. During the 1870s and 1880s, foods and other consumer products began to be shipped great distances by railroad—from the farm to the processing factory, and from the factory to the grocery store. Tin cans were mass-produced, enabling shoppers for the first time to eat canned tuna, peas, and corn—and worrying my grandmother, who only decided as late as 1920 that it was safe to eat fish she hadn't seen swim-ming around the fishmonger's tank with her own eyes. In the nineteenth century, the Quaker Oats and Pillsbury flour companies began to pack grains in bags and seal them at the factory before shipping them to stores. This enabled them to standardize weight and guarantee quality, and also to sell products that had previously appeared to be generic "oats" or "flour" under their own brand names. For their part, shoppers quickly saw the benefit of buying insect-free flour and other staples in one-pound or five-pound bags instead of relying on their local shopkeeper's cleanliness and honesty. They also liked buying milk that was sealed in glass bottles at the dairy instead of ladled out from open cans in the store. The packaging in a universal store made shoppers feel modern.[17]

But these changes subjected shoppers to more controls. Displaying packages instead of exposing the foods themselves made stores cleaner, more predictable, and also—in a paradox of modern aesthetics—more attractive. As manufacturers intended, package design and company logos encouraged shoppers to identify their food needs with specific brands. While branding seemed to increase—or at least to clarify— product choice, it made the social space of the store more uniform. Shoppers knew exactly what to expect, and where to find it, when they went inside. At the same time, with control over food production becoming centralized in the hands of big processors like Swift, for meat, and Pillsbury, for flour, seasonal and regional differences in diet began to weaken.[18] Manufacturers shipped the same products all over the country, ran the same advertisements in newspapers and magazines and on the radio, and painted the same signs on roadside billboards.[19] By 1930, the large grocery chains and five-and-dimes stocked the same products—with some local variations—in all their stores. Independent merchants fought back against the chains' growing power by banding together in voluntary associations, but their stores, though usually smaller, promoted the same brand names and bargain culture.

Both the five-and-dime and supermarket romanced shoppers by romanticizing variety and routinizing sensuality. Like the cosmetics counters in department stores, they offered an unprecedented profusion of colorful merchandise in eye-catching boxes and bottles. Woolworth's, Kresge, Kress, and all the five-and-dime stores chose distinctive red-and-gold signs for their facades and stacked small items in pyramids of profusion in their tall, plate-glass windows. They permitted young women to handle sensational products—red lipstick and nail polish, hair clips, and costume jewelry—and take them home, without parental approval. Children, depending on their age and interest, fingered yo-yos, whistles, embroidery kits, and small carpentry tools. All shoppers loved to touch and smell the paper goods displayed on stationery counters. Schoolchildren looked forward to shopping for Big Chief school tablets and number 2 lead pencils in early fall, and adults liked the Woolworth's brand of Herald Square writing paper, whose fine quality the chain's central management took pains to maintain.[20]

Like Wal-Mart, the five-and-dime thrived by selling the highly consistent, standardized goods made possible by mass production. But like an old country store, it brought shoppers into immediate contact with these goods in a paradise of sensory temptations. "The stores smelled of sweet candies and cosmetics and burned toast from the luncheonette counters along the wall," the architectural critic Ada Louise Huxtable recalls; "they echoed to the sound of feet on hardwood floors, the ringing of old-fashioned cash registers, and the clanging of bells for change. . . . And there was the absolute saturation of the eye with every conceivable knickknack."[21] Woolworth's also kept some aspects of personal service typical of an old general store. Managers tried to keep the same clerks in place at specific counters so shoppers felt they knew them, and clerks scooped and weighed the typical Woolworth shopper's treat of "sweet candies."

"The stores smelled of sweet candies and cosmetics and burned toast from the luncheonette counters along the wall": interior of a Lamston's five-and-ten-cent store, New York City, 1930s–'40s. Wurts Collection, Museum of the City of New York.

Luncheonette counters, first introduced by Woolworth's in 1907, were a fast-food convenience for the swelling workforce of office workers in the city. In small towns, they were a place for local people to gather and socialize over a cup of coffee or a Coke, confirming the store's ability to establish a sense of place. Many Americans were shocked to discover just how powerful a local symbol these lunch counters were, in the early 1960s, when black college students in the South organized nonviolent sit-ins and forced their racial integration. Although Woolworth's executives in New York had anticipated this step, they wanted to leave its timing, in the South, to the discretion of regional managers.[22]

These romantic qualities of the shopping experience—sensual pleasure, near-erotic intimacy with goods, and a feeling of local community—were balanced by the inexorable forces of routinization, as universal stores competed on the difficult terrain of low prices and quick turnover. F. W. Woolworth's great innovation, in the 1870s, was to take the variety store's practice of putting unsold goods on sale for five or ten cents and

Lunch counter sit-in for racial integration, day 2: Woolworth, Greensboro, North Carolina, 1960. Photo by Moebes, Greensboro *News & Record*.

standardize these as everyday prices. With this step, Woolworth's was able to avoid the merchant's bane of "markdowns," and introduced what would later become the mantra of discount stores: low prices, every day. To make a profit under these conditions, the universal store counted on a low-wage workforce and hands-on managers who ran a tight ship and moved the goods.

In the early 1930s, before the federal government raised the minimum wage, most Woolworth's sales clerks worked between forty-eight and fifty-six hours a week, standing on their feet behind a counter, for an average weekly salary of $11, or $13 to $14 in cities.[23] Many clerks were young, single women, and on these wages, they were expected to help pay the household expenses, buy the smocks they wore at work, and eat lunch. Managers tended to send them home when business was slow—or reduce their salaries.[24] Preferring to direct the workforce by a mixture of paternalism and intimidation, management fiercely resisted labor unions. A 1940 exposé of working conditions at Woolworth's reads like a criticism of McDonald's today, comparing the menial qualities of working there with the dehumanizing experience of shopping. "We walk to the counter, pick up what we want, and hand it to the salesgirl. She says very little to us—'Yes,' 'No,' 'Thank you.' The department store salesgirl, the grocery clerk—they sell us things, too, but we talk to them, discuss the merchandise with them, get to know something about them. The Woolworth's girl takes our money, wraps our purchase, gives us our change. That is all."[25]

Woolworth's claimed that the wage increases mandated by the federal government during the New Deal forced them to raise prices above the old ten-cent limit. So they were always trying to recruit new employees who would work for lower wages. Between the forties and the sixties, Woolworth's replaced young salesgirls with older retired women, before eliminating sales clerks in favor of self-service and the checkout cashier. Supermarkets, since they also competed on the basis of price, followed the same path. White-aproned male clerks gradually yielded to smocked female cashiers. Preprocessed and prepackaged products reduced the need for skilled butchers and dairy men. By the seventies, over the labor unions' opposition, supermarkets imposed the use of the UPC bar code that could be read by automated scanners. This eliminated the need to label prices by hand on each item in the store.

In the fifties, when wages rose but price inflation discouraged shoppers, a new kind of universal store reinvented the supermarket and five-and-dime. No-frills discounters took bargain culture to a new level of transparency, both simplifying and rationalizing the shopping experience, and competing head-to-head with both department store chains and small, independently owned stores. Discounters placed all merchandise out on the floor and provided little or no sales help. Decor was limited to counters and pipe racks, bare wooden or linoleum floors, and harsh but economical fluorescent lighting. Shoppers made immediate contact with the merchandise—opening and closing refrigerators, lifting the oven door, comparing sizes of television screens by measuring them with their fingers, and feeling the rush of air through the blades of an electric fan. What was most appealing about the new discount stores, however, was their cutthroat prices. They were a Woolworth's for big-ticket consumer items.

Discounters were able to offer such low prices because they refused to respect state and federal fair trade laws. Instead, they sold goods below the "suggested" retail prices set by manufacturers. Employing so few salespeople kept their labor costs low. According to an academic study done in the early sixties, discounters' total wage bill was only half that of regular retail stores. Regular stores couldn't, or wouldn't, fire their workforce and convert to a no-frills format, so they could not compete with the discounters' aggressive pricing. Besides, department store chains weren't thinking about lowering prices; they were busy expanding into the suburbs, where they focused on "soft" goods like clothing and furniture for a captive market of new homeowners, housewives, and parents. Like corner grocery stores facing chains like A&P and Piggly Wiggly in the early 1900s, department stores in the fifties thought shoppers would never abandon full-service stores.[26]

But the new bargain culture proved to be irresistible. Discount stores won the support of populist members of Congress and state legislators, who criticized manufacturers for keeping consumer prices high. Since the courts refused to penalize discounters for breaking the fair trade laws, these laws gradually fell by the wayside. It is fair to say that from the fifties to the seventies, discount stores oiled the wheels of the postwar economic boom. Americans who shopped in discount stores could afford to buy more refrigerators, televisions, air conditioners, and stereos. Shopping at a discount store appeared to be both thrifty and modern—values that had been at the core of bargain culture since the five-and-dime of the 1870s.

Indeed, the discounters claimed to follow the same philosophy of consumer sovereignty as did the founders of the five-and-dime, the supermarket, and the modern drugstore. Decades earlier, businessmen—F. W. Woolworth, J. C. Penney, Clarence Saunders, founder of the Piggly Wiggly supermarkets, and Charles Walgreen, who started the drug store chain—had declared their goal was to make the customer feel like a queen. But with one eye watching the bottom line, they all walked the same narrow path between rationalizing and romanticizing the shopping experience. It wasn't easy for them to create an intimate encounter between shoppers and goods when they expanded their inventory beyond core categories and tried to cut costs to the bone.

By 1920, however, Charles Walgreen pulled these elements together. He managed to "reestablish the small-town general store in the corner drugstore, a place to which local residents might be attracted daily by a wide range of goods and services. Not only drugs but a continually growing variety of personal care and home products were combined with the services provided by newsstand, tobacconist shop, lunch counter, and soda fountain." Moreover, since Walgreen's stocked a variety of competing products and brands, customers could do comparison shopping without leaving the store. After World War II, these were the elements on which the social space of discount stores would draw—though on a much grander scale.[27]

The corner grocery had offered a familiar space of convenience and sociability for people who were just getting used to the national markets of an increasingly urbane society. Without exaggerating these shoppers' initial tendencies toward self-restraint, we can understand how they bought small quantities of consumer goods according to their needs. But the new social space of five-and-dimes, drugstores, and supermarkets—the combination of self-service, low prices, and variety—encouraged shoppers to develop new habits. Instead of chatting with merchants and neighbors, they shopped alongside—but rarely speaking to—the "autonomous presence" of other shoppers. Like going to the movies, shopping engaged them in public culture—but in a private space of their own. Yet both shopping and moviegoing broadened consumers' perspectives on the world. Together with advertising, the new social spaces of consumption persuaded people to browse and buy more. Supermarket shopping created a mobile public who measured convenience in terms of the time it took them to shop rather than the distance they had to travel to do so, and prized bargain culture over personal relations with store owners and clerks.[28]

Although shoppers still tended to patronize nearby food stores, more of them began to go shopping by car rather than on foot. Supermarket chains bought land wherever it was cheap—building larger stores, but fewer of them. To attract shoppers with cars, they surrounded their stores with parking lots. These arrangements created a different, more diffuse kind of city, especially in Los Angeles and the growing cities of the West. They also created a different hierarchy of stores. By the 1950s, only 5 percent of all American grocery stores were supermarkets, yet they accounted for nearly half of all grocery purchases. Challenged by the greater resources and ambitions of the chain stores, corner stores and small grocery shops could not compete, and gradually disappeared.[29]

Shopping in supermarkets changed us as a public. Our geographical mobility—our ability to range much farther from home in quest of goods—empowered us; it made us feel we had a wider choice. But shopping in the most modern stores, which were not only larger but located at a greater distance from home and work, made shopping more tiresome. And though parking lots, shopping carts, and multiple checkout lines— all in use since the 1920s—made it faster to get in and out of the store, it took longer to escape the supermarket's totalizing environment. From the beginning, supermarkets carried nonfood items as well as groceries, and generally made higher profits from them. But as competition between chains grew more intense in the 1960s, supermarkets followed the same path as the early department stores: they offered more products, and more amenities, to keep us shopping longer. Large refrigerators and home freezers—often bought in discount stores—enabled us to make fewer shopping trips each week, but on each trip, we spent more time inside the store. We were emotionally immobilized by the immense abundance. There were "mountains" of goods; "the vast display overwhelms, physically and visually." The author John Updike ironically wrote:

> I drive my car to supermarket,
> The way I take is superhigh,
> A superlot is where I park it,
> And Super Suds are what I buy.[30]

Though shopping trips became a weekly ritual in every American family's routine, supermarkets and discount stores kept few of the event rituals connected with the "mythical cycle of seasons" department stores had perfected.[31] Instead of seasonal sales and markdowns, supermarkets offered weekly "specials" that varied from store to store. Since each discount store promised the lowest prices, bargains were built into every shopping trip. "Everyday low prices" encouraged everyone to shop, all the time, and feel they were saving money by doing so.

The discount stores founded in the 1960s—Wal-Mart, Kmart, and Target—ushered in a new order of shopping. The size of these stores, their primary location outside of cities, and the scale of purchases they supplied raised shopping to a direct experience of mass consumer society. But like the best new forms of social life, these stores were not completely unfamiliar to shoppers; they bridged the variety stores of the past and the supercenters of the future, and embodied some of the basic qualities of each.[32] Especially in Wal-Mart's mythology, which was inspired by Sam Walton's folksy style, a discount store is a space of community as well as of bargain culture. At the same time, it is a space of both freedom and control. While

Public ritual meets private ritual at the mall: Garden State Plaza, New Jersey. Photo by Richard Rosen, 1975.

liberating shoppers from the narrow choices and high prices of local merchants, each Wal-Mart store is as capital-intensive as a modern factory. To retain and keep track of its huge inventory, Wal-Mart maintains a global system of just-in-time deliveries using the chain's own computerized satellite system, warehouses, and trucks. To move shoppers through the store, Wal-Mart has a well-developed self-service system. And to keep prices down, the chain persuades and threatens its suppliers. Wal-Mart's economies of scale have helped consumers to live larger and larger. "What . . . occurred," Ada Louise Huxtable writes about the shift in scale from the five-and-dime to the discount store, "was a total revolution in the American way of living and buying. Stores grew to warehouse size, and aisles of goods became acres of products."[33]

Just as importantly, discount stores and shopping malls organized a new landscape of consumption. With cornfields and forests obliterated by a grid of interstate highways and subdivisions of suburban housing, big stores and malls imposed an equally rational arrangement of "repetition and banality within unpredictable patterns of consumption."[34] Regions of the country that had been wilderness, as far as shopping was concerned, joined the worldwide consumer revolution.

When Sam Walton started Wal-Mart in Rogers, Arkansas, in 1962, he combined the transparency of the modern discounter with the small-town friendliness of the old variety store. He believed in J. C. Penney's 1913 credo: "Serve the public . . . to its complete satisfaction"; concentrate on fair remuneration rather than high profits; give customers value, quality, and satisfaction; keep training the sales staff to improve service; keep improving "the human factor"; share profits with employees; always ask "Is it right and just?" On these points, Walton did not differ from many nineteenth-century merchant-entrepreneurs.[35]

While F. W. Woolworth, "the Chief," had been "a skinflint with wages," he believed in sharing profits with managers, and was one of the first employers to give employees stock ownership.[36] Walton also used stock ownership—for all employees, not just managers—to compensate for low-wage, often part-time jobs and lack of labor union representation. Like Woolworth, Walton's paternalism camouflaged a refusal to deal with unions and a not-so-subtle gender discrimination.[37] Indeed, most of the elements of Wal-Mart's success were copied from the variety store's business model that was familiar in Woolworth's time. Walton opened stores in small towns where shoppers were eager for new products but couldn't pay high prices for them; he set cutthroat prices that other stores couldn't or wouldn't meet; and he kept very few sales clerks on the floor but closely supervised those he had.

Walton triumphed over his rivals, becoming "the richest man in America" before Bill Gates, by his hands-on management style and hard-nosed business strategies. Like F. W. Woolworth, Walton made frequent personal visits, until his death in the 1990s, to check up on each of his stores. He instituted a severe, no-frills, corporate policy that applied to managers' offices and executives' business trips as well as to store decor. Both the corporate headquarters staff and store managers watched store employees to make sure they always behaved in a friendly, even ingrati-ating style—requiring them to make eye contact with shoppers as they approached within ten feet of them. Walton also required managers to join the local Elks, Chamber of Commerce, and religious organizations, as well as to sponsor local charities and children's groups. Beginning in 1983, every Wal-Mart store hired retired men and women to be "people greeters," who say hello to each shopper as they enter the store. Not only do the people greeters present a friendly, local face at a relatively low wage, they also deter shoplifting.[38]

Sam Walton kept J. C. Penney's credo written out above his desk: "Serve the public . . . to its complete satisfaction." But he also expanded the chain in a methodical, state-by-state saturation of local markets—eventually closing some stores while opening bigger ones nearby. Walton made huge investments in automation—apparently as a leap of faith rather than as a careful business decision. Unlike Sears, with its perennial displays of carpentry tools, hardware, and automotive goods geared to men, Walton courted women shoppers by featuring health and beauty products. Unlike the more expensive department stores, Walton aimed at the middle-income shopper.[39] Most important, beginning in the eighties, Sam Walton aban-doned Woolworth's, Penney's, and Sears's dependence on generic brands, switching to nationally advertised labels.

Brand-name products had mushroomed with the growth of national advertising during the first quarter of the twentieth century. But during the sixties, when television commercials made brand names a ubiquitous image in every home, the appeal of these products grew. Rising incomes, and a sense of entitlement, encouraged shoppers to think they could, and should, buy products for their quality. And brand names seemed to assure that quality without denying the standardization of mass production. More-over, as income differences leveled off, to some degree, during the sixties, blue-collar families sought brand-name goods to confirm their new, middle-class status. By the middle of the decade, trade publications urged discounters to interpret consumers' desires and upgrade their merchandise from the schlocky to the merely inexpensive. Brand names were infiltrating bargain culture.[40]

In the seventies, however, a series of economic setbacks reawakened shoppers' interest in low prices. Several years of recession were followed by an oil crisis that raised prices for heating oil, gasoline, and many consumer goods. Not only did wages fail to keep pace with inflation, many men and women lost their jobs—particularly in the heartland that Wal-Mart served—when the companies they worked for failed to overcome foreign competition. Shuttered factories and labor "givebacks" discouraged a large part of the public from buying more expensive goods—yet they created a situation for discount stores to thrive. Wal-Mart did especially well, becoming the second-largest retail chain, after Kmart, in America.

Nevertheless, during the eighties, Wal-Mart stopped selling generic products and began to feature brand-name goods. Though television commercials and licensing agreements had made brand names universally known, Sam Walton made them universally available. Wal-Mart promoted brand names the way supermarkets use "loss leaders." Though the store might make only a few cents' profit—or even lose money—on some items, it made up for this by selling a huge volume of the items on sale. Besides, bargain prices on name brands—not just on cheap generic items—brought *everyone* into the store. Middle-class shoppers who had never shopped at Wal-Mart before began to regard it approvingly: the stores were big, they offered a choice of goods, and prices were "right." Moreover, the chain's high sales volume enabled Wal-Mart to lean more heavily on manufacturers to make significant price concessions. The five-and-dime store was becoming obsolete, but Wal-Mart updated Woolworth's business strategies. Wal-Mart used modern, automated technology to create not just daily but hourly records of sales, and then demanded that manufacturers pack and deliver fresh supplies of goods to keep up with the pace of items moving off the shelf.[41]

Wal-Mart also updated the marriage of price and convenience that supermarkets offered. Now shoppers could find cheap designer jeans and brand-name appliances in the same store. This one-stop shopping was important to shoppers because nearly all of the chain's stores were located in small towns or on distant suburban fringes, far from any other store that could afford to carry such a wide selection.

The shift to selling nationally advertised brands enabled Wal-Mart to overtake its biggest discount rival, Kmart, as well as the old titans Sears and J. C. Penney. The new policy also attracted more affluent shoppers, reviving the egalitarian bargain culture of the early universal stores. "The space is a giant melting-pot," wrote a reporter who visited a Wal-Mart supercenter in rural, northwestern Virginia, ". . . a place where people from trailer parks mingle with people from designer homes, just as a couple of cappuccino-makers are on sale alongside the ordinary coffee machines."[42] Like Woolworth's in the old days, Wal-Mart created the illusion of a class-less society.

But this *is* an illusion. Wal-Mart's wages are so low that the employees often cannot afford to buy items in the store even when they are on sale. The chain has lost at least one class action suit for forcing workers to work overtime without clocking in the hours. And, like every other store, to keep prices low, Wal-Mart imports a large portion of its merchandise from China. If superstores mean low-wage sales clerks, traffic belching carbon monoxide, and sweatshop jeans, they are "satanic mills," indeed.[43]

Yet Woolworth's and Wal-Mart have had a tremendous effect on both our culture and our economy. By the early twentieth century, Woolworth's had grown into a multinational chain. A hundred years later, Wal-Mart's annual sales are as high as the industrial giant General Motors', dwarfing the gross national product of many countries. Wal-Mart is also the second-largest employer in the United States after the federal government. While the company first suffered setbacks when it exported the Wal-Mart model to other countries, such as Mexico, it has overcome the local competition by the same low prices, brand names, and economies of scale. From Wool-worth's to Wal-Mart, these stores have encouraged us to think "low prices—every day" is a universal human right.

Trying to explain Wal-Mart's success, business writers tend to talk about Sam Walton's relentless cost-cutting, the just-in-time deliveries by Wal-Mart trucks, and the automated distribution centers and satellite inventory system. For their part, the CEOs who have taken Walton's place never tire of praising the store's "humility," its focus on the customer, and its willingness to roll back prices to ensure that shoppers get "full value." But I am sure the real key to Wal-Mart's success lies elsewhere. It lies in the promise every shopper can read in the social space of a Wal-Mart store: the promise that, by shopping for brand names at bargain prices, all shoppers can be "middle class."[44]

That doesn't mean we all have middle-class jobs or incomes. Wal-Mart aims at the real mass market, where household incomes are relatively low and consumers overuse their credit cards. Yet Wal-Mart enables more people to shop their way into the good life then their incomes would warrant.

If we shop at Wal-Mart, we can feel we live as well as the rich do. Like McDonald's and Disney World, like bowling alleys and diners and other spaces of mass consumption, Wal-Mart upgrades our standard of living to match our dreams of a lifestyle. We use our Wal-Mart credit card to buy a new GE refrigerator that the company produces in a strategic partnership with the store. And in that GE refrigerator, we chill a nice bottle of California Chardonnay that E. & J. Gallo produces for Wal-Mart in another exclusive relationship. And when we watch programs on television—the same brand-name television that we buy at Wal-Mart—we see all the appliances and health and beauty supplies and breakfast cereals we have bought, to make our lives better, right up there on the screen. Then we feel we truly belong.[45]

The universal store has made the culture of bargains our universal culture. Just as the "aristocratic shopper" shopped for new items at Woolworth in the 1930s, so Ivana Trump, the former wife of the real estate magnate Donald Trump, now shops at Costco with her chef—and claims to enjoy the experience of getting a bargain. "You go, Wow, $3.99 for a bottle of virgin olive oil," Ivana Trump explains. "I honestly don't know how much it costs normally"—who would, if you can afford to buy a whole villa in Tuscany?—"but somehow they make you feel good about it."[46]

It is no wonder that just when Wal-Mart was beginning to convince the masses that they could afford to shop for luxuries, the historian Daniel Boorstin argued that mass consumption had eliminated differences between social classes. In contrast to the conflict and inequality represented in the past by classes, Boorstin wrote in 1973, people were now united by "consumption communities." The social revolution that began with the five-and-dime brought infinitely more freedom than any movement in the political realm: "consumption communities were quick; they were nonideological; they were democratic; they were public, and vague, and rapidly shifting. . . . Never before had so many men been united by so many things."[47]

Neither had so many women. At Wal-Mart, Costco, or Home Depot, the woman who earns $20,000 a year from a part-time job can shop like Ivana Trump. Connected not by our social positions, and still less by the things we can truly afford to buy, the culture of bargains makes us feel that we are all part of the same society.

Though Woolworth established its own discount chain, Woolco, in the same year that Sam Walton founded Wal-Mart, it never successfully competed with the discount stores. After the 1960s, all the elements of the old Woolworth's gradually disappeared. In the eighties, Woolworth sold its U.S. Woolco stores to Wal-Mart, and in the nineties, it added all the Canadian Woolco stores. In contrast to the clean, well-lighted spaces of Wal-Mart, and its location on the highway, the five-and-dime seemed old, it was tied to the city's decaying downtown, and it sold a crazy assortment of shoddy items. "This Woolworth's on Vermont, in Hollywood," Steve Abee writes, " . . . emits the five-flavor perfume of a crumbling quartz galaxy of pantyhose and jack of lanterns. . . . This is Woolworth's, man. The polyester seams start to unravel before you even get to the car."[48]

In the seventies, Woolworth shut the flagship store on Fifth Avenue in midtown Manhattan. It diversified into athletic shoes and apparel. It sent the last remaining luncheonette counter to the American history museum at the Smithsonian Institution—ringing the death knell on the stores' once-central symbol. In 1997, it closed all the remaining five-and-dimes that were still open, including one in my neighborhood, where I used to buy needles and sewing thread. A year later, they sold the landmark Wool-

Woolworth, Fourteenth Street, final sale. Photo by Richard Rosen, 1997.

worth Building, a skyscraper that had raised the skyline of Lower Manhattan when it was built, in 1913. Then it changed the corporate name. For all practical purposes, by the end of the twentieth century, Woolworth's as we had known it was dead. It was swallowed whole by Foot Locker.[49]

The universal store wasn't dead, however. While Woolworth sank, Wal-Mart rose.

It did so by clinging to small towns and rural areas near the highway, and by blanketing the backwoods and blacktop regions of the country with more big stores and more brand names than residents had ever seen. Sam Walton bet on his ability to turn the countryside into a shoppers' paradise—but to do this, he had to turn country people into shoppers, and lure city dwellers to the countryside to shop.

It turns out that city dwellers really love discount stores—even in the capital of shopping, New York City. Though they don't want the traffic a superstore brings, the vigilant community board in my neighborhood is seriously divided by the obvious attraction of permitting Home Depot to build a new store on the waterfront. And Kmart didn't need a shopping revolution to open the store on Astor Place. Since the early years of zoning, in John Wanamaker's time, the block has been zoned for high-density commercial use. Kmart is perfectly within its rights to operate a 140,000-square-foot store there.

Even so, the City Council still hasn't changed the zoning laws. In 1996, the same year Kmart opened, the council voted down the mayor's plan.

Elsewhere in the city, superstores have found loopholes in the zoning laws. Staples, calling itself a "stationery store," has opened branches all over Manhattan. Despite protests by local merchants and residents, Home Depot said it was a "hardware store" and opened two branches in Queens.[50]

Though I still shop for paper towels at Kmart, I find the discount superstores depressing and soulless. Yet I can see how they function as the heart of a mobile, mass society that lacks other gathering places to express communal grief and exaltation. We have so few means of overcoming our solitude that even a discount superstore serves us as a temple of humanity.

When the stock car racer Dale Earnhardt Sr. was killed in a crash, "his death brought a silence to the Wal-Mart" near the town in North Carolina where he had lived. "After a moment," I read in the *New York Times*, "the silence broke. Women shrieked, and men cried. Then, slowly, they moved to the . . . clothes and toys [with the Earnhardt logo], and began to buy them all." People who had just been casual visitors to Wal-Mart on a weekend afternoon expressed their shock and grief by shopping for both mementos and memorials, and they mourned together in the store.[51]

The great achievement of the universal store is to surround us with both democracy and humanity. In this sense, it is the true heir of the outdoor public market and the great bazaars. Yet five-and-dimes, supermarkets, and superstores don't want to eliminate social classes. They just want all of us to keep shopping, every day.

4

"the perfect pair
of leather pants"

The new Miss Teenager of New York will win a shopping
spree of $1,000 in the form of a prepaid credit card.
The Post-Star (Glens Falls, N.Y.), 1999

Cindy wants to tell me a shopping story. It's certainly not a story of deprivation. She holds a job at a major international organization, lives by herself in an apartment in Manhattan, and has time and money to shop for clothes. Indeed, the object she desires—leather pants—suggests that this will be a story about middle-class narcissism: Cindy will reveal herself to be a shopaholic who has nothing better to do than wander from store to store, buying things most people can't afford and she doesn't need.

But instead, Cindy has a story every shopper can relate to. It's about looking for the perfect solution. And about why stores and marketers don't have a clue. I know that Cindy is a careful shopper. She learned to shop from her older sister—the sister who, when she had a specific item in mind, charged through a store until she zeroed in on it. This sister taught her to appraise clothing carefully for quality, rubbing a fabric between her thumb and forefinger to gauge whether it feels like silk or polyester. Since Cindy once worked at a company that sells luxury goods, like Chanel or Gucci, she has seen plenty of rich people shopping for products that she cannot afford. She doesn't want to be like that.

"Leather is such a classic thing," Cindy begins.

I nod my head. When I was her age, in my late twenties, I never thought that leather pants were classical. In those years, if you wore leather pants, especially black pants, people thought you were some sort of a sexual fetishist—or, at the very least, that you didn't mind being stared at for flaunting a well-honed pair of thighs. Recently, however, leather pants have changed their image. If you wear them with a cashmere turtleneck and houndstooth jacket, they look simple, rich, and casual. They represent the "classic" American sense of comfort with a materially satisfying life.

"I wanted a classic pair of leather pants," Cindy continues. "I didn't want to pay a lot of money, I wanted good quality, and I wanted them to fit really well." She laughs and adds, "I know that's a lot to ask for!"

Hearing Cindy talk about the importance of fit, price, and quality, I wonder what we shoppers really feel about the objects we long for. The simple, iron teapot whose beauty cries out to us from the display case in the Takashimaya department store, the shiny, red, high-heeled shoes we

The object of her desire: a classic pair of leather pants. Photo by Richard Rosen.

spot in a shop window on Eighth Street and whose details we lovingly trace in our minds time and again even though we know we could never walk on heels that high, the high-end stereo system we "visit" at the hi-fi store until we can afford to make it ours—these aesthetic urges to acquire specific objects do not contradict our basic rationality. Why are we prepared to think Cindy is a narcissist just because she wants a pair of leather pants?

For one thing, more than a century of exposure to marketing strategies has encouraged us to be skeptical about the authenticity of aesthetic urges for commodities—especially when we look at other shoppers' urges. We know that any "must-have" item projects our fantasies of a perfect self— often enough, a self that is youthful, cool, and rich—through multiple filters of product design, advertising, and in-store display. As for leather pants, they are neither cheap enough nor common enough to be accepted as an ordinary need. They still have a strong whiff of luxury about them, and neither the fashion magazines nor the stores that sell leather pants are willing to give up this image. The deepest and most devastating reason for suspecting Cindy of narcissism, however, is that she is a *woman* shopper speaking of a product she desires. And when this product is as morally suspect as a pair of leather pants, the woman becomes morally suspect, too.

We have no problem internalizing the guilt. When we women desire goods because of their sensuous qualities, we tend to think these desires are signs of a personal or even a biological flaw. The more sophisticated and self-aware we are, the more we try to distance ourselves from our urges for commodities—or to laugh ironically about them. Deep within our belief in sexual equality lurks a severe mistrust of our aesthetic urges—our *unworthy* urges for goods. We fear these urges today just as women at the turn of the twentieth century feared that they were prone—as their detractors claimed—to kleptomania. Aesthetic desires for goods are examples of object lust, and therefore they're unclean.

"Only women born with the shopping gene can understand why I awake one morning," a reporter writes in the *Los Angeles Times*, "daydreaming of blue jeans. By the time I've reached consciousness, I am gripped by an undeniable urge for new, mean jeans I can see in my mind's eye." Is this a language of desire or of moral pollution? Though the reporter is talking about a normal pair of jeans, she suggests that the desire for them is "genetic"; her object lust is not a flaw shared by all women, but by women who inherit a "bad seed."[1]

Yet the reporter is also reaching out to her readers in solidarity. She believes that all women will feel the same way she does—if not about the jeans, then about another piece of clothing that inspires in them equally intense desires. Oddly, while men "research" and plan their purchases around specific products, and count this as an example of their superior, rational approach to shopping, the reporter's attempt to describe in precise detail the jeans she desires only makes her appear less rational and more obsessive.

"The denim should be slightly stiff and dark," she writes, "the color of night sky. They won't look already dissipated. These jeans will challenge me to break them in. . . . " This language situates the jeans somewhere between an Impressionist painting—the energy of Van Gogh's *Starry Night*—and the sexual dynamism of a rodeo rider. The jeans are animate, alive: the reporter idealizes their sensuous qualities. She imagines how they will *feel*. Most importantly, she fantasizes about how they will make her *look*: "The waistband will hover just south of a . . . T-shirt's edge. . . . an errant sliver of skin might peek out now and then."

Though this may be a vivid daydream, it is hardly a narcissistic fantasy. Daydreams are the wellspring of all desire. They are a perpetual source of our permanent longing for things, a driving force of the "imaginative hedonism" that, in turn, drives modern consumer society. Daydreaming about goods is our attempt to fill the gap between a perfect self and the imperfections of reality.[2] In this case, a daydream fills the gap between a woman's flawed thighs or hips and a physical ideal. It suggests that, even if you don't have a perfect body, shopping for the "perfect pair" of jeans might help you feel comfortable in the body you do have. Moreover, since women are often aware of how important appearance is in determining social status, they tend to be anxious about how they will look in clothes they may buy. Envisioning how they will look is a way of "trying on" the outfit in advance. Though it won't eliminate the trauma of the fitting-room mirror, it is a way of anticipating how you'll look in the outfit, and how it will feel, before taking it off the rack. It's a particularly visual way of making a shopping list before going into a store.

Besides, many women tend to visualize their perfect selves in outfits rather than in physical activities. This doesn't prove that we are obsessed with buying clothes. It does demonstrate that women think of themselves as cinematically performing certain roles, and shopping is the way we get into costume for these roles.

Cindy sees herself in a "classic" role—as a young career woman working for a major international organization: single, solid, feet on the ground; at twenty-nine, she is old enough to spend money, but she wants to spend her money wisely. Crucial to her self-image is the contrast between her current employer, a nonprofit organization, and the luxury goods firm where she used to work. She sees herself as bridging the serious moral purpose of the one and the extravagant fantasy world of the other. So Cindy frames her desire for leather pants by objective standards that most shoppers share. She speaks of the pants as a "classic" item, whose sensual appeal is tempered by fit, price, and quality. From this point of view, her search for the perfect pair of leather pants is a search for the common ideal of consumer society: the ideal value at which price and fit are perfectly balanced with quality.

So Cindy is a *virtuous* shopper. She is looking for a product that is both practical and economical—clothing that will not be pushed to the back of the closet because it has prematurely worn out its appeal, or stretched, or shrunk. She is looking for a shopper's utopia—not buying too much on a shopping spree, but buying *the right thing*.

Yet she already feels this hunt for leather pants is doomed to frustration. Despite the many products and stores that surround us, the continual sales and bargains, and the efforts by retailers to appeal to our emotions, Cindy knows it will be difficult to find exactly what she wants. There are structural factors that limit her possibilities for satisfaction: the seasonal rhythms of clothes shopping, fashion cycles that dictate what's in and what's out, the availability of reasonably priced leather on the world market. And there are also individual limitations: her inability to carry out the search at a large enough number of stores, the decisions of buyers at the stores she goes to, and the amount of money these stores have at their disposal to keep new inventory flowing in. What makes it worse is that Cindy is a small woman. She wears size 2 petite, a very small size that few stores carry.

In fact, when she began searching for the perfect pair of leather pants, "there were no leather pants *anywhere*, except maybe size 16 or 18. Or ones that had been in the store a long time and were store-worn and kind of faded." She "learned," moreover, that it was the wrong season to shop for leather pants. It was "really too late [in the year] to be buying leather pants."

Cindy had begun to search for the pants during the summer. She'd "go in [to Lord & Taylor on Fifth Avenue] and ask, 'Are the leather pants in yet? Are they in yet?'" Now, though the autumn was just turning cool,

Cindy was already out-of-sync with the seasonal cycles of manufacturers and retail stores.

On this point, Cindy's story confirms one of the most common complaints of women shoppers. According to a recent marketing survey, women "can't find anything because things aren't in stock." Like most of these women, Cindy believes these items *should be in the stores* because they are not foolish fads: "81 percent said . . . that they buy things regardless of fashion trends. 65 percent admitted . . . they're actually willing to pay more for *classic looks*."[3]

So Cindy perseveres. She mentally sorts through the advantages and disadvantages of shopping in different stores, calculating the chances that they will have leather pants in her size in stock.

"I even went to Macy's and Bloomingdale's," she says, "and I *hate* them. I always get lost, and I can never find anything there."

Like many shoppers these days, Cindy isn't happy about the large size of department stores and the way they organize their stock in designer boutiques. Despite the common belief among retailers and marketers that shoppers, especially women shoppers, prefer to shop by brand, many consumers prefer the organization of stock by functional category or occasion—the way Macy's used to have departments like "Blouses" and "Evening Wear" instead of "Ralph Lauren," "Lauren," and "Ralph." According to that marketing survey, "two thirds of consumers . . . want to shop by category or end use or occasion. Only 15 percent want to shop by brand."[4]

Cindy's dislike of department stores also reflects her childhood experience of shopping in smaller stores. She grew up in a suburb of San Francisco, where most stores, except for superstores, tend to be branches, and therefore smaller than the main store in the city. Though these stores are not "mom-and-pop" stores, their inventory, which is geared toward rapid turnover, is not exhaustive. Suburban stores provide both limited choice and unlimited convenience: enough of a vision of plenty to satisfy shoppers and reachable by car.

But Cindy now lives in Manhattan and prefers to shop there. "I put all my stock in Lord & Taylor," she says, referring to the chain's mother store on Fifth Avenue and Thirty-ninth Street. "They're my favorite store. They have a 'Petites' section that carries [size] 2P, and they carry leather pants, so I thought this was a sure thing. They have the really nice, black leather pants and brown suede pants. Perfect."

Since Cindy doesn't have time to visit the store every day, she is counting on the sales clerks to let her know when the size 2P leather pants arrive. Like nearly all specialty clothing stores for both men and women, Lord & Taylor uses its sales staff to gain shoppers' loyalty with this kind of "personal service." "You know those salesgirls," Cindy continues. "They're really friendly. They say, 'Do you want me to call you when [the leather pants] come in?'"[5]

"Friendly salesgirls" are one way of looking at personal service. Because of their low wages, the women are eager to make a commission on their sales. Just as waiters learn to read diners' expressions to see whether they will leave a big tip, so sales clerks learn to read shoppers' faces and body language to see whether the shopper they approach will actually make a purchase. They learn to seize the right moment when a customer is wavering to tell her that the outfit she is trying on is "just made" for her or makes her look thin. And they are often hired because they speak various foreign languages that will attract desired groups of immigrant or foreign shoppers—wealthy Brazilians or Japanese on Madison Avenue, a few years ago, or Pakistanis on Coney Island Avenue in Brooklyn. Good sales clerks refuse to be turned away by an evasive "Just looking." They don't just answer a shopper's question, they tell her the item she is tentatively exploring in her mind has "just arrived" in the store or is expected in a shipment tomorrow. At Lord & Taylor, where almost every sales clerk on every floor is female, the saleswomen will take an evasive "Just looking" in stride with a confident smile and tell the hesitant shopper to ask for Marie, or Yvonne, or Anna when she "needs some help."

Though most stores, including Lord & Taylor, are organized for self-service, shoppers do need help. As the Nobel Prize–winning economist George Akerlof has famously shown about shopping for used cars, every market is plagued by imperfect information.[6] Even when they know more or less what they need, shoppers often lack the experience to evaluate specific types of products. The Home Depot chain has triumphed over many local hardware stores and lumber yards to gain women customers, who traditionally know less than men know about hardware and tools, because Home Depot presents its helpful sales staff as "solution providers." Clothes shopping, about which women usually know a lot more than men, carries its own risks. We want to know which styles are new and which are right, whether to wash or dry-clean the fabric, and which outfit makes our body look terrific. Male clothes shoppers, who often will themselves to ignorance about clothes and groceries, feel an even greater need for information. No wonder "87% of women and 92% of men [say] that they choose stores to shop at specifically with the sales help in mind. They need help. They admit it." Fit, price, and quality are only the beginning of the information shoppers require. A good salesperson will also anticipate and rationalize a shopper's fantasy of a perfect self.[7]

But all this doesn't work if the leather pants don't arrive.

"They never called me!" Cindy exclaims. "I was in there every couple of days because I didn't trust them to call. When they finally got the leather pants in, it [took] a couple of days before I found out. And, of course, they didn't have my size!"

The saleswomen have squandered Cindy's trust. She can no longer believe their attempts to forge a special relationship. But she mostly blames the store. And when Cindy calls the store buyer to complain, the buyer blames the manufacturer. "She told me they just don't make them in [size] 2P," Cindy says. "I even went to the Lord & Taylor store in New Jersey." Not even a suburban shopping mall can turn up a size 2P.

Women shoppers always agonize about their size. Unlike Cindy, however, who is very short and thin, most women are anxious about looking fat. Lana, an older woman shopper, went to Kmart recently to buy underwear and came home horrified. "The rolls of fat!" she says about her experience in the changing room. "The way my arm looked! The skin around my waist!" And the conclusion of her shopping trip isn't gratifying—it's mortifying. "My husband says I should exercise," she sighs.

Leather pants exaggerate these body problems. Though leather is supple, it is unforgiving: regardless of the style of the pants, the material shows every bulge. It's supposed to fit "like a glove." All of this puts a severe burden on the shopper's body discipline. My friend Jackie has owned five pairs of leather pants, and she never gains an ounce. My neighbor Claire, on the other hand, owns two pairs of leather pants, but she can only wear one of them for a few months every year—when she's working out regularly at the gym and eating hardly anything at all.

The magazines know how burdensome our bodies can be. A recent issue of the *Ladies' Home Journal* offers "8 Healthy Ways to Blast Off Fat," *Redbook* promises "101 Slimming Fashion Secrets," and *Fitness* presents "Slim and Sculpted in 1 Hour a Week . . . Plus 9 Quick Fat Burners." According to a marketing survey, "60 percent of consumers today . . . have difficulty finding clothes that fit them right" because "the average consumer is a size 12." Manufacturers have tried to deal with our bodies by increasing the range of fashionable clothes in larger sizes—like Tommy Hilfiger Woman, which covers sizes 14 to 22. Even the more expensive stores, whose customers may have personal trainers, have opened special, in-store boutiques for large-size women. And the fastest-growing category of fashion models is no longer waif-thin but "plus"-size.[8]

But women shoppers aren't only getting bigger. More precisely, many women are too fat in one part of their body and too thin in another. Though fashion advertisements idealize our "dream of wholeness," that dream is shattered by the realization that, while our upper torso is an acceptable size 8, our hips (or waist, or thighs) are several sizes larger. Or while our hips may fit quite nicely into a smallish size 10, our chest is a flattish size 6. Women tend to see their body as divided into zones of different sizes—each of which is problematic in its own way. This makes clothes shopping a potentially traumatic experience—especially in a large, collective changing room where other women shoppers look you over when you are in an unclothed state of vulnerability and show off their own, better-proportioned hips, busts, and thighs.[9]

Daydreaming about mean jeans or the perfect pair of leather pants gives us a way of countering the inevitable disillusionment of facing our body in the changing-room mirror. When we look in the mirror, we can neutralize the fat and the odd proportions by remembering how we looked in the daydream—which is how we *ought* to look, or how we *used* to look, or how we *will* look one day. Rachel Colls, who has studied the way English women look at themselves, and at each other, in the changing room, calls these multiple projections "a complex system of looking relations." For Cindy, however, what is complex in the first place is simply finding a small enough size to try on. So now she decides to try the more expensive stores.

"I went to Ralph Lauren, but [the pants] are $900 there, and I just couldn't justify it. Aquascutum, where the queen shops, they had a beautiful pair, and they were only $500."

But these prices are just too high. Even if Cindy can afford to pay $500 financially, she can't *morally* afford it. Good shopping has moral limits—or will Cindy overcome her scruples to get the object she desires?

No, now Cindy tries the cheaper branded stores. But in these stores, she confronts her aesthetic limits: the ambiance and sales help are not up to speed.

"I went to The Gap, but I couldn't find anyone to help me. You know how they have the leather pants displayed, with the lock and chains [to prevent stealing]?

"Well, this salesgirl is talking on her cell phone and is just ignoring me. She finally ends the conversation—on *her* terms—and she knows exactly what I've been waiting for.

" 'So, you want the leather pants?' she says.

"*Thank you very much!* (with sarcasm in her voice).

"But, of course, they're the hipster pants, with the flared bottoms. And I want *classic* pants."

The Gap is not good enough. The sales clerk is insulting, the lack of trust in customers not to shoplift is demoralizing, and the leather pants are styled for the moment—they're fashion-heavy, cheesy, "cheap." They're not the pants Cindy desires.

So she moves the hunt slightly upscale. She tries another branded store.

"In Banana Republic," she says, "I found the best quality leather I've ever seen. They were supple, great leather. Even their suede pants were great. They don't use pigskin, which has those little dots on it. . . . But the pants were $900, and, of course, they were the hipsters with the flare."

Good quality, exorbitant price: Cindy still isn't satisfied. If she were rich, she could go to a tailor and have a pair of leather pants custom made. But since the 1870s, with the onset of mass production, most of us have depended on stores to stock the goods we want rather than ordering them custom made. In the nineteenth century, poorer shoppers still sewed their clothes themselves, had a sister who could make clothes, or knew a tailor, usually an immigrant tailor, in their neighborhood. As factories developed, however, we became dependent on buying all our clothing in stores. If we can't find what we want in the stores (or in their functional equivalent—mail-order catalogs or websites), we are doomed to disappointment.

So Cindy tries the stores in another neighborhood; she travels downtown to SoHo. But the small, trendy boutiques there tend to stock hip rather than classic designs. "I was completely disillusioned," she says. "I wanted to spend a lot of money and get a good pair of pants, but it was impossible." She sighs. This hunt for the perfect pair of leather pants has been exhausting.

At the last minute, with nothing left to hope for, Cindy overcomes her final limit. She decides to try shopping on the Lower East Side, an immigrant neighborhood that, since the late 1800s, has been famous for bargains, especially in the shops owned by Jewish merchants. Though the population and mix of stores have changed considerably since the 1950s, with Latinos moving in and Jews moving out, and, more recently, small start-up stores of independent designers replacing discount stores, there are still a few small clothing and leather goods stores where the owners speak both English and Yiddish and the signs suggest great bargains. But Cindy is reluctant to shop in this alien atmosphere.

"I didn't want to go downtown to Orchard Street," she frowns, "because it's 'discount street.' I didn't want some guy trying to sell me something I didn't want to buy." Thanks to her middle-class background, white-bread ethnicity, and chain store experience—for, after all, Cindy grew up shopping at a suburban mall in northern California—she finds the sales pressures of the uptown department stores more bearable than those of the small stores downtown.

"I mean," Cindy says, "even if I wanted [the pants], I didn't want to go through that pressure."

But when Cindy goes to the Lower East Side, she confronts another limit. She is stymied by the limit on shopping time set by the remaining

Leather shop on Orchard Street. Photo by Richard Rosen.

merchants on Orchard Street who observe the Jewish Sabbath. Not knowing about this, Cindy goes to Orchard Street on a Saturday, when all the shops that sell leather clothes are closed. Still, she perseveres.

"I went back on Sunday," she says. "I started at one end of the street and just started looking."

Cindy starts at zero. She doesn't know the names and reputations of these stores on Orchard Street. She doesn't know what each of them carries, whether they offer standard or discount prices, or whether they'll accept returns. She doesn't know which stores to trust.

"I went into four stores," Cindy reports, "and all of them had my size, except one. And he said he could have it for me the next day."

But could she trust him to do so? Would he get the size from another store down the block, which might be owned by his cousin or his competitor? Would Cindy waste her time if she returned the next day? In a store that isn't part of a well-known chain, and doesn't sell brand-name clothes, whom can a shopper trust?

And these little, old stores are physically uncomfortable to shop in.

"The fifth store didn't have a dressing room. It was really tight, so it was hard to look in the mirror. The racks were like this"—she pushes her hands together to show a narrow, constricted space. I feel a lack of air.

Yet, as unlikely as it seems, in this store Cindy finds "the perfect pair of pants." She smiles broadly.

"They sent me around the corner to get the hems sewn, and that was done in *five minutes!*

"In five minutes I had a perfect, beautiful pair of leather pants! After a year of looking!" Cindy's shopping story has reached a happy ending, and I am happy for her. I smile, too.

"But," she adds suddenly, furrowing her brow, "that was my last resort. *I had nowhere else to go.*"

We normally think that if enough shoppers want certain products, manufacturers will produce them and stores will have them in stock. Yet Cindy's story shows that balancing supply and demand is a tricky business. The problem of not finding the goods we want is only one side of the equation. For reasons no one can completely understand, consumers often ignore manufacturers' and merchants' best guesses of what they will want to buy—or else their demand far outstrips the available supply.

Seemingly trivial products—toys, for example, that are cheap and mass-produced—carry heavy risks for manufacturers and store owners who guess wrong on consumer demand. Many a Christmas goes by without the toy industry finding the magic formula for a sure-fire, top-selling item. As an adult, however, I have lived through inexplicable consumer manias for certain toys that the cleverest minds in the industry have not predicted. I have seen shoppers' desires for pet rocks, Cabbage Patch dolls, Tamegatchi virtual pets, and Tickle Me Elmos cause near riots in Toys "R" Us, leading to declines in the chain's stock price when its supplies run out.

But demand can be manipulated by those who control the supply of goods. Product designers appeal to consumers' aesthetic urges for the new, the sleek, and the erotic. The advertising industry—those "captains of consciousness" who have played on our hopes and fears about the perfect self for so many years—are masterminds of individual and mass psychology. Journalists, especially fashion journalists, work hand-in glove with merchants and manufacturers to stoke desire for this season's styles.[10]

Yet over the past few years, while consumers have seemed most willing to keep shopping and producers have been most able to ply us with an enormous number and variety of goods, stores have suffered a major crisis of confidence. "I don't think the stores are what they used to be," a thirty-one-year-old woman said to *Women's Wear Daily*. "There is so much junk you have to sift through to find the good stuff." "Junk" is not the only problem. Not only have stores lost the shoppers' confidence that they will find items they want to buy, they have lost their own confidence in being able to predict or control shoppers' desires.[11]

The retail clothing industry is practically schizophrenic about this. For years retail merchants have been torn between marketing to shoppers' interest in low prices and to their emotional identification with specific brands. Many stores have gone out of business because they couldn't compete with the low prices offered by discount chains like Wal-Mart and Target. During the 1990s, as department stores continued to lose customers, discount stores increased their market share from 27 to 41 per cent. By the early 2000s, not a single department store remained among the top ten retailers in the country.[12]

Yet at the same time, branded stores like Ralph Lauren and The Gap developed "lifestyle brand[s]" that attract shoppers to the image and status of their name regardless of price. These stores manage to turn the standardization of mass production into individualized images of status and style. Moreover, through a series of shrewd business deals, they shift responsibility for manufacturing to a changing group of offshore, and ever cheaper, suppliers, setting up both "a supply chain . . . [and] all the [retail] space where they can re-create their three-dimensional or lifestyle experience in an attractive area." In the industry, these companies are called "channel captains" because they control all phases of the production and distribution process, from the design studio to the sales floor. Their competitors claim that this vertical integration of all phases of the business gives them an "unfair" advantage. This is true. Though Ralph Lauren's fashion judgment isn't always infallible, and in recent years The Gap's tremendous growth rate has slowed down, the ability to control both production and distribution helps these companies to balance supply and demand.[13]

But the advantages of vertical integration are not new. In the late 1800s, independent merchants voiced the same complaints of unfair advantage against big department stores like Macy's and Wanamaker's and against the national mail-order retailers Sears and Montgomery Ward. These companies bought or set up their own suppliers and put the independent stores out of business by selling cheaper house brands. By the end of the twentieth century, however, these once-mighty titans of commerce were either gone for good or battling for their survival. "It is tough out there. Very competitive," says the head of a market research firm. The typical shopper is "unhappy, she's feeling unloved, she's bored. She's tired of looking around and seeing sameness as far as the eye can see. . . . Over half of consumers today don't feel like anybody . . . is listening [to them]."[14]

Yet stores and manufacturers *need* to listen to consumers. Though they try to seduce consumers into buying the goods they have on hand, they can only attain this goal by selling shoppers *what they want*. For over a hundred years, the entire marketing field of mass consumption has revolved around this conundrum. Like the conquest of outer space, the conquest of consumers' desires rests on strong-willed entrepreneurs carrying out strenuous projects of applied research on unknown territory. It's not as complicated as rocket science, but market research has a hard time finding out what consumers *really* want.

Despite the early triumphs of the advertising industry, in the 1920s, only in the thirties did companies begin to pay serious, systematic attention to "what the public really wants."[15] General Motors was one of the first big corporations to carry out real market research. Until then, advertising agencies counted consumers' brand preferences, compiled indexes of buying power, and analyzed small samples of consumers by occupation and social class. In the late twenties, to compete with the larger, more successful Ford Motor Company, GM had begun to make cars in colors other than black, and introduced annual styling changes. Yet consumers' falling incomes during the Great Depression made it less certain that anyone would buy a new car. Putting their heads together, Alfred P. Sloan Jr., then president of GM, and its chairman, Lammot du Pont, decided to make a concentrated effort to convince old customers to make new purchases. They figured they could accomplish this if they found out what made car buyers unhappy and responded to their complaints.[16]

So General Motors initiated a program of soliciting consumers' opinions about both the corporation and its products.[17] In 1931, it hired Paul Garrett, a former financial columnist for the *New York Post,* as the company's first director of public relations. Garrett began by examining investors' attitudes. He sent out questionnaires to stockholders who had recently sold GM stock, and was delighted to learn that they had not rejected the company because of a lack of faith in it. Garrett also undertook to examine consumers' attitudes indirectly, by analyzing the letters sent to GM by people who listened to *Parade of the States,* a weekly, GM-sponsored "radio program of orchestral music with a local theme." Since these letters were also overwhelmingly positive, Garrett convinced Alfred Sloan that the company had nothing to fear, and everything to gain, from further research.

In 1933, Sloan set up an independent "Customer Research Staff" within GM, thereby making consumer research an "operating philosophy" in all GM divisions. By mid-1934, the Customer Research Staff had received nearly three hundred thousand replies to their various questionnaires. By 1938, the research staff had distributed 1.5 million questionnaires, asking for consumers' opinions of specific styles, prices, and engineering features of GM cars, as well as for their general taste preferences.

GM drew several advantages from doing research "on a highly scientific basis" about "what the public actually thinks." It got specific, exclusive information that it used to plan new models and shape marketing campaigns. Moreover, GM advertised the fact that it did consumer research in order to present the company as both more responsive to consumers' needs and more forward-looking in their strategies. It claimed, in 1934, that GM had "An Eye to the Future—An Ear to the Ground." This may have reassured investors, but, as Roland Marchand points out in his history of public relations, it also convinced consumers that the company was listening to them. General Motors used market research to create an impression that there was a "democratic" relationship between each individual consumer and the giant corporation. This aura of responsiveness was especially important during the thirties, when the economic crisis and criticism from antibusiness groups made Big Business more vulnerable to demands for governmental regulation.

The auto industry was not the only industry to undertake market research during the Depression. Like GM, all the companies that sold consumer products desperately wanted information that would help them to sell more goods. For their part, researchers were fascinated by the purely intellectual question of how people made choices. With more goods appearing on the market all the time, and the range of choices greatly expanded by the growth of national markets, consumers faced more complex decisions than ever before. If researchers could only understand how consumers chose between car models, or radio programs, or presidential candidates, they could develop new psychological and sociological theories. Pressed to answer questions posed by their patrons about specific products, however, the early market researchers quickly moved into applied research.

They began to do extensive surveys of all kinds of consumers, from dress and gasoline buyers to radio listeners. Their research not only created a new collective consciousness among the companies that made consumer goods, it also fostered a new collective consciousness among consumers. As Susan Douglas says in her history of American radio, market research *invented* the audience during the 1930s. Because they were studied—and appealed to—as reasoning subjects, consumers formed a new, modern *public*.[18]

Paul Lazarsfeld, an émigré sociologist from Vienna, and Hadley Cantril, a Princeton University psychologist, used their research on audience reception of radio as an opportunity to study cognition and choice—but in an increasingly applied, business-oriented way. They quickly realized that the medium of radio encouraged people to develop a new attentiveness to sound; together with phonograph records, radio increased people's attraction to all forms of audio stimulation. Radio persuaded listeners not only to make cognitive connections, but also to connect aesthetically and emotionally with both the medium and its message. People made these connections regardless of whether the message was uplifting or commercial, banal or profound.

When people became steady listeners to specific radio programs, they began to identify with the sound of the announcers' and performers' voices. Even if people didn't salivate when they heard the opening bars of their favorite programs' theme songs, they did at least pay attention to the material that followed the theme songs, including the commercial announcements that became a regular part of network radio programs at this time. The more listeners heard the sponsors' voices on the radio in their homes, the more they transferred their loyalty to the sponsors' products in the stores. Both the products and the programs became popular "brand names."

At the beginning of the thirties, research on radio audiences was funded by the Rockefeller Foundation. Yet even under this not-for-profit sponsorship, the surveys focused on practical questions about which radio programs people listened to and why. Within a few years, researchers were computing the survey responses and comparing them in the abstract form of "ratings." Paul Lazarsfeld, who refined the statistical methodology of this field, went on to a distinguished academic career as a sociology professor at Columbia University. He laid the groundwork for several generations of market research, as well as for Pierre Bourdieu's future, critical work on tastes, by placing listeners in categories according to their social and economic "demographics"—by their income, education, and general cultural level. Though Lazarsfeld, like other European sociologists of the time, was interested in raising the cultural level of the whole society, he came to accept the idea that most radio listeners prefer banal or mass entertainment. Moreover, he did not challenge the idea that commercial sponsors should control the content and scheduling of radio programs—an idea that was put into law by the Federal Communications Commission around 1930. In contrast to the strident criticism of "the culture industry" offered by Theodor Adorno, Leo Lowenthal, and other sociologists who formed the Frankfurt School of critical theory, Lazarsfeld legitimized thinking of the radio audience as a new public of cultural consumers who could be exploited for commercial purposes.[19]

Herta Herzog, Lazarfeld's research partner and second wife, developed a more subtle understanding of the radio audience. Interviewing a small sample of quiz show listeners, Herzog found that listeners interactively participated in the program with the on-air contestants. Both comparing themselves and competing with the contestants, listeners experienced an emotional catharsis. Listening to the radio program, they lived through a range of emotions, from stressful to joyous. Herzog argued that radio listeners have a dual role: they are both passive and active agents in the consumption process. Her argument can be applied to shoppers as well. Like radio listeners, consumers make a cognitive, aesthetic, and emotional connection with the goods they desire.[20]

Lazarsfeld and Herzog came up with the basic insights—both quantitative and qualitative—that still drive market research. Just as Lazarsfeld *quantified* consumers' choices by statistical techniques and abstracted them in the "objective" form of ratings, so Herzog conceived of consumers' choices in terms of the *qualitative* attachments of the "subjective" self. To some degree, the continuing tension between these two ways of looking at consumers has exacerbated producers' problems in trying to balance supply and demand. The two methodologies see the consumer as a divided self: as both body and soul, *corpus* and *psyche*.

In the thirties, *corpus* ruled: most market research consisted of body counting by statistical methods. From the forties, however, *psyche* took over, with market research reinforcing the influence of Freudian psychoanalysis. In line with Sigmund Freud's view of the individual personality, the consumer appeared as a seething mass of unresolved contradictions and latent desires, many of which reflect primal needs. Since the source of these desires lies in the "inner self," consumers can more usefully be examined by subtle psychoanalytic techniques than by a statistical analysis of superficial buying patterns. Experts trained in psychoanalysis can uncover hidden needs and motivations that advertisers and producers then "mobilize" by "forming connections between human passions, hopes and anxieties" and specific qualities of consumer goods. The psychoanalytic approach attracted researchers on both sides of the Atlantic at this time. In America, the motivational researcher Ernest Dichter became the guru of marketing managers and advertising agencies, while in London, researchers at the Tavistock Institute studied consumers as psychological, rather than social and economic, "types."[21]

During the fifties, researchers at Tavistock looked at both psychological drives and cultural practices to create theories about the psychological gratification of eating pleasure foods like ice cream and chocolate to alleviate anxiety. Nor were they shy about theorizing that food and other product preferences reveal disguised motivations of sexual gratification. They carried out in-depth studies to answer such questions as how to persuade people to buy ice cream in winter and how to increase consumption of Toblerone chocolate bars. They also devised strategies to persuade women to buy new hair products—not by surveying consumers about their attitudes toward these products, as GM would have done in the thirties, but by examining women's attitudes toward their hair. They adapted their theories to new products as these came on the market. So, in the mid-fifties, researchers at the Tavistock examined the appeal of new, soft toilet tissue in terms of the desire for upward social mobility.

Instead of assuming, as George Akerlof would eventually do, that markets are plagued by a general lack of information, the Tavistock researchers assumed a tension between people's tendency to think that all brands are the same and their fear that some brands are really better. They concluded that consumers keep buying specific brands because it is "psychologically uneconomical" for them to switch around; this avoidance of experimentation is reinforced by "objective dangers and subjective anxieties" associated with certain products, especially cars. Yet the researchers also believed that advertising reassures consumers that they have made the right choice. This led the Tavistock researchers, in the sixties, to invent a new psychoanalytic term. They suggested that loyalty to certain brands reflects positive "brand cathexis," while aversion to other brands represents negative cathexis, based on a bad experience with a product or the company that produces it.[22]

The use of psychological and psychoanalytic techniques to uncover hidden motivations fed consumers' fears. They felt that they were being manipulated, against their will, into buying goods they neither wanted nor needed. This fear was intensified by journalistic exposés of "communist" propaganda and brainwashing during the Korean War and witch-hunts of the McCarthy period. In the mid-fifties, Vance Packard's best-selling book *The Hidden Persuaders* awakened Americans to the possibility they were being brainwashed by the advertising industry. Yet in the sixties, when ads grew more subtle and ironic, market researchers developed new "psychographics" to identify the socio-psychological types of consumer who would be most receptive to specific marketing appeals. These tools were useful to companies that wanted more effective marketing concepts that would speak to consumers' needs.[23]

The sixties' creative revolution in advertising, followed by alternative lifestyles in the counterculture, moved market research in a different direction, more attuned to fine-grained consumer choices. In 1969, Dr. Joseph

Plummer, who was later to become the executive vice president for research at Young & Rubicam, began to do "life-style analyses" for the beer-maker Schlitz, one of the New York ad agency's clients. He found that heavy beer drinkers were "macho people [who] lived life to the fullest and didn't take any crap from anybody"—which led him to propose that televised beer commercials should speak to hearty males. Plummer then turned his attention to analyzing different types of women, based on what they look for in a laundry detergent; he "concluded that the heaviest users of detergent were young middle-class women with large families—women who cared about their families but didn't want to be chained to the laundry room." This led him to devise an appropriate advertising strategy for another of the agency's clients—Cheer.[24]

Also in the sixties, the market researcher Arnold Mitchell began to study the effect of "social values" on consumers' spending patterns. Working at SRI International, formerly the Stanford Research Institute, in California, Mitchell predicted that young adults who reached maturity during the counterculture years would be attracted to advertisements attacking materialist values. He wrote that new, emotional ads should tap into "person-centeredness, direct experience, and . . . intangibles." During the seventies, Mitchell and SRI expanded this approach into a new research program focusing on "values and lifestyles." Their program was based on a hierarchical list of lifestyle types Mitchell devised in 1976, influenced by David Riesman's early-fifties sociological classic *The Lonely Crowd* and Abraham Maslow's psychology of needs. Over the next few years, these lifestyle types replaced the upper, middle, and working classes as the conceptual basis for thinking about consumer choice. By the eighties, values and lifestyles (VALS) dominated the whole field of market research.[25]

In an effort to provide scientific backup for their impressionistic typology, VALS researchers inflicted survey questionnaires on thousands of willing subjects. They asked them not only about their brand preferences, but also about their sexual habits and attitudes toward themselves; they catalogued their pets, credit cards, and programs they watched on TV. During the eighties, these surveys were expanded through the use of intensive focus groups, which placed researchers in small, face-to-face discussions with consumers, who were encouraged to speak at length about brands and products they liked or disliked. These methods painted an interesting, and sometimes even a humorous, composite portrait of "Inner-directed," "outer-directed," "achievers," "need-drivens," and "socially conscious" consumers. But the researchers insisted that advertising, and eventually all marketing strategies, should be pitched to these composites as though they were real. Without either the psychoanalytic sophistication of earlier researchers or the anthropological appreciation of how commodities change meaning in different cultural contexts, lifestyle marketers reduced the complexity of individual desires to abstract categories. They didn't really understand social diversity; they *organized* diversity to persuade people to buy more.[26]

Nonetheless, lifestyle researchers believed that their methods enabled them to visualize consumers as real, complex "individuals rather than statistics." As Plummer defended it, "VALS . . . made consumers less abstract." And the methods appeared to work. "We spent a lot of time kind of hypothesizing about which VALS groups would be receptive to our product categories—and we must have been right," a marketing director at Timex says. "We sold a lot of Timex products." Within a year of adopting the VALS methodology, "Timex had captured 34 percent of the market for electronic blood-pressure monitors; its closest competitor had nine."[27]

VALS could be adapted to market research for any product. By the eighties, it was used by a wide range of consumer products companies, from Clairol to Mitsubishi and REI. It was also used by political candidates to devise campaign strategies that would appeal to specific groups of voters. "VALS . . . is more than a market research outfit," a journalist wrote about the missionary zeal of the researchers who spread the lifestyle methodology; "it's a credo, an aesthetic, a way of interpreting contemporary" thought.[28]

Despite VALS' success, psychographics was only one set of techniques for analyzing consumers' choices. Researchers continued to devise an array of physiological and ethnographic methods of observing consumers' bodies in order to track their attentiveness to specific advertisements, products, and brands. In the fifties and sixties, "biotechnologists" brought consumers into the laboratory and fitted them with headbands to measure electrical activity in the brain. Though they believed that more effective stimuli would generate more noticeable brain waves, these waves proved difficult to interpret. Other laboratory methods tracked consumers' eyeballs as they read ads or watched TV commercials; still others placed people under hypnosis to uncover long-repressed memories of consumer goods and services. All these experimental procedures severed *corpus* from *psyche*, reducing consumers from subjects to objects of research.[29]

Yet researchers still hoped to find the right factors of desire that could be "mobilized" to persuade consumers to buy goods. While focus groups were still in fashion during the eighties, an anthropologist named Paco Underhill believed the body would be the next wave of market research. Underhill watched shoppers as they moved through stores to track their attentiveness to different displays. He found shoppers tend to move to the right in store aisles rather than to the left, and to be repelled by messy changing rooms. These observations led him and his consulting firm, Envirosell, to make proposals on stores' layout and display to client firms; their fee was based on whether these proposals increased the clients' sales.[30]

Other researchers returned to the *psyche*. Taking a different approach to the collective unconscious, a medical anthropologist named Clotaire Rapaille developed "archetypal" research, loosely connecting psychoanalysis and cultural practices. This research traces consumers' memories of, and associations with, different smells, tastes, and colors. Rapaille found smell to be the most powerful stimulus for recalling early childhood sensations— leading him to tell the people at Procter & Gamble who market Folger's Coffee: "Don't care about the taste. You have to own the aroma."[31]

When competition between brands grew more intense in the nineties, companies pressed for more foolproof methods of tracking both *corpus* and *psyche*. Focus groups fell out of favor. They had been overused during the eighties, and now they were criticized because of "interference" by the group leader and dominant members of the focus group. At a loss, researchers returned to more subtle, psychological methods. One advertising agency asked frequent fliers to use crayons to color stages of a journey on a map, with hot colors to show stress and anger and cool colors to show satisfaction. Other researchers went to consumers' homes to look in their kitchens and medicine cabinets, accompanying them while they shopped or drove their cars, and videotaping them as they used products in their homes. The search for new research methods was made more intense by companies' new global strategies. If they wished to position themselves in many regional markets, they had to know how consumers in those markets used different goods and what they "really wanted" from them. But the push for new research methods also reflected the companies' desire to sell more goods in an oversaturated world—"to come up with products that solve problems shoppers [don't] even know they [have]."[32]

Since the nineties, computer technology has made it easier than ever to track consumers' bodies, or at least the movement of their eyeballs and fingertips. Yet if the newer counting methods are fairly unobtrusive, consumers are not too happy about being tracked. The black boxes, mouses, and Web TV that enable interactive participation are parts of a mechanical apparatus that separates researchers and consumers. Moreover, many consumers resent the hidden "cookies" that track their journeys through the Internet, especially because websites sell these data to other firms. The dismay at these invasions of privacy has encouraged software manufacturers to allow users to set security levels on their computers. However, high security settings don't disable cookies; they just block access to web sites that have them. On the other hand, it is not even clear that tracking "clickthroughs" is a meaningful form of market research. Counting how many times a product or an online ad has been seen does not tell us whether consumers remember anything about it. Neither does it tell us whether the product was just seen in passing or was deliberately sought. At any rate, surfing the web casts consumers in the role of unwitting, and often unwilling, laboratory rats. As tracking technology gets faster, cheaper, and easier to install, we become more visible to market researchers—but we also become more reluctant subjects.[33]

The biggest problem with computer-based market research is that it engages *corpus* without *psyche*. We feel free to ignore what we see on the screen in ways we cannot ignore human researchers. Neither is there any assurance that clicking on a website or seeing an online ad leads to the producers' main concern—our buying their product. Like every other kind of market research that has been devised so far, online research cannot trace the sources of our desire.[34]

What market researchers do best is to find consumers who are likely to buy the products in question in the first place—and to sell the data they compile on these consumers. As Eileen Meehan writes about the early twentieth-century radio audience, they were "an audience of consumers rather than of listeners," and networks sold access to them "as the basic commodity." Neither broadcast nor cable television has made this situation more democratic, for to these media the audience is only a set of "audited eyeballs." Though we have learned through our consumption how to be a public, to marketers we remain a commodity.[35]

But, of course, we consumers are not mere objects of research. We are also autonomous subjects who determine our own desires. Just as each one of us is made up of *corpus* and *psyche*, body and soul, so we all combine desires that both respond to and transcend the available universe of commodities.

We do recognize ourselves in the abstract categories market researchers devise. Though we don't think of ourselves in these terms, we can see ourselves as "inner directed" or "outer directed," as young, female secretaries with pink flamingos on our lawns or as people who would look good in leather pants. But I wonder whether the masters of market research have really helped us. Using one method after another, they have torn apart the double helix of our body and soul—selling us more things without ever finding out what we "really want."

I don't know why Cindy wanted "the perfect pair of leather pants." Maybe she saw a really good looking woman in leather pants walking on the street one day, or a friend told her about them, or she saw them in a magazine. Maybe she remembered a pair of leather pants from long ago. At any rate, Cindy wasn't as lucky as Gina: Gina found *her* perfect pair of leather pants for $49.95 at The Gap.

The most important thing about Cindy's story is that she believes she has a right to find the object of her desire in a store. In a democracy, you shop for what you really want. The appeal of a shopping spree is not that you'll buy a lot of stuff; the appeal is that, among all the stuff you buy, you'll find what you truly desire.

5

b. altman, ralph lauren, and the death of the leisure class

> I find that department stores are depressing. . . . They're in the business of numbers. . . . They're not in the business of dreams.
> —Ralph Lauren, speaking to apparel industry executives, 1998[1]

My colleague Tim, who also teaches at Brooklyn College, has never stopped wearing light green Shetland crewneck sweaters and khakis even though everyone else in New York wears black. This morning, he asks me how I like the new quarters of our university's graduate school, which has just moved into the former B. Altman department store—a tall, classical, limestone palazzo built in the midtown shopping district, on Fifth Avenue, around 1900. When I tell him my new office is on the sixth floor of that building, he chuckles and says, in the orotund tones you would expect of a speech professor, "Sixth floor? Isn't that 'Lamps'?"

Like many middle-class people of a certain age in New York, Tim and I both shopped at Altman's. The store went out of business in 1989, after it was run into the ground by L. J. Hooker, an Australian real estate development company, which took advantage of the mergers and acquisitions mania of the eighties by buying several well-known, American retail chains: Altman's, Bonwit Teller, and the Sakowitz store in Houston.

B. Altman had enjoyed a long and respected local reputation, stretching back to its founding as a dry goods store in the mid-nineteenth century by a German Jewish immigrant. It was the kind of store people call "an institution." You could always find what you needed there, and you always knew where it was. Selma, who is married to one of my older colleagues, says, "The salespeople knew everything, and they were civilized. It was old fashioned, it was 'old New York.'"

It really was "old New York." In its first incarnation as a dry goods store, in the 1850s, Altman's was located on Third Avenue near Tenth Street, a block away from A. T. Stewart's new Marble Palace. This was a good location, near the bustling stores of Broadway and at the northern end of the dry-goods district on the Bowery. A horsecar line ran up and down the avenue. German immigrants filled the working-class tenements to the east, while upper-class Dutch and English families lived in the townhouses to the west. Some German Jewish shopkeepers, like the Altman family, were beginning to expand their business and prosper. Merchants who had been peddlers or secondhand clothes dealers on Orchard Street, on the Lower East Side, were moving uptown to open real, American, dry goods stores.

Foot traffic on Third Avenue must have increased dramatically after 1858, when Cooper Union, a school for adult workers, opened its doors. Students attended both day and evening classes, and public meetings were held in the Great Hall, where Abraham Lincoln, then a likely presidential candidate, gave a rousing speech against slavery in February 1860. At any rate, Altman's prospered, and continued to prosper after the Civil War, when the mass production of clothing made it possible for consumers to buy new styles in "ready-to-wear." In the 1860s, Benjamin Altman, then in his twenties, joined his father in the store.[2]

During the next decade, Altman's moved to Sixth Avenue and Nineteenth Street, where horsecars, followed by an elevated subway line, drew a large number of retail merchants and shoppers. Nearly twenty years earlier, in 1858, R. H. Macy had staked out the territory. He founded a "fancy" dry goods store, at Sixth Avenue and Fourteenth Street, where "he sold goods at lower prices than his competitors, bought and sold only for cash rather than credit, and advertised vigorously." The signs up and down the front of Macy's four-story building, above the awnings, advertised every "fancy" a woman could want—"shawls, cloaks, mantillas," as well as "silks, velvets, merinoes, laces, embroideries & hosiery."[3]

By the time Altman's moved over to Sixth Avenue, Macy had bought up several neighboring townhouses and installed a more elegant commercial facade. Soon, Macy's rivals—B. Altman and Company, Hugh O'Neill's Store, Simpson, Crawford, Ehrich Brothers, and Siegel-Cooper—filled the blockfronts of Sixth Avenue from Fourteenth to Twenty-third Street. These merchants built huge, new, multilevel stores, with selling floors of an unprecedented size. They chose columned facades made of a new industrial material—cast iron—providing a "front" that was impressively solid,

Emporium of dreams: former location of B. Altman, Sixth Avenue, 1868–1906. Photo by author, 2003.

in their customers' eyes, but cheap and mass-produced, in the view of those who knew about classical architecture. Gigantic windows, made of another new material—plate glass—embellished the facades above the street floor. Passengers riding in an elevated railway car could catch a tantalizing glimpse of merchandise through the windows as they passed by. These windows illuminated the merchants' sensuous fabrics by natural light, transforming the old, crowded, musty fabric shops into modern department stores, or palaces of dreams.

The more upscale Ladies' Mile, where wealthy women shopped for jewelry at Gorham and Tiffany and for clothes at Lord & Taylor, and prosperous businessmen and professionals patronized Brooks Brothers, was two long blocks away, on Broadway. But it must have been liberating for middle-class women and shopgirls to come to Sixth Avenue on the "el," and find dresses, scarves, or rugs that were stylish, well made, and inexpensive. Whether women shopped at the more exclusive shops on the Ladies' Mile or in the cheaper stores on Sixth Avenue, this was the beginning of the golden age of department stores as "dream worlds": bazaars where beauty, luxury, and elegance were publicly displayed and eminently available.[4]

Department stores were part of an urban mosaic that remade the city's streets at the turn of the twentieth century. Skyscrapers, stores, theaters, and sweatshops created a dense concentration of places for work, entertainment, and public display, where men and women from different walks of life competed for the same scarce space. Although, in the 1880s, the Ladies' Mile was the most fashionable street in Manhattan for luxury shopping, this area was also stigmatized by the presence of prostitutes soliciting on the street and houses of prostitution, or "temples of love." Soon, high land prices downtown, from Wall Street to Canal Street, caused a wave of speculative building of both sweatshops and skyscrapers around the subway and horsecar lines on Fourteenth Street. All these undesirable neighbors persuaded the more prestigious retail merchants to move farther uptown.[5]

B. Altman was the first major department store to move, in 1906, to Thirty-fourth Street and Fifth Avenue. Macy's had announced plans to move a block away, to Thirty-fourth Street and Sixth Avenue, in 1901, but it didn't actually make the move until several years later. Tiffany and Gorham began work on new stores in the neighborhood in 1903. Between 1910 and 1915, the furniture merchants W. and J. Sloane and the clothing firms of Lord & Taylor, Brooks Brothers, Bonwit Teller, and Arnold Constable all built new stores uptown. They settled just north of Altman's, between Thirty-sixth and Forty-fourth Streets.

During these decades of continual commercial expansion, moralists inveighed against women—or women's imaginations—running loose in department stores, where they were free to make important choices without a man's consent. Women were continually accused of being too weak to withstand the temptations of choice; they were charged with spending money beyond their means, abusing their husbands' charge accounts, and shoplifting. Kleptomania was considered to be the middle-class woman's disease.[6] Yet every great city—New York, Paris, London, Berlin, Budapest, Tokyo—tempted shoppers with the bright lights and dramatic displays of its dream palaces and influenced merchants in smaller cities to build their own modest copies.

By 1915, the window displays of the department stores had become a thrilling public spectacle of the streets. In the big city of Chicago, crowds lined up in front of Marshall Field, eagerly waiting for the curtains on the annual fall window displays to be pulled aside. In the twenties, store owners in small towns, like Ypsilanti, Michigan, and Davenport, Iowa, held special "window nights," when unveiling the window displays of new fall merchandise was coordinated with local harvest festivals. The novelist Theodore Dreiser wrote about window-shopping in Manhattan in his diary, in November 1917. "We go across 34th and 5th Avenue [the site of B. Altman], and up to 42nd," Dreiser wrote, "looking in windows. Wonderful display. . . . These stores are so fascinating in the winter."[7]

Shrewdly, Benjamin Altman began to buy land on Thirty-fourth Street in the 1890s—at both Sixth Avenue, along the elevated railway line, and in the more elite block between Fifth and Madison Avenues, near Roland Knoedler's art gallery and the elegant, new Waldorf-Astoria Hotel. By 1905, he had bought almost the entire square block between Thirty-fourth and Thirty-fifth Streets, and Fifth and Madison. Altman commissioned the architects Trowbridge & Livingston, who had designed a mansion for the steel baron Henry Phipps, at Eighty-seventh Street and Fifth Avenue, to design his new store on a similar scale. When it was completed, in 1914, B. Altman's white, limestone-clad palazzo rose to eight stories on the Fifth Avenue side of the block and to twelve stories on Madison Avenue. A genteel restaurant, Charleston Gardens, was located beneath the atrium on the top floor. There also may have been workshops on the higher floors, where some of the clothing sold in the store was made. An article published by T. P. O'Connor, a visiting Irish member of Parliament, in a 1907 issue of *Munsey's Magazine*, described Altman's and Tiffany's as highlights of his trip to New York. "These shops," O'Connor wrote, "were palaces for the magnifico who ruled an Italian city and state in medieval times rather than a mere shop where the ordinary citizen or his wife could go and haggle about their wares." Ironically, B. Altman placed his store on the site of A. T. Stewart's ornate, grandiose, "overdecorated" mansion; Stewart had built New York City's first great department store, the Marble Palace, down-town in 1846.[8]

A photograph of Altman's, taken in 1920, shows a great, glistening, white cube, grand but classically austere, like the porticoed Lincoln Memorial in Washington, D.C.—if the Lincoln Memorial were surrounded by tall, plate-glass windows. At the center of the main entrance, on Fifth Avenue, a dozen narrow, wood-and-glass-paneled doors swing open onto a vestibule, about ten feet deep, where shoppers waited for their carriages,

Palace of dreams: main entrance, B. Altman, Fifth Avenue, 1906. Wurts Collection, Museum of the City of New York.

or opened an umbrella before heading into the rain. Outside, the doors are arched by three scalloped, glass-and-metal portes cochères that recall Hector Guimard's elegant, Art Nouveau entrances to the Paris metro, also designed around that time.

An inner set of twelve more glass-paneled doors leads from the vestibule into a large central rotunda, a typical feature of the grand department stores that were built in the late nineteenth century. The Galeries Lafayette on Boulevard Haussmann, in Paris, still has a rotunda, and so—in an architectural conceit—does its new branch on Friedrichstrasse in central Berlin, built in the 1990s. By the middle of the twenties, however, most department stores, including B. Altman, replaced their rotundas with escalators, which permitted them to increase the size of the selling floor. Like other stores, Altman's also covered the windows around the sides of the store, making it a darker, more private space, and illuminated it by artificial light.

So department stores took a step away from the public street of the shopping arcades, which were so popular in European and American cities before 1890, toward the enclosed shopping malls of the future.[9]

But B. Altman remained a classy store. Its elaborate decor included iron grillwork around the elevator cages, white marble drinking fountains, glass display cases, and globe lamps hanging from the ceiling. The store was so big it had thirty-nine separate elevators. Wood paneling from Benjamin Altman's house was installed in the store after he died, in 1913. There was never a bargain basement. Unlike S. Klein, Filene's of Boston, and the cut-rate shops of Orchard Street, Altman's did not woo shoppers in search of bargains. The crowded counters where shoppers jostled for position to paw through goods, the communal dressing rooms where five hundred women undressed at once, and the clerks on high platforms who watched out for shoplifters that were so much a part of the shopping experience for working-class and immigrant women[10] had no place at Altman's. Instead, like the other great department stores of the time—Marshall Field in Chicago, Selfridge's in London, John Wanamaker in Philadelphia and New York—B. Altman wooed middle-class women shoppers with personal services like hairdressing salons and fur storage and with such amenities as elegant ladies' rooms, restaurants, and post offices. Even in an age when merchant princes routinely decreed that the customer must be made to feel like a queen, Altman declared that, in his store, "shopping was to become a pleasure instead of a task."[11]

Benjamin Altman was also a paternalistic employer. Like R. H. Macy, John Wanamaker, and the Boucicault family that founded the Bon Marché, he tried to make up for low wages with privately funded welfare benefits. B. Altman may have been "the first department store to provide bathrooms for workers, to provide a cafeteria with subsidized prices and a school for the children of employees." When Benjamin Altman died, he left his property, including most of the stock ownership of the store, to a charitable foundation.[12]

After the twenties, Altman's doesn't appear to have made any dramatic changes to either their policies or their image—and that's where the reasons for their ultimate failure lie. While other stores devoted more attention to new suburban branches than to their downtown stores, Altman's opened six branches—among them, one in Manhasset, on the north shore of Long Island, and one in Willow Grove, near Philadelphia, Pennsylvania—but the center of its attention remained the flagship store. Moreover, even though the level of civility at B. Altman remained close to what it had been in 1906, by the sixties the store failed to meet the shifting expectations of younger, more mobile consumers.

My friend Renée, a sociologist in her fifties who grew up in New York, worked at B. Altman as a sales clerk in the early sixties to pay her way through college. "Altman's had an older clientele," Renée says about those years. "Little old ladies with their poodles, diamonds, and rubber boots. By the time I could afford B. Altman, it had closed."

Many New Yorkers were sad when B. Altman shut down. Selma, my colleague's wife, says she hasn't bought a pair of curtains since they closed. The journalist Dennis Duggan writes, "I miss being able to browse in a store where nobody asked you what you wanted unless you asked first." Along with the reticence of the salespeople, a slower, less pressured way of life was lost. "The disappearance of these old stores," Duggan says, ". . . leaves an emptiness behind."[13]

By the sixties, however, women's longing to express themselves in more public ways encouraged them to search for different styles of clothing, and younger shoppers sought out smaller, hipper stores for younger, newer-looking fashions. To compete for these shoppers, Altman's opened a new department, Studio Three, on the third floor, but it never succeeded like the innovative S'fari Room at Bonwit Teller, Henri Bendel's chic Street of Shops, or even Macy's Little Shop. At a time when *Women's Wear Daily* urged all stores to upgrade themselves by offering "superior fashion merchandise" to affluent, educated, sophisticated shoppers, the newspaper criticized Studio Three for failing to develop a distinct personality. The department had too much stock out on the floor, *Women's Wear Daily* complained, and, without brisk sales and rapid turnover, the merchandise never looked fresh enough.[14]

B. Altman seems to have lost its groove during the sixties, when moderation and gentility became hopelessly old-fashioned. In those years, all the "classics" of modern culture became old-fashioned: pre-Beatles rock and roll, corporate glass-box architecture, and even the realistic dramas that were the mainstay of American theater. Looking back on the early sixties, when his work—including *Death of a Salesman* and *A View from the Bridge*—fell out of favor, the playwright Arthur Miller says, "The 60s was a time when a play with recognizable characters, a beginning, middle and end was routinely condemned as 'well made' or ludicrously old-fashioned." Miller blames this decline on the loss of a "unified audience." Like shoppers who abandoned department stores for boutiques, a new, hip group of theatrical consumers went off-Broadway to see avant-garde plays. Broadway then lost its image of good value—a "Shakespearean ideal, a theatre for anyone with an understanding of English and perhaps some common sense."15

But that was the image of value B. Altman represented—civilized, reasonable, a store for shoppers with common sense. "The help was courteous and looked as though they had been working there for more than a day or two," says Dennis Duggan. "They didn't seem to regard your presence as an intrusion on their time. If you asked a question, you got an answer. . . . The store was a shelter from the hurly-burly of the streets outside."

Yet it was just this hurly-burly that the most successful stores began to exploit in the sixties. Shopping was no longer a civilized activity; neither was fashion a matter of "common sense." Manufacturers woke up to the demographic bulge of young consumers with money to spend, who thought of style as a means of rebellion. Department stores, cornered by discounters on one side and small specialty shops on the other, decided to make themselves over into boutiques to experiment with different merchandise in order to lure young shoppers into the store. When fashion changed from a spectator sport to an aggressive free-for-all of self-expression, tremendous opportunities arose for entrepreneurs and intermediaries—especially stores—that catered to a new passion for shopping.

In 1973, the novelist Lois Gould issued an ecstatic description of Bloomingdale's as a new kind of department store, dedicated to the new Fashion. In "Confessions of a Bloomingdale's Addict," Gould breathlessly enumerates a flamboyantly diverse list of shoppers—divided by race, ideology, wealth, and fame—whose only common characteristic is their conspicuous consumption.

> Where else could you find—in a single recent week—Antony Armstrong-Jones [brother-in-law of Queen Elizabeth II] stocking up on no-iron sheets; Marietta Tree [a patrician activist for liberal causes who held a position at the United Nations] stripping in public to try on a sequined pants suit; Mrs. Jacob Javits [wife of a U.S. senator from New York] clutching a bulging United States Senate folder and confessing that Bloomingdale's takes her a whole day to "do" (she starts at the top and works down, like a tourist

covering the Louvre); two small black schoolboys pounding hard-rock hell out of a $400 electronic organ—without anyone in a suit asking "May I help you?"; nomadic tribes of fierce "singles"—all ages and sexual persuasions, sheepskin coats flung wide over silver-studded jeans—cruising the action-packed main floor for Saturday-night dates; and a pair of stringy-haired Yippie-style evangelists letting it all hang out over the UP escalator, shouting gleefully into the crowd: "Greedy, *Greedy!* GREEDY!"[16]

This couldn't have been a more different scene from B. Altman, where the store was still a calm oasis of civility. Unlike Altman's fashion-unconscious shoppers, whose sense of self inhabited a stable social status, Bloomingdale's became a store for people who shopped for status the same way they shopped for lamps or lingerie: openly, enviously, enthusiastically.

Indeed, until the sixties, all department stores and their core shoppers were much more stable than they later became. Grace Mirabella, the former editor of *Vogue*, recalls, "Each store aimed for a certain style, a certain specialty market, and a certain clientele, and you knew the minute that you walked into any one store, and smelled the perfume and saw the flowers and doormen or bargain tables, precisely where you were." The sensory cues that gave each store a specific sense of place were keys not only to the store's dominant style but also to its exclusive contracts with manufacturers, and to the social status of many of its customers.[17]

The contrasts between stores are illuminated by the ironic vignettes that accompany Lois Gould's "Confessions." Written by two young New York women—an author and an editor—these vignettes caricature the distinctive social types that shopped at each of the city's well-known department and specialty stores. While the caricatures ring true to anyone who remembers shopping in New York City in the early seventies, they were, at that very moment, being turned upside down. The growing number of women who began to pursue careers outside the home, the assertive rhetoric of the women's movement, and the incessant hucksterism of the fashion world soon made these stereotypes obsolete. Yet the vignettes also show evidence of change, of women pursuing upward social mobility by switching stores. Ultimately, these women were shopping for a new, more fluid social status—that seemed just within their reach.

Bergdorf Goodman and B. Altman are extreme examples of the old social status: traditional, unquestioned, and unchanging. "The Bergdorf," Joni Evans and Carol Rinzler write, tongue in cheek, about frequent shoppers at one of the most expensive stores in New York City, "has been breeding for more than two generations. She is a thoroughbred. She has always maintained the utmost in taste and comfort and she has not held a job since she sat desk at Wellesley twenty years ago [in the fifties]. The Bergdorf believes in charity balls, formal dinner parties, and when she goes to Europe, she goes by ship." The B. Altman shopper is dowdier and thriftier; yet she is equally old-fashioned. "The Altman," in Evans and Rinzler's words, "wears nylons and heels, even in the coldest and hottest weather, and has never left her house in her entire life without a handbag. . . . She is likely to get more excited over a pillow than a cashmere sweater. . . . [and] may buy a potato masher on impulse, but never a dress."[18]

Meanwhile, the Henri Bendel shopper points to big social changes. "Unlike the Bergdorf," Evans and Rinzler write, "the Bendel is not born, but made. She has worked hard to be Bendel, beginning in the days when, after years of training [as a shopper] at Bonwit's, she made the big move across Fifth Avenue to buy a pair of sunglasses." By this point, they suggest, it is archaic for shoppers to remain loyal throughout their lives to a single store. In a commercial kind of serial monogamy, they move from store to store in search of social status. But in the seventies, a woman's choice of where to shop no longer represents her father's or her husband's social position—the way Thorstein Veblen described conspicuous consumption; it represents her own, active search for status. Switching her patronage from store to store has become not only a rite, but a *right* of woman's passage. Reflecting a new age of aspiration for upward social mobility, and spinning a philosophical pun, Evans and Rinzler declare, "The Bonwit is Becoming rather than Being." But they are quite clear about which store is associated with each stage in the social ladder: "Every Bermuda Shop on her way to being a Bergdorf, every Bigi on her way to being a Bloomingdale has been a Bonwit at some time in her life—and will be again."[19]

Of course, women never did all their shopping at a single store. And in our day, these caricatures are totally obsolete. The idea that each store caters to a different type of shopper, that Macy's and Bloomingdale's sell completely antithetical styles, that we can't cobble together provisional identities by mixing and matching pieces from Kmart and DKNY: these ideas have been superseded by a different shopping culture.

But how did it all begin?

The new culture of shopping began, oddly enough, with lamps—or really, in the home furnishings department at Bloomingdale's.

Marvin Traub, the merchandising executive who led Bloomingdale's from the sixties through the eighties, recounts in his memoirs that when he was hired, in the early 1950s, Bloomingdale's was a low-status store. The only department with any reputation—that was a "destination," as we would now say—was furniture, and maybe also the overflowing "sale" counters in the bargain basement. Traub was hired after getting an M.B.A. from Harvard and working for a short time at Alexander's, a department store with an even lower pedigree than Macy's or Bloomingdale's. But the CEO who hired him away from Alexander's, James Edward Davidson, had a different idea in mind—an idea of upgrading Bloomingdale's to an authoritative store where the merchandise, not the price, would be the center of attraction. The new Bloomingdale's would be somewhat like the venerable Neiman Marcus in Dallas, a store that set standards for both fashion and quality.

Davidson, Traub recalls, "transformed the store by teaching the buyers to focus on the merchandise and the Bloomingdale's level of taste. . . . He had a vision of a store that was defined by the merchandise it carried and the way the goods were presented." The new Bloomingdale's would not cater to the social status of the shoppers it already attracted—which, by all accounts, was fairly low. Instead, Davidson "felt a store should decide what to offer *based on the taste of the customers it wanted to attract.* . . . Instead of the department store being merely a selling agent, *it would become a creative force*; the merchandise would be the star and the buyer would be the arbiter of taste and style. This," Traub says, tooting his own horn, "was a revolutionary concept."[20]

Department by department, floor by floor, Davidson, Traub, and a group of young buyers remade the store in the image of the equally young, upwardly mobile consumers they wanted to attract. They began with home furnishings, the only area in which Bloomingdale's already had some distinction. This area of merchandise also promised rapid growth. In the first economic expansion following the Great Depression and World War II, young couples were buying their own houses or renting their first apartments and furnishing them from scratch.

In 1953, Davidson sent Traub to Spain and Scandinavia on his first overseas buying trip. He gave Traub a special mission, searching out small workshops that produced ceramics, wooden objects, and textiles, using methods of traditional craftsmanship. Davidson's sense of timing was prescient: in contrast to the standardized mass production of most postwar consumer products, and the cookie-cutter mold of new suburban tract houses, Bloomingdale's would offer "old," "authentic," artisanal products in "real" materials. These items would stand out as distinctive status markers for a new middle class.[21]

But because Bloomingdale's wanted to sell a high volume of merchandise, these items had to be mass-produced. Under Davidson's and Traub's directives, their functions and details were subtly altered, without losing their interesting, artisanal look. Olive oil cans were made into lamp bases; French bidets became planters. The rugs Traub brought back from Spain and Scandinavia sold out, he writes, because they hadn't been seen before in the United States. But they were also "well made, reasonably priced, and unique"—a formula the Bloomingdale's team used to enhance the store's reputation.[22]

Davidson and Traub were not the first executives at Bloomingdale's to think of combing Europe for distinctive crafts. In 1952, Traub's immediate boss—another business school graduate, who headed the Downstairs Store—sent a buyer to Europe, and she came back with the idea of organizing a special promotion of Italian goods. The Downstairs manager opened the "Capri Shop" to display Italian imports, as well as craft products, straw baskets, and pottery that looked vaguely Italian; its success encouraged Bloomingdale's to set up a London and a Mediterranean shop—all placed, at first, in the bargain basement.

In the late fifties, Bloomingdale's expanded the small shops organized around European craft products into a series of country-themed "import fairs." These promotions provided a bonanza in publicity, turning the store, like a Disneyland for urban adults, into a center of themed consumption and cross-marketing opportunities. The first promotion, in 1957, focused on Scandinavian design. Two years later, for "Casa Bella," the whole store was turned into a themed experience of Italy: "Italian murals and statues were recreated for the entrance and Italian food and wine were served. But most important," Traub recalls, "each item carried a red tag with a drawing of a cherub holding a candle encircled by the words *Made in Italy for Bloomingdale's*."[23]

These in-store displays and festivals drew upon two older department store strategies. Since the early twentieth century, department stores had shown furniture, fabrics, and decorative products in the themed environments of model rooms. Not only did these rooms raise popular awareness of period styles and decor—thus offering all shoppers an elementary course in connoisseurship, geared to mass-market reproductions—they also aroused shoppers' desires to buy the items on display. Model rooms were the first lifestyle stores. Moreover, in fashion merchandising, Bloomingdale's followed strategies that had been developed at Neiman Marcus. Beginning in the twenties, Stanley Marcus, a son and nephew of the store's founders, introduced weekly, in-store fashion shows, a pre-Christmas shopping night when the store was open just for men, and annual promotions of individual fashion designers, who were flown to Texas from Paris and New York for personal appearances.[24]

By the early sixties, Bloomingdale's had made a significant discovery. There was a place in New York City—fully stocked with stores as the city was—for an authoritative yet democratic department store, one that had a reputation for being highly selective about merchandise but open to all who wanted to shop, and that brought middle-class believers to worship at the shrine of the new, the well-made, and the not-too-expensive. Just as Neiman Marcus, since 1907, had taught Texas women how to shop, so Bloomingdale's "would be the arbiter of taste and style" for the urban—and newly suburban—middle-class masses of New York City.

And who could be better arbiters of taste than Davidson, Traub, and their hand-picked crew of buyers? These were people with high-status tastes working in a low-status store. Like Stanley Marcus and Marvin Traub, some of them had Harvard M.B.A.'s, and Traub's mother was a supersaleswoman in the mold, perhaps, of Carrie Marcus Neiman. Bloomingdale's management team succeeded in identifying new consumers who were, as Traub says, pretty much like themselves: young, upwardly mobile, attracted to authenticity but with "a passion for the new"—the sort of shoppers who would buy a Tuscan majolica urn to use as a vase. In contrast both to their parents', Depression-era generation, which was just one step removed from Ellis Island, and to prestigious, Old Money families, these post–World War II consumers weren't stuck in the social position where they were born. They would achieve a new social status by shopping for it.

Before the sixties, being fashionable was a status a woman was born into. A truly fashionable woman had great beauty, innate elegance, or wealth—and, preferably, all three. But in the sixties, being fashionable was transformed from ascription to achievement. Fashion is "sexy as well as democratic," wrote Marylin Bender, who chronicled the "beautiful people" for the *New York Times*. New fashion icons were imported to the United States from Britain, and came from the working and lower middle class. They included the clothing designer Mary Quant, who popularized the miniskirt, the Beatles, and the young working-class men, known as Mods, who dressed up as latter-day dandies in suits and ties. Although they became famous for looking different, pretty soon all young people wanted to look like them. Refracted through mass production, youthful rebellion was incorporated into fashion.[25]

As fashion changed, so stores changed with it. Some stores led the way, guided by strong women executives like Geraldine Stutz at Henri Bendel and Mildred Custin at Bonwit Teller. Other stores were looking for an "edge" that would set them apart from their rivals. But many stores were not prepared to sell the new fashions; they protested against a trendiness that bordered on "kookiness," which bordered, in turn, on "the weird, the strange, the unexpected, the unusual, the offbeat, the individual," all of which boiled down—in the view of the older generation—to the "unintelligible." Throughout the sixties, retailers and fashion commentators ranted and raged in the trade press, trying to make sense of—and control—a "youthquake" that quickly spread through the ranks of women shoppers. To be left on the other side of the generation gap, as Arthur Miller suggests, was to be completely out of fashion.[26]

"Youth has become a class," the French film director Roger Vadim announces to Marylin Bender in the early sixties. "There used to be the young working class, the young middle class; now those who are young recognize each other. Youth is a rallying sign."[27] If social class as Arthur Miller and other intellectuals understood it was well and truly dead—or if, more likely, "youth" was being recognized as a mass consumer market—these changes were translated into a more aggressive democracy of shopping. Conservative, old-line stores could no longer coast on their reputation; they had to jockey for media attention with upstart boutiques. Rock stars replaced society matrons as fashion icons. While rich consumers who wanted to be "with it" shopped for the latest trends, young people identified downward, with the downtrodden and oppressed—an attitude that would be taken further with hip-hop and rap fashions in the eighties and nineties.[28]

A generation of department store executives, like Bloomingdale's Marvin Traub, made their careers on these sea changes. Bloomingdale's rode the wave of a youth rebellion, a sexual revolution, and a revolution of rising incomes and expectations. By presenting the store as a mirror of the new social aspirations, it displaced its competition. At the same time, the fashion industry, which had long been dominated by the haute couture fashion houses in Paris, was taken over by young designers who presented themselves as the representatives of a rising social class. Not only in Paris, but also in London and New York, new designers aimed for less detail, which represented the arrogance of the past, and more pure sensation, which seemed to represent the self-confidence of the future. This emphasis on a new kind of fashion made fashion into news. Fashion magazines expanded their readership and advertising, and daily newspapers and news magazines published more articles on style. Developments in color photography and printing, and the spread of television into nearly every American home, made fashion images pervasive.[29]

Like urban newspapers in the nineteenth century, and the Internet a hundred years later, magazines, car radios, and television networks shaped "a symbolic language shared by almost all. They were a part of an immediate, widely available, fast-changing culture which was beamed into almost every home and understood by young and old, poor and rich." It wasn't only media images that communicated this new, national culture of consumption. On "interstate highways and jet passenger planes," the historian David Farber writes, "goods, services, and celebrities rocketed around the country."[30]

In this decade, closely observed by the young Andy Warhol, the media manufactured celebrities. Some, like the Beatles, were entertainers; others, like Jean Shrimpton and Twiggy, were fashion models; and one was even a politician—President John F. Kennedy. The whole extended Kennedy family became media icons, as well as influential role models for the new culture of consumption. Everyone knows that JFK was the first political candidate to win a presidential campaign by his appearance on television. His thick hair, healthy complexion, Boston accent, and casual sense of humor created an indelible image of youth, which was so important for selling fashions. And when he went to his nationally televised presidential inauguration without the formal top hat male presidents traditionally wore, he literally destroyed the men's hat industry with his bare head.

Marylin Bender was the first writer to point out that Jacqueline Kennedy had an equally important influence on the culture of consumption. During the sixties, her photograph appeared regularly in every national magazine, and her wardrobe choices—from buying Parisian knock-offs at Ohrbach's,

on Thirty-fourth Street, to ordering gowns designed by Oleg Cassini—
were detailed in newspapers from *Women's Wear Daily* to the *New York
Daily News*. Her children's haircuts made the front page. As Princess Diana
did in the nineties, so Jacqueline Kennedy embodied many women's desires.
In contrast to her near contemporaries among presidents' wives—Eleanor
Roosevelt, Mamie Eisenhower, and Pat Nixon—she clearly liked to shop.
And Jackie, like the other Kennedys, looked terrific. Viewing a documentary film made during the 1960 presidential campaign nearly forty years
later, a *New York Times* critic observes, "At a rally full of men and women
who look as if they have stepped out of a 1950s Sears catalogue, all the
Kennedys seem impossibly glamorous and young." As Marylin Bender
more critically notes, Jacqueline Kennedy was "fashion['s] first supercon-
suming goddess enthroned in the White House."[31]

Jackie Kennedy's "look" was everywhere in the sixties. Her custom-
designed A-line dresses, fur-trimmed wool coats, and pillbox hats were
copied by manufacturers and mass-produced. Her children's velvet-collared
coats, shorts, and knee socks—a look derived from the British upper class—
were copied and sold in all the "better" department stores and children's
clothing shops. Caroline's and John's haircuts were copied by children's
barbers. But the successful merchandising of the Kennedys, through the
mass media, fashion magazines, and women's magazines, shows how quickly
fashion became a double-edged sword. Like the Kennedy "look," the rapid
fashion changes of the sixties were both a means of individualistic expression, especially for women, and a selling tool of mass consumption.

Bender blames the making of "fashion victims" on the lack of sepa-
ration between advertising copy and editorial content in the fashion
magazines. But the sixties were not the first time magazines explicitly
promoted their advertisers' wares. Early twentieth-century magazines like
McClure's promoted products and celebrities in an "informational" style
of journalism. In the thirties, *Good Housekeeping* solicited advertising
from refrigerator manufacturers to complement "educational" articles on
their products. At that time also, Stanley Marcus says, Neiman Marcus
discovered that they could persuade the fashion magazines to mention
the store in the credit line of editorial photographs (as in ". . . This dress
is available at Saks Fifth Avenue and Neiman Marcus.") if they bought
an advertisement.[32]

What was new in the sixties was that "ordinary" women like Jackie
Kennedy became mass icons of fashion. Rich women and, even more so,

newly rich women used fashion publicity to gain social status. And though they often needed their husband's money or connections, they gained status independently of their husbands. Socialites whose names might have been familiar from the discreet "social notes" published in the women's pages of the daily newspapers, and from their charitable activities, now appeared in the gossip columns. According to Marylin Bender, they wanted to get *noticed*. In return for their fifteen minutes of fame, these women, the "willing enhibitionists" of the fashion press, became "the new idols of materialist America." Shopping was their achievement. " 'I was terribly proud of myself,' recalls Nan Kempner, the Park Avenue socialite, who got on the [well-publicized Best-Dressed] List several times in the mid 1960s. . . . In that time, it mattered a great deal. It was a kudos."[33]

While being named to the "Best-Dressed List" required that a woman have a lot of time and money to shop for clothes, the way the list was described in the sixties suggests an ideal of meritocracy to which all women can aspire. "Money helps but is not the last word," *Women's Wear Daily* explains, when Jacqueline Kennedy "topped" the list of the "world's" best-dressed women in 1960. "Beauty helps but is not all, . . . youth is a good ingredient but not everything." Status—in the traditional, sociological sense of the honor accorded by others—now reflects individual achievement rather than birth into an exalted group: "The personal flair that shines through, that *'quelquechose'* with clothes are the qualities that excite international admiration."[34]

Yet, for many years, most of the "best-dressed" women were merely beautiful, expensively dressed, and married to exceedingly rich men. They were, in Marylin Bender's words, "superconsumers of fashion." Their dual achievement consisted mainly of knowing how to spend money and how to wear clothes. And yet, they did have a meritocratic effect on fashion. They encouraged the idea that all women could shop for social status.

The promotion of fashion also promoted the reputations of designers, who now achieved a celebrity status. Until the sixties, the New York fashion industry—the "rag trade," as it was unflatteringly called—was controlled by immigrants and ethnic manufacturers, usually Jews or Italians whose families had come to America in the great wave of immigration from 1880 to 1910. The designers who created the product seldom had their names on clothing labels; instead, manufacturers provided the brand names. For their part, the designers tended to come from the lower middle class; they were often, though not always, gay men. These low-status entrepreneurs and designers, like their counterparts in Hollywood in the thirties and forties, "always yearned for . . . social acceptability." Now, in the sixties, the fashion media's quest for something new to write about made them stars. "Hand in hand," Marylin Bender writes, "the woman who wears the dress and the man who designs it have become fashion celebrities and leaders of the new pop society."[35]

Maybe these were signs of the "democratization" of fashion, as the French sociologist Gilles Lipovetsky says.[36] But the emphasis on fashion innovation gave more power to the media and manufacturers. Ultimately, the quest for self-expression through this "democratic" kind of fashion made shopping for status into a mass obsession.

While shoppers, stores, and the media were changing fashion, the creative center of the industry—the Parisian haute couture—was in total disarray. For at least a hundred years, this handful of designer-led firms had monopolized fashion innovation. Throughout the nineteenth century, transatlantic ships brought display dolls and paper patterns from Paris so Americans could make their own copies of Parisian styles. Beginning in the 1900s, American stores sent delegations of buyers to Paris to view the seasonal collections of the couture houses and to place orders for clothing they could sell back home. When Neiman Marcus opened in Dallas, in 1907, Carrie Marcus Neiman traveled to Paris to choose the best of the latest styles for the store. By the 1930s, Russek's, on Fifth Avenue in Manhattan, sold copies of Paris fashions two weeks after they were shown on the runway, and in the sixties, Ohrbach's, on Thirty-fourth Street, sold these "line for line" copies more cheaply than could be imagined. In this way, an international hierarchy of fashion was established, with Paris at the creative center, stores like Saks Fifth Avenue and Neiman Marcus selling authorized styles to their richest customers, and lower-price stores like Russek's and Ohrbach's selling copies to the lower middle class.[37]

Since the end of World War II, however, the fashion houses in Paris had been limping along on their reputations. Given jolts of revival by Christian Dior's postwar "New Look," in the late forties, and, a decade later, by Yves Saint Laurent's sack dress or chemise, the haute couture was basically producing the same discreet luxury and well-turned seams as in the past. But during the sixties, changes in the fashion world challenged the couture's centralized power.

To ensure their financial survival, couture houses expanded the lucrative licensing arrangements that made it possible for shoppers who weren't rich to buy Dior scarves and Chanel No. 5 perfume. But they also embarked on a new strategy they had previously regarded with disdain: developing their own lines of ready-to-wear. Despite these efforts to revive their business, members of the Parisian haute couture now had to share the high status of fashion authorities with newly influential designers in London and New York (and eventually Milan)—including Mary Quant, Zandra Rhodes, Halston, Calvin Klein, and Ralph Lauren. More ominously, couture houses that had rigidly controlled the sale of high fashion in the most exclusive department stores, as well as in their own salons, had to compete with new channels of fashion in popular boutiques.

The power of the Parisian haute couture has always been based on both a huge concentration of creative energy and the skills to translate this creativity into luxury fabrics, superb tailoring, and unique ornamentation. Unlike the American fashion industry, the Parisian couture was a closed, guild system. Young designers apprenticed at the feet of older masters, whose professional association set strict rules of entry. These rules specified that each couture house must introduce at least a certain minimum number of elaborate new styles each season, thus mandating a high level of aesthetic performance as well as financial investment by every member. In return for its exclusivity, the association guaranteed an aura of authority around all couture designers. The combination of absolute creative freedom and exclusive cultural authority attracted talented young designers, from Charles Frederick Worth and Mainbocher to Yves Saint Laurent, who flocked to Paris from foreign countries, French colonies, and the provinces. The lure of Paris fashion was absolute.

Styles created in Paris were spread around the world in monthly magazines like *Vogue*, *Cosmopolitan*, and *Harper's Bazaar*. Like department store buyers, the staffs of these magazines—including editors, illustrators, and, eventually, photographers—enjoyed traveling to Paris to report on the seasonal showings of the fashion houses. Magazines competed to select the most remarkable styles and describe them in luscious detail for their readers. Perhaps the most authoritative reporting was in *Women's Wear Daily*, which was anxiously read by American store owners and garment manufacturers who wanted to attract shoppers with the latest styles.

By the early sixties, however, *Women's Wear Daily* began to criticize, rather than just report on, the couture collections. In 1961, *WWD* panned Dior's collection, which was designed by Yves Saint Laurent, while applauding the designer André Courreges as "a comer" because he presented styles that looked different from everyone else's. The mainstream fashion industry was slow to adopt these styles. During the first half of the sixties, the traditional designer Balenciaga was the most copied by American manufacturers. Yet the newcomers—especially André Courreges and Pierre Cardin, who presented radically different looks—gained more media attention. So did new designers in London and New York—as well as young people trying out new styles on the streets. The haute couture was no longer the center of fashion innovation. Even European designers came to New York—and returned to the Old World "bearing blue jeans, button-down shirts, flowered sheets and barbecue equipment."[38]

The fashion press claimed that clothes made by traditional couture designers—by Dior, Balenciaga, and Givenchy—looked old and dowdy, compared to the expressive, unstructured new styles created in places where young people gathered: Carnaby Street in London, the Left Bank in Paris, and New York's Greenwich Village. The old way of shopping—going to dressmakers' fittings at the couture salons—was a bore. Under these new cultural pressures, even the rich older women on the "Best-Dressed List" began to dissociate themselves from the image of the haute couture. "Those stiff, cutout little Givenchy coats didn't give a damn," said William J. Cunningham, who wrote a fashion column for *Women's Wear Daily*. "People thought the [women wearing them] were arrogant."[39] In this time of rapid social changes, the Kennedys, and seemingly democratic consumption, being "arrogant" was out of fashion.

Like the haute couture, department stores also seemed dated. Shoppers learned about new styles by shopping in inexpensive boutiques that catered to young people. When Yves Saint Laurent opened his first boutique of women's ready-to-wear in 1966 in Paris, his chief financial backer advised him to place the boutique on the *rive gauche*, or Left Bank, near the student quarter of colleges and cafés, surrounded by bookstores and art galleries. Both the store's name—Rive Gauche—and location crystallized a new alignment of art, youth, and fashion. "Yves had created a whole new market, a veritable revolution in fashion merchandising," says Marvin Traub, who was then in charge of merchandising at Bloomingdale's. Saint Laurent's Rive Gauche boutique showed that the dominance of the old stores, and of the old couture, was dead.[40]

During the sixties, boutiques supplanted department stores as significant places of consumption. The great department stores of the past had offered women shoppers an opportunity to move about freely in public space. Boutiques now offered public spaces in which women could construct—could *shop* for—their individual identity. Yet they were, after all, just stores.

The first generally recognized fashion boutique was opened by the innovative Parisian designer Elsa Schiaparelli in 1935, as an annex to her haute couture salon. During the first half of the sixties, however, boutiques—or small shops showing highly "edited" selections of clothing—became tremendously popular not only in Paris but also in London and New York. They quickly spread to many other cities, where shoppers had neither the money nor the cultural capital—the necessary "arrogance"—for haute couture. In some boutiques, you could find "outrageous" new styles; in others, you could buy lower-priced—but hardly cheap—ready-to-wear by couture designers. Regardless of the styles, the social space of the boutique fed a desire to express individuality without necessarily being a radical feminist. Boutiques in the sixties created a new experience of shopping as a *personal* expression.

As the place where consumers found a cultural rapprochement between "high" and "low" fashion, boutiques moved the dialectic of mass production and identity shopping to a new synthesis. On the one hand, as Marylin Bender says, "the essential meaning of boutique . . . is a place where a woman can find self-expression in wearing apparel. In the inexorable, world-wide drive toward mass anonymity, the boutique is an oasis of identity."[41] On the other hand, boutiques democratized and popularized the mass consumption of designer labels. Boutiques inherited the charisma department stores had lost—and yet they eventually strengthened the standardized formulas of mass production.

The first retail merchant to install boutiques in a large specialty store was Geraldine Stutz, who was named the president of Henri Bendel, in New York City, in 1958.[42] She divided each floor of the store into tiny shops, and gave each one a special name: The Bottier for shoes, The Gilded Cage for cosmetics, and The Jean Muir Shop for clothes by the young British designer. She bought items from young European and American designers, and encouraged publicity both by and about Bendel's customers, who included the major fashionistas of the day. Anyone who read *Vogue*, *Harper's Bazaar*, or *Women's Wear Daily* during the sixties knew which actresses, entertainers, and other glamorous women shopped at Bendel. Stutz "created a superboutique," Marylin Bender says, "for the woman who uses fashion to proclaim her definite, contemporary style."[43]

By 1965, rising stars like Bloomingdale's, and even low-status stores like Alexander's, were creating in-store boutiques to sell the merchandise of well-known designers. According to Marvin Traub, the major reason was financial. The small size of boutique departments limits the store's financial risk on any single designer, product, or style. Especially in the sixties, when styles began to change rapidly, "boutiques made good business sense.

Boutiques make news: crowd staring at Twiggy, the British model, in the window of Paraphernalia boutique, 67th Street and Madison Avenue, 1967. Photo by Bernard Gotfryd.

You could experiment with new fashions, but in small amounts. You could display the most fashion-forward designs that would give you the image, while still selling more mainstream items. This was the same strategy that worked so well in home furnishings."[44]

But department store boutiques really reflect the competitive dynamics of selling fashion. Competing with Bendel and Bonwit Teller, Saks Fifth Avenue claimed to be the first store to adopt the "total design boutique concept," when they opened a special department for the sportswear designer Anne Klein, in 1965. According to *Women's Wear Daily*, the Saks shopper "leaves [the boutique] with a complete wardrobe and a complete look. . . . [W]hat they really get is the security that they look their best." In other words, Saks presented their boutiques as a comprehensive, anxiety-free way to shop.

Over the next few years, in-store designer boutiques multiplied. Saks opened a boutique to highlight clothing by the American sportswear designer Stan Herman, while Bonwit Teller opened separate boutiques for André Courreges, Pierre Cardin, and the American designers B. H. Wragge and Luba. Bonwit's S'fari Room featured a smaller, changing assortment of edgier designers, where women could hunt for the "big game" of new fashion. Despite the focus on specific designers, the underlying marketing strategy was, according to *Women's Wear Daily*, "the total sell." Moreover, as Helen Galland, the merchandise manager for accessories at Bonwit's, explained, the visual and conceptual coherence provided by a single designer encourages shoppers to buy. "Showing people a look is more important than showing them [individual items of] merchandise," she said. "We try to do within a department what other people are doing with boutiques."[45]

Boutiques attracted new shoppers, and more shoppers, into the stores. In 1968, when Yves Saint Laurent opened his first U.S. boutique for ready-to-wear, on Madison Avenue, police barricades were set up for ten days to keep the crowds under control. The shop quickly sold out its supply of Saint Laurent's "city pants," and couldn't get enough new stock to satisfy demand.[46]

The men's clothing industry soon followed the boutique mystique. Men's departments and specialty shops began to be reorganized by designer in 1967 or 1968, with special displays for Oleg Cassini's shirts and Pierre Cardin's "Euro-cut" suits. When Ralph Lauren designed his first items—men's neckties—in 1969, he negotiated with Bloomingdale's for his own, in-store boutique. But despite stores' efforts, throughout the sixties, to persuade men to buy newly changing styles, reorganizing the social space of the men's department into designer boutiques "was like a culture shock to customers," recalls John Fresco, who was an executive at Saks Fifth Avenue when Saks introduced an Emilio Pucci boutique for men. In Philadelphia, an owner of a large, center-city men's shop remembers this period, when the store began to sell Pierre Cardin's new, "youthful," close-cut silhouette, as introducing a momentous change in both merchandising and conspicuous consumption: "It was like you were wearing the label *on the outside.*"[47]

Imported from Europe after World War II, the social space of the boutique overtook larger, more experienced, infinitely better financed department stores. During the next twenty years, it evolved from a small, independently owned shop with a heavily "edited" point of view that recalled the charming little streets and cafés of Paris, Florence, or Greenwich Village, to a generic store of any size, or even a part of a department store, selling items "that have a natural affinity for each other." By this point, you could find almost any kind of merchandise in a boutique—from women's clothing and jewelry to men's neckties and pet supplies. Yet the social space of boutiques still suggested the core elements that made shopping more popular than ever in the sixties: intimacy, selectivity, and individuality.[48]

In a thoughtful article published in 1967 in *Stores*, a magazine for the retail trade, an architect named Peter Copeland traces the adoption of the boutique in America to both a crisis of competition among stores and shoppers' changing social tastes. Customers were tired of "the bustle and confusion of the large department store," Copeland says, "and longed for the intimacy and greater selectivity of the small shop."[49] Faced with the continuing loss of customers to both small stores and discount chains, department stores created ever more specialized departments. Boutiques had demonstrated that they could draw shoppers, especially young shoppers, into stores.

A large part of the excitement surrounding clothes shopping in the sixties came from the perception that clothing boutiques were a new, separate, public space for the young—a foreshadowing of fashions "for us, by us." In the United States, this perception was based on new stores like Paraphernalia on Madison Avenue and Patricia Field's eccentric clothing boutique in Greenwich Village, the used-clothes, book, and music shops in hippie neighborhoods like the East Village and Haight-Ashbury, and, on a somewhat larger scale, The Gap—whose name initially referred to the "Generation Gap"—and Tower Records, which were both established in the sixties in the Bay Area around San Francisco.

Surrounded by this competition, department stores were desperate to find "the next new thing." They needed more than a new store design; they needed distinctive product—designers—to bring shoppers into the store. Under these conditions, in 1968, Mildred Custin, the chairman of the board of Bonwit Teller, discovered Calvin Klein. A recent graduate of the Fashion Institute of Technology, Klein had borrowed $10,000 from a high school friend to manufacture a few "samples" of women's coats for his first collection. When Mildred Custin gave him his first order—$50,000 for fall coats and dresses—he rushed through production in the Garment Center of midtown Manhattan and delivered the goods himself, pushing a coat rack up Fifth Avenue to the store on a Saturday morning.[50]

Meanwhile, over at Bloomingdale's, Marvin Traub was also trolling for new designers. Now in the position of general merchandise manager, Traub wanted to upgrade the store's fashion image the way he and his buyers had done with rugs and lamps. For more than a year, Traub negotiated with Yves Saint Laurent to open his first U.S. ready-to-wear boutique in Bloomingdale's. But at the last minute, Saint Laurent refused, and chose, instead, to open a freestanding shop on Madison Avenue. A year later, Traub was promoted to president of Bloomingdale's—and discovered Ralph Lauren, who was designing interesting new ties for men. Just as Mildred Custin offered a contract to Calvin Klein, so Traub offered Ralph Lauren a strategic relationship with Bloomingdale's.[51]

Almost immediately, Traub's judgment was shown to be correct, when Lauren won two of the annual Coty Awards, given by an association of American fashion designers, for his menswear designs. For Bloomingdale's, this was a coup. "In Ralph," Traub writes, "we had our first exclusive, our first home-grown designer."[52]

Ralph Lauren and Calvin Klein went on to design distinctive lines of clothing for men, women, and children, as well as to license shoes, socks, eyeglass frames, perfumes, dishes, and bed linens. But their crucial contribution to the culture of consumption in the sixties is that, with the department stores' strategic support and media coverage, they placed their names, rather than the names of manufacturers, on their labels: "Polo"—a brand name bought from Brooks Brothers—"by Ralph Lauren" and "Calvin Klein."

By striking out on their own, these designers took the first step toward creating the mass culture of designer labels. But they also separated the concept of design from the physical process of production. This in turn contributed to a dramatic split in the fashion industry, and in all industries, between image creation and manufacturing. Image became the most important product a designer could create. Freed, moreover, from financial responsibility for manufacturing, designers could expand their licensing arrangements across a broad array of product lines. Like the Parisian couture houses, American ready-to-wear designers discovered that their licensed products—perfumes, scarves, sunglasses, and, eventually, jeans— were infinitely more profitable than their most expensive fashion lines. By the eighties, when Ralph Lauren opened his own, freestanding boutique in the old Rhinelander mansion on Madison Avenue, he placed all the products he designed—for body and home—in a thematically unified shopping environment. "Ralph was not interested in being just one line of a company," Marvin Traub reminisces, not unkindly. "He wanted to be a whole brand unto himself."[53]

When Stanley Marcus, of Neiman Marcus, wrote his memoirs in 1974, he dismissed Ralph Lauren as a mere necktie designer, and he didn't even mention Calvin Klein.[54] But, by then, the stunning changes of the sixties had utterly transformed shopping. The "youthquake" was in full force, all women wanted to look different, the department store was changed into— or returned to its origins as—a bazaar of separate shops . . . and the designer stood alone, as a dazzling commodity.

Despite the example set by New York specialty shops, department stores throughout the country were not so quick to jump on the bandwagon. They had a lot of fixed capital in large, functional departments, like "Evening Dresses," "Blouses," and the "Men's Shop." Older managers were often not attuned to new marketing strategies, and most young M.B.A.'s did not want to pursue a career as retail merchants. Most shoppers, moreover, wanted both the stimulation of new products and styles and reasonable prices. So department stores remained squeezed between the "rock" of boutiques and the "hard place" of discount stores.

But fashion writers and marketing consultants continually nudged stores to change so they could attract young shoppers. "Stores must be contemporary," a 1967 issue of *Women's Wear Daily* warns. "They must be hangouts on Saturdays and after school for young junior customers using juke boxes that play all day, pop artists, and beatnik guitar players." Market researchers pointed to the positive example of Sanger Harris, a dignified store in Dallas, that shed its old dowager image—similar to B. Altman's!—and "keyed [all its marketing] in a deliberate and sometimes overstated way to woo the emerging, young, affluent and adventurous customer with fashion interest and an upscale taste level." In order to "reinforce the new image of a young, fun-loving and swinging store," Sanger Harris stopped selling work clothes, paints, hardware, pet supplies, and drugs, and concentrated on fashion.[55]

Over the next twenty years, most stores moved in the same direction. They eliminated "hard" goods, from televisions to trash cans, and bargain basements, and stopped competing with discount stores on appliances and the emerging category of electronics. Focusing on "soft goods," especially highly changeable fashions, and the youth market, they subdivided their large selling floors into designer boutiques. By the late nineties, the entire bottom half of Macy's flagship store, on Thirty-fourth Street, was turned over to displays of men's and women's fashions, with variously priced lines of the most popular designer labels—Tommy Hilfiger, Ralph Lauren, and Calvin Klein—on every one of the first five floors. Macy's famous food department, similar to the food halls of Harrod's, in London, was moved to the cellar, folded into a cookware and cuisine department, and eventually replaced by brand-name men's athletic wear. Both Macy's and Bloomingdale's also reorganized their children's departments so that most of the clothing was displayed in small designer boutiques, miniature versions of mom's and dad's floors. In the children's department at Saks Fifth Avenue, representatives from DKNY and other companies worked several days a week in their own, in-store boutiques—giving the companies, as they say, direct contact with shoppers' needs. By contrast with Macy's, Saks, and Bloomingdale's, according to retail sales analysts, a fine old store like Sears suffered from a fatal problem. Sears continued to focus on men's hard goods—automotive products and hardware—without paying enough attention to women's fashions.

But the rise of designer labels brought about the decline, and eventual demise, of most of the department stores that had nurtured them. Shoppers so wanted these designer labels that they followed them out of the department store, to designer boutiques. When the labels remained in department stores, they negotiated to be displayed in prime locations, and pressed store owners to accept more than one of their lines. They spread their "look" around different stores, making it hard for the stores to differentiate themselves. Moreover, long-term economic and demographic changes hurt department stores' business. During the sixties, all retail stores experienced a wave of mergers and acquisitions, and, during the eighties, they became targets for takeover by ambitious investors. Many department stores had atrophied during their customers' decades-long exodus to suburbia, which intensified after the urban riots of the sixties. Department stores like Macy's and Bloomingdale's, whose names and flagship downtown stores were local landmarks, appeared ripe for a corporate takeover.

The main reason department stores attracted investors' attention had nothing to do with fashion; it was that their stocks were undervalued. Stock prices were cheap compared with the potential earnings analysts foresaw if management could be changed or converted to more aggressive marketing. These stores also controlled large plots of valuable land, both in the suburbs and downtown. The stores' names were well known and trusted; they represented an irresistible asset at a time when Wall Street investors were willing to risk their shirts and suspenders to buy high-risk, high-yield junk bonds.

Some investors—like the Canadian real estate developer Robert Campeau and the Australian speculator George Herscu—took flying leaps into the retail sector. They were aided and abetted by investment bankers and attorneys who earned gigantic consulting fees. While Campeau, through a series of mind-boggling deals, was able to buy both Macy's and Bloomingdale's—and to buy and sell the distinguished men's clothing firm Brooks Brothers—Herscu bought Altman's, Sakowitz, and Bonwit Teller. Neither new owner could manage retail stores, however, or install a competent management team. By the end of the eighties, Macy's was in receivership, Marvin Traub was out of the top job at Bloomingdale's, and B. Altman had closed its doors.[56]

These changes ignited a spark of nostalgia for the old-style department store that had been both the dowager of downtown and an oasis of civility. While *Fortune* magazine, in 1986, restated the familiar argument that stores, like other businesses, must respond to shoppers' boredom, *The American Scholar* complained of "A Sad Heart at the Department Store." What had been lost, according to Marjorie Rosenberg, who wrote this article, was the amenities that gave an air of civility and graciousness to the grand department stores of the past. In Rosenberg's view, the old department stores had been benevolent and worthy of shoppers' trust. Now, benevolence was replaced by financial wheeling and dealing; the goal of increasing sales volume overshadowed the ideal of service.[57]

Shortly afterward, however, *American Heritage* magazine published a reply by the business writer Peter Baida. Titled, in contrast to Rosenberg's lament, "A Happy Heart at Bloomingdale's," Baida's piece points out that, by the eighties, all the amenities department stores had offered to attract women shoppers in the past simply cost too much. If shoppers had to pay for these amenities by paying higher prices, they would walk away. He answers Rosenberg's complaint about the disappearance of trust by showing that some stores, like Neiman Marcus, were still locally rooted and supported local charities. Finally, Baita argues, if shoppers don't like these changes, they can choose not to shop. "Choice shapes the economy," Baita says. "People who find department stores intolerable will cease to tolerate them."[58]

Most shoppers had already made their choice, and they chose shopping for status instead of "civility." Women were more explicit about wanting to express themselves both publicly and privately, and they identified this expressiveness—aided by fashion designers and magazines—with youth and style. More women had careers outside the home. For the first time in history, young, unmarried women and men had the time, the money, and the autonomy from their parents to be frequent shoppers. During the sixties, moreover, new celebrities, including designers themselves, emerged as icons of style, and emphasis was placed—beginning with the face but gradually encompassing the whole body—on image and appearance.[59]

These changes subjected shoppers, especially women shoppers, to enormous pressures. While cultural values and social status became more fluid, women's traditional role in shopping for status grew more intense. More choices among products and styles brought more anxiety; more rapid fashion changes meant more chances to be wrong. In the chaotic world of new products and lifestyles, designers' names were elevated to landmarks, replacing those of the old department stores.

The culture of shopping no longer depended on a leisure class of women shoppers who had the time and energy to spend in "civilized" department stores. Thorstein Veblen's leisure class was now divided into wealthy "ladies who lunch," as well as shop, and working women, rich and poor, who have to schedule grocery shopping, clothes shopping, and gift shopping, often with kids, into an already overscheduled day.

In the fifties and sixties, when my friend Harvey was growing up in suburban Baltimore, his mother spent much of her time shopping. She would return home at the end of the day, exhausted, collapse into an armchair, and moan, "I've spent the entire day at Hutzler's." By the end of the sixties, however, this kind of shopper was beginning to disappear. Not only were more suburban housewives working in jobs outside the home, they were also more involved in organizing their time and their children's time, planning for career advancement, and scheduling leisure activities. They couldn't spend their weekdays cruising the aisles at Altman's or Hutzler's, and making demands on patient sales clerks. They could no longer eat leisurely lunches in the stores' tearooms and restaurants. Women "used to sit on the beach at the end of the summer and . . . flip through the September [fashion] magazines and do their fall clothes shopping," the editor in chief of *Elle*, the women's fashion magazine, recalls. "Now what woman has time to do that?"[60]

Women shoppers in the sixties were newly anxious about status, about "looking right," and about no longer being young. But the old department stores did not provide the assurance of status they wanted. Paradoxically, the revolt of the masses against the fashion industry led to their being enthralled by new, more aggressive, and more pervasive forms of status consumption.

In the 1960s, Fashion sounded the death knell for classic department stores like Altman's. But this was a new public sphere of Fashion that shaped— and was shaped by—new stores, new intermediaries, and new "personalities." Fashion was no longer the privileged sphere of well-born, elegant women and the custom fitters of the haute couture. Fashion was a status you could achieve—if you shopped hard enough. Tragically for department stores, however, we learned to shop for status by designer labels rather than by stores.

B. Altman had its own problems. While their management rejected, or was slow to adapt to, the new culture of shopping, the flagship store at Thirty-fourth Street and Fifth Avenue was not in the best location. Almost from its opening, this stretch of Fifth Avenue was filled with immigrant workers from the lofts of nearby garment manufacturers, and these workers, according to the merchants of the Fifth Avenue Association, scared women shoppers away.[61] The construction of the Empire State Building diagonally across the street from Altman's, during the Great Depression, did not improve on this situation. Affluent tourists followed the more expensive stores, like Tiffany and Bonwit Teller, that moved farther north, to Fifty-seventh Street. Other shoppers looked for bargains farther west on Thirty-fourth Street, where low-price clothing and shoe stores filled the long block between Ohrbach's and Macy's.

Civility exacts a price, after all. Since our expectations of shopping have changed, we want stores to offer us status, variety, and excitement. When I ask my friend Rachel, a literature professor, whether she ever shopped at B. Altman, she says, "Not really. Altman's was a dull store, you know."

Believe me, I know exactly what she means.

6

artemio goes
to tiffany's

The crew here is working hard to please you. We're
constantly scoutin' for the best new fashion on the
streets of New York City! Check back often!
———www.urbanwhere.com, 2000

My student J, who will graduate from Brooklyn College next June, is
chatting with me in my office. He is an intelligent young man, articulate in class discussions, though often silent. So I am surprised when he
tells me he is an aspiring rap performer.

I think he can help, however, with a question that has bothered me since
I began to write about shopping.

"Why do so many rap musicians, and the kids who follow them, wear
clothes with a brand-name label?" I ask him. "Tommy Hilfiger, Nike, Polo,
Nautica," I tick off some of the brand names associated with rap
performers and, through them, with the many dark-skinned teens I see on
the street, in the subway, and, often enough, in the classroom. "How did
it begin?"

J looks serious, and I notice that none of the rather quiet clothes he's
wearing today—a dark blue turtleneck, blue jeans, and boots—is sporting
a logo.

He points to the turtleneck. "Armani," he says. He points to the jeans.
"Guess." Finally, he nods toward his feet. "Timberland."

Not a logo in sight. J settles back in his chair and gives me an appraising
glance to see whether I appreciate his taste, now that he has pointed it out
to me.

"We rebel," he says, in answer to my question. "But we're socialized."

J's clothes, and the finely honed consciousness of status distinctions that he shows, point to a remarkable merger of popular culture, mass fashion, and racial identity in the early 2000s. During the last few decades, expensive brand-name clothes identified with designer labels have gone through a curious double migration. They have moved from the privileged terrain of country clubs, ski resorts, and designer boutiques to "the streets," and from the bodies of dark-skinned "urban" youth to those of suburban white teenagers whose familiarity with city streets comes from watching music videos.

Like rap music and professional basketball, certain designer labels have made a racial crossover. Identified as "black," they enjoy enormous commercial success among all shoppers, but especially among teenage males; their advertisements in fashion magazines play on the dubious dangers of the streets and the outward signs of criminal cultures; and, as their sales in department stores and specialty shops increase around the world, they attract the interest of Wall Street analysts and investors. No doubt about it, black is hot these days, but only if it sells.[1]

The financial value of these fashions rests on the curious ability of mass-manufactured clothing to represent the cultural value of cool. Jeans and logoed sweats, baseball caps worn backwards, gold chains perhaps, and definitely athletic shoes: these have long since been elevated to their own fashion category of "urban wear," a business that is worth several billion dollars a year. That so much money is at stake signals a paradoxical triumph of both countercultural symbolic coding and corporate decision making, which hangs, in turn, on creating a fragile balance between the changing body images of two volatile groups—teenagers and blacks.[2]

It used to be that being cool was *outside* fashion. And if you think about the various body images of male coolness that have dominated popular culture since the fifties, you can visualize them separately in black and white. A capsule history of rebel chic would have to include flashbacks to the dark glasses of jazz hipsters (think Miles Davis), the black leather jackets of motorcycle gangs and greasers (think Marlon Brando in *The Wild One* or James Dean in *Rebel Without a Cause*), and the longer, more tailored leather coats and berets of Black Power militants and rude boys (no matter how young you are, you've probably seen posters of Che Guevara, Eldridge Cleaver, and Richard Roundtree as the original Shaft). More recently, we've had the torn, mismatched outfits of rockers, punks, and grunge musicians (look at album covers for the Ramones, Sid Vicious, Kurt Cobain) as well as the occasional dashiki and dreads (Bob Marley). Although teenagers copied these looks, they weren't mass-manufactured in advance by clothing companies. Prior to the eighties, the styles were never "in fashion." And the sources of mainstream fashion weren't black.

Yet there were conflicting signs even in the early years. The writer Norman Mailer confessed, in the fifties, that he wanted to be a "white Negro" like cool jazz artists. In the sixties, an astute market researcher named William Capitman warned the fashion industry that young people—the emerging mass-consumer market—identified themselves with the "disenfranchised," especially with "Negroes." For the most part, however, in those years, black kids and white kids still had separate styles.[3]

In the urban North, some white kids wanted to be black, or wanted what blackness represented to them—a body language that was both understated and physically graceful, a verbal language cut loose from formal rules, and a manner of presenting oneself that seemed free of artificial social restraints. At least as far back as the middle of the nineteenth century, these were the cultural qualities that "whiteness" lacked, and that persuaded white audiences and performers to patronize, and often copy, black entertainers.[4]

It wasn't until the 1980s, however, when black performers and athletes won lucrative contracts with major professional sports teams and recording companies, when they were routinely well paid for celebrity endorsements, and when—most important—they regularly performed in National Basketball Association games on network television and in music videos on MTV, that blackness became a mass-market phenomenon. But no one knows whether it was the black celebrities' commercial success that white teens wanted to copy—or their cultural estrangement from the homogeneity of a suburban mall. Certainly the marketing of both the NBA and MTV during the eighties brought vivid images of leaping, rapping, and break-dancing black performers into millions of black and white homes. If white kids mimicked darker-skinned teens, they were acting out the marketing strategies of ambitious clothing manufacturers and even more aggressive media, sports, and entertainment corporations.[5]

Yet this fashionable blackness mocks the historical disenfranchisement of black consumers. And getting black players into the NBA, and black rap videos on MTV, was only achieved by challenging the initial resistance of their corporate owners. Like many white-owned businesses, professional sports teams and entertainment companies were reluctant to alienate white consumers by seeming to cater to blacks. African American entertainers were supposed to serve their white audience rather than join them in box seats—or in the dressing room. For this reason, athletes like Jackie Robinson and entertainers like Sammy Davis Jr. were ambiguous figures in the black community, where they were seen as both symbols of universal achievement and tokens of racial integration—especially since stars like Davis were barred from swimming in the hotel pool when they played nightclubs in Las Vegas in the fifties and sixties. Mohammad Ali spoke out prominently against white control over black athletes' careers, but he was criticized by many whites for his conversion to Islam and his political views, and deprived of his world boxing championship for refusing to serve in the military during the Vietnam War. By the early eighties, when black athletes formed a significant presence on professional basketball teams, both black and white artists began to question not only the value of individual players but the value of black men, in general, to corporate marketing. Jean-Michel Basquiat painted a picture of a large ball under the ironic caption "Famous Negro Athletes," and Jeff Koons created a parody of a poster advertising Nike athletic gear that showed the basketball player Moses Malone standing alone in a desert, holding a basketball in one hand and a staff in the other. It was obvious that the success of a few superstars did not pull African Americans as a whole out of the ghetto.[6]

The contradiction between using dark-skinned people as marketing icons and failing to welcome them in the store recalls the whole troubled history of race in America. If African Americans, as the writer Toni Morrison argues, have been the ever-present figure against whom the major white characters of American literature are formed, they have rarely received recognition for it. And if, as rumors claim, African Americans are responsible for the success of brand-name labels like Tommy Hilfiger and Timberland, other rumors say that the heads of those companies deny it. Faced with these contradictions, dark-skinned shoppers develop the dual consciousness that W. E. B. Du Bois famously described in *The Souls of Black Folk*: "One ever feels his two-ness," he wrote in 1903, "an American, a Negro; two souls, two thoughts, two unreconciled strivings." Though this dual consciousness speaks to the experience of ethnicity in American society, it also exposes an illusion about the experience of consumption: that shopping makes possible *anyone's* upward social mobility.[7]

Artemio, a brown-skinned Latino in his early thirties, tells me a story that is every shopper's nightmare. A few years ago, he went to Tiffany's flagship store, at Fifty-seventh Street and Fifth Avenue, to buy his girlfriend a meaningful present. He had never been to a store with such a pricey reputation, and he was looking forward to every delicious moment of shopping there.

"I had on black jeans, sneakers, and a black sweatshirt," he begins with a smile, "and a pocketful of money."

Now, Artemio is sharp, a native New Yorker, and he is obviously aware that he is breaking one of the most important rules of shopping in an exclusive store: you've got to dress for it. He didn't think about the problems his outfit would pose before he set out. He is wearing urban wear, the kind of outfit that brings big bucks to the manufacturers of "urban" labels, but that also brings some extra social baggage. If most people—black or white—see a young man wearing this kind of outfit on the subway, hunkered down inside his hoodie, they go out of their way to avoid him; he looks like—so he is—an outlaw. Even if the cool authenticity of "the streets" influences this year's couture collections, a young black man can't go into an expensive store wearing a sweatshirt and sneakers . . . unless maybe they're Prada. And I think Artemio knows this.

"So I'm not dressed that nice," Artemio repeats, making it clear he does know the rules. "But," he says, with a pause for emphasis, referring to the democratic illusion that drives shoppers on, "I've got a pocketful of money."

He sets the scene, pointing to something I wouldn't notice at first, or at least I wouldn't notice it with the same sharpness he does. "There's guards by the door inside," Artemio says. "Black guards. Colored people. I told them at the end of it"—shaking his index finger—"that you shouldn't treat people like this.

"So I go in, and I don't try to avoid the guard"—a touch of honesty I find appealing but strange, since the security guard, a small, silent presence at the door for me, looms so large to him—"and I asked him where I would find the silver section."

Tiffany has several floors, and though they're fairly small, if you haven't been there before, you wouldn't know where to find what you want without asking. But who would ask a security guard? Surely Artemio should know enough about stores to look for a directory near the entrance or the elevator, or even approach a sales clerk. But he doesn't do either of these things because he is a brown-skinned Latino from Brooklyn who has never been

Tiffany & Co., Fifth Avenue: main entrance with security guard. Photo by author.

to Tiffany before. He approaches one of the security guards—who are "black," or, at least, "people of color"—because he feels more comfortable speaking to him than approaching a sales clerk.

Besides, the sales clerks are busy. And, while most security guards in New York City are dark-skinned, most sales clerks at Tiffany are not.

"So he tells me I need to go up the escalator or the elevator, and he escorts me to the elevator. At this time, I figure he's just being nice."

Artemio grimaces and shakes his head. Poor Artemio, I think. He is unsuspecting, but not above suspicion. And he doesn't know it.

When they arrive at the proper floor, "it's huge," Artemio says, spreading his arms. "It's crowded. And everyone's all dressed up, in suits. And everyone's white."

Now Artemio's anxiety starts to kick in. Is it a racial issue? Is it a matter of his social class? Or is it that he lacks the necessary camouflage of a suit? Although Artemio has "a pocketful of money," he isn't *known* at this store; or rather, he is known by the brown face and "urban" clothing people see. And he looks like a working-class Latino guy who doesn't belong at Tiffany.

He doesn't immediately find the silver items, and, unsure of himself, he approaches a sales clerk. "I ask her, 'Can you help me?' She gives me this dirty look, and looks me up and down, and says no, and walks away."

He makes a pushing motion with his hand, to show me how strongly he felt the sales clerk's rejection. She didn't just dismiss him with a polite smile of regret; she gave him a real refusal, bordering on insolence. I know you can get the same treatment from the clerks at Macy's, or at the post office, but what does it mean at a store like Tiffany, especially if you're not dressed right, and your face is brown?

Artemio keeps walking around the counters, and eventually finds his way to the silver. But he has a peculiarly heightened sense of being *seen*. "I felt like a cameraman was right on top of me all the time," he says.

This isn't strange, considering the high-tech surveillance system they must have in a famous jewelry store like Tiffany. Neither is it strange, considering the cinematic view of life we all have in this age of movies and video. In *The Ville*, a nonfiction book about an African American teenage boy in Brooklyn, the boy obsesses about Polo brand clothes and dreams of a career in the movies. He and his friends call themselves the Lo-Lifes, in a homage to Polo, and go out of their way to shoplift only this label on their expeditions to Bloomingdale's. At a party, the group preen, and pretend they're modeling clothes on a runway or in a music video.[8]

But Artemio is not in a video; he is under the immediate gaze of Tiffany's security guards. Artemio is aware of both their looks and their bodies as they press in on him.

"There were two guards at the elevator," he recalls, "and I looked around for the other guard, and he's right beside me. Three people are supervising me, and I can't find anyone to help me!"

The classic shoppers' lament—"I can't find anyone to help me!"—gets a deeper, sadder refrain in the racial profiling experienced by dark-skinned shoppers: there are too few salespeople, and too many security guards. At some small stores, the salespeople double as guards, working both the sales floor and the buzzer at the door. They decide which shoppers should be admitted. If they see a "round brown face" peering in the plate-glass door, they just refuse to press the buzzer, miming from inside the window: We're closed.[9]

If there is no door buzzer, and people can enter freely, salespeople are covertly instructed by management to follow dark-skinned shoppers around the store. Certainly this violates the shoppers' civil rights. But don't merchants assume, law professor Regina Austin says, that all dark-skinned people belong to "a nation of thieves"?[10]

"So at the silver counter," Artemio goes on, "I ask this saleswoman if she can help me, because there's something I want to buy. And she says, 'Are you sure you want to buy it here?'"

Artemio raises his eyebrows. Forget the suspicion, this is a total blowout! What good is his pocketful of money and his dream of leaving the shop with one of those cute little robin's-egg-blue Tiffany bags if the saleswoman questions his right to buy something—to buy anything—in the store? Doesn't he have a right to be there? Doesn't he have "a pocketful of money"? Anyway, isn't the customer always right?

"'Yes,'" Artemio answers, with the proud persistence we muster in the face of a sales clerk's unbridled snobbery. "'I want the whistle, and the pen, and I want them now.'"

Check it out: he doesn't even ask about the price.

On a normal shopping expedition, you would ask the price of a potential purchase. You would pause to think about it, you would show the sales clerk you were making up your mind. In some fly-by-night discount store, or with a street vendor, you might hesitate a minute or two, and try to bargain, in order to drive down the price. But at Tiffany, challenged by the sales clerk, you want—you need—to assert your right to be in the store. You need to show you can buy anything you please, even if it drives you to the poorhouse.

"'And how will you be paying?'" Artemio mimics the saleswoman's fastidiously polite voice.

The question is always asked at this point in a sale, so the salesperson knows whether she should prepare a credit card form and ask for a customer's identification, or tap a mysterious code of letters and numbers into the computer. I imagine I'm shopping in Artemio's body, however, and as Artemio, I find the question more insinuating, more personal, and even sinister.

"'Cash,'" Artemio answers. "The only reason she didn't say anything else was because there were clients all around." He frowns. "She was so rude."

It's interesting how we expect to be treated as the equal of any other shopper in a store. We don't even pause to question it. Sociologists call this a "universalistic" norm: we believe that if we have money, we can go into any store, no matter who we are. We usually say money has no color. Everyone wants to make money, and everyone wants to spend it. Merchants will sell to anyone. Sales clerks must be polite. But are they really polite to everyone?

"So I reach into my pocket to get my money," Artemio says, "and I feel two guys right behind me. One by my left shoulder and one by my right shoulder. Two guards."

He spreads his arms out to either side, as if trying to make room. I'm conscious, again, of being in Artemio's body—and of the guards' bodies literally intervening, coming between me and the other shoppers, between me and the sales clerk, between me and the items I want to buy. I'm feeling that my freedom is being chipped away, my pleasure at finally being able to enter Tiffany is drying up, and I'm beginning to get angry.

"So she brings out the two blue boxes, puts them into a blue bag, and then into a white bag. And I'd noticed that for all the other customers, she would bring out their credit card and their bill on a little plate. But with me, she puts the bag down, slams the receipt down on the counter, slams my change down, and just walks away."

Bingo! Poor service!

"So I'm getting pissed off," Artemio says. "Now I have a bag and a receipt. I got something. Now I'm gonna browse!"

Artemio knows he has paid his dues. He has made a small, symbolic purchase to show he "belongs" in the store. Many of us have done the same. In some circles, it might be a little white shopping bag from Prada; in others, a red, yellow, and blue plastic drawstring bag from The Athlete's Foot. But in each case, we buy something small to show we have the right to be there. And then we carry the symbol of our belonging—the little shopping bag—in triumph around the store and down the street. "Look, everybody," the bag says, "I can buy something at Tiffany."

But the bag isn't just a proof of status, it's a free-access pass in a system of apartheid. The little shopping bag gives us the right to move freely through the store. And this brings up another universalistic assumption about shopping: our right to browse.

Doesn't every shopper have the right to browse, to wander aimlessly through each and every store, to gaze at and caress each leather coat and sneaker, even if it's chained to the rack, and to ask questions of any sales clerk, even if she can't answer them? But you don't really feel you have possession of this right until that little shopping bag is dangling from your hand.

"*Now* they're not going to harass me," Artemio says. "I'm like, F___ it. I want to check this out. This is where rich people shop."

Okay, now that Artemio has bought something, he can settle down to the joy of shopping for his own research. He wants to see how rich people live, the way they shop, and what they shop for. He wants to see whether the rich are really different from you and me. He wants to see whether he and they belong together, if only for a little while, in public.

"So I'm looking around, looking at the watches that cost 14 thousand, 20 thousand [dollars]. I'm like, I could drive this watch! If I had that much money, I'd put it on a house or a car."

Artemio chuckles. He wants to show me that he's thrifty, that he has a rational sense of value. He's not a status shopper who blows everything on a fancy watch. He has *real* values.

"I'm having a good time," Artemio says, "looking around." He is proving that the best "entertainment retail" is simply shopping in a store that you haven't been in before. "Then"—uh-oh—"the guard comes up to me.

" 'Can I help you?'

" 'No, I'm just browsing.'

" 'Do you know what you want?'

" 'No' "—Artemio decides to stand on his rights—" 'That's the whole point of browsing!'

" 'Are you done yet?'

"That got me pissed off! I'm like, 'Take it easy.' I figured he'd at least be sensitive to the situation, him being a black man. And he's trying to act like he doesn't care, like this is okay."

Oh, Artemio! He assumes the security guard will feel some solidarity with him, or at least some empathy for the shopper who is placed under suspicion because he's dark-skinned and looks like he comes from "the streets." Doesn't the law stand on Artemio's side—the U.S. Civil Rights Law of 1964 that assures everyone equal access to public facilities? And isn't this story taking place many years after that law was passed—and in the North? Hasn't it been settled that anyone can enter a store anywhere in the United States and expect to be served with respect? It's nothing personal, it has nothing to do with Artemio or the security guard: it's the law.

But what about racial profiling? Security guards routinely watch dark-skinned shoppers; Kwame, Alicia, and their friends from East New York have been watched in stores. Not so long ago, ten unarmed black teenagers—six boys and four girls—who were shopping for tuxedos for their senior prom were stopped, handcuffed, and searched by the police in

West Orange, New Jersey, after an anonymous caller to 911 reported—wrongly—that one of them was carrying a gun. Half of the black men, and a quarter of the black women, questioned in a survey by the *Washington Post* said they had been stopped unfairly by the police. My student J and his brother were seized by a security guard at a club in Manhattan one night, when the guard chased a robber out to the street, and J and his brother were passing by.[11]

Now the guards at Tiffany are physically, verbally, and literally intervening in Artemio's shopping experience.

"So I'm talking to the guard," Artemio says, bringing me back to the story, "and everybody stops for a quick second."

Again Artemio feels he is on camera, being watched. He sees the store in a freeze frame. Time stops.

"The whole floor stops and watches me talking to the guard," he says.

Whether or not the other shoppers are really watching, Artemio *feels* he is the center of attention. He is humiliated. And he begins to admit to himself that the security guard's intervention, like the saleswoman's slights, have got to him.

"I'm thinking," he says, "What am I doing in this place?"

But then, the security guard says something to him.

"The guard says, 'You should be on your way.' In other words, 'Quit giving me a hard time and get out of here.'"

Artemio goes on the offensive.

"I say, 'I got money. My money's no different from theirs. What're you stressing me for?'

"So he says, like off the record, 'What are you doing in a place like this? Most people that come in here, they're spending five thousand dollars. Are you gonna drop five thousand dollars?'"

The drama, then, the stress of shopping at Tiffany, comes down to a showdown between these two men—the outsider and the insider, both of them resisting and yet also playing off their similarities: their dark-skinned bodies and their social class.

"He was trying to be nice," Artemio says, "telling me to go back to Canal Street or somewhere I can afford to buy. So I'm pissed off."

Canal Street: New York's headquarters for discount jewelry stores and knockoff designer handbags. Is Artemio the right shopper in the wrong place? The guard has exposed the subtle hierarchy of shopping, the hierarchy that shopping tries to make us forget, the idea that we can move up in social status by shopping in the right places—but only if we're the right shoppers in the first place.

Directly provoked and feeling the brunt of the guard's disrespect, Artemio moves into a more personal mode of expression: the mode of the street.

"I take out my money and I show it to his face. I knew I had more money in my pocket than he ever did. He was comparing me to these white people, and I was comparing him to me. I wanted to break it down to what he could understand."

But it is Artemio who doesn't understand. When he walks into Tiffany, he compares himself to the other shoppers, and he thinks, maybe just for a moment, that appearance doesn't count. Maybe he isn't dressed the same as the "white" shoppers, and maybe he doesn't have as much money in his bank account, but he has "a pocketful" of cash. (In fact, most shoppers at Tiffany pay with credit cards—a point Artemio barely mentions.) In his eyes, Artemio is only one of many shoppers. And he is their equal.

Yet from the moment he walks into the store, the security guards see him differently. Like them, he is dark-skinned; therefore, he is under suspicion.

At moments like these, security guards occupy a pivotal position. They're authority figures, doorkeepers, watchdogs, poised to look out for thieves. But if they're dark-skinned, they have probably been thought of as members of the "nation of thieves" themselves. Guards may have been harassed by police officers or by other security guards when they were out of uniform in a public space. They may have been stopped and frisked on the street, or in their cars; they may have been cursed at or spoken rudely to, or even falsely arrested or killed.[12] Yet when they're on the job, dark-skinned security guards use their uneasy intuition and peer closely at dark-skinned shoppers. For Artemio, assuming solidarity with a security guard, and counting on the guard's understanding, is fraught with risk.

"So he says, 'Are you done?'"

"And I say, 'No. I'll see you later,' meaning, I was going to browse."

Artemio is really pushing the envelope now. He doesn't accept that it is the guard's duty to suspect he's a thief; he's insisting on his rights as a shopper.

"And I stayed there 20 minutes more, and it was like I had control of a camera."

Artemio goes into cinematic mode again. This time, though, he feels he has control of the camera. He strolls around the store, leaning over the counters, looking at rings, pens, bracelets, scarves, and even china. But does he really have control?

"And the saleswoman would be right there, and the guards; it was like going from wide angle to close-up on me."

He has the camera, then, but he is not in control. He is still under the camera's scrutiny. It's not even a question of whether he has enough money to buy more things. His worst fears have been confirmed. Although he has bought something at Tiffany, he doesn't have the right to browse there. The shopping dream has turned against him. He'll never belong.

"When I left, two guards followed me down the escalator and two guards were waiting for me at the bottom. I said to them, 'You guys are f___ed up. You're black men, and you shouldn't treat a brother like this. You're racist against your own kind.'"

I don't know whether they answered him. Despite his outburst, there's no dramatic turnaround, not even a fight. Artemio has his moment of passion. And then he leaves the store.

Although Artemio is a Latino, his story is a common one for all dark-skinned shoppers. Most black shoppers believe they will be treated with disdain by sales clerks in expensive stores, even if they haven't actually had this experience.[13]

Why not think so? American blacks have a history of disenfranchisement from consumer society. In the old days when shopkeepers kept flour, sugar, and beans in barrels, they often short-weighted black customers' purchases and sold them stale supplies. Neither did they serve them as courteously as they did white shoppers. Of course, it wasn't practical for store owners to exclude dark-skinned shoppers completely. No merchant turns customers away. Yet in the rural South, blacks weren't permitted to join the cracker-barrel socializing, dominated by white men, at the general store. Throughout the South, and even in some of the border states, restaurants had separate entrances for blacks and whites. White clothing store owners, fearing not only the loss of white shoppers but also violence, tried to prevent black shoppers from using the dressing rooms to try on clothes. In the North, white merchants looked at dark-skinned shoppers suspiciously, sometimes cheated them, and followed them around the store. The very products blacks shopped for mocked them. Until the middle of the twentieth century, advertising posters as well as packaging frequently pictured dark-skinned people in racist stereotypes: happy-go-lucky, primitive, and servile. The mammy figure on the box of Aunt Jemima pancake mix was benign compared to many other logos.[14]

In northern ghettos and southern towns, shops patronized by African Americans sold inferior products at higher prices. When black shoppers sought an assurance of quality in brand names, and shopped at chain stores rather than at the corner grocery, whites tended to sneer at them for acting "uppity." When blacks chose to pay premium prices, whites made fun of what they considered their tendency to show off and derided their ambition to shop for the best as a caricature of conspicuous consumption. Conflating the arrogance of class and race, whites looked down on blacks, first, for having little money, and then, for spending what little they had on such useless status symbols as gold teeth, Cadillacs, and fancy footwear.[15]

There's nothing subtle about these racist stereotypes. Yet if they hold any truth at all, social scientists tend to find the sources of blacks' conspicuous consumption in their history of exclusion. "A Cadillac has its point," says an article published in 1951, "as a weapon in the war for racial equality. . . . To be able to buy the most expensive car in America is as graphic a demonstration of . . . equality as can be found."[16] We can understand this point intuitively, as Artemio does: people who shop for the same things—and can afford to buy them—are equal. Buying something that is considered to be the status object of the dominant group—a Cadillac, a Jeep, a Lexus—is a graphic way of declaring equality.

But sociologists and psychologists go farther. They have theories to explain what they take to be a group's tendency to shop too much. They expect dark-skinned shoppers to shop as women do: to compensate for their being excluded from legitimate sources of social status, to make up for not having great wealth or high positions in business and politics. Yet dark-skinned shoppers—again, like women—are also supposed to find in shopping a realm of freedom, in contrast to the constraints of segregation and inequality. Either way, these theories predict that as long as they are divided by status differences, black people will shop differently from whites. As late as the 1980s, according to Bart Landry, a sociologist who studied middle-class blacks, African Americans spent disproportionately more money on groceries and home music systems than middle-class whites did. Landry says this reflects blacks' habit of entertaining at home, in the continued expectation they will be denied access to, or treated badly in, public places of consumption.[17]

During the 1950s, the economist Marcus Alexis did an exhaustive study of whether African Americans shop differently from whites.[18] Years later, when I met him, he told me he had been angered, as a young man, by the persistent stereotype that blacks, even poor blacks, buy big luxury cars like Cadillacs. Reviewing every study that had been done to that time, Alexis found a number of reasons that blacks might shop differently from whites; however, he discovered little support for the stereotype of blacks' conspicuous consumption.

Alexis found black shoppers to be keenly interested in both price and quality. Not surprisingly, they shopped at stores that offered credit and guaranteed full satisfaction, even if these stores were more expensive than others. Lagging behind whites in car ownership, blacks tended to spend more money than whites on public transportation. And as for racial differences in buying those Cadillacs, Alexis found no evidence at all.

Even if many blacks did spend a lot of money on clothes, we needn't try to explain this by saying they're less rational than whites. Until the sixties, as Alexis points out, many blacks still held low-wage, uniformed jobs as maids, mechanics, and factory workers, and were required to wear work clothes chosen for them, and often provided by, their employers. The employers also offered workers hand-me-down clothing and leftover food to take home to their families. These payments in kind would lower black workers' household expenses, allowing them—if they wanted—to splurge on clothes for social occasions. Being kept down in low-wage jobs would even encourage conspicuous consumption of clothes—to spite the white employers, establish an alternative public sphere, and keep up appearances.[19]

That certain consumer goods have a deeply racialized meaning suggests that shopping in America rarely elevates the color of money over the color of people's skins. There is, in fact, a malicious symmetry between whites' stereotypes of blacks' conspicuous consumption and marketing strategies that target black consumers. Black shoppers get the same treatment women shoppers do. They are courted by advertisers and then condemned for going shopping.

Yet for many years, black shoppers were not courted at all. Not until after World War II, as Alexis points out, did companies begin to think about developing the black consumer market, or even hiring blacks as salespeople. And even if they could afford it, many blacks may have held themselves back from spending money. By the fifties, a magazine like *Ebony*, which was oriented toward the black middle class, actually urged its readers to spend lavishly. Not only did wealthy blacks deserve their success, the magazine said, they should not be criticized by other blacks if they could afford luxuries. Flouting the stereotype that would inspire Alexis's research, *Ebony* urged its readers to buy Cadillacs.[20]

But Cadillac wasn't interested in selling cars to *Ebony*'s readers. The companies that advertised in the black media sold low-status products like food, cigarettes, and liquor, as well as candy, soda, and men's clothes. While black entertainers and athletes appeared in some advertisements—Duke Ellington promoting Lucky Strikes and Jackie Robinson endorsing Chester-fields—brand-name appliances and other big-ticket items were pictured with white models.

During the early sixties, market researchers, especially the few blacks in the field, tried to interest companies in blacks' spending power. They emphasized "the growing power of the Negro market," as an article in the November 1961 *Public Opinion Index* termed it, and urged companies to advertise and organize promotions for black shoppers. Some of these efforts look clumsy and offensive to us now. Just as Jackie Robinson appears in a cigarette advertisement, so the booklet put out by the tobacco industry, "Brown Skin and Bright Leaf," thanks African Americans for their role in tobacco production. D. Parke Gibson, the author of *The $30 Billion Negro*, published in 1969, endorses the "gracious hospitality" lessons offered to black women's groups in Philadelphia by alcohol distillers.[21]

For their part, African Americans have not been docile consumers. Throughout the twentieth century, blacks organized boycotts against white-owned stores, both North and South, for refusing to hire blacks or serve them. During the war years in the forties, and again during the militant sixties, police harassment sparked destructive riots against white-owned stores in black neighborhoods. In 1960, moreover, black and white college students led sit-ins to integrate Woolworth's lunch counters and local department stores in the South. As a result of these protests and many more dramatic confrontations, the Civil Rights Act of 1964 outlawed racial segregation in all public spaces. It was time for the racial etiquette of shopping to change. If there really was a "$30 Billion Negro," D. Parke Gibson reminds his readers, he had to be addressed as "Mister."[22]

Department stores all over the United States still relied on their sales clerks to maintain an informal system of racial intimidation. Black shoppers continually had to make their presence, and their spending power, felt. In southern cities like Birmingham, Alabama, this struggle had been under way for years. During the thirties, more affluent, black women shoppers pressed for better service at downtown stores. They were gradually joined by poorer blacks, who were forced to shop downtown when small neighborhood shops disappeared.[23]

For the same reasons, black shoppers also became a more significant presence at downtown department stores in the North. By 1965, "the percentage of Negro trade" at major department stores in Philadelphia, St. Louis, New York, and Washington, D.C., generally ran to about 35 to 50 percent, with lower percentages at more exclusive shops. In downtown Atlanta, New Orleans, Chicago, and Detroit, up to 90 percent of the shoppers at some stores were black, as they were in the emerging black ghetto of south-central Los Angeles.[24] While these numbers should have encouraged more department stores to cater to blacks, the stores simply stopped investing downtown. Following their white customers, they moved to the suburbs.

Between the sixties and the eighties, shopping opportunities in black neighborhoods became even more constricted, and more black shoppers visited suburban malls—even though those malls were deliberately located far from public transportation. The new black middle class sought high-quality goods in the better class of stores, which were now often located in the suburbs. Since more blacks owned cars, they could drive to the mall.

Yet taking advantage of shopping opportunities wasn't easy for everyone. Many poor blacks still lived in urban neighborhoods bereft of supermarkets and chain stores. The presence of black teens in malls—especially boys—scared whites and middle-class blacks as well.[25] Salespeople always suspected them of stealing.

With little money and few attractive stores around their homes, poor and working-class blacks had a rough time shopping. The anthropologist Elizabeth Chin, who studied the consumption patterns of low-income African American families in New Haven in the early nineties, found few possessions in the children's rooms. Most of their toys cost less than $5, and few children owned licensed goods like the action figures based on movie characters, except for the ones that are given away with fast-food meals. One grandmother started saving money in July to buy Christmas gifts in December. A mother asked her child to write out his Christmas wish list in October so she could buy his gifts one at a time, when she could afford them. Sometimes children were the only family members to receive gifts. Moreover, since the neighborhood that Chin studied lacked big stores and supermarkets, and many families didn't own cars, they couldn't make the rounds to stores to comparison shop. Neither did parents try to negotiate with their children over purchases; their tight budgets—including government-issued food stamps—didn't permit them any leeway.[26]

Yet during the eighties and nineties, black teens, especially boys, cut a fashionable figure. Break-dancers and hip-hop performers rose from the streets of the Bronx to become popular entertainers on street corners in midtown Manhattan, in subway stations, and in public parks. Their performance style was picked up by the New York-based media and music industries, and gradually brought into the mainstream. Eclectic hip-hop culture spread through black and Latino communities on both the East and the West Coasts.

As major music companies competed to sign young black and Latino artists, some of these young performers became highly visible commercial properties. Like the basketball players who were beginning to dominate both the Olympics and the NBA, some young black men started to make big money. They were a dark counterpoint—a doubling, if you will—to the suddenly rich stock brokers and investment bankers—the yuppies—of the eighties, and they provided some of the labor in image-producing industries that were beginning to fly high on Wall Street.

Of course, most young black men were not getting rich in the stock market. Crack cocaine and heroin traffic plagued black communities, and continued persecution of the "war on drugs" led to high rates of black imprisonment. Blacks were still more frequently unemployed than whites. Moreover, playing basketball or break dancing is often something young men do to combat idleness; it becomes more prominent when other means of gainful employment dry up.[27]

While a small number of black basketball players and rap musicians seemed to become supremely successful, black men continued to be dogged by lurid sexual and criminal stereotypes.[28] The photo of Willie Horton, a convicted black rapist, that was trotted out by Republicans to discredit the Democratic presidential nominee in 1988 helped George H. Bush to win the election. Bush, who had served as vice president for eight years under Ronald Reagan, rode a wave of resentment that had seethed against Democrats throughout the seventies and eighties for supporting blacks, women, and gays. Although Reagan and Bush did not use the language of race, their lack of support for civil rights, affirmative action, and other issues that benefited minorities clearly signaled a different attitude toward racial equality. Moreover, code words like "welfare queens" that the Republicans condoned contributed to a stereotype of blacks as an "undeserving," if not also a criminal, poor minority. Fears of losing control over social space— in the neighborhoods, the public schools, or the stores—fueled widespread fear, among whites, of losing their place in society and encouraged many of them to abandon even lip service to the goal of equality. It also brought back the racist stereotype of blacks as icons of conspicuous consumption that had gone underground during the sixties.[29]

As crime rates increased and an epidemic of illegal drugs affected all racial and ethnic groups, a line was drawn equating fashion, race, and danger. Magazines showed skinny, disheveled white fashion models who were said to be suffering from "heroin chic," and newspapers reported that young black men were mugging other teenagers to steal their brand-name clothes. In city after city, waves of muggings targeted teens who were wearing leather jackets, gold chains, Nike, Reebok, or Adidas sneakers, Polo, Nautica, or Eddie Bauer shirts—and any other item whose label happened to be, at least momentarily, hot.[30]

For many kids in the city, this desire for brand names posed real problems of physical safety. At the same time, for many white kids, linking fashion and danger just dramatized the appeal of designer clothes. In the late eighties, when the rap group Run-D.M.C. sang about how much they liked "My Adidas," and various gangsta rappers talked about the brand names they preferred, they stretched white consumer society to an extreme. Within the next few years, however, when Mary J. Blige sang about "my Tommies," and Snoop Doggy Dogg appeared on the television show *Saturday Night Live* in Tommy Hilfiger clothes, another meaning emerged. In an ironic doubling of black shoppers' striving for quality, blackness and brand names were suddenly linked in fashion.

It wasn't just about selling clothes. Race was a token of the intense competition between consumer goods companies—a drastic confirmation of the high-stakes position they assumed in the new symbolic economy of fashions, media, and entertainment. Each company had to differentiate itself from the rest of the pack. If a product was associated with blackness, it looked different and new, it had a story outside fashion, and it promised sales to the expanding market of young consumers—which was now worth between four and seven billion dollars a year. In an age of inauthentic products, a product associated with blackness looked real. Though this seemed to mark a reversal of status shopping—with more affluent white teens copying working-class blacks—it was really the culmination of the "democratization" of fashion that had begun in the sixties, when market research said that young people identified "downward," with the disenfranchised.

In the sixties, identifying downward helped white people to think about blacks trying to register to vote, go to school, and use a public rest room, especially in the South. It brought them together with the blues of the Mississippi Delta and with gospel music, some of which was transcribed and marketed by the Motown record label. But in the eighties, identifying downward meant identifying with the drug trade, with gangsters, and with gangsta rap. This was neither as noble nor as modest as before, but it would sell products that appealed to a young men's market: sneakers, jeans, CDs, and advertising time on televised basketball games. It would get media coverage. And—most important—it would excite the imagination of financial analysts on Wall Street, who were constantly searching for the next new thing.

Companies competing for market share in the "sneaker wars" used race as a last resort, with Nike—the upstart company that became so powerful—as the crucible. Nike had always invested a lot of effort in shoe design, but their designs were geared to athletic performance rather than to fashion. This paid handsomely through the late seventies, when most Nike fans were young male athletes, especially runners. At the moment the company went public, in 1980, financial analysts' enthusiasm propelled share prices to twenty-one times earnings, and, in 1981, Nike took first place in *Forbes* magazine's annual survey of returns on investment by major corporations. But at this point, Nike's rivals—Adidas, Reebok, and New Balance—started to make shoes for the large number of men and, increasingly, women who were now training for fitness rather than running races. And one Wall Street analyst declared that Nike's dominance was dead: "What do you need in a mature market?" he asked. "A hot new product to excite people to go out and buy it."[31]

To recharge its connection with the core market of young men, Nike decided to change its focus from running to another popular sport. Since Fila had already used tennis players for product endorsements in televised championship matches, Nike turned to basketball. Puma had marketed "Clydes," a model named after Walt "Clyde" Frazier, the stylish New York

Teenagers shopping, Houston Street and Broadway. Photo by Richard Rosen.

Knicks guard, in the seventies. But the shoes didn't have staying power. In the eighties, Nike found a great African American rookie player—Michael Jordan—on the Chicago Bulls, and made a deal with him for an exclusive endorsement. Thinking of Jordan as a marketing concept before they even had a product in mind, Nike decided to "take him out of the realm of colored sneakers and into style." They would "make Michael Jordan a label. Take him into the realm of Ralph Lauren." The company signed Michael Jordan for $2.5 million in 1984.[32]

Signing Jordan helped Nike, as marketing gurus say, to expand the "franchise" of the brand. Literally, however, their franchise benefited from the franchise of Jordan's nationally televised basketball team, the Bulls. This relationship set a precedent for the mutually beneficial cross-marketing of sports, media, and fashion. While Nike used Jordan as a walking logo on the court and in commercials, the National Basketball Association used television to establish a bigger presence in American homes. But unlike in earlier years, the vast majority of NBA players were now black. A large, mainstream audience began to identify with them because they brought a different style of play to national TV; they jumped higher, dunked harder, and ran like crazy up the court. They also wore different uniforms—with longer, baggier shorts, like those worn by high school kids on the streets. And Jordan, of course, wore his signature shoe—Air Jordans—which were made by Nike. "It's TV that defines the athletes," Nike's cofounder and CEO, Phil Knight, said. "They perform on television, and we just expand on the image."[33]

Air Jordans pushed Nike ahead of its competitors, to the unanimous praise of the business press. "Nike Catches Up with the Trendy Front Runner," trumpeted *Business Week* in 1988, dismissing Reeboks as a "fad." In fact, Nike specialized in getting the endorsements of black athletes while Reeboks were endorsed by musicians regardless of race. Aside from Michael Jordan, 265 of the 320 NBA players wore Nikes. Mick Jagger, Bruce Springsteen, and Lionel Richie wore Reeboks.[34]

Athletes' endorsements have been used for years—but Nike paid so much money for them that they created a unique conflict over the athletes' loyalty. At the 1992 Olympics in Barcelona, Michael Jordan led the gold medal–winning U.S. basketball team in a refusal to wear the logo of Nike's competitor, Reebok, despite the explicit directive of the Olympics committee. Though the team dressed in the required uniforms for the awards ceremony, they covered the Reebok logo so it would not be seen on worldwide television. This avoided a final confrontation with the Olympics committee, but it only confirmed the view that the leading black athletes were on Nike's payroll. And it also confirmed the importance of the televised logo. When Michael Jordan retired from the NBA, Nike's stock price momentarily fell, but the company pressed on to buy endorsements from athletes in other sports—including the phenomenal, mixed-race golfer Tiger Woods, and the $90 million high school basketball player LeBron James, whose name would help Nike battle Reebok for a sweet distribution agreement with Foot Locker—formerly a part of Woolworth—stores.

Consumer culture in the eighties was shaped by television, by designer jeans, and by the use of celebrities—including white tennis stars and black basketball players—as walking logos. "We're socialized," my student J said. He didn't have to add: "We're socialized to shop."

What's the appeal, then, of developing styles "on the streets"? The idea of cool hunting—looking for new fashions, reporting on them to industry executives, mass-producing the designs, and selling them back to teens—seems to reverse the old cultural model of fashion "trickling down" to the poor from high-status groups. In this it suggests a final degree of democratization. But we live in an age of permanent image production, when the acceleration of the fashion cycle makes styles bounce from one medium to another because all producers are desperate to find the next new thing. Companies compete to sell more shirts, or shoes, or stars, but they're also competing for an image of growth in the media. The success of "urban" fashion really rests on the union of more ominous processes: the fetishization of black men's careers in sports and crime, the effort to impress financial analysts, and the branding of consumer products companies in the media-fashion-sports-and-entertainment complex. Buying a certain style of clothes doesn't imply respect for the people wearing it. Except when they begin to earn real money and, like Michael Jordan, Sean Combs, or Jennifer Lopez, they become brand names themselves.

Artemio discovered this when he went to Tiffany. Even if you have money in your pocket, you can't go shopping for status if you're urban, and poor, and brown.

7

consumer guides
and the invention of lifestyle

If shopping isn't the universal language, what is?
—Ernst & Young, *Global Retailing 1997*

At the Jefferson Market, a full-service grocery store where I like to shop, you can't buy a chicken to cook for dinner without being surrounded by taste tests and testimonials. On top of the refrigerated showcase in which identical chickens repose, you'll find a brochure claiming that Bell & Evans chickens, raised without antibiotics, are hormone-free. "Participants in national taste tests" have rated them "the excellent chicken," and they are endorsed by such authorities as *Good Housekeeping*, the *New York Times*, *Cooks* magazine, *Prevention*, *Cooks Illustrated*, the *Washingtonian*, and the *Boston Globe*. But then you'll see a clipping from the *New York Times*, taped to the glass front of the case, which challenges this claim. "The best" is a competing brand of chicken—raised as "free-range" in Canada, flash-frozen in Montreal, and flown to New York by jet plane. This Canadian poultry is recommended by several well-known chefs and—in the ultimate endorsement—it gets an article all to itself in the Dining section of the Wednesday *Times*.

How do you reconcile this conflict of values? In the store, you face competing brands of chicken that are all healthy, guaranteed to taste good, and carry the endorsement of cultural authorities. But at home, you've got a grocery budget, a spouse who likes a leg of lamb, and a daughter who is a vegetarian. Besides worrying about the chicken, you worry that you, as a shopper, will fail the test. You're immobilized by the anxiety of making the wrong choice.

The language of shopping deals with this anxiety. To the extent that it is a universal language, it speaks to our desire to be rational rather than to our desire to buy. It doesn't speak of "must-haves" or status items. Instead, countering every aesthetic urge and advertisement, it offers clear standards of value: "four stars," "worth a journey," "two thumbs up," "best buy." Though the language of shopping doesn't teach us to deny ourselves pleasure, it pushes us to find the best of every kind of goods. Because we learn to have absolute belief in it, we become smarter, less anxious shoppers. We know which chicken to buy.

It's not just about the chicken. Shopping for a car or a computer, we check the product ratings in *Car and Driver* or *PC World* and access other consumers' opinions on www.Epinions.com. Before dining out, we count the number of stars a restaurant has received or look it up in Zagat's. I have waited to buy a new book I saw in a store until I went home and read the reviews on Amazon.com. And browsing among the bottles of Chateauneuf-du-Pape at the wine store the other day, I saw another shopper, a young man, take furtive looks at a printed list he pulled out of his pocket, which, I could see by looking over his shoulder, was a list of the *Wine Spectator's* "100 Most Exciting Wines of the Year." I wondered whether he was interested in the 1998 Chateauneuf-du-Pape Guigal, rated 89 by the *Wine Spectator* and 90 by the *Wine Advocate*: " 'The finest Guigal has produced since 1990 . . . a full-bodied classic . . . copious quantities of kirsch liqueur, pepper, balsam and spicy aromas' (Robert Parker)."[1]

Taking advantage of our willingness to pay attention to these ratings, shops and service providers do not hesitate to use them for self-promotion. Like the advertisements for movies that feature an array of glowing blurbs, even the humblest restaurant in New York City tapes reviews from local newspapers and dining guides on its plate-glass windows. The take-out menu of a pizzeria on Bleecker Street presents favorable reviews from two going-out guides before it boasts, "Mona Lisa offers more than your average slice."

I don't blame the "honest brokers" or cultural authorities who write these reviews. In fact, I myself pay a great deal of attention to what they say. Reading their reviews is often the first step of my shopping experience. Their rhetorical flourishes and the numerology of their lists and charts have become our universal language. And why not? The honest brokers are so sincere; they seem to be just like us. They place themselves on our side in the endless struggle for value, when they earnestly ask: "Is the product any good? Is it worth the journey? The price? Or the effort? Is it truly 'the best'?"[2]

Would you eat here? Dining guide reviews, Indian restaurant, First Avenue. Photo by Richard Rosen.

Unlike the "hidden persuaders," as Vance Packard called advertisers in the 1950s, or the "captains of consciousness" who try to manipulate consumers' minds through marketing,[3] the honest brokers speak for us consumers. They speak from our position in society—the anxious position of shoppers who are trying to balance price and quality. We read movie reviewers and art critics at the high end of consumption—*The New Yorker* and the *New York Times*—for their ability to write learned essays that place cultural products in an analytic history of their genre. But we also read the honest brokers who write reviews of dustbusters and toaster ovens because they tell us whether we will *like* these products. We don't care whether they know everything about their inner workings. But we trust them if they guess right about what works for us.[4]

Though some honest brokers appear on television and become media celebrities, we don't know them personally. We know them only by their judgments, and they don't know us at all. They earn our trust by expressing what the sociologist Pierre Bourdieu calls a "homology"—"a perfect . . . harmony between . . . [our] expectations . . . and . . . [our] dispositions."[5] They speak for us when they earnestly try to balance the objective qualities of money and materials against the subjective qualities of pleasure and style. They personalize the objective qualities and objectify the subjective elements of what we like. By taking our position, they seem to understand us. And that makes us feel more secure.

But honest brokers are only partly like us. They are helpless and incompetent like us, especially when they don't understand what's really inside the hard drive of a computer, but they are also cultural authorities because they tell us which hard drives work better than others. Their position in the middle, between consumers ("us") and producers ("them"), deepens our perception of their sincerity.[6] Yet it also deepens our dependence on them.

In years gone by, a young man relied on his father's or master's advice about choosing the right tools for his trade; a young woman would receive her mother's or mistress's advice about proper cookware and sewing needles. Today, we depend on the advice of honest brokers who teach us how to choose the best automobiles, microwave ovens, and take-out pizzas. By teaching us about the "tools" we need to survive, the honest brokers teach us how to live.

They certainly teach us how to live more rationally. The honest brokers' words and images unify the thousands of different goods and services that are available to us on the market, their separate places of display and manners of presentation, and the various ways they can be used, abused, or abandoned. When *Car and Driver* compares the transmission of six different models of cars, or *Consumer Reports* tells us which VCR is easiest to operate and will last the longest, we feel more confident about our final choice. Honest brokers also speak to our inner feelings about products. They guess what matters most to us, and they express our concern. They say we should buy the Acura Integra LS because of "its smooth powertrain, pleasant ride, and high fuel economy." They recommend we see the movie *Unbreakable* because it "shows Mr. Shyamalan's remarkable growth as a director." They tell us to buy the Canadian chicken because it is "the best." This language becomes our cultural currency. We use it because it represents a common ground between producers and consumers, between us and them. It represents our deepest longing for value.[7]

The honest brokers have given us a powerful language—in which consumers seem to hold their own against producers. They have placed a framework of rationality around our choices: it's market research in reverse. But this language also balances two primal motives of modern life—the desire for both rationality and pleasure. It applies the aesthetic judgments of high culture to products of mass culture. And it eases people who would otherwise suffer bloody conflicts over wages and power into a more peaceful, though still competitive, concern with consumer goods. Above all, the honest brokers' language transforms the conflict-prone struggle for a higher standard of living into a more ambiguous struggle for a better "lifestyle."

Early twentieth-century social critics focused on the irrationality of consumption, in general, rather than criticizing the qualities of specific goods. The best-known critic, the economist Thorstein Veblen, lashed out against conspicuous consumption—the wasteful process by which wealthy people lavishly spend resources, from idle money to leisure time, in order to demonstrate their social status to their peers and neighbors. Veblen singled out women as both subjects and objects of conspicuous consumption. With an anthropologist's eye, he explained how women in almost all societies are status trophies for the men who pursue them. Yet in modern times, women themselves are status shoppers; they select, nurture, and conspicuously display the consumer products, from curtain fabrics to fancy gowns, that determine their family's social standing. Veblen and other writers were upset by what they took to be Americans' loss of their traditional moorings in work and thrift. From the robber barons of the Gilded Age to the immigrants who came in a great wave to America's shores, the country appeared to be awash in a new preoccupation with consumption. This behavior made people greedy and tore them away from family and community values.[8]

Veblen was regarded as a scold. By contrast, the influential economist Simon Patten urged Americans to welcome a new era of abundance. Self-sacrifice may have been appropriate in times of scarcity, Patten wrote, but, with the development of industry and technology, Americans had to learn to spend their wealth rather than save it. Patten's view gradually prevailed, especially among the intellectuals who were becoming prominent in public life. During the 1920s and 1930s, economists, sociologists, and psychologists shifted from criticism to acceptance of mass consumption. They created a moralistic halfway house, in which ascetic rationality was balanced by aesthetic pleasure. "What intellectuals preferred," writes the historian Daniel Horowitz, " . . . usually centered on lives passionately lived, in which restraint obtained for material goods and commercial experiences but not for expressive, communal, or sexual aspects of life."[9]

The idea that consumer goods are a source of pleasure as well as of convenience was widely publicized by popular magazines like *Woman's Home Companion*, *Ladies' Home Journal*, and *Good Housekeeping*, which began to write for a middle-class readership around 1900, just when Veblen published his *Theory of the Leisure Class*. The magazines kept up a steady stream of information and opinion about consumer products, not only through feature articles but also through editorial columns and advertisements. They developed the approach of "practicality, 'inside dope,' and proprietorship" about consumer goods that is familiar to us from today's lifestyle magazines. Typically, an article in the twenties would instruct readers about the advantages of a refrigerator over an icebox, while a nearby advertisement for General Electric refrigerators reinforced the point.[10]

The balance between rationality and pleasure was even more authoritatively struck by a new field of economics that emerged in the early thirties:"consumer economics." Economists in this field shifted the focus of the "dismal science" from production to consumption. They also discussed consumption as a matter of individual choice—or subjectivity—rather than of an aggregate, and thus less personally interesting, demand for goods. This approach complemented the rise of Keynesian macroeconomic theory. While Karl Marx and other nineteenth-century economists had already warned that "underconsumption," based on the workers' lack of money to buy the goods they produced, would pose continual problems for capitalist economies, John Maynard Keynes urged that the government increase its spending to increase people's "propensity to consume." The economics in Keynes's *General Theory of Employment, Interest and Money*, published in 1936, supported the government's jobs programs during the New Deal. After the recession of 1937, political conservatives accepted Keynesianism, and some form of "consumerism," as a necessary, though quite limited, form of social welfare.

The first consumer economics textbook in the United States, *Economics for Consumers*, was published in 1939 by Leland J. Gordon, a professor at Denison University, in Ohio. Beginning, like Veblen, with a critique of waste and of manipulation of consumers by "producer-made wants,"

Gordon suggests that consumers learn "wiser consuming practices" that "promote human welfare." He calls upon his readers to become rational, disciplined consumers by "develop[ing] the art of buymanship." At a certain point, however, Gordon breaks with Veblen and sounds more like Patten. "Consumption is an art," he says, "which Americans have too long neglected. It is the task of future generations to match the productive genius of their ancestors with cultivation of the art of living."[11]

The women's magazines, especially *Good Housekeeping* and the *Ladies' Home Journal*, had already worked out their own idea of "buymanship." For years, they had been offering advice to readers about which household products to buy, based on their "scientific" comparisons of consumer goods. In 1909, under its founding publisher, William Randolph Hearst, *Good Housekeeping* set up an "institute" to analyze and evaluate products that were advertised in the magazine. The magazine presented this institute as an independent testing laboratory. Vacuum cleaners, washing machines, refrigerators, scouring cleansers, and laundry detergents that passed its tests carried a special "Seal of Approval," and manufacturers were permitted to reproduce the seal on product labels and in advertisements. The Good Housekeeping Institute also investigated readers' complaints about products that were advertised in the magazine. If tests showed that the product was defective, the institute guaranteed that the manufacturer would replace it or refund the purchase price. The institute worked differently from the testing labs at Macy's, Bloomingdale's, and Piggly Wiggly, where technicians in the stores' employ checked the quality of the hundreds of thousands of different products made by the stores' suppliers. Yet today we might consider its relationship with manufacturers to be a strategic partnership or even an early example of cross-marketing.[12]

The institute's claim to be an honest broker depended on its utter objectivity—its position in the middle between producers and consumers. On a "Guaranty Page" inside each issue of *Good Housekeeping*, the editors stated that fewer than 30 percent of consumer products that had been awarded a Seal of Approval were advertised in the magazine. An article marking the thirtieth anniversary of the seal, in December 1939, declared there was "no charge to manufacturers and no requirement that they advertise in" the magazine. "These policies—unchanged for thirty years—enable the Institute to do its work *with strict impartiality*." For these reasons, the *Good Housekeeping* Seal of Approval carried great symbolic value.[13]

But the very first edition of *Economics for Consumers* cast doubt on the institute's reputation. Though Professor Gordon praises it for declaring it had turned down $1 million of advertising offered by manufacturers who were eager to gain the Seal of Approval, he criticizes the institute for failing to make its standards public and omitting information about test conditions and prices. Neither did the institute publish comparisons of goods in the same category. These points led Gordon to conclude that the Good Housekeeping Institute was not an honest broker. His suspicions were soon confirmed by the U.S. Federal Trade Commission, which exposed the Seal of Approval as a fraud. According to the FTC, the institute's testing procedures were either inadequate or nonexistent, and the magazine regularly received kickbacks from manufacturers. Far from being an objective judge, the institute sold use of the seal to any manufacturer who wanted to buy it.[14]

These charges demanded rapid revisions. By 1941, *Good Housekeeping* changed the formerly unconditional approval to a "limited guarantee": manufacturers would replace, or refund the purchase price of, products that turned out to be either defective or "not as advertised." Eventually, the limited guarantee disappeared, and the seal itself was retired. By the time Professor Gordon published the fourth edition of his textbook, in 1961, *Good Housekeeping* offered only to replace the item, or refund the purchase price, if it "verified" a consumer's complaint. Instead of awarding a Seal of Approval, the magazine now published a twice-yearly *Buyers' Guide*.[15]

Though the form and contents of a "buyers' guide" spoke to the same urge for rational decision making as consumer economics, there were no *consumer* guides in the United States until 1936.[16] Before the thirties, such guides existed only as catalogs for trade buyers, expanded versions of the business directories that had been published by local chambers of commerce since the late nineteenth century. A brief "study guide" prepared in 1935 by the Committee on Standardization of Consumers' Goods, of the American Home Economics Association, seems to be the forerunner of the consumer guides that we know; it was intended to be a more objective source of product information than the brand names, labels, advertisements, and salespeople that represent the *producers'* interests. Shoppers urgently need unbiased information, the study guide says, because more new products, "marketed without any definite information as to quality and performance, ha[ve] made wise selection increasingly difficult." To help consumers, the guide offers practical suggestions about how to buy hosiery, blankets, and sheets—nearly all of which, we can assume, were purchases made by women—and urges shoppers to ask pointed questions about the contents, durability, sizing, and weight of specific items.[17]

The idea that shoppers in the thirties would need guidance to choose among new consumer goods contradicts our image of the Great Depression, with its urban breadlines and shantytowns, unemployed youths riding the rails, and rural poverty. Yet not everyone was on the dole. New service industries, new technologies, and new consumer products were expanding, and workers who kept their jobs could buy more goods, at lower prices, than before. At the high end, demand for luxury goods was not affected by declining wages. Yet price consciousness still ruled most consumers' minds. And many consumers, especially women and African Americans, organized around consumption during the Depression to protest social inequality.[18]

Consumer militancy was encouraged by President Franklin D. Roosevelt and the activist government of the New Deal. A month before his election, in 1932, Roosevelt proclaimed: "In the future we are going to think less about the producer and more about the consumer." During the next few years, the National Recovery Administration and other federal agencies invited consumer representatives to serve on important commissions and boards, and the Congress passed laws on product content and labeling. The president was prodded by his liberal advisers and a number of new consumer organizations that were speaking out—Consumers' Research, founded in 1927; the Consumers' League, to which the young Eleanor Roosevelt belonged; and Consumers Union, established by staff members who broke away from Consumers' Research in 1936. The League of Women Shoppers, also organized in 1936, included prominent socialists, writers, and Democratic Party reformers—among them wealthy, socially conscious New Yorkers who wore their fur coats in winter to walk on picket lines. These women boycotted department stores for paying their workers too little and requiring them to work too hard; they published the exposé of working conditions at Woolworth that I quoted earlier. By 1940, according to a right-wing attack on the group, the League of Women Shoppers had thirteen local branches, mainly on the East and West Coasts— and they had been accused, by the Dies Committee on Un-American Activities of the U.S. Congress, of being a Communist "front."[19]

For the most part, the new consumer organizations simply tried to help consumers become more rational shoppers. Copying the idea of the independent testing laboratory, they allied it with consumers rather than with manufacturers. The earliest and best-known organization, Consumers' Research, published a magazine that rated products as "recommended," "intermediate," or "not recommended," and indicated which prices were fair. After the founder of Consumers' Research, F. J. Schlink, refused to raise the staff's wages above $16 a week, or allow them to join a labor union, some staff members broke away to form a competing organization, Consumers Union, which also "conduct[ed] research and tests on consumer goods and . . . provid[ed] consumers with information which . . . permit[ted] them to buy their food, their clothing, their household supplies and other products most intelligently." Like Consumers' Research, CU rated products as "best buys," "also acceptable," or "not acceptable." But like the League of Women Shoppers, "the directors of Consumers Union [did] not feel . . . they [had] done their job when they. . .provided information which permits the saving of a few pennies, or even a few dollars, by buying one brand instead of another." They continued to investigate and publicize the conditions in which products were manufactured, so they could help "workers to get an honest wage."[20]

From the outset, neither Consumers' Research nor Consumers Union accepted advertisements in their magazine, which enabled them to take a critical stand on manufacturers' claims. Typically, an article in the first issue of *Consumers Union Reports* exposed misleading practices in the marketing of milk—then, as now, a basic commodity in the American diet, especially for children. In those years, milk was marketed in two "grades" according to butterfat content. Grade A was presented as having a higher fat content and higher quality and was, accordingly, priced higher than Grade B. But when CU technicians analyzed fifty-seven samples of both Grade A and Grade B milk from two large dairies, they found practically no difference in butterfat. The article therefore urges consumers not to pay higher prices for Grade A milk. It instructs "the housewife" about *scientific* indicators of product quality—bacterial count and pasteurization, which was just coming into common use—and cautions her not to "accept the word of the milk companies." Thumbing through the magazine, we see the same critical approach applied to all the consumer products that were becoming basic commodities in American households: "What Soap?" "How to Select a Toothbrush," "The High Cost of Octanes." We can sense both the consumers' bewilderment, as they confronted a confusing array of competing products and advertisements, and the honest brokers' self-righteousness, as they advised consumers to inoculate themselves with a strong dose of skepticism about producers' claims.[21]

If consumer magazines and economics textbooks developed a rational language of shopping that was appropriate to toothbrushes and milk, other new media of consumption created a more aesthetic language. Duncan Hines's restaurant reviews, *Cue*, the going-out guide, and *Gourmet* magazine were also founded in the thirties—between the end of Prohibition and the start of the New Deal. Though they were concerned with cocktails and dining, travel, and entertainment, they also carried out rigorous comparative tests and tried to educate their readers. After all, to compile a "list of 167 excellent restaurants in 30 states," Duncan Hines must have eaten a lot of meals.[22]

The tremendous postwar boom in mass consumption increased the need for honest brokers. Manufacturers, designers, advertisers, and sales clerks actively encouraged shoppers to buy. But many consumers were still cautious about spending money. Their experience of material deprivation through fifteen years of Depression and war was not easily overcome by the new prosperity. When inflation spiked, moreover, during the Korean War, shoppers balked at paying higher prices. Their attitude encouraged merchants to open the discount stores I have already described, and persuaded Congress and state legislatures to abolish fair trade laws. Yet with so many industries trying to seduce consumers with new cars, hi-fis, televisions, and washing machines, and so much spending power in postwar households, shoppers really needed objective information about what products were available on the market and how to make rational choices between them. Between 1940 and 1960, Professor Gordon's consumer economics textbook went through two new editions. The Schwann Catalog started out in Boston as a twenty-six-page typed list of classical recordings and developed into an "invaluable" listing of all recorded classical music for sale in the United States. *Road and Track, Car and Driver*, and at least eight other automotive magazines began publication. And by the early sixties, the magazines of Consumers Union and Consumers' Research were read by nearly five *million* men and women.[23]

The car magazines intrigue me because they reached out to male readers with both a rational and an aesthetic language of consumption. They printed detailed technical reports about fancy sports cars and "cars of interest" to expert drivers, as well as "interesting" and "meaningful" critiques of ordinary models for Sunday drivers and the average buyer trying to choose a family sedan. In each case, the automotive magazines subjected cars to stringent road tests and compared them on the basis of such objective factors as speed, reliability, and roominess. They gradually adopted the charts and numbers approach of *Consumer Reports*, rating "roadability" and "reliability" on a scale from one to five. "I would rate a Ford or Chevvie as four," a writer named Bob Yount declares, "which doesn't necessarily mean that it will run longer than a three rated foreign job with less trouble, but that parts and service are more apt to be available."[24]

Detailed explanations of ratings were devised to relieve new car buyers' anxiety. When a letter to the editor of *Car and Driver*, in November 1955, begs for "honest, or as honest as can be, evaluation[s]," the editor replies that the magazine has expanded its program of comparative road tests and replaced numerical ratings by specific adjectives ranging from "poor" to "excellent." When a later letter writer, in July 1960, worries that the road tests are based on the writers' pet peeves instead of on the models' objective specifications, the editor tersely says that road tests are "based on performance on the road, not merely on a study of specifications," and affirms that performance is "very definitely based on the likes and dislikes of the . . . staff." There is a universal language of shopping for cars, the editor implies, which offers clear, transparent, and precise criteria for evaluating them.

But admitting that even the most objective product review is based on the reviewer's subjective judgment represents a new understanding of the honest brokers' role. It opens the door to a more variable appreciation of consumer goods—and to a more aesthetic kind of criticism. Alongside comparative tests of cars' speed, roominess, and reliability, the automotive reviewers looked for pleasure, beauty, and the satisfaction of, as Susan Sontag wrote about creative artists at the time, a "new sensibility." The sixties were, in many ways, a golden age for cultural critics—but these were no longer high-culture critics, they were honest brokers of mass consumer commodities like cars.[25]

The "new sensibility" shifted standards of value from a morally committed, scientific evaluation of a product's usefulness to a cooler, more pleasure-oriented subjectivity. This development ran parallel to a generational shift from the labor-oriented, Old Left politics of the 1930s to the cultural, New Left politics of the 1960s. It also marked a transformation in art and literary criticism. Younger, well-educated reviewers began to revel in products of mass consumption, while judging them by the aesthetic standards of high culture. In the fifties, these critics liked hot rods, sex, and rock and roll; in the sixties, they adopted the counterculture, French food, and Pop art. But it took at least ten years for the critics to develop a coherent voice—and to turn it into our shopping language. Oddly enough, this language was born with the Beat authors and avant-garde New York poets of the 1950s, who rebelled against both the standardization of mass culture and the pretension of highbrow cultural authorities. The Beats spoke for the repressed desires of a young generation who wanted to create an aesthetics of everyday life. Their deliberately casual attitude and sophisticated tastes were the first postwar example of a "lifestyle" explicitly chosen in counterpoint to mass-consumption tastes—the guys dressed in blue jeans and the gals in black tights, both drinking bitter black espresso instead of percolated "American" coffee.[26]

But it was Craig Claiborne, the restaurant reviewer for the *New York Times* in the 1960s, who brought this new lifestyle sensibility into the cultural mainstream. Highly influential not only in New York, Claiborne was acknowledged to be—along with Julia Child, James Beard, and the cookbook author and teacher Michael Field—one of the "Big Four" figures of the American Food Establishment. According to a *Los Angeles Times* survey of food writers and restaurant owners, he was this country's first writer of "honest, serious food criticism." Craig Claiborne invented the restaurant reviews that we take for granted today; he went beyond *Consumer Reports* and *Car and Driver* to create the modern grammar of our shopping language.[27]

Claiborne was the first restaurant reviewer to insist that food writing was straight news rather than an element of household management to be buried on the "women's page." He was also the first to write *negative* restaurant reviews rather than pieces of fluff that praise the owners, ignore the chefs, and flatter the newspaper's advertisers. He insisted on observing professional standards—standards that were weighted toward the aesthetics of the producer, or chef, but which also represented the rational demands of the consumer.[28]

Claiborne's reviews introduced Americans to the quantitative ratings of restaurants that the *Michelin Guide* had developed in France since 1899. For the first time in the history of American newspaper reviews, the *New York Times* awarded each restaurant between one and four stars. (The

Michelin Guide uses one to three toques or chefs' hats.) Moreover, in the manner of *Consumer Reports*, Claiborne's reviews included explicit comparisons—in his case, between New York restaurants and a general model of fine restaurants in Europe. These innovations made his critical voice both more rational and more aesthetic than that of any previous American restaurant reviewer. "It is sufficient," Claiborne might say with a gourmet's expertise and an expert's cultural authority, "that each of the dishes is prepared in the best classic tradition."[29] Or he would praise a dish in sensory as well as logistical terms, as when he described "a stuffed turbot, imported fresh from European waters but as sweet in flavor and as tender in texture as if it had been pulled within the hour from the waters off Long Island." You could practically taste his pleasure with every bite—and his criteria would be as familiar to readers of *Consumer Reports* as to those who learned about pastries from Marcel Proust.

Claiborne's considerable enthusiasms did not overwhelm his capacity for negative judgments. "It must be said," he tempers his praise of a very fine restaurant, " . . . that there are flaws in each and every paradise. . . . The coffee on occasion tastes raw and bitter." A restaurant of this caliber, moreover, "should not admit corned beef and cabbage to the menu even on a trial basis." Likewise, the service is "well above the New York average, but it still lacks the pride, precision and finesse that is found in certain European restaurants."

Though Claiborne always offered his opinions modestly, in the third person, as "one man's taste," he clearly expressed criteria that were accepted by growing numbers of readers. Like him, these readers were first of all consumers. They lacked the training and experience that would enable them to produce for themselves the products under review; neither could they form an independent judgment of culinary products. Like Claiborne, they wanted aesthetic fulfillment at rational prices. They liked rating restaurants on the basis of numerical ratings or "stars" because the rules were clear, transparent, and precise.

If Craig Claiborne was the solid rule maker of restaurant reviews, Gael Greene is their diva. Greene has been the main restaurant reviewer at *New York* since the magazine began weekly publication in 1967; at that time, she was a young college graduate. Though she had no training in cuisine, she had already published a profile of Le Pavillon, New York City's most famous French restaurant. And like Craig Claiborne, Greene loved to eat, had traveled in Europe, and knew how to write. So she was hired by Clay

Felker, *New York*'s founding editor, "to compete" with Claiborne, whose reviews appeared every Friday in the *Times*. Felker expected her, Greene recalls, to "tell it the way it was," as Claiborne did, but also to produce "more stylish writing."[30]

Clay Felker's reasons for hiring Gael Greene as a restaurant reviewer are a good example of Pierre Bourdieu's "homology." He hired her to write, she says, for "people like me. People who loved food. A mixture of very affluent, established New Yorkers and upwardly aspiring, young career people." While she was greatly impressed by Craig Claiborne's "enthusiasm and his seriousness," she wanted to infuse her criticism with sensuality and a love of pleasure—that "new sensibility" making its way from art and literature to shopping. This was the same direction in which the entire magazine was heading. "We felt," Clay Felker recalled years later, "one of the major activities of people was being consumers." Unlike the mass-circulation *Consumer Reports*, however, *New York* aimed to attract "educated, affluent people . . . who, broadly speaking, consumed print." As Felker realized, these were middle-class people with a great deal of cultural capital, who would also consume a wide range of information about real estate, business, celebrity gossip, new plays and movies, and fashion. These topics would become the basic features of the urban lifestyle magazine.[31]

The shift from Craig Claiborne to Gael Greene illustrates the way lifestyle journalism—and our ideas about lifestyle—developed during the sixties. Claiborne's language is straightforward, a little straitlaced, and heavy on the adverbs. "The Chauveron is scarcely more than 10 years old," Claiborne wrote of a well-regarded French restaurant in 1968. "But it has an old-guard patina. The decor may seem a trifle dowdy, but the kitchen is meritoriously old-fashioned and classic." Greene, by contrast, is personal, explicitly sensual, and rebellious in her flaunting of adjectives. "With my chronic Puritan hangover," she writes of the same restaurant in 1969, "I feel rather decadent waxing lyrical over mere food. And lapsing into sexual metaphor seems sacrilegious. . . . Café Chauveron . . . justifies both decadence and sacrilege. Great staggering feasts to stagger home from giggling, pleased with the sheer brilliance of having chosen so well." This language fits its aesthetic overload to a rational core, but it also points the way toward food consumption as both an art form and a form of status competition. "In my crowd," Greene writes in another typical, over-the-top declaration, "uncorking a '66 Bordeaux [only four years later] is infanticide."[32]

New York made a great leap by presenting consumption to a middle-class public as both an art form and a way to shop for status. It did this, to some extent, by covering both chic and cheap consumption—often, by publishing two different restaurant reviews in each issue. While Greene wrote high-culture reviews of expensive, well-known, usually "French" establishments, the "Underground Gourmet" produced mass-culture reviews of cheap, little-known, "ethnic" hangouts. Yet people who read one of these reviews also read the other, marking the convergence of an aesthetic appreciation of both high and low culture—a sensibility that liked both a kosher pickle and a rare Bordeaux. "Multicultural" it was, before its time, but *New York* also developed a split consciousness about shopping—what cultural theorists would call a "hybrid subjectivity." The educated upper-middle-class men and women who read *New York* magazine shopped to satisfy their aesthetic and emotional needs—but they wanted to do so as rationally and as cheaply as possible.

This hybrid subjectivity infuses one of the magazine's early features, "The Passionate Shopper." Directed to both women and men, "The Passionate Shopper" joined a new aesthetic appreciation of traditional products with a nostalgia for traditional social spaces outside the standardized core of mass production. The Passionate Shopper doesn't go to Macy's, but to little-known, out-of-the-way shops in "the neighborhoods," tucked amid the remains of rapidly vanishing ethnic and work communities. Significantly, she becomes most impassioned about foods—the products most redolent, as the market researcher Clotaire Rapaille would say, with primal longings.

Indeed, "The Passionate Shopper" that appeared in *New York*'s first issue as an independent publication, on April 8, 1968, suggests that shopping is a voyage of discovery and even rediscovery. What do you find on this journey? The Passionate Shopper finds an Italian American worker, who has deboned fish at the Fulton Fish Market for the past thirty years, working on the seasonal arrival of fresh shad. She visits the daily fruit auction at Pier 28, in the Produce Terminal, where you have to arrive before 7 A.M. to get in on the action. She likes the large duck eggs that come "fresh each day from New Jersey" to "a dark little store [on] 75th Street." And she is excited by her discovery of Drew's Scottish Bakery, an outpost of the Highlands in Bay Ridge, an ethnic neighborhood in Brooklyn that is now dominated by Irish and Italians. Like the letter to the editor about pickles published in the same issue, The Passionate Shopper challenges "this era of mass production" which "sanctif[ies] the ersatz": she mourns the death of authenticity.

Despite her sophisticated nostalgia, The Passionate Shopper lacks the production knowledge that earlier generations commanded. By the sixties, Americans no longer knew how to milk a cow, make a bagel, or build a car out of a soapbox or a packing crate. Even in New York City, the home of so many ethnic goods, most consumers depended on products brought to them by department stores and supermarket chains. To be a smart shopper, *New York* suggests, you have to know your way around the small suppliers, neighborhood shops, and few wholesale markets that didn't disappear with the city's dying port. Instead of production knowledge, The Passionate Shopper needs craft knowledge: a sensory appreciation of a product's qualities, a modest understanding of different production techniques, and the imagination to construct a product's "back story"—a social narrative of the cultural tradition from which the product comes. As *New York*'s readership grew during the sixties and seventies, the magazine made this sort of craft knowledge another basic part of our shopping language.[33]

"The Passionate Shopper" disappeared around 1972, but other features in the magazine applied the same approach to an array of products and experiences, including private schools, art auctions, and shopping for antiques, that were new to middle-class experience. Though this may have reduced anxiety about making rational choices among unfamiliar things, the urban middle class at the time felt anxious about the roots of their whole style of life. White families—the historic core of the city's middle class—were leaving for the suburbs. The public schools, which groomed future doctors, teachers, and lawyers, were demoralized by aging and crowded facilities and racial tension. Many neighborhoods bore the fresh scars of bulldozing for uncompleted urban renewal plans, and the revitalization of blocks of brownstone houses in Park Slope or on the Upper West Side was just a dream. Moreover, under the strains of paying for both domestic programs and the Vietnam War, the national economy had recently fallen into a recession. Not surprisingly, *New York*'s readers wanted to get the best *life* for the cheapest price. As Gael Greene expressed the magazine's lifestyle mission, *New York* teaches its readers "how to eat rich, though poor. Or, more realistically, how to eat with the rich at austerity prices."[34]

The magazine's innocent enthusiasm for passionate consumption soon turned into an easily caricatured obsession. In the very first issue, in 1968, the central feature "Best Bets" was a listing of wildly diverse cultural events. It sampled high and low culture, from the premiere of an off-off-Broadway play and the first American poetry reading by Jorge Luis Borges to the annual display of Easter lilies at Rockefeller Center and the television broadcast of the Academy Awards. During the seventies, "Best Bets" continued to be an eclectic listing of events, and, even after *New York* was bought by the Australian publisher Rupert Murdoch and a new group of editors emphasized the magazine's "service" features over hard-hitting political articles, the feature kept readers in touch with both mass-market and high-culture innovations. In 1980, however, after Murdoch also acquired *Cue*, the going-out guide, "Best Bets" was changed to a shopping feature. Now it carried a different subtitle: "The best of all possible things *to buy*, see, and do [my emphasis]." Like "Best Bets," the entire magazine now appeared to be dedicated to "using, enjoying, and finding" the best consumer goods—a point that was not lost on media critics.[35]

In its earliest years, Clay Felker recalls, *New York* published "endless lists of what's the best this and that,"[36] and these "best" lists gradually became the magazine's most noted—and most notorious—feature. Everything was rated in groups of ten, from the best and worst movies of the year (1969) to the best dresses (1970) and biggest power brokers (1973). Of course, Americans have always been transfixed by "bests"; before *New York* was conceived, there was already a long history of "bests," from early twentieth-century collections of baseball statistics to Andrew Sarris's annual list of the ten best films of the year, first published in the *Village Voice* in the late fifties. But *New York's* "best" lists expressed a new shift in cultures of consumption during the seventies. Looking for "the best" signals the burgeoning sense of entitlement of upwardly mobile, middle-class consumers. They want to shop for pleasure without taking risks.

At the same time, consumers were jolted by a new set of honest brokers who spoke of nothing but risks. In rapid succession, student activists of the New Left and young lawyers allied with new environmental and consumers' movements challenged The Passionate Shopper's innocent pleasure in consumption. Both groups revived old ideals of ethical consumption that harked back to the moralistic scolding of Thorstein Veblen. Though only slightly younger than most of the staff of *New York* magazine, and equally middle class in their background, these activists called on consumers to "reject dominant lifestyle choices"—social and economic, as well as environmental.[37]

Their willingness to think critically about consumption was stoked by writers who adapted Marxist concerns with economic oppression and alienation to postwar society. The philosopher Herbert Marcuse, author of *One-Dimensional Man*, attacked mass consumption for fostering widespread false consciousness; according to Marcuse, consumer society led men and women to abandon the fulfillment of unique, creative human needs in favor of pursuing ever more standardized commodities. Taking a different approach, the sociologist C. Wright Mills, author of *White Collar* and *The Power Elite*, criticized big corporations for fostering conformity among their employees and subverting democracy in their pursuit of economic power. To a generation of young readers raised on cheerful Hollywood musicals, spreading suburbs like Levittown, and their parents' satisfaction with buying a piece of the American Dream, the conclusion was clear: corporations engaged in "domestic imperialism." Not only did they exploit workers, they also "manipulated and harassed" consumers, creating a pervasive sense of alienation in the private sphere.[38]

The New Left's critique gained a wider audience when it focused on consumers' growing concern with industrial pollution and distrust of corporations for foisting unwholesome products on an innocent public. Creating a new language of rational consumption, the young lawyer Ralph Nader put himself forward as a "consumer advocate." He gathered together a team of idealistic young lawyers, researchers, and student volunteers who documented how corporations profited from selling products that were actually dangerous to consumers, and proceeded to sue them for redress. Initially, "Nader's raiders" only tried to persuade or shame manufacturers into admitting their guilt and correcting dangerous or defective products. By the early seventies, however, this organization and the "public interest" research groups with which it was allied were also pressing the government to regulate business more severely. They wanted government to ensure product safety, occupational safety, and a safer natural environment. Aside from workplace regulation, protecting consumers from defective products and industrial pollution became the basis of "public interest law."

Nader's raiders scored their earliest and most famous victory against automobile manufacturers—the industry that most clearly symbolized postwar consumers' lifestyle. The report they issued in 1965, *Unsafe at Any Speed*, accused the largest automaker, General Motors, of knowingly selling cars with fatal flaws. Closely examining consumers' complaints about one of GM's most popular cars, the Chevrolet Corvair, Nader's group found that GM had failed to warn Corvair owners about the low tire pressure that caused all models to have turning problems. Though the company offered optional features to correct this flaw, they didn't publicize the features, so few car owners knew enough to request them. By 1965, the Corvair had been involved in so many accidents that GM faced more than 150 lawsuits just on this car's account. According to *Unsafe at Any Speed*, the company tried to settle each lawsuit quietly, without making a public disclosure about defects in the Corvair's design or recalling the car. This behavior, the report's authors said, was typical of the auto industry as a whole. All car makers ignored safety factors while concentrating on superficial design changes that would sell more cars: "From instrument panels to windshields, the modern automobile is impressive evidence that the manufacturers put appearance before safety. . . . The car makers seem to value their concept of appearance over the driver's right to see." And neglecting safety wasn't all. Car makers also ignored their role in causing air pollution so they wouldn't have to pay for solutions: "The industry left it to [us] to discover the harmful side effects of the product it manufactures, refused to recognize the need for prompt and effective remedy, and moved in the direction of emissions control only under the compulsion of law and imminent competition."[39]

Unsafe at Any Speed had a devastating effect on consumers' confidence, similar to that of Rachel Carson's somber examination of chemical pesticides, published in the early sixties in *Silent Spring*.[40] Carson wrote about toxic chemicals so simply and dramatically that everyone could understand the dire consequences of their use to the natural environment. Because she also emphasized the dangers pesticides posed to people's health, Carson—like Nader—was seen as the ultimate consumer advocate. Both consistently took the consumers' side against big companies who played an important role in the postwar economy—in Nader's case, the auto industry, and in Carson's, the giant petrochemical producers. Their work pushed the consumers' movement beyond individual complaints, to class action suits against producers and a more systematic critique of irrationality in mass consumption.[41]

While Rachel Carson and Ralph Nader strongly influenced the fledgling environmental and consumers' movements, they also molded consumer culture. Their rational evaluation of products entered the public sphere, mobilizing citizens, elected officials, young activists, and even apathetic nonvoters around a revitalized "public interest"—that of the *consumer*. Moreover, after eight years of a pro-business, Republican administration in Washington, D.C., the Democratic presidents John F. Kennedy and Lyndon B. Johnson swung to the consumers' side. A rising groundswell for what Professor Gordon had called "consumerism" created the widespread perception that big social changes were under way. "For the first time," Gordon writes with a coauthor in the preface to the new, 1967 edition of *Economics for Consumers*, "two presidents [Kennedy and Johnson] have sent messages to Congress devoted entirely to consumer interests. Congress has responded with new legislation." You can find "scores of books and research reports . . . [on] such life and death issues as the misuse of chemicals, the increasing use and abuse of drugs, the relationship of smoking to health, and the safety of automobiles and automobile tires." Consumers' interests are now discussed in every area of life, from "the moral issue" of "burial practices" to such "pocketbook issues" as "marketing, pricing, accuracy of weights and measures, use and abuse of credit, [and] investment practices."[42]

Indeed, Ralph Nader's "study groups" soon targeted banks. Like *Unsafe at Any Speed*, a new report issued in the '70s argued that a major industry whose products support consumers' lifestyle deliberately and systematically perpetrates abuses. Specifically, the consumer group charges that Citibank's lending policies discriminate against low-income borrowers and black-owned businesses. The public was not aware of this, for just as General Motors had failed to disclose fatal flaws in the Corvair, so Citibank failed to disclose their lending criteria. Neither did they publicize the fact that they offered lower interest rates on loans to preferred customers. Moreover, by examining the interlocking directorates that connected Citibank's board of directors with the boards of other major financial corporations, the Nader report implicates the entire banking industry. It concludes by recommending the adoption of a wide array of new regulatory rules by local, state, and federal government agencies.[43]

With these proposals, consumer advocates moved from writing exposés of producers' misconduct to devising strategies of "consumer empowerment." This phrase expressed the militant, self-interested spirit of the times—a spirit inspired by both social activism and anxiety about health. The U.S. surgeon general's report linking cancer with cigarette smoking was being widely discussed, as was Ralph Nader's charge, published in *The New Republic*, that the coal industry, the coal miners' union, and the federal government colluded in a refusal to confront the occupational causes of black lung disease. Sensing a crusade, media stepped up their investigation of consumers' claims, and public interest research groups were founded and staffed by volunteers on college campuses in every state. Their work, which included lobbying state legislatures for new regulatory laws, resulted in many of the labeling practices, generic products, and "truth in testing" safeguards that we take for granted today.[44]

Consumer Reports kept pace with both affluence and anxiety by adapting its product reviews to consumers' more sophisticated tastes. Like the 1936 article demystifying the butterfat content of Grade A milk, a 1968 article on scotch whiskies debunked the illusion of quality surrounding expensive labels. There was no noticeable difference between the most and least expensive scotch, *CR* researchers declared—yet consumers were often fooled by appearances: "It has become our opinion that for most people a Chivas Regal bottle filled with, say, Clan MacGregor (nearly $4.50 a fifth less expensive) is a bottle of Chivas Regal." When laboratory technicians separated whiskeys by body, aroma, and flavor, and analyzed these factors by age and price, "the results were another blow to the mystique."[45]

New York magazine refused to be left behind. In 1970, the magazine published a year-end "Guerrilla Guide for Consumers," which "feature[d] complete instructions for how to break the supermarket code and guarantee your food is fresh." Along with a prescient article by Gloria Steinem promoting "Ralph Nader for President," and one by Chris Welles on the Naderites who had exposed GM, *New York* introduced this guide as a tear-out handbook of "the sort of information and advice to keep the consumer movement going and growing." Yet the editors didn't abandon their hybrid subjectivity: they published a long article on "comparison shopping for Vitamin C" along with tips on where to buy vintage champagne for New Year's Eve at bargain prices.

Though it might seem as though a wide gap separates Nader's raiders from *New York* magazine, they both developed a language in the sixties and seventies that changed the dominant culture of consumption. This language spoke to both the rational and aesthetic sides of consumer choice. As in the concurrent debates over the right of abortion—for the Supreme Court made its momentous *Roe v. Wade* decision legalizing abortion around this time—"choice" became a keyword for individuality and freedom. Yet choice led individuals to differentiate themselves by adopting alternative ways of life. While some people in the counterculture opted out of mass consumption, others used their considerable "entrepreneurial energies" to set up new retail stores like The Gap and restaurants like Berkeley's Chez Panisse. In these establishments, consumers could engage in collective strategies of lifestyle shopping. [46]

The self-help movement in psychotherapy, which became enormously popular at this time, also had an influence on consumer empowerment. Guidebooks that had taught consumers to check products' quality and durability were replaced by manifestos urging them to "fight back." Increasing numbers of "survival manuals" told them not to get ripped off— a phrase borrowed from the counterculture—or "conned" by any store, manufacturer, or service provider. Though thirty years had passed since the publication of *Economics for Consumers*, Americans still seemed to lack either the traditional production knowledge or the new craft knowledge that was needed to make a rational choice. Moreover, as more consumer transactions involved services rather than goods, they required "performance" rather than judgment of materials or workmanship; consumers had to *act* as though they knew enough not to get cheated. The self-help approach encouraged consumers to create a good performance. Yet, in contrast to the sociological approach of the counterculture and the public interest research groups, self-help was apolitical. It tied the language of consumption to a culture of individualism.[47]

During the seventies, Americans confronted a dual crisis of higher bills for importing oil from overseas and lower revenues from exporting goods abroad. Economists coined the term "stagflation" to describe the combination of high prices and interest rates, and stagnant wages, that stymied both producers and consumers. Responding to the crisis, consumers changed their shopping habits. They gave up—at least temporarily—the giant, gas-guzzling autos made in Detroit in favor of small, fuel-efficient, imported "economy" cars. They bought cheap T-shirts and jeans made overseas. And they shopped in ever greater numbers at discount stores, feeding the growth of Wal-Mart and Kmart. Though they often looked for cheaper goods, consumers did not give up on status competition. If few women could attain the perfect "10" score of the young Romanian gymnast Nadia Comaneci, who triumphed in the 1976 Olympics, they could still shop for a pair of the new designer jeans. Consumers didn't want to shop less; they wanted to shop *smarter*—and this made them even more attentive to the honest brokers' "bests."[48]

The increasing polarization of incomes and goods gave rise to a polarization between the vicarious consumption of celebrities' lifestyles in *People* magazine and the costly purchase of "bests." Yet even rich people were dissatisfied by the endless repetition of stores and styles that were standardized by mass production, and publicized by mass media. In *Quest for the Best*, the retail magnate Stanley Marcus sadly reflects on an earlier age when shoppers were not so influenced by brand names and the media and individually owned stores, like his family's Neiman Marcus, were supreme arbiters of style. He mourns the disappearance of craftsmanship in luxury goods, which he blames on corporate takeovers of stores and "the decreased discrimination of customers"—even rich ones. And he complains that luxury stores no longer provide real personal service, as they did when sales clerks and store owners knew their customers' likes and dislikes and recommended goods accordingly.[49]

Though Stanley Marcus expressed an elitist view, the crisis of consumer confidence spread through all levels of society. Government tried to deal with it—but the results were contradictory. The deregulation of industries and financial markets that began under the Democratic administration of President Jimmy Carter was introduced as a way to foster business competition and lower consumer prices. But the strongest effect of competition was to goad companies to lower costs—resulting in lower wages, transfers of production overseas, and the closing of factories. The real dollar value of most people's incomes continued to fall; fewer employers offered job security. Yet voters resented President Carter's urging them to cut fuel costs by lowering the thermostat in their homes and pursuing a more rational standard of consumption. In fact, deregulation and corporate restructuring lowered many workers' standard of living while making executives and investors rich.

After Ronald Reagan was elected president in 1980, his Republican administration declared carte blanche for entrepreneurs and reduced taxes for the highest income brackets, while systematically reducing the safety net for both poor people and organized labor. Reagan's appointees supported business interests by pushing for big military contracts at home and free trade abroad. This encouraged American companies in finance, technology, and consumer products to expand into global markets. The resulting rise in stock values rewarded those wheelers and dealers who knew how to make strategic investments and—more important—were able to convince others of these deals' worth.

In this overheated financial climate, entrepreneurs and their investment bankers became visible symbols of status consumption. They were pandered to by gossip columnists, accompanied by fashion designers and models, and profiled on television's hot new program *Lifestyles of the Rich and Famous*. But if the new rich bought Rolex watches, Armani suits, and cellars of fine Bordeaux, there was an explosion of consumer products and venues for the lower classes as well. The eighties introduced moderately priced Murjani and Gloria Vanderbilt jeans, opportunities to use personal computers at home and Nautilus fitness machines at the gym, and ever larger, ever cheaper discount stores.[50]

For most people, prices were still a major concern. Married women could only pay household bills by going out to work, and even dual-income families used credit cards to deepen their debt. Though few people realized it at the time, the income differences between rich and poor had already begun to widen, and the middle classes developed a "fear of falling" down the social scale. Not only high prices, but marketing appeals, designer labels, and celebrity role models raised the level of consumers' anxiety. As Professor Gordon asks in the 1977 edition of his textbook: "Is the consumer really king?"

Yet all Americans had come to depend on an expanding array of consumer products and services. From the basics of cars and houses to former luxuries like dining out and travel, people were constantly making decisions about what and how to consume. They craved more information from honest brokers, and they needed to know that the honest brokers were "just like us." Toward the end of the seventies, two young lawyers in New York—Tim and Nina Zagat—began to develop a new kind of consumer guide that spoke to these needs. Using both Craig Claiborne and Gael Greene as models, they published a booklet of brief restaurant reviews based on a small survey of their friends. At first, compiling the reviews was only a hobby. They printed the booklet privately, at their own expense, and distributed it informally among people they knew—somewhat like when Schwann began to hand out his lists of new LPs at the end of the forties or when a Swarthmore College student began mimeographing and self-publishing *Crawdaddy!*, a pioneering 'zine of rock music, in the mid-sixties. The Zagats placed their survey in several New York City bookstores, but few copies were sold, and after three years, they decided they either had to stop losing money or turn this into a professional business venture. Setting up a company to publish the reviews entitled them, at least, to deduct the cost of restaurant meals from taxes as a business expense. But after the Zagat's survey was mentioned favorably in *New York* magazine, the slim red book took off. In the eighties, "sales jumped from 40,000 copies a year to 75,000 a month, almost overnight."[51]

The Zagat's survey succeeded because it was a new kind of honest broker: it expressed the consumers' voice at a time of high anxiety. Consumers wanted a semblance of power in the marketplace that producers—and President Reagan's pro-business government—were unlikely to grant them. Indeed, borrowing the rhetoric of the consumer movement, Tim Zagat calls the restaurant survey an example of consumer democracy. The restaurateur and food critic George Lang likewise calls it "*vox populi*," the voice of the people. I prefer to call it market research—but turned inside out to represent the interests of the consumer.[52]

Zagat's authority as an honest broker begins with the large number of people who submit reviews. More than 18,000 Zagat's reviewers come from New York City, and 125,000 come from other regions of the world. The survey's sincerity also reflects Craig Claiborne's rules: no advertisements, negative as well as favorable reviews, and standardized, numerical ratings. Moreover, Zagat's style is very readable. The language is slangy, making points by quick jabs and a good sense of humor. It resonates with pop culture idioms. Most important, Zagat's is not a snob. If it satisfies consumers, even the humblest restaurant can get a great review. "Critics say 'it's a barn, all right—all that's missing is the trough,'" says the 1993 Kansas City Zagat's about a popular restaurant in Stanley, Kansas. "But the low-cost buffet's country cooking is a long-established magnet in suburban Johnson County." The editors are sharp enough to realize they're not in New York City anymore.[53]

While Zagat's has expanded horizontally, since the eighties, into forty-five "major markets," and vertically, into shopping guides, movie guides, and guides to the best golf courses, each survey retains the authenticity of the consumers' voice. By fashioning reviews from small snippets of direct quotes, the editors reproduce the process of weighing pros and cons by which consumers make their choices, and suggest how often we settle for the optimum rather than get the absolute best. Each review is rich in local knowledge. "An oasis in a culinary desert," begins an entry in the 1998 London Zagat's. "This 'Italian gem' would 'do well in a better location,' but Putney locals are pleased to have it around for its 'very fresh, interesting' fare supported by a 'fantastic wine list' and 'helpful service'; prices are more West End [expensive] than suburban." By the same token, an Indian restaurant in a central location is pretty good—"not like your local curry house"—but it's a "shame the service is 'so slow.'" Even if the culinary products are totally unfamiliar, the grammar has become so ingrained in us that we have no problem understanding the language. In the 2001 Zagat's guide to Tokyo, an "*udon* specialist wins raves for its 'al dente noodles' and *nikomi-udon,* flavored with various kinds of *miso;* many are 'uncomfortable' with the modern decor, which doesn't look like your typical *udon* joint, but the fair prices put even frugal types at ease." Zagat's ability to subject a wide variety of consuming experiences to the same boilerplate criteria of price and quality makes the language of shopping even more universal. And who knows whether this language really comes out of the consumers' mouths, or is adroitly edited by the staff?

Since their origin in the 1930s, consumer guides have relieved the anxiety we feel when we confront the vast and ever changing array of goods and services in the marketplace. But they themselves have changed over the years. They acknowledge our greater aesthetic concern with pleasure while elaborating more detailed measures of rationality. Partly this reflects the sophistication of postwar, and postglobal, consumer tastes, as more goods become available in the marketplace and prices of many consumer products—relative to wages—decline. Partly, too, the acknowledgment of pleasure in consumption represents less participation in material production, with fewer consumers making the products they—and others—consume.

Consumer Reports and consumer economics set out in the thirties to pursue the issue of collective well-being. They initially posed the problem of consumption in terms of how to assure men and women a higher standard of living, as both producers and consumers. After World War II, and most markedly during the sixties, this problem was gradually reinterpreted as an individual (or a household) matter—and no longer in terms of the standard of living, but in terms of "lifestyle." Between the sixties and the eighties, the development of lifestyle in the media reflected a growing sense of consumption as a matter of entitlement. Though our obsession with "the best" represented our desire for rational consumption, it also reflected our feeling that we are *entitled* to the best.

"Lifestyle" emerged in the pages of consumer guides as a way to reconcile two types of shopping: shopping to associate ourselves with a set of *collective* qualities like social status, and shopping to advance a set of *individual* qualities, like beauty or pleasure, related to the self. This accounts for the success of a guide like Zagat's—it speaks less about the absolute qualities of consumer products and more about our insecurities. We need these guides because they impose some degree of certainty on an anxiety ridden world. As Terry Eagleton says of the literary critics' role during a period of social turmoil, we want them "to explain and regulate [social] change as much as to reflect it." In an era when consumption is so defining, we want our honest brokers not just to address our needs, but to unite us across the chaos of the marketplace and re-create us as a public: "[A critic] must actively reinvent a public sphere fractured by class struggle, the internal rupturing of bourgeois ideology, the growth of a confused, amorphous . . . public hungry for information and consolation, the continued subversion of 'polite' opinion by the commercial market, and the apparently uncontrollable explosion and fragmentation of knowledges."[54]

Today, as in the late nineteenth century of which Eagleton writes, people are driven apart by ideology, and money and social status are up for grabs. At times like these, then, a consumer guide is not just a guide to goods; it is a guide to the longing for clear, precise, and transparent standards in the public sphere. We read consumer guides because we want to reconcile our individual desires with our collective dreams.

8

how brooks brothers came to look like banana republic

Lifestyle Factory
—Sign on furniture store, Brooklyn-Queens Expressway, 1998

I'd like to think that doing all this research on consumer culture has made me immune to the lure of brand names, but I still have my little weaknesses. Why do I always buy Scott's toilet paper and never even look at Charmin'? Have I ever abandoned Band-Aids for a cheaper generic? I tend to swear by Bounty, while the usually rational Marge Simpson gets passionate about "Burly"-brand paper towels: "You're about to get a lesson in value!" Marge excitedly tells her daughter Lisa, rapidly tearing off towel after towel to wipe up puddles all over her kitchen floor. Even cartoon characters develop an emotional attachment to brand names.

The brand name speaks to both our open anxiety about making choices and our partly submerged desire for status. From Ivory Snow and Crest to Yves Saint Laurent, a brand name on consumer products assures us of quality. This marketing strategy wasn't born in the status-conscious, "best"-listed eighties. Branding goes back to the birth of modern trademarks and packaged goods—with the packaging of "Quaker" Oats and "Uneeda" Biscuits, in the 1870s. For more than a century, brands have developed close—and even intimate—relations with our bodies and our lives, and certainly with our aspirations for value.

The connection between branding and value plays an important part in consumer culture. During the 1980s, consumer products companies decided to capitalize on our anxieties about value. They emphasized the charisma of brands and extended it over a wider range of products. Tried-and-true brand names acquired a snazzy new image, and corporate managers attempted to ride this image all the way up the Dow Jones stock market average. Who could resist, they asked, the power of brand names?

But the evolution of Brooks Brothers, from a clothing store to a brand, illustrates the pitfalls of branding's power. When I walk into Brooks Brothers' flagship store on Madison Avenue, I sense value all around me. I feel I am returning to that classical period, in the early twentieth century, when a great store was an oasis of civility. The six-story building is much smaller than B. Altman's, but they are of the same generation, and Brooks Brothers is even more of a cultural icon of old New York. I half expect to see a little brass plaque, like the kind you see on the wall of a fancy tailor shop or teashop in London, certifying that this firm enjoys the patronage of royalty. At Brooks Brothers, however, the whole ensemble—dark wood paneling, pale blue button-down shirts and rep ties lined up in glass-fronted display cases, elderly, dark-suited salesmen, and, until recently, the absence of escalators—all discreetly announce that this is a store of the American aristocracy.

Brooks Brothers was founded in 1818, near the waterfront in Lower Manhattan. Over the first hundred years, the store moved northward as the commercial center of the city shifted—first to Union Square, next to lower Broadway at Bond Street, then to the Ladies' Mile, and, finally, just after the turn of the twentieth century, to Forty-fourth Street and Madison Avenue. In these various locations, Brooks Brothers has sold white shirts, dark blue pinstripe suits, linen handkerchiefs, and regimental striped ties to generations of the American power elite—to Democrats and Republicans, to presidents, business leaders, and military generals—and also to celebrities. Through the efforts of their managers, as well as the visibility of their clientele, Brooks Brothers has introduced tailored forms and fabrics that, while never exactly in fashion, are classic examples of American style.

In 1830, Brooks Brothers created frock coats made of lightweight seersucker; in 1845, it produced the first American ready-made men's suits. In the 1890s, it invented the silk foulard necktie, and designed the button-down, polo collar shirt that men and women have worn, at work and at play, for more than a century. After 1900, Brooks Brothers introduced in rapid succession the Shetland sweater, the English polo coat, the rep tie, and clothes made of madras fabric. In 1930, they developed the three-button—followed, thirty years later, by the two-button—suit. If these innovations didn't entirely create the reputation of the Ivy League, they nonetheless made the store, according to its official history, "a national icon

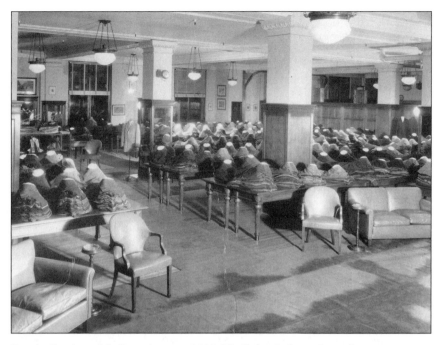

Brooks Brothers, Madison Avenue, 1915. Until the sixties, suits and trousers were displayed inside out on counters, so customers could examine the hand stitching. Club chairs and ash trays were placed in the waiting area for customers' convenience. Photo courtesy Brooks Brothers.

revered for the correctness, quality, and classic elegance of its merchandise and services."[1]

Yet like most conservative men's clothing stores, Brooks Brothers was almost oblivious to style. "While fashions come and go," their official history says, "Brooks Brothers has demonstrated that the desire for quality and good taste remains constant." For many years the store prospered while remaining true to its founder's ideal: "to deal with people who seek and appreciate . . . merchandise of the finest quality."

This sounds like B. Altman's philosophy, though applied to a richer, more powerful clientele. Indeed, as the managerial class expanded in the 1930s and '40s, shopping at Brooks Brothers began to symbolize, for many men, entry into the corporate world. Wearing a Brooks Brothers shirt showed an ability to play it safe, to avoid any sort of personal flamboyance or exoticism—to be a thoroughly predictable, and perhaps even wealthy, WASP (white Anglo-Saxon Protestant). But if this cultural style was safe, it was also boring. Trying to describe his dismay with New York City nightlife in the fifties, the critic Gilbert Millstein snipped, "Everybody wears Brooks Brothers suits."[2]

The store's location on Madison Avenue, surrounded by bank headquarters and advertising agencies, and just a block away from the great commuting hub of Grand Central Terminal, confirms its connection with the "organization man" of the fifties. Portrayed in detail by the journalist William H. Whyte and the novelist John Cheever, as well as by the sociologist C. Wright Mills, the organization man had a middle-management or upper-level job in a national corporation whose headquarters was inevitably in Manhattan. He wore his hair short and his collar buttoned-down; he smoked Winston cigarettes; and he commuted home to the northern suburbs every evening on the 6:24 train from Grand Central. The club car was filled with guys like these, loosening their ties and drinking gin and tonic, before they toddled home to their wives and children. No wonder New York nightlife was stunted. But Brooks Brothers' style, or lack of style, remained popular through both the countercultural onslaughts of the 1960s and '70s and the casual Fridays introduced into many offices in the 1990s. "In the American imagination," says the journalist Rebecca Mead, in a recent profile of the store, "Brooks Brothers remains a purveyor of Cheever camouflage, the outfitter of a kind of unreconstructed suburbanite."[3]

So the store has a specific place in the cultural imagination. It is an icon of class and power. Though its image is bland, smug, and conformist, the name "Brooks Brothers" has significant image value.

In the 1970s, the firm, like many other businesses, began to trade on this value. Acquired by the department store chain that owned Garfinkel's, in Washington, D.C., Brooks Brothers went global. It opened branch stores in Japan, and, in the early eighties, when preppy style was revitalized by the interest of a new generation, Brooks Brothers expanded both at home and overseas. By that time, the entire Garfinkel's chain had been bought by a bigger retail chain, Allied Stores, in an initially hostile takeover. In the mid-eighties, like B. Altman, Bonwit Teller, and other retail stores, Brooks Brothers attracted the attention of multinational investors, and the company was sold again.

The Canadian investor Robert Campeau bought the entire Allied Stores chain with financing supplied by junk bonds. But Campeau had no experience in retail. Overextended on the bonds, he was caught in a bind between the need to invest in operating and updating all the stores he had bought and financing his debt. Brooks Brothers, for its part, was caught in a value warp—between a potentially high sales volume that would reflect the value of its name and the actually low level of sales that reflected an aging customer base and diminishing appeal to younger shoppers. Miraculously for Campeau, the British retail chain Marks & Spencer soon took Brooks Brothers off his hands for $750 million—a purchase price that was regarded, within the business community, as either extremely generous or completely misguided.[4]

Though Marks & Spencer immediately introduced new, trendy styles, Brooks Brothers' earnings fell disastrously. The store's old clientele refused to buy the English-cut suits and tank tops Marks & Spencer placed on the racks. Since many of these customers were well placed in the media, they published angry diatribes in leading newspapers and magazines, complaining about the store's "hideous trendiness." But Brooks Brothers' new styles didn't attract new customers either. The management team that Marks & Spencer installed had the bright idea to open outlet stores, where they shipped unsold inventory; the outlet stores soon became the fastest-growing part of the business.[5]

During the nineties, Brooks Brothers operated more than fifty outlet stores and almost seventy-five retail stores in the United States, as well as sixty-five stores in Japan and two in Hong Kong. Yet younger shoppers still stayed away. They either bought sleek linen suits by Italian designers or flocked to Banana Republic for casual khakis. Searching for ways to attract the younger, "impulse" shoppers they desperately wanted, Brooks's managers hired image consultants. But the image these consultants came up with didn't change radically enough. In 1991, three years after being acquired by Marks & Spencer, Brooks Brothers still offered shoppers "authenticity, integrity, family, [and] guarantee of quality."[6]

Four years later, Marks & Spencer recruited a new CEO for Brooks Brothers from the women's clothing store Ann Taylor. Not surprisingly—for he had worked in merchandising at The Gap with Millard (Mickey) Drexler, a hands-on CEO—Joe Gromek placed a high priority on visual display. After arriving at Brooks Brothers, he brought in bright-colored shirts in peacock hues, which appeared alongside shirts in the store's traditional, muted pastels. Displays were opened up so shoppers could feel the materials. Salespeople got younger. Gromek increased the selection of more casual clothes, replacing pin stripes with less fussy styles, and, again not surprisingly, expanded the women's department. Over the next three years, sales increased by more than a third, and the customers' average age decreased from fifty-five to forty.[7]

Perhaps the biggest change, however, was the building of a new Brooks Brothers store at Fifth Avenue and Fifty-third Street. Following the corporate trend to "two-tier marketing," Brooks Brothers' management felt they needed two different stores, in different locations, for different clienteles. Like Prada, they would have a more traditional store, on Madison Avenue, for older, "local" customers, and a flashier "lifestyle" store, on Fifth Avenue, for tourists and younger shoppers.[8]

Sharing more than just an address at 666 Fifth Avenue with the National Basketball Association (NBA) Store, the new Brooks Brothers is equally brand-conscious and equally dedicated to lifestyle shopping. Unlike the old, flagship store, the new one is sheathed in glass, and follows the pattern of two-story-high display windows which is set by other upscale chain stores—Versace, Armani A/X, and Banana Republic—nearby on Fifth Avenue. In contrast to the dark wood interior of the flagship store, the new Brooks Brothers glistens with honey-stained, cherry wood paneling and stainless steel. You enter the new store, as you do its neighbor, the NBA Store, under a steel marquee. Suggesting a theater, or at least an event, these marquees prime shoppers for an "experience." Departing, again, from the style of the old, flagship store, where the women's department is squirreled away in the attic, the new Brooks Brothers features women's clothing on the first floor, where it is visible to passersby through large plate-glass windows. But the focal point of the entrance is the prominent display of men's shirts and sweaters in a rainbow of magenta, electric blue, lime green, and bright red, with variations in thick and thin stripes and windowpane checks.

Strangely enough, as you gaze around the new Brooks Brothers store, you can't help thinking about all the other upscale chain stores on Fifth Avenue. For all the obvious attention to design, it looks a lot like other "contemporary" clothing stores—like Ann Taylor, where Joe Gromek worked before he came to Brooks Brothers, and like the current market leader, Banana Republic. The same huge plate-glass windows. The same light wood and stainless steel. The same natural light pouring in the windows. The same T-shirts and sweaters piled up on counters, in bright colors, like gumdrops in a candy store. The same names on Madison Avenue and Fifth Avenue, on North Michigan Avenue and Market Street,

Brooks Brothers, Fifth Avenue, open in 2001. Photo by author.

in the gallerias and in the outlet malls, in Paris and London, Miami, Tokyo, and Beverly Hills. Each of them is a corporate vision of the same branded image Brooks Brothers chose when the new store opened: "Distinctive, Correct, Casually Elegant, Genuine, Eclectic, Smart, Sexy."[9]

How could this happen to Brooks Brothers? Why did the store reject its past, promise us it would be totally different, and wind up looking like Banana Republic?

Just a few years earlier, so many new shops were opening—flashy mega-stores specializing in one brand, like Niketown; "category-killer" super-stores for discount sneakers, books, and office supplies; outlet malls; and designer boutiques—that the *New York Times* devoted an entire issue of its Sunday magazine in April 1997 to the theme: "The Store Strikes Back."[10] Although the magazine focused on stores in the city, it also looked at shopping places throughout the United States and, with multinational chains and global brands, throughout the world. Whether these stores reflected a truly new wrinkle in the profit motive, or were overly hyped by publicists and marketing consultants, they tried to make the encounter between shoppers and goods a more spectacular experience.

Like the great department stores of old, the new stores used technology—electric light and escalators, in the old days, and, in our time, interactive media—to convince us that shopping was sensational. "The merchandise is almost secondary to the experience of being in this store," Paul Goldberger, the architecture critic of the *New York Times*, said of Niketown. And this "experience . . . bears more than a passing resemblance to a theme park. Niketown is a fantasy environment, one part nostalgia to two parts high tech, and it exists to bedazzle the customer."[11]

A lot of money was spent to bedazzle us. Starting in 1991 with its flagship store in Portland, Oregon, Nike built a series of giant, multilevel, glass-and-steel attractions to display its products and flaunt its brand. "Part Disneyland, part MTV," a journalist described the Portland store, and the same description fits a large number of stores that have protruded into the urban landscape since then, especially the Niketowns that appeared in rapid succession in Chicago, Atlanta, Boston, and London. Five years after opening the Portland store, Nike spent $28 million to build a Niketown in New York, on one of Manhattan's most expensive shopping streets—Fifty-seventh Street just off Fifth Avenue—on the site of the old Bonwit Teller. You wouldn't just wander into this store if you passed by, or go in to check out new styles and prices; you would make a *pilgrimage* to Niketown.[12]

Once you pushed your way through the subway turnstile at the entrance and checked out the clacking black-and-white squares of the notice board, just like the old arrivals-and-departures boards at train stations and airports, you could throw back your head and gape at the four levels of athletic equipment and clothing, arranged by sport and color, that ringed the central atrium. As you worked your way up or down the different levels, you'd pause to gaze respectfully at the artful displays of running shoes, sneakers, and cleats, baggy basketball shorts, bats, rackets, and balls of various dimensions arranged in showcases like ancient Greek artifacts in a museum. The merchandise suggested both frozen movement and awesome grace. There wasn't a statue of Michael Jordan in the store on Fifty-seventh Street, as there was in the Portland and Chicago Niketowns, but the displays of products and sports memorabilia intentionally recalled Jordan's leaps toward immortality, when he played basketball for the Chicago Bulls and served as Nike's most famous, extravangantly paid, celebrity endorser.[13]

The glass cases and "Team Nike" caps, high school gym, with its wooden floor and bleachers, and giant video screens, where promotional videos for Nike products were shown four times an hour: the whole shopping environment was shaped, as Goldberger says, "to give its merchandise sex appeal and establish Nike as the essence not just of athletic wear but also of our culture and way of life."

Niketown wasn't built to satisfy a local demand for sneakers. My students at Brooklyn College never go there; if they need shoes, they shop at Modell's or Dr. Jay's in Brooklyn. So one morning, I stood inside the entrance to Niketown, on Fifty-seventh Street, to see what kinds of shoppers were coming in. Almost all of them carried a shopping bag from the Warner Brothers Studio Store, then located across the street, or from the Disney Store, on Fifth Avenue. This almost certainly meant they were tourists. Most of them were also wearing athletic shoes—in contrast to most people walking down lower Broadway or riding the subway, who tend to wear black leather shoes. Since the tourists coming to Niketown were already wearing athletic shoes, they couldn't have a desperate need to change their lifestyle. No, they were coming to Niketown as a "destination," as they visited the Empire State Building or the Metropolitan Museum of Art; they wound up seeing the store as the ultimate branded product and experiencing shopping as the obsolescence-defying spirit of our times.

Nike wasn't the only company to invest a lot, during the nineties, in upgrading the social space of the store. Research shows that the more time we shoppers spend in stores, the more we buy. If a store's environment fascinates us, encouraging us to move from "attraction" to "attraction," as we do at Disney World, we'll spend more time in the store, and we'll buy more things. Research also shows that the overwhelming portion of any store's sales—80 percent—are made to only 20 percent of shoppers. To increase sales volume, then, a store has to lean on those of us who actually buy something with all the means at its disposal: enveloping us in a sensory paradise of goods, creating displays that are vignettes of desirable lifestyles, and offering us more and more merchandise under the same popular brand names.[14]

Merchants had begun to invest more money in upgrading their stores in the early eighties, despite constantly complaining about higher costs. Over the next ten years, "merchandising"—a vague term that encompasses all the visual techniques and environmental strategies that aim at enhancing shoppers' direct encounters with goods at the POP (point of purchase)—

grew from a $5-billion to a $25-billion-a-year business. Although some stores, like Wal-Mart, invested heavily in computer technology, and others, like Nordstrom's, raised wages to hire experienced salespeople, most companies put their money into building larger stores, with more elaborate POP displays, as a means of "reenchanting" the shopping experience.[15]

The sobering fact, however, is that the whole country has been "overstored" since the 1970s. "Too much selling space is chasing fewer sales," a 1995 article in *Business Week* pessimistically declared. "Competition is rampant," says the publisher of *Barnard's Retail Trend Report*. "Too many stores look alike." Finding themselves under intense pressure to increase sales and lower costs, many stores—like manufacturers—try to become "lean and mean." They stay in business by reducing the number of employees, outsourcing to cheaper suppliers, and cutting inventory. But "lean and mean" stores don't enchant us shoppers. *Business Week*, trying to explain shoppers' pervasive discontent, says: "Selections are unsatisfying, prices unappetizing, service unsatisfactory, and hours and locations inconvenient. From cars to food to clothes, shopping is a pain."[16]

It's not that shopping has got worse, however; it's that years of experience with shopping have raised our expectations. We want the convenience of a corner store and the wide selection of a supermarket, the intimacy of a bespoke tailor and the stylishness of a designer boutique, the magic of Woolworth and the prices of Wal-Mart.

By the nineties, many shoppers felt that stores weren't delivering on any of these promises. The long-term financial crisis of department stores, made painfully acute by junk bond financed buyouts and hasty acquisitions, weakened their inventories and their hold on shoppers' imaginations. Local merchants were menaced by the ceaseless expansion of chain stores and the building of larger, regional supercenters. Though all of us still had to shop, we cut back on our routines, visiting fewer stores on each shopping trip. Women, who do the major share of every kind of shopping, from bottles of wine to men's underwear, felt especially stressed. They had to sandwich shopping trips between their household responsibilities and their jobs—which made us "tightfisted, . . . and [with a] lower tolerance for all the imperfections of retail." In 1974, each square foot of retail space generated an average of $175 a year in sales; in 1995, it accounted for only $166.[17]

But businesses exist to sell us things, and the economy of everyday life is geared to buying and selling. Economic recessions, terrorist threats, and chronic inequality do not contradict the fact that America is still the world's largest consumer market. To keep this economy going, in the eighties and nineties, credit card companies extended credit to even the modestly employed, especially if they were women; new variations of basic products were churned out under old brand names; and stores continued to open at a rapid pace.

This wasn't just a normal process of some stores opening while others folded. This was an *acceleration* of "storing." At the low end of prestige and price, Wal-Mart crept steadily from the rural heartland into the suburbs—opening more stores, and larger stores, every year. At the high end, multinational companies that made luxury goods, and those that just wanted to establish a presence, opened new stores in prominent urban locations.

One of these was the Disney Company. When a new executive team, led by Michael Eisner, took charge of Disney's management in the early eighties, they tried to devise ways to increase the company's value on the stock market. Until then, Disney products consisted mainly of animated films and the theme parks in Florida and California—neither of which lent themselves to retailing, except for souvenir shops at the theme parks. But now Disney executives began to think about marketing products related to Disney movies in freestanding stores. These stores did not have to be limited to the theme park locations; they could sprout in urban shopping districts and suburban shopping malls—promoting Disney films and theme parks, and spreading the Disney aura, throughout the world. If these stores could also turn a profit on toys, pajamas, and sweatshirts that were produced cheaply in Haiti or Taiwan, so much the better.[18]

Stores that sell a single company's products, whether these are Ralph Lauren's or Walt Disney's, signal that the company is a *contender*. When the Sony Company took over the AT&T building, on Madison Avenue, it opened retail stores on the ground floor as showcases for both its traditional core products—electronics—and the music and films it produced with its recent acquisition of Columbia Records and Columbia Studios. It called these Sony Space and Sony Style; shoppers couldn't fail to make the connection. Identifying the company behind the diversity of products is important for big media conglomerates, where the underlying corporate unity isn't always apparent. In the mid-nineties, Viacom—the entertainment company that owns *Star Trek*, Nickelodeon, MTV, VH-1, Nick at Nite, Paramount Pictures, and Blockbuster Video, as well as the publishing firm Simon and Schuster—opened a 30,000-square-foot store on North Michigan Avenue, in Chicago. To establish a coherent corporate presence, the store set up displays where shoppers could play interactive games and small boutiques where they could buy clothing, skateboards, board games, and dogtags with the logos of Viacom's most popular movies and television shows.[19]

Branded stores also suit the strategies of real estate developers and stock market investors. Placing stores in upscale shopping areas like North Michigan Avenue, Madison Avenue, and Market Street, in San Francisco, fulfills a company's desire to establish its name as a global brand and also provides a "story" to financial analysts. Even if the company loses money on high-rent space in these districts, keeping a store there is a major form of self-promotion. "It is like an advertisement, especially for someone who wants worldwide visibility," says a New York real estate broker about the luxury shops on Madison Avenue. "It's better to have an outstanding boutique [on Madison Avenue] than a full-page ad in *Vogue*," says a manager of Yves Saint Laurent's Rive Gauche boutique.[20]

Like the expensive products that they display, these stores are simultaneously produced in multiple copies, or branches, and infused with an aura of luxury. This contradicts Walter Benjamin's view that original works of art lose their special aura "in an age of mechanical reproduction." How, then, do these stores succeed? Some of them are truly conceived as original works of art, like the Comme des Garçons boutiques of the fashion designer Rei Kawakubo, "whose store interiors are just as idiosyncratic and carefully considered as her clothing." During its first five months, Kawakubo's new store in the emerging art gallery district of Chelsea was written up no fewer than three times in *The New Yorker*'s weekly listing of art exhibitions; this was the only occasion on which I have ever seen that magazine consider a store a work of art. More often, luxury chain stores benefit from the Planet Hollywood effect: their aura derives not from their uniqueness, but from shoppers' familiarity with their name, and from repeated encounters with their image.[21]

Branding has always been an exercise of power. When brands were introduced into the modern business world, between the 1880s and the 1920s, they relied on new federal trademark and copyright laws protecting companies' claims to make truly distinctive things.[22] From the manufacturers' point of view, putting a brand name—or a trademark—on a product is a completely legal way to create a monopoly. If it's given the right placement in store displays, and paired with the right images in advertisements, a brand name differentiates a product from its competitors; it controls the meaning of a product, designer, or company; and, most important of all, in the current age of rapid image circulation, it tells a product's story—a story that compels us to believe.

Branding is also a clever way of getting consumers to accept new products. In the early twentieth century, as the historian Susan Strasser shows, manufacturers developed new supplies of raw materials, which enabled them to produce more goods than the public had ever bought. Under those conditions, branding became a means for unknown and untried products to develop a familiar identity. This identity was confirmed by advertising, especially in national magazines, which popularized brand names by repeating specific images and slogans. Visual repetition strengthened shoppers' ability to recognize products when they saw them in a store, and, eventually, the repetition created a relationship. By the 1920s, mainly because of the print media, more than 75 percent of grocery shoppers in Chicago asked for baked beans by brand name; in nearly every grocery store, one brand—Campbell's—outsold all its rivals.[23] In the thirties, the enormous popularity of radio broadcasts strengthened sales of all nationally advertised brands. With the federal government's consent, the new national radio networks brought frequent commercials, corporate sponsorship of weekly opera and orchestral performances, and celebrity spokespersons for consumer products companies into everyone's home. "What the manufacturer could name, he could advertise," the marketing professor Richard Tedlow writes. "The result was something more than a name. It was a kind of supername—a brand."[24]

If these early branding strategies made shopping more predictable for shoppers, they also made the ebb and flow of consumer demand more predictable for manufacturers. According to Strasser, branding "offered . . . protection against competition, against industry price fluctuations, and even against the effects of business cycles."[25] Yet the success of manufacturers who were able to capitalize on brand names gave them disproportionate power over stores. Big companies, like Procter & Gamble and Kellogg, demanded the lion's share of shelf space for their soap bars and cereal boxes, even if the store owner made a higher profit from private labels, and even if shoppers preferred to choose among competing brands. On the other hand, a strong brand identity sometimes created so much demand for a specific product that shopkeepers had trouble keeping it in stock. Even today, the CEO of Wal-Mart admits, despite the store's computerized inventory system, a weekend "run" on a popular brand-name product like Tide can provoke a crisis—and irritate shoppers, as well.[26]

Branding not only establishes an identity for individual products, it also draws attention to the company name behind them. In the 1920s, diversified corporations began to use branding to promote the whole range of products that they made. General Electric—like Viacom—revealed itself to be the maker of both light bulbs and refrigerators, while General Motors—GM—stood behind Frigidaire refrigerators as well as a whole "family" of car brands. Branding eased consumers' anxiety that they were becoming dependent on giant, impersonal corporations, which would not be as responsive to their needs and complaints as small, local producers. And it did turn out to be a good strategy for making consumers less wary of a company's size. Brand names personified companies that the public perceived as too big—like GE, which, in 1911, was accused of price-fixing by the federal government—but they also magnified companies that were considered too small—like GM, which, until the mid-twenties, was seen as Ford's weaker rival.[27]

Branding does more than establish a corporation's charisma. It is also a practical strategy to raise prices. Shoppers who insist on buying brand names pay a premium price for that name recognition, though—like Marge Simpson and her "Burly" paper towels—they may justify the added expense by the perception that they are getting greater value. Moreover, by increasing the sales volume and showing growth, branding often helps to raise a company's share price on the stock market. When General Electric and General Motors pursued a branding strategy in the twenties, their share prices rose—a lesson that was taken, much later, by Nike and Tommy Hilfiger.[28]

During the early 1900s, there was constant friction between manufacturers, store owners, and state and federal legislators over manufacturers' use of branding to charge premium prices. A&P's campaign to establish itself as a "high-value" grocery store chain was especially vexing to manufacturers, since the company lured shoppers by charging very low prices, including "loss leaders" on popular items. In 1915, the Cream of Wheat Company refused to sell cereal to A&P because the grocery chain was pushing the price too low. After the company stopped shipping to A&P, the chain sued Cream of Wheat under the Clayton Antitrust Act for an illegal "restraint of trade." Nothing limited A&P, however, from developing its own store brand of cereal as well, and selling it at even lower prices; sales of these house brands thrived during the consumer boom of the twenties as well as the Great Depression. House brands were given an added boost by new government regulations that prevented manufacturers from making exaggerated claims for brand-name products in advertisements. From 1938, the Federal Trade Commission required advertisers to state specific reasons why a brand was good, rather than simply saying it was "superior," or playing on radio listeners' Pavlovian reflex and connecting the brand name to a catchy jingle.[29]

During World War II, shortages of raw materials and the rationing system limited the availability of brand-name products. But by the end of the war, Procter & Gamble, anticipating a great surge in consumer demand, reorganized its marketing into a "brand management" system that made one manager responsible for all aspects of each brand the company produced. The brand manager was, in effect, the head of a quasi-independent company—which pitted the managers against each other if they represented competing brands. Other companies soon followed Procter & Gamble's lead, reorganizing the firm according to brand names instead of product lines. Strong brand franchises soon developed for all consumer products, from laundry detergents and bathroom tile cleaners to electrical appliances and automobiles. And, with the rise of daytime television, new chains of supermarkets, and suburban shopping centers, Procter & Gamble's marketing strategies for Ivory soap spread to a whole family of products under the Ivory name, from laundry detergent (in powder, flake, and liquid forms) to dishwashing liquid.[30]

With new products multiplying in number, format, size, and style, the task of shopping became more complicated. Brand names served as landmarks in uncharted seas; they signaled a product's consistency and integrity, and that mysterious ratio of price and quality which indicates a good value. Brands make products "easier to read," the author of a book on "strategic brand management" says. They are "the only truly international language—a business Esperanto."[31]

Brand managers in the fifties plowed huge sums of money into advertising and fiercely competed for shelf space in stores.[32] To reach consumers more effectively, they supported a growing army of market researchers, advertising copywriters, and marketing consultants. They reengineered production systems to make products better, cheaper, and faster. They

increased their studies—especially the cases studies of business school—
to learn from different companies' success and failure. As a result of all this
work, basic household products became not just standardized, but virtu-
ally identical. By the mid-seventies, as *Consumers Reports*' scathing review
of scotch whiskeys shows, brands were distinguished more by "intangibles"
than by such "real factors" as size, ingredients, price, and effectiveness. And
shoppers knew it. When they stared at tubes of Colgate, Crest, and Aim
on the drugstore shelf, and acknowledged, in their hearts, that each toothpaste offered exactly the same protection against cavities, they chose one
because they liked the image of the brand. But market research was one
step ahead of them. Researchers in the seventies shifted from studying
shoppers' social and demographic characteristics—which didn't tell enough
about their choices—to studying the images they held of brands. If ingredients couldn't be manipulated to make completely different products,
images could: it wasn't a new formula for cola, but "youth" and "fun" that
distinguished "the Pepsi generation." This manipulation of images is what
branding is all about.[33]

Though some researchers began to use the VALS methodology to deconstruct consumers' personalities, others began to deconstruct the "personality" of the brand. Because brands are ultimately projections of human
minds, however, their personalities have to be defined by what *humans*
think and feel about them. But different humans may have entirely different
views of the same brands—especially if they are manufacturers and
consumers. To deal with these contrasting perspectives, researchers at the
Young & Rubicam advertising agency came up with two opposing
concepts. On the one hand, "brand personality statements" express what
manufacturers, retailers, and designers "*want* consumers to think and feel"
about their products. On the other hand, "brand personality profiles"
describe "what consumers *actually* . . . think and feel" about different
brands. The researchers left it to merchandising and marketing strategies—
design, advertising, and in-store displays—to bridge the gap, by manipu-
lating the personality of a brand so that "profiles" of shoppers' expectations
would eventually match producers' "statements." If they matched, shoppers would show "brand loyalty": they would keep buying a brand of toothpaste, or jeans, or automobile, regardless of whatever practical inducements
were offered to switch brands.[34]

The manipulation of intangibles led to the creation of special branded
stores and placing them in new consumer environments. During the seven-

ties and eighties, many retail merchants placed them in "urban entertainment destinations," or UEDs. These projects appealed to several influential groups—not only to consumer products executives who were trying to establish an image for their company, but also to national, and even multinational, real estate developers and local elected officials desperate to find new economic opportunities. They believed that revitalizing the retail trail would create an excitement that, in turn, could stimulate tourism and investment; in city after city, they were proved right. The restoration of Faneuil Hall and Quincy Marketplace in Boston, and the redevelopment of Baltimore's Inner Harbor, turned old industrial warehouses and derelict downtown streets into a "festival marketplace" of shops and restaurants. The Lower Manhattan loft neighborhood of SoHo entered the retail boom, with art galleries competing for space against dozens of new clothing, shoe, and furniture stores. In San Diego, the architect Jon Jerde, working with the development firm Ernest W. Hahn Inc., transformed the declining downtown into a colorful shopping district called Horton Plaza. UEDs soon became the fastest-growing form of commercial development from Maine to Hawaii. Despite their varied designs and local heritage, they all provided a standardized backdrop for tourism, leisure play, and shopping— an ideal environment for branded stores.[35]

Critics charged that UEDs just moved the uniform design package of a suburban mall—initially inspired by lively downtown streets—back into the city's core. But Jon Jerde insisted he was designing a more social, and more humane, environment. He wanted to recreate the dynamic public centers you still find in towns in Tuscany and Umbria, and install them in the decaying centers of modern cities.[36] Jerde used oversize neon signs, bright colors, and decorative water fountains to establish a sense of place and scale and to enhance the experience of strolling around. To the degree that he did recreate some of the sensual qualities of old Tuscan cities, he did so within an entirely modern grammar of plate glass, electricity, and commuting by automobile—which was also the lingua franca of the suburban mall. Since Jerde was hired to design similar downtown developments around the world, the same elements pervaded the Fremont Street Experience in Las Vegas, CityWalk in Los Angeles, and Canal City in Fukuoka, Japan—all of which were dedicated to shopping, eating, and tourism and offered the experience of shopping in branded stores. This made a pleasurable environment to be sure, but it also created a more standardized space of shopping than had ever existed. The lovely Canal City,

located on an island that was reclaimed from industrial wasteland, has
fountains shooting up in a random pattern from the granite ground, upscale
clothing boutiques, and Chinese and fast-food restaurants—but all this is
as typical of Los Angeles as it is of Fukuoka.

By the eighties, consumer goods companies faced a dramatically unstable
business environment. Though steadfast brands like Tide and Levis still
earned the greatest profits, consumers wanted more individualized products that also offered good value. Companies' overseas rivals made the same
products, or knockoffs, at a lower cost. At home, a volatile stock market
played havoc with their share prices, while aggressive investment managers
pressed them to increase shareholders' value. Finance, not manufacturing,
seemed to rule the world, setting new priorities. Responding to these
changes, the CEOs of such giants of the industry as Procter & Gamble
and Nabisco replaced the brand managers who had led them through the
postwar consumer boom. They wanted new ways to sell their products.[37]

Like the steel- and automakers who also found themselves in a crisis
situation, consumer products companies tried to modernize. Conservative
boards of directors began to take greater risks. Board after board replaced
experienced, but often stodgy, CEOs with more dynamic salesmen, and
aimed for the gigantic corporate size that would annihilate smaller rivals.
After all, big firms enjoyed many advantages. They got discounts on advertising rates from magazines and television, rolled out campaigns in many
cities at once, and pushed stores aggressively to promote their brands.
Equally important was their ability to master "market segmentation."
Marketing ten different kinds of cookies, or automobiles, or jeans, gave a
company the opportunity to capture consumers in ten different ways—or
to capture ten different groups of consumers. Dominating a market niche
enabled big companies to establish a near monopoly.[38]

Beefing up their presence in the marketplace was important to consumer
products companies because many brands had been around for so long,
they had little potential for growth. Marketing managers viewed the groups
of consumers they had courted and nurtured since the sixties—teenagers,
women, and affluent households—as increasingly sophisticated but also
footloose shoppers. After decades of reading consumer guides, shoppers
were more demanding than ever and no less unpredictable. If they were
captivated by a new style or product—Air Jordans or soft cookies, to take
two product innovations of the eighties—they simply switched brands,

making or breaking a company's sales volume and causing extreme variations in its share price. Companies had to appeal to consumers' imaginations in order to show hard numbers to stock analysts.

Marketing different brands of the same basic goods enabled companies
to compete for the discretionary spending of the many baby boomers who
were setting up homes, raising children, and nearing the peak of their
earning power. This age group had a deep interest in aesthetically distinctive products. Their attraction to cultural difference had been stoked since
the sixties by writers, chefs, artists, and all sorts of reviewers, while media
like *New York* magazine, and increasingly the *Times*, waxed critical of standardized commodities. With the "sneaker revolution" quickly following
the success of designer jeans, formerly humble products that were dominated by a seemingly generic brand name—like canvas "Keds" and denim
"Levis"—morphed into dynamic, expensive, "aspirational" brands.[39]

As the building of Niketown suggests, companies hoped that the social
space of the store would promote this process. But how? The archetypal
shopping spaces of the previous century had been "disenchanted"—or
reached a point of exhaustion. Big department stores continued to decline,
and the five-and-dime seemed hopelessly old-fashioned. Supermarket chains
saturated the market, and shopping malls competed for the same mobile
shoppers. Asked to come up with a new type of store, market researchers
connected the social space of the store to the personality of the brand. By
chance, perhaps, they stumbled back to a concept created by the marketing
expert Pierre Martineau in the fifties, when he wrote about "the personality of the retail store."[40]

Pierre Martineau says that stores don't only offer an array of goods, they
offer symbolic values—a "wide range of intangibles." He emphasizes that
shoppers perceive a store "partly by its *functional* qualities and partly by
an aura of *psychological* attributes." Maybe a shopper will tell you she
chooses a store on the basis of price, he says, "but plumb her mind . . . and
you will find that she is not the 'economic woman' that American businessmen have so long and glibly assumed." She wants even the most routine
stores—supermarkets—to provide "a *pleasurable* experience." According to
Martineau, a rich shopper is the most attentive to these intangible values.
Like the middle-class women whom I interviewed, she wants to know
"whether the symbolic meaning of the store reflects her status and her style
of life." Martineau also describes how a store that is mainly oriented toward
men can create a space for aspirational shopping as well. He praises the

owner of a successful sports car dealership, who "has imbued his establishment with the symbolic appeal of the foreign sports car." "All the salesmen are . . . recognizably British," and have appropriate accents; they wear linen pants and blazers decorated with Sports Car Club of America emblems. This automobile showroom is an amazing prototype, thirty years ahead of its time, of Ralph Lauren's flagship store on Madison Avenue. It demonstrates how the social space of the store can be manipulated, in Martineau's prescient term, as a "total environment."[41]

Though Martineau notes that women shoppers, the rich, and members of ethnic minorities often hold different views of the same store, he is interested in a store's ability to *exploit* social differences rather than minimize them. In the thirties, as we have seen, Woolworth's could attract women of all social classes; by the late fifties, however, higher-status women want to escape from the pseudodemocratic mingling and the lack of discrimination among shoppers that they find in such stores. "The upper-status woman cannot conceive of herself shopping in the subway store [i.e., the bargain basement] of a large department store," he writes. "Regardless of bargains, she is repelled by the thought of odors, milling crowds, poorly educated clerks. Conversely, the wage earner's wife is not going to expose herself to the possibility of humiliation by shopping in the quality store, whether it be Bonwit Teller or Neiman Marcus or Lord & Taylor—even if she has the money to buy something there." Like the "status seekers" described in Vance Packard's best-selling book, which also appeared in the late fifties, Martineau's shoppers choose where they shop to distinguish themselves from lesser mortals.

Yet Martineau fails to discuss the other social advantages that a store can offer. Stores are not only a means of affirming social status, they are also a means of seeking, and expressing, intimacy, sociability, and community. The women whom Martineau interviewed emphasize how much they value chatting with sales clerks and store owners—though these interactions, especially in bigger, more bureaucratic stores, tend to reflect and reinforce social status differences. "The upper-status woman expects a respect and a restraint from the salesclerk that would be interpreted by the wage earner's wife as formal and forbidding," Martineau says. "The family atmosphere and the great emphasis on savings which attract the Sears customer are distasteful to the Marshall Field shopper."[42]

Shoppers' loyalty to specific stores seemed unshaken in the fifties. By the seventies, however, the future of many traditional retail stores was in doubt. High labor costs discouraged merchants from hiring more sales clerks and training them better. Discount stores undersold them dramatically. Automation enabled them to shift more of the work of shopping to self-service, but it also raised the prospect of "push-button shopping" that could be done at home, at the shopper's convenience—though this remained, until the development of Internet shopping two decades later, a figment of the science fiction imagination. Most important, retail stores competed with more channels of distribution than ever before, from mailorder sales to catalog showrooms and warehouse stores. Yet researchers argued that shoppers would always prefer to shop at a store that provided meaning and symbols. So they urged merchants to manipulate the intangible values: "services, fashion, and prestige."[43]

Most stores were not ready for a makeover. The transparency imposed by universal stores—symbolized by the iconic shopping cart, price tags, and standardized displays—blocked efforts to reimagine a store's "personality." And besides, many stores sold the same products in the same range of brands—the big brands that were advertised on national television. To offer consumers what they saw on TV, both department stores and drugstores sold Revlon cosmetics, and all supermarkets sold Campbell's soup. These brands enjoyed name recognition—but they were not associated with the "personality of specific stores.[44]

It's odd to think of The Gap following in the footsteps of Yves Saint Laurent. Yet The Gap was one of the first American retailers, and surely the most prominent chain, to set up its stores as if they were Rive Gauche boutiques and capitalize on their personality.[45] The Gap had begun, in the sixties, with a distinctive image value. Founded in the Bay Area, around San Francisco, as an "alternative" to traditional clothing stores, it specialized in casual clothing sold in an informal atmosphere. Immediately, The Gap was recognized as a space for, and a symbol of, the youth market. Sales grew dramatically when the seventies commercialized the sixties' counterculture, and young people shopped for products that had special appeal to their own age group, in their own kinds of stores. After The Gap expanded into a national chain, the store's founder and owner, Donald G. Fisher, became one of the four hundred richest men in America.

By the early eighties, however, The Gap had run out of steam. It was seen as a store where teenagers shopped for cheap jeans. Since it was still associated with the dress-down, hippie counterculture of the sixties, it did not attract either an older crowd that was now more interested in dressing for success or younger shoppers who wanted to buy designer jeans. Instead of admitting defeat, however, Fisher looked for new managers to remake the business. He hired as CEO Mickey Drexler, who had begun his career at Bloomingdale's under the merchandising master Marvin Traub; Drexler had recently breathed new life into the women's specialty clothing chain Ann Taylor by building on the store's "personality." Drexler transferred the image value of a designer label to the store, giving Ann Taylor, and then The Gap, a special aura.[46]

Working directly with the store's director of visual display, Drexler recast the entire array of merchandising strategies by which The Gap created image value. He had the walls of all Gap stores painted bright white, and piled the jeans and T-shirts on counters, in neat stacks, by color, like gumdrops. He changed the lettering of the logo. Most important, he had this logo placed on the label of all products sold in Gap stores. From a manufacturing point of view, Mickey Drexler reduced The Gap's dependence on its major supplier, Levi Strauss, and put the retail chain at the center of a network of contracts with numerous small factories around the world. From a cultural point of view, however, he transformed The Gap from a store where you shopped for a durable, stable, inexpensive commodity—jeans and a T-shirt—to a store where you shopped because the place, itself, was cool. The Gap took generic products like jeans that were previously associated with traditional manufacturers, and no-brand generics like T-shirts, and used them to brand the store.

These branding strategies led to a great expansion. "In the early 1980s," according to a brief biography of Drexler, "the Gap Inc. was a moderately successful apparel chain that sold ho-hum casual wear at bargain-basement prices. By the next decade, the company had mushroomed into a $2.5 billion fashion empire comprising over 1,200 stores known for selling hip, designer-quality clothing to millions of Americans of all ages from all walks of life."[47]

In the annals of the retail industry, The Gap's success is much more impressive than that of Yves Saint Laurent's boutiques. The Gap showed that trading on image value can work just as well for a casual clothing store chain as it does for a famous designer. After Drexler and his team developed a strong visual image for The Gap, this image was reproduced all around the world, in every material and personal medium—from product design and in-store displays to shopping bags, advertisements, and employees' dress and attitude. The coherence of the image ensures that the products and the social space of the store reinforce each other, and the word for this reinforcement is "branding." Oddly enough, Gap shoppers never felt exploited by these strategies. As VALS researchers would say, they felt The Gap expressed their identity.

During the eighties and nineties, branded stores were adopted by a huge number of consumer products companies, many of which—like Patagonia and REI—made clothes, but most of which—like Disney and Nike—had never even operated a mail-order catalog. At first glance, it seems paradoxical that a film company like Disney would think a *store* could strengthen its public image. But branded stores are like movie theaters; they offer individuals access to a central image and give shoppers entry in to the world of meaning—in Disney's case, a world of "fun" and "family"—under the company's control. It is vital to remember that branded stores do control a world of meaning. Just as the collaborative team consisting of a film's director, producers, and actors controls the images projected to the audience seated in a darkened cinema, so the company that owns a branded store controls the images projected to a mobile crowd of shoppers. In some ways, a branded store is the *best* way to capitalize on image value. It makes a company's image concrete and coherent and creates a synergy between its different product lines, while eliminating the presence of rival products. By 2000, when Disney had opened more than seven hundred stores around the world, the company proclaimed: "For some people, [the stores are] the only tangible, three-dimensional experience they get with the brand." The store makes the brand's aura real.[48]

But branding transforms the social space of the store. When I stood inside the door of Niketown and looked at shoppers' faces, I realized that they weren't coming because of low prices, high quality, or a wide selection of goods. Neither were they coming to socialize with the owner or sales clerks. They were coming to be with the *brand*. This accounts for the aura of the branded store. We go to the Louvre to commune with the *Mona Lisa*; we go to Niketown to commune with the brand. From the company's point of view, branded stores deepen consumers' loyalty to their products. From the shoppers' point of view, branded stores deepen our ability to commune with mass culture. We actively make this culture ours by *shopping* in branded stores.

This is especially important because branded stores further the illusion that consumer culture is democratic. No one is excluded from shopping in a Gap or Disney store, and if you can't afford to shop for shoes at Prada, you can go to the less expensive, but equally branded Steve Madden or Nine West. More dramatically—but just as inclusively—the Ralph Lauren company provides access to the brand's aura at different price points without offending anyone's social status. We can buy "Ralph Lauren" by passing under the gaze of a uniformed doorman at the Madison Avenue flagship store, or by taking the escalator up to the "Ralph" boutique at Lord & Taylor and the "Lauren" boutique at Macy's. We can even buy "Ralph Lauren" house paint at a Home Depot store. By separating product lines into separate but equally branded spaces, the company has solved the conundrum of how to capitalize *democratically* on image value, despite the fact that shoppers are still segmented by income, age, and social class.

Branded stores tell shoppers that the best way they can have access to the brand's charisma is by having fun. The Pleasant Company, a small mail-order firm that manufactures dolls representing a girl's life in different eras of American history, runs a multilevel store on North Michigan Avenue, in Chicago, where you can shop for the dolls and their accessories, attend a fashion show, and order a teatime snack. At the NBA Store on Fifth Avenue, you can buy a basketball jersey with your favorite player's name and number on it, watch the tape of a professional game on a video monitor, and toss balls at hoops on a small but serviceable court. Shopping in a branded store is a form of amusement.

Like branding itself, this isn't new. In the nineteenth century, the United States was the first nation to insert amusements concessions into the exhibition space of world's fairs and to add popular entertainments like horse racing, minstrel shows, exotic food stands, and ethnic restaurants to the agricultural demonstrations at county fairs. The great department stores offered shoppers restaurants, musical performances, and art exhibitions. They gradually reduced and finally eliminated these attractions—until the seventies, when economic recession and stagflation forced merchants to think again about providing "atmospherics." In the long run, the "entertainment" in a UED means "spending money."[49]

Retailers justified the changes they made during the entertainment-conscious nineties by emphasizing "bread"—the cultural value of the goods we buy—and "circuses"—the sensual and emotional high we get from being in a crowd-pleasing attraction. I musn't be too playful here, for both approaches capitalize on shoppers' aspirations and feelings, rather than on the quality of merchandise or bargain prices. With bread and circuses, the social space of the store *engages* us, and overcomes our resistance to buying.[50]

Whether we go into The Gap, Ralph Lauren, or Sneaker Stadium, we enter a world that deliberately projects who we are and what we want to be. The merchandise is displayed in vignettes that show a specific attitude, and we shoppers are skilled at reading their subtle meanings. Instead of connecting an item of merchandise—a shirt, a bookcase, or a pair of shoes—with a quality of *goods* shoppers admire, the social space of the store connects an entire range of products—and thus the image value of the designer or retailer—with the quality of *life* we desire. This romanticization of life through displays of goods is turned into "lifestyle." And stores can be frighteningly efficient at embodying it. "When our products and store environments become truly interdependent," a visual display director at Old Navy writes, "we create a synergy—a 'lifestyle' if you will—that actually consumes the consumer." [51] Help me, please!, I want to shout: the model room has come to life.

But in these models we see our daydreams. We see ourselves enacting a role in the "movie of life."[52] In an IKEA display of blue-checked bed linens and Scandinavian pine, we are homey; in a video at Sneaker Stadium, we are competitive runners. Amid the gardening tools and potted herbs at Smith and Hawken, we are purposeful but gracious cultivators of our nest; we are the very image of the brand—a tasteful blend of New California and Old England.

Beneath the surface of freedom and fun, lifestyle shopping demands that we submit to the retailers' vision. As if to deny our claims of uniqueness and individuality, the settings in which we play out this drama are reproduced in thousands of chain stores "in better malls across the country" and around the world. If we want to play, we have to buy the dream. "Stores . . . offer a Faustian bargain," Paul Goldberger cautions. "Step into our commercial world, and we will give you the kind of communal excitement that is hard to find this side of Disneyland." In other words, to get the pleasure, we have to be a *buying* public.[53]

Disneyland has shaped much of our thinking about the social space of stores. As a merchandising model, Disneyland suggests the advantages a store can draw from providing "circuses"—attractions besides the merchandise—in order to give shoppers a "memorable experience." Expanding on this point, the business consultants B. Joseph Pine and James H. Gilmore argue that we now live in an "experience economy." Whatever it's selling,

they say, a store must try to "touch" customers by some emotional or spectacular element, so shoppers take away with them a feeling of joy—and
perhaps also of awe—they will always remember. Pine and Gilmore see
this strategy not only as a means of reenchanting the store, and contributing
to businesses' drive to improve the bottom line, but also as the beginning
of a historically new stage of economic development—one characterized
by more abstract commodities. Yet aren't these abstract commodities the
"intangibles" that branding experts have talked about for years? What makes
them special is that shoppers will pay a premium price for experiencing
them—as long as the experience is truly "memorable."[54]

Like branded stores, "experience retail" responds to a crisis of consumption, in which too many goods chase too few buyers. As the marketing
experts tell us, experience retail is a store that tells a story. But we shoppers are not the only audience. By the 1980s, capturing the attention of
Wall Street analysts was vital to all firms' ability to raise investment capital.
And these analysts, in their own way, shop for value. Though they are trying
to buy—and sell—stocks rather than underwear or personal computers,
they are looking for bargains in the form of "undervalued" stocks; they are
attracted by brand names when they evaluate a company's potential for
growth. So operating a branded store is not only a way of making a
company's intangible aura tangible to consumers, it also sends an important message to Wall Street.

By the end of the twentieth century, Wall Street was no longer interested in the tangible qualities of products. Financial analysts regarded
companies as assemblages of brands. When they applauded Ralph Lauren's
acquisition of the small Canadian clothing chain Club Monaco, for
example, they didn't care that the new division didn't conform to Lauren's
core vision. They loved that he was diversifying his product lines and
hedging his financial risks. According to the chief economist at one investment firm, the array of stores that Ralph Lauren now controlled would
"take market share on Wall Street" for the company as a whole. "Ralph
certainly sees Club Monaco as a branded retail strategy," another analyst
said. "A branded retail strategy can be successful and highly competitive."
Though these comments are a million miles away from the designer's image,
they emphasize how important it is for his story to interest Wall Street.[55]

And all for the payoff of raising the value of shares. During the nineties,
some of the most prominent designer-led companies, like Donna Karan,
went public, or were acquired, like Jil Sander and Helmut Lang, by larger,

multinational corporations, led by Prada and LVMH (Moet Hennessy Louis Vuitton). "If you're going to be public [i.e., publicly owned], you have to play the game," the president of Chanel Inc. told *Women's Wear Daily*. "Wall Street demands a growth curve that's at a very steep angle, and if you don't want your executive stock options to be used for wallpaper, you have to meet Wall Street expectations." The president of Lola Inc., a "contemporary" clothing company that sells the XOXO brand, confirmed, "The stock market is relentless. They want volume. They want growth."[56]

Lifestyle stores seem to provide what Wall Street requires. More than an interactive framework for the exchange of goods, these stores surround us with delightful products we can smell, touch, and buy, and awaken our emotions in a densely imagined environment—all in all, fulfilling our aesthetic sense of value. But lifestyle stores also trade in image value. They connect the narratives of designers' displays to our daydreams of self-improvement, and then they connect our daydreams to investors' dreams of profit. The designers' drive to create desirable products; the shoppers' longing for bargains, variety, and social status; the investors' demand for sales volume and growth: the big plate-glass windows of lifestyle stores reflect these different, and often contradictory, demands for value.

But a most perplexing problem remains. How, over time, can a brand maintain its value? For investment analysts, it is important to grow the business, to drive up sales volume and stock prices, usually by rolling out the brand and its derivatives in as many arenas as possible. This is how to strengthen *financial* value. But for designers, the most important goal is to maintain their products' integrity, their overarching uniqueness, and their *cultural* value. To prevent "diluting" the identity of the brand, designers want to keep their products exclusive—which often requires keeping the sales volume low. It requires them to set up their own branded stores. Calvin Klein jeans would not be "Calvin Klein" jeans if you could buy them at Sears.[57]

Lifestyle shopping is really a business model. Even if the image of any brand, whatever it is, can be mechanically reproduced, the model suggests that the aura will remain. So I'm not surprised when the design of the Brooks Brothers store on Fifth Avenue becomes a template for the chain. The Kansas City Brooks Brothers store, on Country Club Plaza, uses the same limestone and brushed stainless steel facade, marble and cherry wood floors, white walls, and natural light that were used to make the store on

Fifth Avenue distinctive. "The old store was very, very dark," the store manager in Kansas City says. "The Fifth Avenue store in New York and the Post Street store in San Francisco have this design, and this [is] a perfected version of those."[58]

Yet Brooks Brothers would do well to begin searching for the *next* new image. Trying to establish a brand that will appeal to the same group of young, impulsive, fashion-conscious shoppers leads to an endless duplication of products and massively standardized stores. Banana Republic, Ann Taylor, and J. Press all directly compete with Brooks Brothers on pretty much the same stylistic terrain. Ironically, not long after the Fifth Avenue store opened, HartMarx, a men's suit and sportswear manufacturer, created yet another lifestyle store at 666 Fifth Avenue, sandwiched between Brooks Brothers and the NBA. HartMarx wants to use this store to promote its Hickey-Freeman label as a "traditional, yet sexy, American brand." How many lifestyle stores can one block of Fifth Avenue provide?[59]

The competition between branded retailers isn't limited to the social space of the store. Brooks Brothers and the other main contenders for the casual-Fridays market—J. Press and Banana Republic—also operate mail-order catalogs and websites. At one point, Banana Republic experimented with bringing the social space of the store to three dot-com and investment banking firms, whose employees were assumed to be too busy to shop. At each firm, Banana Republic presented an evening fashion show, supplemented by a bar and entertainment, and followed this with a three-day, in-office ministore, complete with sales clerks and personal shoppers.[60]

Just as all branded stores don't succeed, however, so branded stores don't succeed all the time. They are most successful during periods of economic expansion, when shoppers have the money to pay premium prices for name recognition. And like any other kind of store, branded stores eventually run into trouble. Some begin to look déclassé because they have traded on the same image for so many years. Others neglect to develop new products that might attract new, and younger, shoppers. Companies that lose their momentum in an economic downturn can't afford to maintain the spectacle. During the Asian economic crisis that began in the late nineties, Nike stopped opening Niketowns and sent tons of unsold shoes to outlet stores. It remodeled the store on Fifty-seventh Street, so now it looks less like an airport and more like The Athlete's Foot.[61]

I know what the phrase "lifestyle factory" means. We have reached the point in mass consumption where the store as well as the manufacturer mass-produces an image. Image value is enhanced by constant repetition and reproduction—on every street, in every mode, in every channel; on billboards, TV, and pop-up Internet advertisements; in multiple branches, mailboxes, and wireless apps. But the sellers' desire to bring the store to us, and our own desire for convenience, have altered shopping for the worse. Despite all the claims that are made about "experience retail," shopping has become a less social, and a more abstract, experience. We go to stores to commune with brands rather than to make a community.

When I pass the new Brooks Brothers store, I daydream that I am in a horizontal shopping mall composed entirely of upscale chain stores. They all look alike. Whether I am on Fifth Avenue or at the Galleria, in Chicago or Milan, I am in a lifestyle factory—the empire of brand names.

9

the zen
of internet shopping

"I think, therefore I save."
—Advertisement for Priceline.com, 2002

I have always been a skeptic about shopping on the Internet.

When my friend Paul said he preferred to buy khakis online from Lands' End instead of rooting around on shelves to find his size at The Gap, I thought he was overreacting.

When my colleague Ted smiled and said he'd rather shop on the Internet so he wouldn't have to deal with the snippy clerks at Bloomingdale's, I was sure he was teasing.

When Wall Street analysts praised Jeff Bezos, the founder of Amazon.com, and Pierre Omidyar, the eBay guru, I remained unimpressed by the dot-com hype.

So I felt as though I had been right all along when dot-com stocks crashed in the year 2000. And I was smug when Marian Burros, a senior food writer at the *New York Times*, said you couldn't trust online grocers to send you the freshest green peas in season, and, one by one, like peas in a pod, the online grocers failed.

But then I watched my friend Colin sell his late father's economics books on eBay, and heard him brag about selling stray sections of Nixon-era copies of the *Times*, which he found in a drawer around the house, for eight or ten dollars apiece. And my editor, Dave, bought a half-dozen CDs of bands he liked for half price on Amazon. Adam proudly told me that he buys Greek soap on the Internet from a distributor in Chicago. Even Phil bought a rice cooker on the Internet when he didn't have time to go down to Chinatown and look around in the little stores.

So I watched carefully to see what my cousin Jerry would do after he decided to get into digital photography.

He needed a digital camera, of course, and this posed the usual problems of how to shop for a piece of complicated equipment. Though the technology of digital photography is still new, there are already so many models to choose from. And like computers, new digital cameras are getting smaller all the time. Jerry thought he would have to hold them, one by one, in his hand, feel their weight, and get used to their shape—so different from the bulk of traditional cameras, even the fairly small 35 mm's. A camera is such a personal thing, too. He'd have to place each one carefully next to his eye, squint through the lens, pretend to focus on a shot, and click the shutter—no, with a digital camera, you actually look at the monitor and press the button. Too many things to think about! So Jerry decided to begin by buying a scanner. He will need one eventually, and, after buying the scanner, he can continue to take pictures with the cameras he already owns and view the negatives on his computer.

Jerry's shopping begins when he turns on his PC and logs onto the Internet. But this is the way most of us shop for electronics equipment these days.[1] Julia, Maria and Anna, the teenage girls I interviewed in East New York, and Cindy, who wanted the perfect pair of leather pants—they all do research on new clothes by making the rounds of different stores. But men, who are still the main buyers of electronic equipment, do research on items they want by shopping around on different websites. Jerry does his research on the Nikon, Minolta, and Polaroid websites. Just as if he were prowling the aisles at Bloomingdale's or Circuit City, he sizes up the models and prices and takes note of discounts and rebates, as well as special deals on delivery fees. Like the people who travel out of New York City to shop at a suburban mall, he searches for out-of-state vendors who don't charge sales tax. He prints out the details on models he likes, and then he looks up reviews of these and other scanners on www.imaging-resource.com. For comparison shopping, he checks the Pricewatch and PriceSCAN websites. Though Jerry thinks these sites do not have good prices on digital cameras, he does like their prices on scanners.

When he wants technical information, however, Jerry picks up the phone: he wants to talk to someone "in person." During the whole shopping process, the only kind of conversation he really enjoys is a good give-and-take with a technical support person at Nikon, Dell Computer, or the DSL department at Verizon. Between making these calls and going online,

"Go home and shop!": ad for Internet shopping site, 2003.

Jerry relentlessly buttonholes friends who already own a scanner or know something about electronics. "After all," he says, "a scanner costs three thousand dollars."

During the next three weeks, Jerry keeps going back online to see whether prices have come down. Like a day trader who accesses the Internet every hour to check stock prices, Jerry goes online every day to check scanners' prices. He briefly wonders whether he should look for a scanner on eBay, but then he remembers the friend of a friend who bought a defective IBM Thinkpad on eBay, and the vendor wouldn't give his money back. Anyway, by this point, Jerry has decided which scanner he really wants, and he gets on the phone again. A real conversation with another person provides more of an opportunity for bargaining, and he has been lucky in the past. Sometimes calling a vendor directly nets him an even cheaper price than the one listed on the web, especially when the vendor wants to move an old model or clinch a deal.

When he dials a merchant's "800" number and the salesman he talks to names a pretty good price, Jerry decides to wait no longer. He never places an order online, not even on a secure site, not since the credit card company called and told him about the two thousand dollars of charges someone racked up against his account, and Jerry suspects they got his account number from a website where he recently made a purchase. This time, after giving the salesman his credit card number over the phone, all he has to do is to wait anxiously for several days until United Parcel Service (UPS) brings the package to his door. So Jerry joins the twenty-six million Americans who go online every day and buy something—the same number of people, small but growing, who use the Internet to search for a map, look up an address or a phone number, listen to music, or share files.[2]

It sounds easy, right? But as Jerry's story shows, Internet shopping is filled with paradoxes.

Until we began to shop electronically, in the 1990s, we actually believed it would make shopping easier. Science fiction writers, beginning with Isaac Asimov, had been predicting since the sixties that some form of automation—smart machines—would enable us to satisfy our daily needs for food and clothing quickly, efficiently, and rationally, without moving from our living rooms or agonizing over choices. Though these visions rested on the introduction of futuristic robots that would take our orders and serve us with goods, it was more mundane innovations, carried out by human workers, that gradually brought those predictions to life.

The interstate highway system, begun in the fifties, made it possible for the already familiar, chocolate-brown UPS trucks to deliver packages faster. Bigger planes and cheaper fuel enabled start-up companies like Federal Express, which depended on air shipments, to compete with UPS. These companies made "overnight" deliveries a part of our shopping language. But shippers were only able to begin processing our orders because they had every expectation of getting paid. Riding a boom of their own in the early seventies, bank-issued credit cards—now known as Mastercard and Visa—coordinated the swelling flows of long-distance purchase payments. And "800" toll-free telephone numbers, first used in 1978, communicated the desire to buy from shoppers in Seattle to merchants in Maine.

Innovation came more swiftly in the computer field. Personal computers began to sell widely in the eighties, and a few forward-looking users hooked themselves up to the World Wide Web as soon as access to it became available outside of the military and scientific research establishment in the early nineties. At first, the technology just didn't exist to move easily around a website, which is important to shoppers who want not only to read verbal descriptions of goods but also to see pictures of them. This was the same problem faced by the first generation of catalog merchants back in the 1870s. When Montgomery Ward and Sears, Roebuck started the mail-order business, there was no way they could print illustrations alongside the text. A whole generation of their customers had to grow up before the development of lithography enabled the merchants to add black-and-white line illustrations to their catalogs. But in the 1990s, when at least four different teams of computer programmers in the United States and Europe worked feverishly to develop software that would make it easy to view pictures online, it took only a few years for them to create GUI (graphical user interface) browsers. After Marc Andreesen, working in a research lab, developed an easy-to-use browser that placed images on the same screen as text, and marketed it vigorously on the Internet, it took only six months for the recently formed Netscape company to bring the "point-and-click" technology to a broader public. At that moment, in 1995, shopping with the newly named Netscape Navigator seemed dramatically easier than getting into your car and driving to the mall.[3]

Rapid improvements in Netscape's software, followed by Microsoft's eagerness to supply its own browser—Internet Explorer—for free, encouraged many more people to use the web, and a burst of creative effort by new entrepreneurs and web designers led to explosive growth in the

number of sites to browse through. Amazon and eBay, the major innova-
tors, were founded in the mid-nineties, and they were closely followed by
hundreds of websites selling airplane tickets, groceries, clothing, automobiles, houses—anything you could think of selling, including stocks and
pornography.

The novelty of using high-tech computers to make routine purchases
caught everyone's imagination. Interest in Internet shopping enflamed the
media, which chronicled venture capitalists and status consumers with
equal enthusiasm. By1999, just four years after the Netscape browser went
on sale, Internet shopping struck the media mother lode. With twenty-six
million people logging onto shopping sites each *week* of the holiday shopping season between Thanksgiving and Christmas, *Time* magazine put Jeff
Bezos on its cover as Person of the Year. Even if you hadn't yet shopped on
the Internet, you couldn't help reading about Amazon.com.[4]

Internet shopping rapidly became easier to handle. Downstream, clever
writers of computer code made websites quicker and more logical to navigate. Upstream, new automation at the warehouse processed orders faster.
Pickers used bar code scanners to find items on the shelves, and sophisticated conveyor belts brought the merchandise to a giant assembly line that
sorted orders and loaded them onto trucks. Catalog merchants like L. L.
Bean built state-of-the-art order fulfillment centers that included their own
FedEx facilities.[5]

All these technological innovations are subverted, however, by a stunning discovery. The unprecedented speed of viewing merchandise, processing an order, and delivering goods to our door does not decrease the
time and effort we invest in shopping. Regardless of how fast we get
the goods into our hands, we're actually shopping more.

What the Internet does accomplish is to minimize the social space of
shopping. Whether you're like Ted, who hates to deal with snippy sales
clerks, or Paul, who never finds what he needs in the store—or if you're
like Artemio, who had that nasty run-in with the security guards at
Tiffany's—electronic shopping promises to filter out all the social "noise"
and bother of going out to shop. The Internet promises to help us make
a detour around all the gatekeepers, and put our hands on what we value.

But what do we really value? Both market research and common sense
tell us that we cherish time, money, and a wide choice of goods. Like the
physical space of supermarkets and malls, however, the virtual space of
Internet shopping works against—rather than for—these values.

Retail websites want to be "sticky"—which means that once we enter, we have to spend more time on them. And the longer we remain on a site, the more money we'll spend. This is true no matter what we do when we're on a site—in fact, the more caught up we get watching multimedia presentations on REI.com, ogling the models in a fashion show on Victoria's Secret, or downloading music files illegally from the early Napster, the more we tend to buy.[6] Even if we go online with the specific purpose of paying the lowest price for an item we have already chosen, we can't reduce our shopping time, since a single website never offers *enough* information to make satisfactory comparisons. So, regardless of how many minutes we spend online, it's never enough—as Paul would like—to prevent us from shopping more. Neither can we shop—as Artemio would prefer—without revealing who we are, for through the widespread use of "cookies," electronic databases constantly collect information on where we browse and what we buy. Nor can we shop—as Ted says he wants to do—without being badgered to buy more, for the Internet continually bombards us with pop-up advertisements and banner promotions. Even worse, like the snippiest sales clerk in the snootiest store, the variable pricing programs used by many consumer sites favor new users and frequent customers over occasional shoppers.

But the subtlest insult of all is that online shopping encourages us to commune more, rather than less, with commodities. Whether we go online to shop at work, or at home, or in the wee hours of the morning, shopping infiltrates and overcomes our lives. And we become less critical shoppers; we become more likely to just sit down and buy.

Paradox #1: The Internet Makes Us Shop More

Though we think of the Internet as a means of easing the burden of shopping, it really keeps us online and buying goods. At first, this seems impossible. Our home computers vie for our attention with other means of distraction—radio, television, telephone, chats with partners, quality time with kids—as well as with routine chores like cleaning out the refrigerator and going out of doors. Like the TV, a PC can be turned off as well as on. And just as we switch channels on television, so we also surf the web. Marketers complain that our ability to turn off a website gives us "multiple exits."

When you think about it, moreover, shopping on the Internet gives us very little sensual pleasure. You don't get a strong whiff of perfume or freshly baked bread while logging onto a shopping site the way you do when you push the revolving door into a department store or bakery. It's not like seeing the vibrant panorama of fresh fruits and vegetables at the farmers' market. Neither are there immediate giveaways to bribe you for your attention—no offer of a free spritz from the nicely dressed woman holding out an atomizer at the cosmetics counter, no sample of crackers and dip from the man in an apron at the end of the supermarket aisle.

Even when you buy something online, the Internet does not deliver it for your instant gratification. You have to deal with the conveniences and conveyances of consumer society: the security passwords, credit card approvals, delivery schedules, and—I speak from personal woe—perfidious DSL lines that are extremely fast at bringing images to the screen but have a too frequent habit of going down. The timing may be no better with a hybrid "clicks and mortar" arrangement, that lets you order merchandise online and then pick it up at a nearby store. When the "Online Shopper" who writes a weekly column for the *New York Times* tries to buy her ideal car online, she finds the closest match on a dealer's lot hundreds of miles away, and it will take the factory at least three months to produce this model.[7]

There is, nonetheless, an aura of instant gratification that Internet shoppers buy into. "You order it, and the next day it's in your home!" says Ted. Speaking more realistically, if you shop at work or during the night, you can make a purchase immediately instead of just thinking about it until you can go to the store. In that case, gratification comes from the act of making the purchase rather than taking possession of the thing you have bought.[8] This is a more abstract kind of gratification than we are used to. Instead of declaring "I'll take it—wrap it up!" to a clerk in a store, when we make a purchase online, we press the mouse, hear it click, and watch a check mark appear on the screen: we learn to feel gratified by the *anticipation* of taking possession of the thing we have bought. Though the waiting period is far shorter than when we "visit" a stereo or an expensive pair of shoes in the store for weeks until we can afford to buy them, it separates the act of buying from taking possession. These changes in the cognitive stages of shopping move the moment of gratification to the act of buying, rather than getting, new things.

Using a point-and-click browser does give us the *feel* of instant gratification—but only in the tip of our right index finger. In the digital culture, we win by clicking the mouse on Buy it Now! and seeing an item pop up in our "shopping cart." The deadline on bids imposed by auction sites like eBay drags out the suspense of whether we've bought, and the competition of bidding intensifies the high that we get from "winning." Outside of the auction sites, we feel pleasure because the Internet just gives us a chance to "cut" the line: electronic shopping means you never have to wait for the slow-moving queue of people to reach the cash register at Macy's when the store is crowded on a Saturday afternoon. This lesson was taken by Amazon.com from the beginning, when they patented their "1-click" technology for making purchases quickly.

As the Amazon people also know, a retail website must provide a good "flow experience."[9] Clickthrough technology has to pique our interest with content or anticipate our needs with options, so that we keep clicking away on the site, moving from item to item, and making purchases. Good navigational software reproduces the no-tech way we flip through glossy magazines and mail-order catalogs with our thumb, going forward and backward in no particular order, stopping to look whenever a picture or headline catches our eye. But providing content that will guide this flow to a purchase is a great challenge to online marketers. There's no narrative in online shopping; it's just an episodic journey prodded by the interaction between shopper and text.

So online marketers turn to the science of statistics, devising on-screen prompts based on Bayesian statistics about which displays will move us on a given path.[10] You might think the website has magically divined your individual taste in novels or lingerie, but it's all a matter of good guesswork using mathematical probabilities. In marketing terms, the prompts are a means of "up-selling"; they're trying to persuade us to increase our order. When we look at a book on Amazon.com, and the website suggests more books for us to look at, it's only mimicking the counter worker who suggests French fries and a coke to go with our sandwich. On Amazon, the software shifts our attention to books that other shoppers have looked at; this is sometimes amusing, but it always catches our interest, because it relates us to a larger and somewhat mysterious social network. If I find it annoying to leap across categories, however, and see my book choices compared to clothing selections, the prompts may lose me as a shopper. It's more effective to appeal to my rationality, the way J. Crew and L. L. Bean do, when they show me photos of a T-shirt, belt, and shoes to go with a pair of jeans. Or on the Abercrombie website, you get a "changing room" that pairs visual images of T-shirts with different styles of jeans. Websites mimic the way we flip through a catalog, and, like a catalog, they suggest a universe of infinite choice. More efficiently than flipping through a catalog, every screen we click on acts as a node of connections to more products that we're likely to buy. Maybe we don't consciously feel it— except when a website moves us across categories of merchandise—but we are being prompted to buy something we don't need.

On the screen at Amazon, the main text consists of objective product information, which is bordered and embroidered by an endlessly spooling stream of subjective associations. We cannot escape from lists of items we have previously browsed through and put aside, lists of other people's "favorites," and our own, semisecret wish lists—all of which are prompting us to buy. The one-click browser makes it easy to flip through these screens—but to what end? As the *New York Times'* Online Shopper discovered when she bought three books by the same author on Amazon instead of the single book she was seeking: "The ease of the shopping experience . . . lured me into making an impulse buy." In fact, according to a study of online shopping sites, nearly every one of these features encourages us to buy items we didn't plan on—to lose our self-control and make an impulse buy.[11]

Removing shopping from the social space of the store or mall alienates us from the sensory stimulation of the marketplace. Like the pages of a mail-order catalog, a shopping site lays out endless rows of boots, parkas, T-shirts, cameras, printers, scanners. Whatever the items are, they lie passively on the screen with their name, serial number, the briefest of descriptions, and a price. What we see before our eyes is the singularly unromantic, functional minimalism of the market. The flatness of the screen highlights our alienation from these goods. But this kind of visual display has become natural to men and women, and especially children, who are raised under the scopic regime of mail-order catalogs, self-service stores, and television. You don't have to be a genius to get the subtext: it's a lot of capitalism plus a little semiotics.

When used by business—and especially by the media—this scopic regime encourages us to shop. It trains us to look, choose, and buy. "I think any reasonable girl would not want to spend *a lot* of time looking at a page of makeup sponges," says Kim France, the founding editor of *Lucky, the Magazine for Shopping*. "But she ought to be able to look at that page and say, 'Yes, I need that,' or 'I need that.'" The editorial pages of magazines like *Lucky*—or *Vogue, Seventeen,* and *InStyle*—not only report on new fashions, they also give us the addresses of stores and shopping sites where we can buy them. And merchants appreciate this. About *Lucky*, an executive of Nine West says: "It is readable and it is actionable." Or as the founding editor of *InStyle* puts it: We "take that last, final step and say, 'P.S., You can have it.'"[12]

This way of *seeing* is also a way of *being* with goods. Like the mail-order catalog, the magazine or the website has become another version of the universal store. And like the minimalist display of the universal store, the flat display of the website and the magazine is understood to be "very user's manual . . . very egalitarian." No one takes offense: we think it's just us shoppers and the merchandise.[13]

Laid against this visual gestalt, the text of product reviews influences us more when we read it on the Internet than when we read it in magazines. But it's the mere presence of reviews, rather than anything they actually say, that persuades us to buy. They confer the rational legitimacy of *Consumer Reports* on our voyeuristic lack of self-control. By tightly framing our voyeurism on the screen, however, they deprive us of the freedom *not* to buy. Negative reviews just push us to click on another item, while positive reviews—the more stars, the better—push us over the ledge of doubt. It doesn't even matter whether the reviews are positive or negative, for websites that provide reviews keep us reading longer. They simulate a community of common interest and invite us to join; they polish the image of a vendor's integrity—all of which makes a website stickier. And we don't really object. When we're not meeting the merchant face to face, and we can't personally examine the merchandise, reading other consumers' reviews creates trust in products, trust in vendors, and trust in the very act of buying. No wonder consumers love eBay's system of rating online sellers, and consider Amazon's website, which was the first to integrate a catalog of merchandise with abundant product reviews, to be number one.[14]

Since we, as a society, spend more time each year clicking our way through retail websites, we must get something out of it. More than half the shoppers who buy holiday gifts online think they're saving money, and more than 80 percent believe they're saving time.[15] But what are we really saving? Shoppers were slow to start using shopbots, the software that finds the cheapest prices on websites, and only 4 percent of Internet users do comparison shopping online.[16] "Shoppers who invest in using shopbots end up with a lower price," writes Hal Varian, an expert on Internet marketing, "but at the cost of a more elaborate"—that is, a more time-consuming—"search." And the need for searching never ends. The ease and speed of Internet use allow online merchants to keep track of their competitors' prices, enabling the swiftest among them to change prices faster than shoppers can respond.[17]

Why, then, do we still think that Internet shopping saves us time? Maybe it's because a third of us shop online while we are at work. It's the ludic—or playful—quality of stealing time from the job for our own use that persuades us we have made a net gain. Or, if we shop at home at night, we think we're gaining because we steal time from sleep. As the author of a book about the Internet says, it's "a 24/7 bazaar."[18]

Whether we take work time or sleep time, the availability of Internet shopping has the same effect on our lives as the repeal of local "blue laws," which prohibited stores from operating on Sundays when I was growing up. After town councils in many communities eliminated these laws, in the 1960s and '70s, Sundays lost their quiet, restful—even sleepy—quality. Instead of going to church, having big family lunches, playing outdoors, or just lying around, we began a new routine of having brunch, piling into the car, and going to the mall. The Internet drives these habits to a farther extreme. When we can shop anytime and anywhere, we wind up shopping more.

Paradox #2: The Internet Is a Lousy Marketer

Though the Internet was initially seen as a way of making transactions easier for everyone involved, it soon showed greater potential as a marketing strategy. In fact, the dot-com boom of the nineties occurred just at the moment when branding seemed to falter—when The Gap's profit rate declined and Nike stopped opening Niketowns and began to sell women's clothes. Companies believed that the Internet could be more effective and cheaper than stores, by giving them "multiple channels"—a direct pipeline—to shoppers. Moreover, with its decentralized technology, which enables companies to communicate simultaneously around the world, the Internet is a perfect medium of globalization.

But with a medium like the Internet, users have to "tune in" to, or deliberately access, a website. And they have to pay attention to it. Though a computer with broadband service, like a radio, may be turned on all the time, unlike a radio, it doesn't provide ambient noise that people can listen to while they're doing something else. Users must *look* at and *navigate* a website—it compels a constantly high degree of our attention by sharp combinations of content and software. And just having the Internet turned on all day encourages people to use it more. The more we use it, the likelier we are to use it for shopping. Broadband users buy more products on the Internet than dial-up users, they look up more product information on it, and they take part in more online auctions. Though we broadband users may not start out as Internet shoppers, we very rapidly become shoppers.[19]

It takes more than technology to bring shoppers to specific sites. Amazon and eBay began modestly enough, attracting their first customers by word-of-mouth recommendations. But most websites, including these two pioneers, quickly embarked on massive advertising campaigns. They plastered their URLs in front of our captive eyeballs, filling space—and creating new space—to promote the image of their website as a brand. From big billboards on the sides of New York City buses to those pervasive pop-ups on other websites, advertisements for Internet shopping multiplied and spread. Even after the dot-com crash, Internet users were bombarded with ninety-four billion ads a year, most of which promoted other websites.[20]

The effort to advertise was more expensive than many online merchants had planned. Quite a few sites went broke in the dot-com bust of the year 2000. Not only did they face severe problems, as all new stores do, with breaking through to a potential market, delivering purchases, and managing customer service. They also had to figure out how to communicate their message through the new medium of the Internet. Jeff Bezos had thought this through in the early nineties, while working for a firm of business consultants. Taking a cue from the Internet's infinite capacity for storing information, he studied the top twenty products in mail-order sales and decided that he would set up a website to sell books. No mail-order catalog could have enough pages to present the vast array of books in print, he reasoned, and no bricks-and-mortar bookstore could be built big enough to hold them all. Improving on the bulk of the Montgomery Ward catalog of the early 1900s, which had more than a thousand pages, and on the business strategy of the exhaustive Schwann catalog, which didn't sell records but only listed them, Bezos created the first online bookstore—and Amazon immediately offered shoppers a practically infinite degree of choice.[21]

But after other websites also began to sell books, the terms of advantage changed. Shoppers' commitment to a website could be neither stronger nor more fickle than their "brand loyalty." Yet if websites offer the same books at the same prices, with the same customer service, why buy from Amazon rather than Barnesandnoble.com? In a flat medium, there are no "intangibles." How can a website re-create the "personality" of a store?

For many mail-order merchants, the problem is pretty well solved by the time they transfer their catalog experience online. The sites of "lifestyle" products like Patagonia and Teva become lifestyle websites, presenting stories about kayakers or mountain climbers who use these products on their trekking adventures. The stories continue to sell the brand: if you bought the story in a catalog, you'll buy the product online. The largest offline store, Wal-Mart, came up with a similar solution. Slow to develop a presence on the web, Wal-Mart eventually decided to follow the same line as in their stores: they emphasize price. If you want a standard product at a predictably low price, you'll shop online at Wal-Mart.

But luxury goods merchants face a special problem. Their sales depend so much on intangibles—the aesthetic qualities of the product, the atmosphere of the store, and the snob appeal of the brand. If the Internet is a universal medium that allows for little subtlety, it surely has little chance of conveying a luxury brand's distinctiveness.

Yet "it's important for a brand like ours to be on the Internet," says a young executive in charge of brand development at LVMH (Louis Vuitton Moet Hennessy), the luxury goods conglomerate that owns the couture house of Christian Dior. "The Internet is the future." So LVMH asked John Galliano, the eccentric head designer at Dior, to create a line of women's sportswear for their very own website, eLuxury.com. He needed to create a product that would suggest "luxury" through the flat display of the screen—a product that would be, in his words, "readable on the Internet." But how? Selling luxury isn't as easy as selling books online. Galliano had to downscale—to alter, in fact—his creativity. Instead of showing outrageous cuts and bizarre combinations of fabrics and colors, the kind that sell for astronomical prices in Dior's Paris salon, Galliano's Internet line was reduced to "sportswear." Its snob appeal relied on a designer name, Galliano's Girl, on its association with other LVMH brands—Louis Vuitton, Baccarat, Bottega Veneta—and on relatively high prices. It's the same logic that has driven all of fashion branding since the early years of Yves Saint Laurent's Rive Gauche.[22]

But how does "luxury" look online? Alas, eLuxury.com does not look as good as a Rive Gauche boutique. It looks no different from other websites. With the Internet's flat display, categorical icons, and universal clickthrough, there's no chance for either nuance or novelty.

When you enter eLuxury.com, the image on the first screen reminds you of the cover of an advertising supplement in the Sunday newspaper. It shows a full-color head shot of a blonde woman whom you're sure you have seen before. She's holding a heart-shaped crystal pendant from Baccarat—a gift suggestion, no doubt, for Mother's Day, which is coming soon—and the price is a high, but not outrageous, $175. Icons of "favorites" are splayed across the bottom of the screen, with small pictures of accessories from the LVMH stable: a saddle pouch pocketbook from Dior, a Louis Vuitton wallet and accessories bag, a pair of Seven jeans, and a bracelet from Marc by Marc Jacobs—another designer's cheaper line. "The ultimate destination for what's hip, hot, and hard to find," you read on the screen called Overview, but an unremarkable set of categories runs across the top: Women, Men, Gifts, Beauty, and, hello, what's this? "Shop by Brand." Where's the aura? "Shop by Brand" lowers the image of eLuxury.com to that of the many other sites that invite you to do the same, from Activision.com, a Website for a company that manufactures computer games, to bluefly.com, a website for—heavens!—*discount* designer goods. When the side panel tries to grab your attention, it only flashes the forlorn signals that are overly familiar from displays that have been used forever—at least since the sixties—by stores and magazines: Fashion Watch, New Arrivals, Hot Looks. Humbug, you mutter: this could be the aisles of Kmart. What I *think* status shopping should be—closed to public view, sensual with exotic fabrics and scents, and, for both of these reasons, somewhat mysterious—has been lost. And, since eLuxury struck a deal to link its site with Amazon's, the aura has only weakened.

But maybe the point of a "luxury" website isn't exclusivity. Like licensed sunglasses that proclaim the Armani name and overpriced Christian Dior lipsticks, a website is a means of advancing an ensemble of *brands*. Galliano's weird couture styles, like Dior's and Yves Saint Laurent's more traditionally glamourous creations, are watered down for sale in the stores, and watered down still farther—reduced to the essential *name*—for their appearance on the Internet. What we get on eLuxury.com isn't the whole sensual complement of luxury, with its threat of going over the edge into incomprehensible detail, but the more readily understood *sign*, as the semioticians say, of luxury: not the Galliano-designed gown, but the T-shirt with Galliano's name on it.

Maybe other websites do luxury better. Let's click on LVMH's rival, the website Style365.com. "So much of what is done today on the Web is done by kids in their teens and 20s who have no sense of aesthetic offline," scoffs its founder, Terron Schaefer, a former marketing executive. Schaefer believes in "editing," the kind of culling and choosing that is done by the owner of an exclusive boutique. But how can free access to a site on the Internet be compatible with an aura of exclusivity?

Schaefer opted for suggesting status by a high-concept layout design—like *Harper's Bazaar* in the fifties and sixties. He created a board of advisers from prominent architects and designers and posted the work of the fashion photographer Bruce Weber. Since he didn't have his own stable of designers, he made strategic alliances with high-status suppliers. But these partnerships only placed him in bed with Dior's rival, the Yves Saint Laurent brand, which now belongs to LVMH's competitor, Prada. It looks like warfare by proxy armies, yet Schaefer dares to describe Style365.com as "a finishing school." Clicking through the screens is supposed to be an education in taste.[23]

An education in taste? Style365 is slightly more varied than eLuxury. com, but, alas, it doesn't look too different from an upscale mall.

When it was launched in 2000, before the dot-com bust, Style365.com did convey a distinctive sense of style aimed at an affluent, mobile readership. Clicking on the site one day, I found photographs of strange sand and mud buildings in Timbuktu, with a brief and knowing description of the city and its inhabitants: "Stately Tuareg and Songhay people move through meandering alleys in embroidered robes and indigo turbans. . . . If you go, don't expect to find a Ritz. . . . Highly recommended is a sunset trek on camelback to a nearby Tuareg village."[24] There were also links to unusual suppliers like Pain Poilâne, a bakery in Paris from which you could order a loaf of sourdough bread for $37. But after the Internet bubble burst and investors looked hard at the bottom line, Style365.com settled down to offering middle-of-the-road, mass-produced merchandise with links to standard mail-order firms.

On entering the website now, you find the usual set of categories overlapping things to buy and the multiple meanings behind them: Gifts, Featured Shops, and Featured Products. Under Featured Products, "Indulgences" sounds promising, but it only offers links to such corporate retailers as Bang & Olufsen, Sony Style, Palm, and Power Shot. "Featured Shops" is even more disappointing, for it connects you to Barnes & Noble, Stylocracy—which yesterday was showing $17 nail clippers, and Sur La Table, a store and mail-order business for cookware and kitchen equipment. Clicking through takes you farther downscale—to catalogs that are familiar to any middle-class shopper who has bought an item from L. L. Bean or Pottery Barn and found herself on their common mailing list—Crate and Barrel, Williams-Sonoma, and Martha by Mail. They've got the merchants, but where's the style? Though I'm not likely to pay $17 for nail clippers, I regret that Style365.com has retreated from the goal of providing high-concept shopping on the Internet. That would have made my voyeurism more fun.

Despite the Internet's "democratic" potential to support an abundance of idiosyncratic sites, it's hard to find different "personalities" of the online store. Within the first few years, the Internet's ability to provide an infinite variety of goods and ways to package them succumbed to the standardization of marketing by brand and big merchants' oligopoly. This loss of choice is partly due to our own behavior. Though we spend more time shopping online every year, we tend to visit fewer sites. And we spend much more time on our favorites than on the runners-up. Moreover, since most new Internet users—especially young ones—are less affluent than those who are already online, the effort to target new younger and poorer users will likely promote even more standardization. If this is the key to future growth—much desired by investment analysts—websites will follow the examples of Amazon and eBay, as well as commercial television. The web will be filled with a small number of "platforms" for an enormous number of mass-market goods. Doesn't this spell oligopoly?[25]

Yet it won't kill off status shopping. The higher a household's income, the greater its Internet use. And, much like the "ladies who lunch" who shop at Bergdorf's and the working women who go to Macy's, richer and poorer Internet users tend to shop on different sites. Internet users whose annual household income is higher than $75,000 shop at LLBean.com, Lands' End, and Nordstrom, while those who earn less than $40,000 shop at Fingerhut.com, Sweepsclub, and Wal-Mart. It's not as though the rich aren't price-conscious, for plenty of them shop on Costco.com. But for some mysterious reason, the rich also choose SprintPCS.com, while the poor shop on SwitchtoATT.[26]

Internet shopping also differs by gender. Though women have caught up with men on using the web for shopping—especially for holiday gift shopping, which remains a "woman's" concern—they tend to shop for different things. Women shop on the Internet for their home and family. But men, like my cousin Jerry, use the Internet to shop for computers, high-tech goods, and cars.

Despite the democratic potential that anyone can produce content for the Internet, we have wound up very quickly with multiple channels to the same old stores. Internet consumers tend to re-create an oligopoly of merchants and brands. And it's hard to turn Internet shopping into a dream world like the old department store when universal access and flat display make it more like the five-and-dime.

Paradox #3: The Internet Makes Every Buyer into a Seller

The genius of eBay—the Internet's first auction site and, for a long time, its only profitable shopping site—is that it promises to take us outside the box of shopping mall conformity. Like its mirror image, Amazon, it offers a practically infinite array of goods. But unlike Amazon, which is, after all, a catalog, eBay is antiroutine. By re-creating a narrative of accident, discovery, and exploration—with no fixed prices—in a world of standardized, branded goods, eBay re-romanticizes the entire shopping experience. You never know what you'll find on eBay, and you never know whom you'll meet. But also: you never know who you'll *be* on eBay—for the truly transformative power of the site turns shoppers into entrepreneurs. There is no such thing as too much shopping on eBay. For on eBay, shopping will make you rich.

The eBay mythos arises out of the lowly Pez dispenser. When Pierre Omidyar set up the website in 1995, just a bit later than Jeff Bezos created Amazon, he envisioned a communal trading post where consumers, as equals, could buy and sell hard-to-find goods—cheap, mass-produced goods like Pez dispensers from the 1950s, which are desired as collectibles. Omidyar had neither the aggressive drive of Jeff Bezos to harness the Internet for profit nor the business-building skills of Steve Case, the founder of AOL. Omidyar "had a typical programmer's view of the Net," says the seminal 1999 article about eBay in *Time* magazine. "He saw it as a free-wheeling, authority-defying medium, and he was proud of his fledgling site's noncorporate orientation."[27]

Yet Omidyar's vision was soon expanded by eBay's professional managers and the increasing participation of full-time merchants in online sales. Aside from Omidyar, most of the men and women who run eBay have a background in the retail business; they joined eBay not to work for "a global garage sale" but to turn the website, on the demand of Wall Street investment analysts, from a "secondary collectibles marketplace" into "a [diversified] trading platform" that can eventually compete with Wal-Mart. Though collectibles are still the largest single category of goods, more than half of eBay's sales are in "practicals"—products people use everyday. Even more suggestive of the website's growing ambition, 16 percent of sales are not auctions, but fixed-price items. By identifying so strongly with its customers' desire for a story, however, and letting that story emerge so variably from thirty million registered users' own concerns, eBay has succeeded in branding the "personality" of the online store. It's democracy, it's community, it's the worldwide bazaar.[28]

The romance of eBay is to turn every shopping experience into a story. Most of these are stories starring us. At its purest, the auction is a trope of individualism: each seller, and each item, stands alone; each bidder competes against all others. When we go on eBay to search for a specific item, we don't feel as though we're wasting time in yet another tiresome shopping trip; we're on the road in a heroic quest. In our eBay stories, we defeat the corporate monster and find exactly the product that we want, whether it's cheap, prosaic, eccentric—or merely unavailable in stores.

I have heard and read hundreds of these stories, and, despite their element of surprise and the excitement of the teller, I think they can be summed up by four basic themes:

- I found it on eBay! (The Online Shopper for the *Los Angeles Times* located exactly the Japanese blended yarn she needed on eBay, when even the manufacturer could not supply it.[29])
- I won it on eBay! (Alex overpaid on the old subway map, but he beat out thirty other bids.)
- I didn't know it existed! (Pat bought a 3-D camera that was made by a man in Ohio, who attached cable-releases to two Minoxes and glued them together.)
- I didn't know I wanted it! (When I heard about an eBay auction for a 1912 edition of the Michelin red guide—the *Guide Michelin*—I was sorely tempted. But since I didn't buy it, maybe mine is not really an eBay story.)

The most interesting story isn't ours, however. As at a flea market or an art-house auction, the most interesting story is that of the thing we buy. Even a cheap, mass-produced commodity like a Pez dispenser is romanticized when it becomes the object of an auction. With eBay's super software, the commodity is described in words and digital images, given a mysterious or historical provenance, and classified among other items of its kind: it becomes a *serious* object. Unlike a souvenir, which is categorized by its significance to our lives, the eBay commodity is categorized by its significance to other goods: it is the object of serious contemplation. Usually this is a privilege only the collector enjoys. But on eBay, we learn the history of commodities that are so modest, they don't yet form the core of anyone's collection. They are so modest, we didn't even know they had a history. But they do . . . and by consuming these histories, we develop a vast amount of often archaic production knowledge. Like a collector, then, we become, in a sense, the producer of these objects. When my colleague Pat shops in the auction of old cameras on eBay, she learns about the manufacture of three-dimensional cameras in Germany before World War II. For a writer in *House & Garden,* the auctions are a means to learn about the markings that were made on antique American levels—carpenter's tools—that he cannot find described in books. "EBay isn't just about buying," he says; "it's about learning."[30]

In contrast to both the slick persuasiveness of advertising and the footnotes of scholarly texts, the naive and misspelled descriptions by sellers on eBay make the objects more valuable. Their words suggest the unstudied speech of country people who readily appreciate the inner qualities—the truth and beauty—of goods. And the clumsier these descriptions sound, the more trustworthy the sellers appear. "I liked the sweet honesty of the sellers' descriptions," says a journalist: " 'It's got a couple of small dings and looks nice.' "[31] "I'm not sure who made this pottery pitcher," a seller writes. "It is rather primitive [*sic*] looking and quite old I am sure." This is flea market and yard sale psychology: though the item is old and mangy, it's got a history, and this gives it value. But since the object has a history, it's no longer a commodity. Once it's lifted out of the commercial world, it's automatically authentic. And it's this authentic experience of the object that we're buying on eBay.[32]

Of course, the items listed on eBay are all commodities. But they are also goods with a specific history to which we can relate in different ways. It's not just Aunt Helen's old glass butter dish, or even a remaindered butter dish, that is being sold: it's a 1940s-vintage, green, pressed glass butter dish—the kind your grandmother set on the table when you were a child. Or you admired this glass butter dish in a museum exhibition, read about it in a magazine column on collectibles, or saw a modern copy of it in *Martha Stewart's Living.* Your experience of this butter dish may be intensely personal, or it may be mediated by other modes of display. In any case, when you buy it on eBay, you're buying someone's story.

The bigger eBay grows, however, the less amateurish these stories become. The "power sellers," or owners of small businesses, who sell an increasing share of the goods on EBay, the liquidators who post large inventories in separate auctions, and the thirty giant companies—including Home Depot and Sears—that use eBay to unload returned or hard-to-sell items: their thrust is to persuade shoppers they are just getting a colossal deal. "You are looking at one of the finest names in men's fashion!" says threads4less, a designer outlet in Phoenix that maintains a "store" with 125 separate items on eBay, including more than 70 in women's clothes, when I check the site today. "Those of you familiar with Armani know that brand black label is one of the finest merchandis [*sic*] Armani makes . . . has all original price tags still attached. . . . The material is 100 percent cotton . . . and is made in Italy! . . . This Armani Black Label shirt is . . . sold in your upscale department store for $215." When threads4less describes a women's coat, the listing sounds like the spiel of a nineteenth-century barker at the door of a dry goods store, or like Ron Popiel doing an informational for the Vegematic on late-night TV: "Ladies are you ready for this . . . then feast your eyes on this brand new Armani Coat retailing for $1195 . . . WOW is all I can say. . . ."

Competition from these heavy-breathing power sellers presses the amateur sellers to develop professional-looking postings. They, too, want to make their auctions pay off. They are helped by eBay's software: since the site makes a profit on all transactions, eBay's managers are constantly trying out new web designs in order to make more sales.[33] In 2000, listings were linear; you had to click on the "headline" for a description and on the camera icon for a picture. But since that time, practically every listing shows fancy digital photographs—four or five full-color views of each ceramic pitcher and "runway photos" of the Armani coats. Since 2000, eBay has also organized paying workshops—they call them eBay University—in cities around the country. EBay staff members, outside experts, and successful sellers teach would-be sellers the most effective techniques of presenting merchandise online. "Presenting an item is a delicate balance between being sophisticated yet appealing to buyers' bargain-hunting instinct," says a video technician who moonlights by selling posters on eBay. "Also, there's color coordination. When I sell photos, the color of the background affects the price. When I have brighter colors, I have less bids. When I used more neutral tones that complemented the photo, the number of bids tripled for the same photo."[34]

Many listings claim expert authority. A woman who sells vintage Hermes handbags on eBay explains the difference between the hardware used on purses twenty or thirty years ago and now. A power seller in Bavaria posts a full-size violin, "a work of German craftsmanship," which "was made by Eduard Meyer Herford in 1953 and was carefully checked by a specialist." Though the violin has been repaired, it has "mint-condition" qualities: "Warm volume on G and D strings and good projecting brilliant sound on A and E strings. Sound is very pleasing and has a fine and aristocratic touch." OK, but how much is it worth? The first bid was $270; there have been seven bids so far. The going price is $355 when I look, and there are three days till the auction ends.

Still, some listings are so blatantly amateur, I can't believe they're not deliberately calibrated to produce the naive effect. The posting of hand-painted replicas of famous paintings offered by a Dutch seller—Van Gogh's *Irises* for one dollar!—begs us to believe in the aura of the handmade good, if not the unreproducible aura of the original art: "Please realize that this is a hand-painted oil painting and not a print." The artist, disgusted by "mass products," assures us that the painting is the same size and has the same colors as the original: "It has taken a specialized artist one full month to paint this very detailed replica." Yet in the same auction category, I also find an "original Willem de Kooning" of a nude offered for $35,000. The seller, in Ohio, says that the painting comes "from the estate of a person close to" the artist. And what a bargain: "Paintings of nude women by him (painted the same year) sell up to 15.6 million U.S. dollars." I'm not sure which is the better bargain—the $1 replica of Van Gogh's *Irises* or the "original Willem de Kooning" for $35,000. The aura of the unique product, or the work of the famous artist: eBay teases us with the way we've been taught to shop for goods. Let the shopper decide which standard of value to use. It's an inversion of consumer society, a throwback to the one-on-one exchanges of the marketplace.

For eBay's biggest story is that of the market, itself. Depending on what you read, eBay is the "24/7 bazaar," "the perfect store," or "a rapid retreat of the horizon" to a "truly global" marketplace.[35] Though these glowing comments describe the Internet's real ability to unite buyers and sellers across great distances, at any hour of the day or night, they apply just as well to the website's ability to romanticize the *idea* of the market. Buyers meet sellers without an intermediary. All information is available to all buyers equally. Buyers decide how much they will pay. No wonder eBay seems to embody the economists' idea of a perfect market. This idea is dramatized and simplified by eBay's auction mechanism, which abstracts commodities from the men and women who first produced them and the conditions under which they work. This eliminates any need to think about sweatshops, labor unions, or an oligopoly of sellers; it creates the impression that buying and selling is a simple, one-to-one transaction. It suggests that market power can be grasped by anyone.

Above all, the Internet's interactivity enables *everyone* to become an entrepreneur. A group of women in Atlanta, who call themselves eBabes, hold monthly meetings to thrash out their selling strategies. Thousands more readers find encouragement in the popular paperback *eBay for Dummies*. "Take a look around your house," chapter 1 begins. "When was the last time your toaster actually turned a profit? When you connect to eBay, your PC or Mac magically turns into a money machine."[36]

But this market ideology doesn't work in a cultural vacuum. My colleague Stuart reminds me that there's a huge subculture of Americans who often wonder "How much can I get?" from selling their baseball cards, sixties-era bellbottoms, Pez dispensers, or toasters. EBay didn't *invent* collectibles, which have always suggested that you can make a killing from items of less-than-museum quality. The charm of the eBay "community" isn't based on altruism; it's based on the possibility of getting the highest financial value for something you own. The insistence that this market is a community doesn't hide the fact that eBay stimulates us to experience life as if everything is all for sale: *things*, in the most basic, material sense, are alienated from experience.

Selling things is based on a legal doctrine of alienation. The Dutch were able to "buy" Manhattan in the seventeenth century because the Munsee Lenape tribe had no sense of land—or other possessions—as alienable property, something apart from themselves and their community that they could trade for something else. But even in a market society like ours, eBay flies against traditional ethics: it encourages us to treat everything as alienable, to trade all the time, and to buy things *only* in order to sell them. No sale is taboo. Fragments of the space shuttle Columbia, which crashed to Earth on February 1, 2003, were offered for sale on eBay soon after scavengers discovered where they fell. After the terrorist attack of September 11, 2001, eBay accepted auctions of relics of the Twin Towers—until formal protests from the New York City government forced them to stop. Malcolm X's sister learned about some journals her brother had kept when she was surfing on eBay and saw them posted in an auction at Butterfield's, an eBay subsidiary. I heard a story on National Public Radio about a man who decided to travel to Argentina immediately after that country fell into an economic crisis; his goal was to buy goods cheaply for U.S. dollars and then sell them on eBay. "I bought it on eBay" quickly turns into "I can sell it on eBay." I don't think this shows an unselfish motive to recycle goods; it shows an entirely selfish way of looking at the world. Or it's an admission of utter defeat, like when the Dartmouth College swim team listed itself on eBay to raise money, or the town of Bridgeville, California, sold itself on eBay for half a million dollars. Even if the website tries to be a good citizen and polices the postings for cheats and frauds, the abstraction and pervasiveness of an Internet auction lure us into morally suspect territory. It's the old question consumers ask, but now it's asked of us: What do ethics matter as long as the product can be sold?[37]

We have not become, as eBay enthusiasts say, "a nation of collectors";[38] we have become a nation of sellers. When all is said and done, Internet shopping naturalizes market ideology and ritualizes market behavior. The Internet has quickly used up its democratic potential by producing a pseudodemocracy where everything is for sale and anyone who is smart enough to buy things is even smarter when she turns around and sells them. The "revolution" that the Internet brought us has transformed shopping into an entrepreneurial opportunity: Buy it Now, Sell it Later.

Many websites offer us what seems to be a space of freedom—where we can post unedited reviews of products and services, gripe about "lemons," and share accusations of devious merchants. But these sites only engage us more deeply in the market system. Most postings in the "official" chat rooms about Beanie Babies hosted by the Ty Corporation seem to come from adult women, who use these postings to suggest new models to the company and to complain that the supply of Beanie Babies doesn't meet their demand. These women show us how invested we become in our own seduction, and how the Internet reinforces this investment.

"Fixed branches," the CEO of E*Trade, an electronic brokerage firm, recently said, referring to the physical space of a bricks-and-mortar store, "are monuments of stupidity."[39] But they are also legacies of one of the oldest forms of human interaction. Shopping in a store places the act of choosing goods in a serious social communion with people and a sensual communion with material things. Though the Internet may make shopping easier in many ways, it reduces our sensual ability to "get lost" in things and reduces the social space we have available. It deprives us of the chance to go "out" into the public sphere. It fails to make us free.

10

zagats
"r" us

News images showed Afghan men using their new freedom to
do what men do: they went out and bought television sets.
—*New York Times*, November 18, 2001

No matter where we go or who we are, shopping dominates our lives.
Brightly lit stores give life to city streets, and asphalt and concrete
malls mark the vast suburban landscape. Billboards and websites speak to
us all day and night, while commercials are on continuous replay in our
minds. Bargains, discounts, sales, and ratings taunt us with the eternal
questions: Does it fit? How much do I need? Can I find a better price? Am
I making the right choice? Cultural theorists are only half right when they
say that by choosing products, we create our identity. Our identity is
formed by the whole activity of shopping—an activity that we experience
as both freedom and necessity.

Necessity is easy to understand. We shop because we have no other way
to hunt and gather the things that have become our means of survival—
groceries, a house, a car, computers, medical care, vacations, and school
for the kids. Even if we have little money to spend, or depend on public
institutions to satisfy our needs, we shop around for the best deals we can
find. In fact, the less money we have, the more we must shop around and
the better shoppers we must be—we must be better informed, more
demanding, and more adept at bargaining. But often we feel we're no good
at shopping. We have too little money to spend, or lack easy access to stores.
We can't find what we want. And the sheer routine of shopping—the
endless repetition of daily, weekly, and seasonal cycles of need—falls upon
us as a kind of oppression.

Every museum needs a gift shop: Tate Modern, London. Photo by Richard Rosen, 2002.

It seems self-evident that we experience shopping as freedom, yet this is really a tricky proposition. Above all, we think of shopping as the area of social life where we exercise free choice. In the middle of the nineteenth century, Karl Marx wrote that men and women were so alienated in their work lives that they felt "freely active" only in "eating, drinking, procreating" and especially "in [their] dwelling and in dressing up." This is still true today, when the nonshopping parts of our daily lives—beginning with work and passing through war, politics, and family—are no less stressful than in the 1840s. Despite the dull aspects of routine—and despite Marx's denigrating these consumer activities as "animal functions"—we deliberately set shopping apart from work; we see them as opposites because shopping offers us an alternative world of dreams and—at least potentially—self-gratification. Certainly shopping presents us with some of the raw materials of freedom. For more than a century, especially in the United States, mass production has supplied an abundance of products to choose from, and competition between companies, between workers, and between stores has provided us with a variety of goods, of reasonably good quality, at consistently low prices. In the early 1900s, when the German economist Werner Sombart asked why the American working class wasn't trying to make a revolution, he found that though prices for food, clothing, and housing were similar in the United States and Germany, American workers ate better, wore more elegant outfits, and enjoyed larger, more comfortable living quarters than their European counterparts. In recent years, prices have been kept low by the prevalence of imports from low-wage countries, with the result that Americans, on the whole, have literally been freed from the tasks of producing goods and—theoretically, at least—have a lot more time to choose them. With more discretionary time and income at our disposal, we do a lot more discretionary shopping—for things that are convenient, or efficient, or just nice to have.[1]

Constant technological innovations also offer us the freedom to move up through a constant stream of products—"new, improved, and more powerful," as ads for mouthwash and gasoline say, or "smaller faster smarter cheaper," as Amazon.com describes a new digital camera it's trying to sell. And the speed at which business absorbs new technology has made it ever faster and easier for us to get these products into our hands—although the consequences, as we have seen with Internet shopping, are ambiguous. All in all, if workers' consent with the system is "manufactured" on the job, by their being allowed to fashion a compromise between what they must do and what they can do, then consumers' consent is "manufactured" in shopping—by our being allowed to fashion a compromise between our dreams of perfection and what we can afford to buy.[2]

Consent is not only guaranteed by the momentary act of purchase. Neither is it entirely due to the conscious decisions of politicians who invoke a democratic consensus based on our willingness to spend, or to the shrewd manipulations of captains of consciousness who try to persuade us to buy. The whole array of activities that are included in the shopping experience promote our acceptance of the system; they "naturalize" the market economy. Julia's browsing in high-class stores to do research on luxury goods, Cindy's dreaming about the perfect pair of pants, Jerry's hunting through the Internet for the best price on a digital camera, and my checking out restaurant reviews in Zagat's: through these everyday practices we internalize the idea that everything we want is available to buy or sell—and that these two aspects of exchanging goods make up our singular function in modern life. Whether we are pushing our wire cart around the warehouse club or sitting at our personal computer connected to Lands' End, we adopt the signs and codes of the retail economy to pursue our dreams. And, as we focus more of our energies on this pursuit than in any previous era, we accept—without really thinking about it— the idea that we all have equal freedom to do so. We are, at last, a public of shoppers.[3]

The seeds of this process were sown long ago, not when middle-class shoppers like me began to wax euphoric about extravirgin olive oil imported from Italy, but when the first rich housewives of Pompeii or ancient Rome decided to buy only the sweet, green olive oil of a certain merchant near the Forum whose terra cotta amphorae bore his own, individual seal—his brand. The process continued with the building of the first shopping malls in Elizabethan London and the construction of the famous arcades of Paris in the early nineteenth century. In modern times—in the long century of mass production and consumption stretching from the 1860s to the 1960s—the expansion of factories, department stores, and mail-order catalogs not only allowed women and men of modest means to acquire the highest-quality bedroom furniture or automobiles they could afford, and dress in pretty much the same black suits or navy-blue blazers as the richest folks in town, but also provided a common point of entry into the public sphere for every social group. Middle-class women, who were otherwise confined to running their homes and visiting their families, strolled unaccompanied in department stores. Rich and poor women shopped side by side in the five-and-dime. African Americans demanded the right to shop together with whites in department stores down South and at exclusive stores like Tiffany. Shopping was experienced, in short, as a space of empowerment.

Yet at some point, the broad expansion of shopping tended to narrow our focus. Shopping for need, and shopping for pleasure, yielded to the voice-inflected, eyebrow-elevated shopping of excess. Historians often trace this narrowing of social consciousness back to the "roaring" 1920s, when spending on new consumer goods excited both the business owners who were riding high on stock market and real estate speculation and the factory workers, supervisors, and office clerks who were buying household radios and Model T Fords on the installment plan. Others locate the origins of consumer society earlier, in the 1880s and '90s, when, for the first time, mass production made it possible for everyone, even new immigrants and workers, to buy a ready-made suit, hat, or dress that materially demonstrated they were just as good—and just as "American"—as everyone else. Alternatively, the urge to shop was ratcheted up in the economic boom that followed World War II, when the return to a civilian economy and the buildup of the suburbs provided jobs, housing, and a determined pitch—especially to women—to buy more things. Or, according to the affluenza explanation, when stock options and bonuses for "stars" in every field created the pervasive image of a decade of greed, during the 1980s and '90s, the rapid rise of high-end incomes produced a new era of copycat shopping, with millions of consumers succumbing to "luxury fever" and conspicuously overspending, even if they could not afford to do so.[4]

Clearly there has been a continuous increase in consumer spending from the moment mass production began. There has also been—and this is what gives us pause—a continuous *intensification* of shopping, with all the pressures on money and time, and the status-driven competition, that implies. Finding different dates for the origins of consumer society just confirms my suspicion that the intensification of shopping proceeds in waves, each of which is marked not only by the availability of more goods and higher incomes but by a different culture of consumption. This culture is made up of a new mentality that distinguishes each generation of consumers from their parents and a new set of institutions that makes shopping broader, more inclusive, and ultimately more compelling. The cumulative effect of these changes is that they alter our worldview: they persuade us to see the entire world as a shopping experience. Ultimately, a new culture depends not just on the production of consumer goods but on the production of consumers.

The institutions of today's culture of consumption were put in place as early as the 1870s, with the establishment of the first department stores, mail-order catalogs, and five-and-dimes. These were not only channels of distribution, as economists call them, but also social spaces where shoppers were literally surrounded by goods and where they learned to stroll around, compare, select, and pay for them. The displays of stores and catalogs prompted new ways of looking and also of living. The cosmopolitan *flâneur* of city streets had a counterpart in the male or female browser, whose casual disclaimer to the sales clerk—"Just looking!"—expressed the mobility and lack of commitment that are typical of modern life. The shift of responsibility for shopping to women and children gradually brought everyone into the market economy, where each person developed a strong awareness of the power of money and the seductions of price—if not yet the hyperattention to brand names that we know today. The new immediacy of goods made it easier to want them, dream about them, and plan to get them—a process that follows just as easily from use of the Internet in the early 2000s as it did from the introduction of self-service a hundred years ago.

Prominent displays of goods at every price level—especially with the breakthrough arrangement of the five-and-dime—made bargains a key part of consumer culture. Low prices opened shopping to everyone and made it universal. Setting prices the same for all shoppers, and posting them in the stores, made the shopping experience transparent, and further broadened its appeal. Meanwhile, the pyramids, rows, and towers of boxes in the windows of the five-and-dime, arranged according to the rule "Sell them cheap, pile them high," strengthened the connection between seeing and getting. Not only did packages become elements of aesthetic pleasure, but shoppers learned to associate the rationality of standardized production with their personal fulfillment—a way of thinking that shaped the fascination of later generations of shoppers with catalogs, designer labels, and branded stores. Shopping became a means of satisfying the urge for both aesthetic pleasure and rational calculation, and gradually brought the two modes of thought together in a single activity.

The mentality of consumer culture also depends on our willingness to accept, and ability to internalize, images of goods. Beginning in the 1880s, magazines and newspapers, and, eventually, radio and television, spread these images into every home. By making goods visible even to those who could not afford the embarrassment of entering an exclusive store, they diminished the barriers between social classes without leveling their substantial differences. Widely diffused images of goods also reduced regional differences, establishing shopping as a part of the foundation—after the English language, religion, and the U.S. Constitution—of national culture. Though these processes began with the early mass-circulation magazines, they speeded up and became more pervasive during the early days of radio, in the 1930s, and—even more spectacularly—with the universal acquisition of television during the 1960s. Since the eighties, this hard wiring of the consumer mentality has established a global culture, as transnational media organizations like MTV or SkyTV and new satellite technology both standardize images and adapt their delivery to geographical, ethnic, and linguistic communities. Surrounding these images of products, of course, are appeals to buy them: advertisements. If I have not gone into detail about advertising in this book, it is only because many other writers have fully described its importance to consumer culture. I can only emphasize that ads are our common texts; the products they feature, our phantom companions: they populate our dreams. Advertising expands and prolongs the shopping experience. And—Tivo and other technological innovations aside—we cannot shut it off.

But mentality depends on both image and language. In contrast to the commercial messages of advertisements, the seemingly objective language of product reviews has not been sufficiently appreciated for its ability to stimulate and shape consumer culture. I don't think this culture really got off the ground until the 1930s, when the first consumer guides developed a specific language for shoppers to use; by the eighties, this language had become our universal pattern for evaluating most of the things we encounter in daily life—not just commodities—and communicating how we feel about them. "Best bet!" "Worth a journey!" "Four stars!" "Best Buy!" Like all native languages, the language of shopping is easily learned; it transmits ideas and shapes our worldview. We use it to talk about both our subjective choices and general standards of value. This language is, in fact, a lot like money: it objectifies value.

Consumer guides are the basic textbooks of contemporary consumer culture. Beginning in the thirties, they established shopping not just as a routine way to get provisions, but as a cultural "field," with rules that have to be learned, places to learn them, and people—the honest brokers of consumption—who serve as our mentors. *Consumer Reports, New York* magazine, and all the other consumer guides I have described created not only a language but created us as self-conscious consumers. They have parallels in other times and places. Describing the rise of gastronomy—which is, like shopping, a field of consumer culture—in nineteenth-century France, Priscilla Ferguson emphasizes how printed books of culinary criticism, or "gastronomic texts," created consumers for an emerging French cuisine. Written as culinary diaries, or collections of recipes, or sometimes even primitive restaurant reviews, these texts provided men and women with rules for how to produce and, just as importantly, *how to consume* fine food. Even today, whether they are reminiscing in luscious detail over a juicy casserole or describing the "celestial" scent of a white truffle fresh from the woods, food writers subject what they eat to a categorical critique—and in doing so, they both stimulate and educate the readers' palate. At the same time, they transform their own subjective preferences into objective norms of value. When Ferguson says that "gastronomic texts ... [are] key agents in the socialization of individual desire and the redefinition of appetite in collective terms," she could just as well be describing the effect of product reviews on shoppers. Product reviews evaluate goods, but they also make us yearn to have them. They teach us how to appreciate, use, and talk about them. These texts transform economic, or *practical*, practices of exchange into *cultural* practices of consumption.[5]

The earliest reviews of consumer products stimulated the first wave of an intensified consumer culture. Reviewers taught a mass public what to expect—and what to look for—in the shopping experience. By doing so, they not only predigested the range of goods and services available on the market and compared their prices and performance to producers' claims; they also prepared consumers to want these products. Reviews of toothbrushes and high-octane gasolines may look primitive to us now, but they socialized a public that was not used to desiring them by pointing out their fine distinctions. *Consumer Reports* managed to combine the scientific professionalism of twentieth-century industry with an older working-class solidarity—at least until the witch-hunting and red-baiting of McCarthyism in the early fifties drove the editor to drop the interest in work conditions. From then on—until the environmental movement of the seventies and the current movement against sweatshops and globalization—the language of shopping would be wholly dedicated to choosing goods by their intrinsic qualities, rather than by the social situation of those who made them or by their effect on the common good.

After the thirties, the next big wave of intensification came in the sixties, when social changes shaped a new consumer mentality. Higher rates of upward social mobility, the entry of many more women into the labor market, and movements for sexual equality sparked a franker, more open, and more elaborate discussion of consumption in which men and women joined. As Susan Sontag noted about the art world, a casual and sensual sensibility was in the air; in fashion as in pop culture, everyone wanted to be young and to try new things. And, with the shift from manufacturing to the service economy, a new generation became totally dependent on shopping; few consumers had the faintest idea how products were actually put together or made. If shopping had long been identified with "not working," then by this time it was also identified with "not making" goods—which intensified the effect of shopping on our lives. These changes in society fundamentally changed consumer culture, as critical consciousness moved from analyzing work and politics to searching for bargains and pleasure. Shopping was, ironically, how the dominant culture absorbed the critical edge of the counterculture: its social critique of dominant styles of life was converted into lifestyle shopping.

"Lifestyle" was where the entrepreneurial energies of the counterculture met the evangelical fervor of the marketing establishment. The word crystallized a new need to shop more intensively, slipping into our language between the counterculture's search for alternative symbols of self-identification and marketers' efforts to supply them. Initially, stores and manufacturers were confused by what seemed to be widespread public resistance to their appeals to buy. Guys who had been known for their crewcut hair and crewneck sweaters now grew ponytails and beards and "let it all hang out." Women threw away their high heels and burned their bras. People of African origin, and those blessed with any degree of curl, let their hair "go natural." For a while, it must have looked as though the era of social movements marked the end, and not the beginning, of modern consumer society. But most men and women were rebels in appearance only. Not everyone was a hippie, a feminist, or a Black Power advocate. If these movements appealed to large numbers of people beyond their specific groups, it was mainly because of the release from social pressures that they implied, a release that could be achieved by "changing your lifestyle." You could change the way you looked, what you ate and drank, whether you exercised at the gym or drove a big car. So the personal quality called lifestyle operated independently of factors like social class. It could be used for a while and then discarded, and—since you signaled it to others by your choice of consumer goods—it could be shopped for. Nothing could be more modern . . . or more American.

For years, many observers, from Tocqueville on, had noted that America was a social democracy in which men and women talked, dressed, and addressed each other pretty much as equals, regardless of their social position. This theme was repeated in Sombart's research, which suggested that the rigid distinctions of social class were, to say the least, amorphous, or maybe even obsolete, in the United States. By the fifties, the postwar boom in mass consumption placed home ownership, as well as most household goods, within reach of a majority of Americans, which encouraged many people to think that social class, and the ideologies it spawned, were dead. The new social movements of the sixties—focusing on social and political rights more prominently than on labor inequality—for the most part underlined this conclusion, which was confirmed by changes in consumption patterns at both ends of the social scale. At the high end, access to a college education and higher income jobs reduced differences in cultural capital between the upper and middle classes. At the low end, a real reduction in income differences and an equally real expansion of shopping opportunities in supermarkets and discount stores gave the working class access to goods that represented a middle-class style of life. These changes had an impact on the broader political culture, reviving Tocqueville's ideas about social equality. According to the historian Daniel Boorstin, who expressed the liberal position, mass production had once and for all destroyed social class divisions in the United States by creating "consumption communities," which "were quick; they were nonideological; they were democratic; they were public, and vague, and rapidly shifting." This interpretation revitalized the cold war belief in consensus that had been badly depleted by the social movements of the sixties. "Never before," Boorstin wrote, "had so many men been united by so many things."[6]

If the idea of social class was dead—or just buried alive under shopping opportunities—social status was still as important as ever. Like other aspects of identity, status was reflected in choosing the right style of things—like a car, a bookbag, or designer jeans—which intensified the process of shopping for them. Lifestyle represented a means for marketers to tap into consumers' desire for social status without relying on the old distinctions of social class; this was especially important because surveys showed that consumers' preferences for different goods or brands or media could no longer be predicted on the basis of social class. Instead, consumers' tastes seemed to cluster together on the basis of attitudes—the way they felt about the products, or about life, or about themselves. Lifestyle gave marketers a handle on these clusters, regardless of how unusual or "alternative" it was.[7]

Clay Felker, *New York*'s founding editor, must have been familiar with the marketing studies done for *Time* and *Holiday* magazines in the sixties, which highlighted the lifestyle of "creative consumers." These men and women "went out a great deal [and] were heavy buyers of new products and premium brands." As described by the market researcher Emanuel Demby in 1974, they "were also heavy users of media (especially print media) and they thought of themselves as more imaginative, more outgoing individuals."[8] This is the social group that Felker recruited as both writers and readers; they were honest brokers of consumption, as Gael Greene says, for people like themselves. They used media like *New York* and, eventually, daily newspapers like the *New York Times* to develop their interest in consumption, communicating an interest not only in certain kinds and brands of goods but in shopping as an all-consuming experience. These highly articulate, self-conscious, but not seriously rich consumers spoke up for a new sense of value. They spoke up for both low prices and designer labels; they taught us to seek "the best." The creative consumers were, in fact, upper-middle-class intellectuals: Bourdieu's "dominated part of the dominating class." Yet they were, as Pierre Bourdieu might say, the new arbiters of distinction.[9] Though their lists of "bests" and their aesthetic claims of lifestyle research reached a high point in the eighties, their influence still permeates mass culture; we have continued our efforts to get the best of everything we consume. Our pursuit of the best intensifies our concern with shopping. It's our *duty* to shop for the best, the cheapest, the newest, and the most prestigious brand name. And our willingness to internalize this duty encourages us to think of consumption as a right of entitlement.

What are we entitled to? Consumer culture translates even our most idealistic desire for beauty, equality, and social acceptance into a need for commodities. The social spaces and honest brokers of consumption are, at bottom, inspirations to shop. And—to give it the specific American spin—the universal quality of consumer culture is felt to be a form of democracy. But it's not our desires that are at fault. I can empathize with Cindy, who dreams of a perfect pair of leather pants as a way of creating a perfect self. And with Artemio, who suffers from the illusion that having money in his pocket will enable him to fit in at Tiffany. And with the teenage boys of East New York, who think they can buy a genuine logo cheap—but find that they have to be better shoppers to gain respect from their peers. It's not wrong that we want to live happier, more comfortable lives—it's wrong that we think that products alone will make us free.

If Karl Marx were alive today, he would write about shopping as the new class struggle. We shop to find the bread, jeans, and homes—or baguettes, Miss Sixties, and McMansions—that we need to survive. Though we don't make these things ourselves, we work at shopping to produce them in our lives. We spend hours, and sometimes months, doing research on the things we need, and then we spend more time doing research on the prices and stores where we can buy them. The smarter we want to be as shoppers, the more work we have to do. And the more money we want to save, the more we need to buy.

It's hard to say, however—as Marx would want to know—who is exploiting whom. It's clear that we take part in a global chain of production in which we indirectly exploit the workers in low-wage countries, who produce the imports we buy at such affordable prices. Ironically, Wal-Mart shoppers, living on their own low wages, are the major oppressors of factory workers in China. And, with the worldwide expansion of that discount chain, those Chinese factory workers also shop at Wal-Mart. But shopping involves us in our own exploitation: the more emotionally invested we are in consuming goods, particularly in consuming specific brands, the more time we spend thinking about them, the more likely we are to buy them, and the more money we will probably pay. We often rationalize our self-exploitation by interpreting shopping as an entrepreneurial investment. With a Honda (or maybe a BMW), we'll impress the boss; with an eye shadow from Sephora (instead of Maybelline), we'll get the guy. If we're thrifty at the supermarket, we'll show our family that we love them. EBay has transformed this entrepreneurial motivation into a means of self-employment and a way of life. On eBay, buying exists for selling—and shopping can't be exploitation when you buy things cheap and sell them high.

Shopping hides the means of exploitation. Though we shop to buy someone else's work, we know very little, if anything, about them. We don't know how many hours they worked to make our computer or our Nikes, or whether it was physically hard, mentally tedious, and not very well paid for them to do so. Shopping seems to absolve us from responsibility for knowing these things. Whether it's our distance from direct production, or the time we put into shopping, or the fact that we also have to work to buy things, we feel that shopping is on a completely different, a completely individualistic plane. If shopping has anything to do with our collective life, it gives us a place to pursue public dreams of a better society by fulfilling private dreams of a better self. The social spaces of stores represent our dreams. It's not just the ads, the merchandise, or the atmosphere; it's the stores' ability to embody the dream and allow us to move within it.

If Marx were alive today, he would condemn the lack of intimacy in stores as a source of alienation. The replacement of small neighborhood shops by branches of multinational chains, the superlarge size of stores and the number of products on their shelves, and the inexorable movement from cash registers to self-service checkout lines: these changes in business and technology have made shopping a more abstract activity, which may be more efficient in some ways but less satisfying in others. If people who live in small towns and exurbs find a sense of community at Wal-Mart, it is only because Wal-Mart is the only store in town.

I have often heard people say, however, that websites like eBay create community. But is this really a community, with a sense of common good

Alienation: shopping mall, Tokyo. Photo by Richard Rosen, 2001.

and a common fate, or a market—a network of potential buyers and sellers? The eBabes, who meet face-to-face to discuss their business strategies, are a limited-interest group that focuses on profit. The consumers who use eBay to learn about Hermes handbags or early American woodworking tools, and the chat rooms of Beanie Babies fans or BMW owners, relate to each other not through the paths of their daily lives but through commodities.

Daniel Boorstin interprets this relationship more positively than I do. Back in the seventies, before the Internet existed, he described mass-produced commodities as "vehicles of community," connecting people more benignly than "possession and envy" or ideology.[10] I can understand that point of view. Commodities defang the specter of social discontent; they can restore, rather than steal, our souls. But I can also see how the scale and intensity of shopping have gradually overtaken more traditional kinds of community. The universal auction site has replaced the community trading post. We have fewer spaces—and fewer thoughts—that are not connected to the market economy. We have produced, as Jean Baudrillard apocalyptically predicted in 1970, around the same time that Boorstin was writing about consumption communities, a real consumer society: a "total organization of everyday life," which links producers and consumers and "runs from affluence . . . through interconnected networks to objects, to the total conditioning of action and time, and finally to the systematic atmospherics built into those cities of the future that are our [stores, supermarkets,] . . . and modern airports." The modern airport has, in fact, become another shopping opportunity. And we think of ourselves, for the most part cheerfully, in terms of the things we buy and the places where we find them. When asked by a reporter to describe himself, a New York City police detective says he is a "Starbucks, Barnes & Noble kind of guy." Markets, not communities, define us.[11]

If Marx were alive today, of course, he would be more interested in markets than in communities. And I think that he would trace the most recent intensification of shopping, beginning in the 1980s, to the increasing influence of the stock market. During the eighties, the government of Ronald Reagan encouraged corporate managers to be more entrepreneurial, but it pushed them toward raising values in the stock market rather than creating jobs. A company's "growth" was now measured in higher share prices. And stock analysts believed in two sources of growth: cutting production jobs so businesses could be "lean and mean," and turning best-selling products into megasellers based on brand names.

This attitude affected all businesses, but it fell especially hard on firms that made and sold consumer goods. Department stores were in a long cycle of decline. Manufacturers of household goods and foods—the Procter & Gambles and Nabiscos of the world—had failed to create new products that would expand "franchise" brands like Oreos or Ivory Snow into new formats and boost sales. The push to be entrepreneurial was transmitted by corporate takeovers that turned over control to new management teams who were more attuned to share prices than were their predecessors in the postwar boom years and the recession-laden seventies.

Some of these new managers tried to milk their companies of assets and lacked additional capital to modernize—which resulted in Macy's filing for Chapter 11 bankruptcy protection, B. Altman's going out of business, and Brooks Brothers' acquisition by Marks & Spencer. Others initiated more aggressive policies of product development that sought to capitalize on their beloved brands. The competition to create new monopolies in sales was mirrored by an enormous volatility of share prices in the stock market—which drove managers to push sales further, since many of them were now being paid in stock options on increased share prices as well as in wages.

And some companies turned—as if it were a new idea—to opening *stores*. The Disney Company set an important example. Mandated by investors to modernize the Disney Company and stimulate growth, a takeover team led by Michael Eisner used stores to morph the company's corporate identity from that of a producer of intangible entertainment in the form of films into that of a seller of Disney-branded goods. Not coincidentally, Eisner was one of the first CEOs whose financial compensation depended in good part on raising the company's share value. The Disney team reasoned that stores would provide a material way for consumers to get acquainted with the company and attach themselves emotionally to the whole range of products that it offered—its brand. Even if its films bombed at the box office—and this was, after all, only the incubation period of video sales—Disney could always sell Little Mermaid T-shirts and *tschotschkes* in the likeness of Mickey Mouse. Like movie theaters and theme parks, stores were now thought of as a space for representing the company directly to consumers. And unlike department stores or gift shops, they were a space the company directly controlled. For Disney, as well as for many other channel captains like The Gap, Ralph Lauren, and Nike, stores provided both a means and a space of representation that increased sales, impressed the media, and—through the media—also impressed Wall Street analysts. If they wanted growth, consumer goods companies needed to grow shoppers.

Consumer culture doesn't thrive because we are manipulated by business or ideology. It thrives because of the million small decisions we make every day—buying a latte at Starbucks, clicking on Amazon, using Homestore.com to do research before buying a house. And driving over to the mall on Sunday afternoon because we want to be with other people.

The cultural theorist Walter Benjamin, who wrote about the arcades of nineteenth-century Paris—the ancestors of our shopping malls—emphasized the very elements of shopping that are still so striking today. He describes the arcades as a social space and a space of representation, a marketplace where crowds mingle, and also a vehicle—through the mesmerizing power of commodities—of social control. Benjamin brings together a history of architecture based on iron girders and glass, a devastating critique of fashion in terms of the rising fascination with—and availability of—novelty, and a critical view of the world as a continual exhibition, where everything is for sale. He suggests how shopping can institutionalize both structural changes in the economy and a new awakening of the self—simultaneously creating a modern public and a modern public culture. As a Marxist, Benjamin defined his work as a way of unmasking the commodity fetish. This gave him, he thought, the opportunity to transform consumers into revolutionaries; the mass dream of individual consumption would turn into a politically utopian, collective vision.[12] But the many notebooks he filled with his research on, and speculation about, Parisian stores—as well as about streets, markets, and fashions—suggest that he was both fascinated and repelled by shopping's importance. And so, after all, am I.

Humans have an endless capacity to dream of pleasure, and commodities—products, goods, merchandise, fashions—are readily available to dream on. We dream of shopping for beauty, truth, and perfection, and if we do not shop for a perfect society, at least we shop for a perfect self. If the social spaces and cultural institutions of shopping produced nineteenth-century Paris, so they have also produced America today.

epilogue
what shopping should be

The consumption of products such as tobacco, tea, and sugar may have been one of the very rare ways in which British workers of the mid-nineteenth century achieved the fulfillment of the promises implicit in the political philosophy of a century earlier. Particularly for the working poor, eating more and more food with substantial amounts of sucrose in it was an appropriate response to what British society had become.
—Sidney W. Mintz, *Sweetness and Power* (1985)

In contrast to the pixilated visions of community drawn by niche markets, the Internet, and TV, I like the face-to-face encounters of real people in real time and space. I like the touch, smell, and sight of goods—whether they're boxes of computer software, rolls of paper towels, or more colorful and sensual cashmere sweaters, spools of embroidery thread, Biedermeier furniture, and bread. Though I can appreciate the surge of emotion that swept through shoppers at that North Carolina Wal-Mart when they heard about the race car driver Dale Earnhardt's death, that kind of discount superstore doesn't do it for me. Yet while I was working on this book, it seemed as though Wal-Mart and the World Wide Web were taking over the world we know. Every business decided to sell merchandise on the Internet, and Wal-Mart grew to become the largest store, and then the largest business, on the planet.

But those marketplaces aren't the only good models of community. While stores have gotten larger, more pervasive, and less personal, we have sought refuge in the old forms of farmers' markets. I'm not the only shopper who swears by the arugula or goat cheese of a certain producer I meet once a week at a stand; all over America, shoppers are showing greater awareness about where and how their food is produced, and demanding closer relations with their suppliers. Despite growing demand, the supply of independent farmers is constantly shrinking. Threatened by land prices, taxes, and competition from both pesticide-bristling agribusiness and health-conscious corporations that have bought up organic farms, farmers are a dying breed. Every town and city wants a farmers' market—but there aren't enough farmers to go around.

I'm lucky that New York has had a citywide network of Greenmarkets since the seventies. Reflecting the consumer consciousness of that time— the twin desires to eat healthy and eat well—a small number of food writers, urban activists, and philanthropists challenged the political clout of the city's supermarkets and the short-sighted modernism of the city government. As the conflict over zoning for superstores shows us, New York supermarkets are small but influential; for many years, according to my friend Marshall Berman, they were also able to deny farmers the right to transport their produce into the city and sell it directly to consumers. For their part, city officials were eager to please big property owners and real estate developers. Acting in concert with their interests, the city government during the sixties forcefully uprooted the wholesale fruit and vegetable market from its historic place in Lower Manhattan to redevelop the land for "higher," more prestigious uses like the World Trade Center. Rising property values, both real and imagined, made everyone who had even a little bit of power insist that the only marketplace for raw food products belonged at Hunt's Point, in the Bronx.

But through the efforts of an urbanist named Barry Benepe and the J. M. Kaplan Fund, the first Greenmarket was set up during the Lindsay administration. Luckily for me, it was set up at Union Square.

At first, I was suspicious of the market. How could really fresh tomatoes make it from the country to the middle of Manhattan? Where were the peasant grandmas who would sell fresh cheese? But once I began to shop at the Greenmarket, I became a true believer. Not only were prices lower than in the stores, but the quality was superb. Arrayed in crates, Mr. D'Attolico's heads of organically grown lettuce looked as precious as the emeralds spread out on velvet mats at Harry Winston, the Fifth Avenue jeweler. Each leaf of chard, thin Japanese purple eggplant, and green bean from Ryder Farm was the essence of elegance, and—though it was all

Intimacy with the onions: Greenmarket, Union Square. Photo by Richard Rosen.

organic, too—it never suffered from insect holes or a scrawny size. When Ryder Farm had raspberries, you had to get there by 8 A.M. on Saturday morning, or they all sold out. Mr. Gibson used to cross off items from his handwritten sign when they were gone, and on this sign, he also noted the time of the last sale.

Knowing the minute and hour when the last berries got away places you in a much closer relationship with the fruit you buy. And knowing the name of the farmer who grows your berries or beans makes you feel pretty good about buying them. Being able to talk to the farmers about weather conditions, soil, and the relative merits of different types of seeds creates the illusion that you bear some responsibility for the growing process— and this is a happier responsibility than posting reviews on a website. One of my happiest moments at the farmers' market came when I presented Mr. D'Attolico with seeds for *frisée*—curly chicory—that I brought back from France. It was great when he thanked me by presenting me with three pale, green-and-white heads of the *frisée* he eventually grew from the seeds—and wouldn't accept payment for them—but I was thrilled when he traded some seeds with his fellow farmers, and soon several stands were selling "my" *frisée*. Since living in the city deprives me of the chance to garden, the farmers' market is my only means of getting close to nature; it is also, no doubt, the only way I'll get even the slightest idea of what it means to be self-sufficient. But chatting with the farmers isn't all heady talk about the fine points of *frisée* or haricots. The talk makes you more realistic about what there is to buy. Despite my begging, Mr. Gibson wouldn't plant any more of his Asian long beans, whose nutty taste I loved, because the deer tore them up and ate them. And there are always weeks when I can't find any lettuce, or green beans, or some fruit or vegetable I want, because there hasn't been any rain . . . or it has rained too much. Shopping at the farmers' market puts you in touch with the weather and seasons. You understand the limits of your climate and place, and you begin to accept them.

You can't overestimate how far most of us have been removed from nature—or from the growing of our food supply. Not only have we got used to the weirded-out taste of peaches picked unripe, thick-skinned toma-toes, and watered-down zucchini, we actually think that fruits and vegeta-bles grow in freezer boxes or plastic bags. I like to see nursery school and elementary school teachers bring their classes to the Greenmarket, and I have often heard children express surprise to see a carrot, or an apple, in its natural form. Even adults are pressed to drop their traditional notions about food's "natural" appearance. I saw a man contradict a farm woman selling cauliflower because she said the brownish color was "the way it comes." "My father taught me to choose the whitest head," the man says before moving on. "And he came from Palermo."

With or without blemishes, produce at the Greenmarket looks more real than when it is sold in other places. At the market you would never hear what a man said to me one day at Dean & Deluca, when we were both gazing with admiration at wild mushrooms that cost $40 a pound: "In Italy, where I come from, we just go into the woods and pick them."

Usually shoppers don't contradict the farmers; they earnestly seek their opinion. "Should I refrigerate the apple muffins?" a man asks the woman selling them. "Only after you get home from work today," she replies. "And that's only because we don't want to use preservatives in our baking." Often, shoppers ask farmers how to cook the produce they buy. The men as well as the women selling at the stands are always happy to offer instructions. You don't hear a complete recipe, but you get a good sense of how to treat the beans, or purslane, or Jerusalem artichokes. More often, shoppers ask the farmer how long it will take for the pears, or peaches, to ripen. "Just put them out on the counter," a farmer will say. "They'll be ready—and really sweet—by tomorrow." Unlike the fruit you buy in the stores, this fruit does ripen overnight. It doesn't rot prematurely because it was picked green, packed up tight, and flown across a continent.

The farmers' market clearly benefits us consumers. But the policy innovation of the Greenmarkets is to benefit local farmers, too. Sure, the farmers get to sell their produce directly to consumers, eliminating the middleman, and making a profit from charging retail prices. By the same token, the farmers travel up to five or six hours to get to New York City. They have to work a full day in the fields, catch a bit of sleep, then get up at 1 or 2 A.M. to load the truck, and drive it—or hire someone to drive it—into the city by 7 A.M. Then they have to stand around and chat with us consumers at the stand all day, packing up to drive back home after 5 or 6 P.M. The Greenmarkets have a rule, however, that helps farmers to remain on their family property. Only local produce can be sold at the market; if you don't grow it, bake it, or can it in the greater New York region, you can't get a stand. This rule helps to keep farmers on their land by providing them with a means of selling to a critical mass of retail customers. The relatively small properties, and working families, many of whom also work at jobs off the farm, are linked more closely to their market. Another benefit to the farmers is that the Greenmarket loosely organizes them into an interest community. They socialize, share news, and exchange produce with one another: the woman who sells eggs trades with the woman who runs a large vegetable stand, and the maple syrup people barter with everyone. They also communicate with each other, and with the city government, through the market organization.

This citywide network of farmers' markets still depends on subsidies from the J. M. Kaplan Fund and the private Council on the Environmental or New York City. But because there is so much demand for them, the farmers' markets have expanded to all five boroughs—and many of the neighborhoods—of the city. Meanwhile, the Greenmarket remains the great magnet of Union Square, where it has been an impetus to remodel the park, gather inside it, and live nearby.

Though I can't claim the farmers' market has all the features of the ancient Greek agora, as a public space, it comes mighty close. Political candidates come to the market to shake hands in election season (the best

I've met there is one of our U.S. senators, Chuck Schumer), and there are always people collecting signatures on petitions or asking passersby to join their civic organization. On Saturdays, I always see at least one violinist or guitarist playing music and leaving out their hat, or instrument case, to collect money. Serape-wrapped flute players from the Andes were constant performers a few years ago. Unlike in a shopping mall, the streets are not privately owned, so there is never any fuss about the legal right to take part in any of these activities. On many market days, a local chef or visiting cookbook author is also sharing recipes or signing copies of their book. (One recent summer day, the great Alice Waters, owner of Chez Panisse in Berkeley, was signing copies of her newest cookbook at the market manager's stand; "Yeah, we called her up," joked the fellow from whom I buy baguettes. "We told her we'd give her fifty dollars if she sat across from us.")

But best of all, even if you're by yourself at the farmers' market, you're never shopping alone. Unlike in stores, strangers often talk to each other. "Is all the corn small this week?" a man asks me one day in the middle of a drought. "They're pretty mushy today," a young man tells me about the apricots. "Is this good? Is this good?" a woman asks her friend as she peels back the husk on each ear she picks up. "I do that, too," a woman says to me, when she hears me tell my husband we should buy a bunch of basil today to make pesto. "I fill the sink with water, wash the basil, and then dry it well."

This is my idea of the marketplace as a community. It offers us a weekly, face-to-face encounter in a world where we don't know our neighbors' names, but we do know the names on the shelves at Wal-Mart. No eBabes or Tommy Hilfiger for me. I like the idea that by shopping at the farmers' market, I take on a small measure of social responsibility.

I also like the consumption community that has been built up by the National Public Radio program *Car Talk*. In contrast to eBay, or to Daniel Boorstin's consumption communities, the program's audience is not connected through ownership of commodities, but through their use of commodities. Tom and Ray Magliozzi, who are brothers from Cambridge, Massachusetts, keep the program going at a quick pace with their detailed knowledge of cars and somewhat raunchy humor. Many of the questions that they answer, however, are complaints about personal relationships that are played out in cars—like the stories of listeners who call in to air their irritation at driving with a know-it-all spouse. I like it that the brothers freely criticize the authorities and powerful figures who limit our enjoyment of cars, including auto manufacturers, garage mechanics, and Boston traffic cops. I also like it that they put on the air comments which are socially taboo, like when they got a phone call from a listener who had found a large sum of money hidden in a car he had recently bought: "You're Italian, and I thought you'd know what to do." But what I find most endearing about *Car Talk* is the way the brothers combine old-fashioned production knowledge about cars and disdain for the new consumer society. When Matt calls in to complain about oil leaking into the body of his truck, the brothers advise him to buy an additive: "Go to a *real* auto parts store, not one of those at Wal-Mart!" And when Liz from Rochester calls, they ask whether she knows anyone who worked at the former carburetor plant in that city which has shut down: "It's probably a Starbucks now!" This speaks of the sense of a common destiny that real community implies.

A lot has changed since I began to write this book. Wal-Mart expanded to China, but the store was sued by employees for forcing them to work over-time without pay. Kmart filed for, and emerged from, Chapter 11 bankruptcy protection. The Gap's growth rates fell. Nike stopped building Niketowns. Disney started to close its stores. Brooks Brothers was sold once again, and, after the attack on the World Trade Center and stock market losses, luxury goods sales dropped.

But more people are shopping on the Internet every month. My cousin Jerry, after buying his scanner, bought a laserjet color printer, special paper to print photographs, a CD read-write, and a new 80 GB hard drive with a PCI card for his computer. "Next, I'll have to throw the whole thing out," Jerry says with a laugh. "Once you've bought it, it's obsolete."

My shopping routines, which I thought were cast in stone, have been permanently altered. When my daughter, at the ripe age of eleven, decided to become a vegetarian, I stopped shopping at the Jefferson Market. Though I don't completely share her moral commitment to stop the killing of animals, I did stop buying beef and lamb, so I no longer had any reason to visit the butchers. A good organic-foods store opened up near my home; it's convenient to shop there during the winter, when few vegetables are available at the farmers' market, and I shop there for the fresh fish and chicken my daughter permits me to buy. Since it also has a frequent buyers' program, I have become devoted to the store.

I still shop at least once a week at the farmers' market. But since Mr. Gibson retired from active duty at the market and set up a consumers' cooperative at Ryder Farm, I no longer rush to get there before 8 A.M. My closeness with the other farmers has also changed. Mr. D'Attolico died of a heart attack several years ago; though his son has taken over the farm, and is just as pleasant as his mom and dad, shopping at the stand isn't the same. Elizabeth of Breezy Hill is so busy running the farm that she doesn't come to the market anymore, except when the first apples of fall arrive, and she stands there cutting off slices for shoppers to taste. At other stands, I have watched children who learned to make change for customers while their granddad weighed apples grow up and take over the farm. There's still a direct line between me and the farmers. But time, and the market's very success, have made a difference. With the *New York Times* praising the eggs from free-range hens that I buy there, so many customers want to buy them (as well as the chickens) that a long line forms around the stand. And these days, Keith's stand is rated by Zagat.

I am also doing what all mothers do, at the proper time. Since my now-teenage daughter discovered that she likes to shop for clothes, I am teaching her how to shop. Like the mothers I interviewed in East New York, I often lecture her about the illusions of brand names; and like the teenage boys, she convinces me to go with her—to see if we can buy "just one thing"—at the Abercrombie or Urban Outfitters store. She doesn't believe that, when I grew up, there were no branded stores.

Like everyone else who dislikes chain stores yet buys a lot of books, I constantly worry about whether it's OK to shop on Amazon.com or at Barnes & Noble. I *feel* so much more like reading when I leaf through the books in an independently owned store. But when I compare the prices at St. Marks Books or Shakespeare & Co. with the big discounts on Amazon, I often can't hold out. And when Barnes & Noble at Union Square organized an event for a book that I produced, I actually felt some affection for the store.

All this goes to show that a shopper's life isn't easy. Our choices of stores, and choices of products, often contradict our ideals. Though our shopping patterns and preferences change over time, we have every right—and should take every opportunity—to make them express our creative and ethical self. Yet it may seem strange that I defend shopping when we are so deluged by appeals and places to buy. Telemarketers invade my home by calling night and day to offer me "free" credit cards and purchase plans.

Martha by Mail knows my address. When I walk down to SoHo, I see advertisements plastered everywhere along Houston Street on giant vinyl billboards. During the past thirty years, the amount of retail space per person in the country has *quadrupled*.

This doesn't mean that we should either demonize shopping or give it up. Not when it gives us pleasure, sharpens our sense of value, and creates a public space like the farmers' market. Pursuing these ideals, rather than buying things, should be what we use shopping to achieve. And we can only develop that critical consciousness if we understand why, and how, we shop.

notes

chapter 1: a brief history of shopping

1. "Objectification" of value: Georg Simmel, *The Philosophy of Money*, ed. David Frisby, trans. Tom Bottomore and David Frisby (London and New York: Routledge, 1990); also see Daniel Miller, *Material Culture and Mass Consumption* (Oxford: Basil Blackwell, 1987).

2. Wal-Mart: company history distributed by Public Relations Department, Wal-Mart, 1999. L. L. Bean led: "World Business: L. L. Bean, Preppiness Has Bean and Gone," *The Economist*, October 22, 1983, 81. More than six thousand specialty mail-order merchants: Frank Lipsius, "Specialist Onslaught Reshapes the Market: Mail Order in the U.S.," *Financial Times*, August 22, 1985. Credit cards: *Affluenza*, television documentary, PBS (KCTS, Seattle), 1997.

3. Annual retail sales: report for 2000 of the National Retail Federation, discussed on *Marketplace: Morning Report*, National Public Radio, July 6, 2001. Consumer Confidence Index: this survey was begun in the 1960s by the Conference Board, a business research organization in New York City. It gained wider currency in the 1980s when it was mentioned by President Ronald Reagan and began to be reported in the flourishing business media.

4. A nation of shoppers: while consumption has always been important in the American economy, the tilt toward acknowledging its importance began, as Lizabeth Cohen argues, during the Great Depression, and much of the infrastructure of consumer society was put in place during the fifties and sixties. Lizabeth Cohen, *A Consumers' Republic: The Politics of Postwar Consumption in Postwar America* (New York: Knopf, 2003). More shopping malls than high schools: *Affluenza*. More Americans travel to shop: Travel Industry Association of America, www.tia.org, accessed August 18, 1999. Airline excursion fares: Gwen Florio, "Devoted Shoppers Find Airline's Holiday Special an Irresistible Bargain," *Philadelphia Inquirer*, December 4, 2000; *Affluenza*. Wal-Mart sales: company history from Wal-Mart. Per capita retail space quadrupled: Professor Kenneth Stone, Iowa State University, quoted in "Target vs. K-Mart," *Morning Edition*, National Public Radio, August 29, 2001. Stores increase size: Leslie Kaufman, "A Glum Season for Retailers," *New York Times*, January 5, 2001.

5. Off-Broadway theater: Elinor Fuchs, "Theater as Shopping," *Theater* 24, no. 1 (1993): 19–30, quote at 24. Economists: Robert H. Frank, *Luxury Fever: Why Money Fails to Satisfy in an Era of Excess* (New York: Free Press, 1999); Juliet Schor, *The Overspent American: Upscaling, Downshifting, and the New Consumer* (New York: Basic Books, 1998). "Your messiah speaking": Vera Frenkel, "This Is Your Messiah Speaking," in *Queues Rendezvous Riots: Questioning the Public in Art and Architecture*, ed. George Baird and Mark Lewis (Alberta, Canada: Walter

Phillips Gallery, the Banff Center of Fine Arts), 1994. For artists' continuing fascination with the objects and displays of consumer society, see *Shopping*, ed. Christoph Grunenberg and Max Hollein (Ostfildern-Ruit: Hatje Cantz, 2002). Thanks to Martha Hostetter and Andrea Kahn for the theater and exhibition references.

6. Archeological traces of social power: Walter Benjamin, *The Arcades Project*, trans. Howard Eiland and Kevin McLaughlin (Cambridge, Mass.: Belknap Press, 1999).

7. Broadway in 1850s: Edwin G. Burrows and Mike Wallace, *Gotham: A History of New York City to 1898* (New York: Oxford University Press, 1999), 668. Darkened loft buildings: Sharon Zukin, *Loft Living* (Baltimore: Johns Hopkins University Press, 1982).

8. Nineteenth-century department stores: this brief sketch draws on the most extensive part of the scholarly literature on shopping—the interlinked history of department stores and modern cities—and, specifically, on the history of department stores in New York City in Burrows and Wallace, *Gotham* and William Leach, *Land of Desire: Merchants, Power, and the Rise of a New American Culture* (New York: Pantheon, 1993).

9. Shift from outdoor to indoor markets: see Dorothy Davis, *Fairs, Shops, and Supermarkets: A History of English Shopping* (Toronto: University of Toronto Press, 1966); James M. Mayo, *The American Grocery Store: The Business Evolution of an Architectural Space* (Westport, Conn.: Greenwood Press, 1993), 48; Daniel Bluestone, "The Pushcart of Evil," in *Landscape of Modernity: Essays on New York City, 1900–1940*, ed. David Ward and Olivier Zunz (New York: Russell Sage Foundation, 1992), 287–312. Mayor Rudolph Giuliani's prosecution of vendors at the Fulton Fish Market for consorting with organized crime groups, and his use of the police to clear African street vendors from the main shopping street in Harlem, in the 1990s, are only the most recent campaigns in this never ending battle.

10. Expansion of chains: Richard S. Tedlow, *New and Improved: The Story of Mass Marketing in America* (New York: Basic Books, 1990).

11. Corner stores: for an intimate history of corner stores in a different location—Texas—see Ellen Beasley, *The Corner Store: An American Tradition, Galveston Style* (Washington, D.C.: National Building Museum, 1999).

12. Ladies' Mile: M. Christine Boyer, *Manhattan Manners: Architecture and Style, 1850–1900* (New York: Rizzoli, 1985), 43–129; movement of stores in 1920s: Robert A. M. Stern, Gregory Gilmartin, and Thomas Mellins, *New York 1930* (New York: Rizzoli, 1987), 317–21.

13. A piecemeal process: see Cohen, *A Consumers' Republic*, 257–89.

14. Pay higher prices: David Caplovitz, *The Poor Pay More: Consumer Practices of Low-Income Families* (New York: Free Press, 1967).

15. Shopping in poor neighborhoods: see Sharon Zukin, *The Cultures of Cities* (Cambridge, Mass., and Oxford: Blackwell, 1995), 207–37, and Camilo José Vergara, *The New American Ghetto* (New Brunswick, N.J.: Rutgers University Press, 1995), 78–94.

16. Teenagers in Haiti: remark of a Brooklyn College student in class discussion, 1999. Home Boys: Brooklyn College student research, 1998. Queens Center Mall: Eric Lipton, "Nothing Gaudy but Sales Figures," *New York Times*, February 2, 2000.

17. Times Square: see Zukin, *Cultures of Cities*, 133–42 and "Times Square," in *The City A-Z*, ed. Steve Pile and Nigel Thrift (London: Routledge, 2000), 256–58.

18. Shopping districts and economic development: the general trend is toward the

replacement of locally owned, low-price shops with stores financed by outside investment that can provide goods of higher aesthetic quality; after a higher-income shopping base has been established, these shops are driven out, in turn, by chain stores which can pay higher rents. Like residential gentrification, this commercial gentrification seems to operate on the basis of consumer preferences and prices rather than public- or private-sector plans. Alternative to suburbanization: see, for example, Elaine Louie's article about NoLITa: "Not a Mall, and a Lot Cozier: For Downtown Shops with a Personal Touch, Follow the Beaten Path and Then Go East," *New York Times*, May 31, 1998. After September 11, 2001: from this date, articles about retail shopping in the press shifted from boastful to poignant, for example, when they discussed the annual holiday decorations in store windows or the opening in Times Square by Toys "R" Us, of "the largest toy store in the world" (*New York Times*, November 15, 2001). Because of the concurrent recession, discussions of whether shoppers were buying much, or buying at all, ranged from deeply mournful to moderately hopeful.

19. Human beehive: See William Cronon's floor-by-floor discussion of the Montgomery Ward headquarters in Chicago, based on the picture on the cover of their 1900 mail-order catalog, in *Nature's Metropolis: Chicago and the Great West* (New York: Norton, 1991), 330–40.

20. Totalizing institution, mental hospital: Erving Goffman, *Asylums: Essays on the Social Situation of Mental Patients* (Garden City, N.Y.: Anchor Books, 1961). Classic studies of power: Michel Foucault, *Discipline and Punish: The Birth of the Prison*, trans. Alan Sheridan (New York: Pantheon, 1977).

21. Discipline of the body: Foucault, *Discipline and Punish.*

22. Raucous carnival: see the tradition of late-twentieth-century writing influenced by Mikhail Bahtin, *Rabelais and His World* (London: Midland, 1984); Peter Stallybrass and Allon White, *The Poetics and Politics of Transgression* (Ithaca, N.Y.: Cornell University Press, 1986); Don Slater, "Going Shopping: Markets, Crowds and Consumption," in *Cultural Reproduction*, ed. Chris Jencks (London: Routledge, 1993), 188–209.

23. General store: Gerald Carson, *The Old Country Store* (New York: Oxford University Press, 1954).

24. Mobile public/displacement through times and spaces: in supermarkets—see Richard Longstreth, *The Drive-In, The Supermarket, and the Transformation of Commercial Space in Los Angeles, 1914–1941* (Cambridge: MIT Press, 1999); in movie theaters and shopping malls—see Anne Friedberg, *Window Shopping: Cinema and the Postmodern* (Berkeley and Los Angeles: University of California Press, 1993). For an earlier sense of displacement through the early modern marketplace as a liminal space, see Jean-Christophe Agnew, *Worlds Apart: The Market and the Theater in Anglo-American Thought* (New York: Cambridge University Press, 1986).

25. Plate-glass windows: Leach, *Land of Desire.*

26. "Life-crushing disenfranchisement": Patricia J. Williams, *The Alchemy of Race and Rights* (Cambridge: Harvard University Press, 1991), 43.

27. If a man goes unaccompanied: by the same token, a store can present merchandise and organize the sales force in ways that reduce social barriers. Home Depot is a prime example of how a hardware and home repair store can reorient itself from marketing to presumably knowledgeable men to equally helpless men and women.

28. Fulfill moral obligations: see Daniel Miller, *A Dialectics of Shopping* (Chicago: University of Chicago Press, 2001).

29. Significant others we buy for: Daniel Miller, *A Theory of Shopping* (Cambridge, England: Polity Press, 1998), 15–72.

30. "Diderot effect": Grant McCracken, *Culture and Consumption* (Bloomington and Indianapolis: Indiana University Press, 1988), 118–29.

31. The dressing room mirror: aside from personal experience, see the interviews reported by Rachel Colls, a student at the University of Sheffield, in "An Exploration of the Spatial and Embodied Experiences of Women's Clothes Shopping," paper presented at the annual meeting of the Association of American Geographers, New York City, February 27-March 3, 2001.

32. A critical language: on the importance of criticism to the development of the public sphere, see Terry Eagleton, *The Function of Criticism* (London: Verso, 1984).

33. Public sphere: Jurgen Habermas, *The Social Transformation of the Public Sphere*, trans. Thomas Burger (Cambridge: MIT Press, 1989 [1962]).

34. Heterotopic space: Kevin Hetherington, *The Badlands of Modernity: Heterotopia and Social Ordering* (London: Routledge, 1997). Totally constructed shopping: B. Joseph Pine II and James H. Gilmore, *The Experience Economy* (Cambridge: Harvard Business School Press, 1999).

35. By and for women: see, for example, Mica Nava, "Modernity's Disavowal: Women, The City and the Department Store," in *The Shopping Experience*, ed. Pasi Falk and Colin Campbell (London: Sage, 1997 [1996]), 56–91, and Victoria de Grazia with Ellen Furlough, ed., *The Sex of Things: Gender and Consumption in Historical Perspective* (Berkeley and Los Angeles: University of California Press, 1996).

36. Shoplifting and kleptomania: Elaine S. Abelson, *When Ladies Go A-Thieving: Middle-Class Shoplifters in the Victorian Department Store* (New York: Oxford University Press, 1989). Although women, teenagers, and children—that is, socially vulnerable groups—are considered to be the most common shoplifters, perhaps they are also, disproportionately, the most frequent visitors to stores. By the end of the twentieth century, however, shoplifting, like shopping, may have become a less gendered activity. In the song "Been Caught Stealing," recorded by Jane's Addiction in 1990, a male and a female sing about shoplifting together.

37. Women as producers of status: Randall Collins, "Women and the Production of Status Cultures," in *Cultivating Differences: Symbolic Boundaries and the Making of Inequality*, ed. Michele Lamont and Marcel Fournier (Chicago: University of Chicago Press, 1992), 213–31. Advertising copywriters: Malcolm Gladwell, "True Colors," *The New Yorker*, March 22, 1999, 70–81.

chapter 2: julia learns to shop

1. Conversations about the food: Russell Baker, "Worse than Gluttony," *New York Times*, January 4, 1986, and Sharon Zukin, *Landscapes of Power: From Detroit to Disney World* (Berkeley and Los Angeles: University of California Press, 1991), 202–15. Status consumption: Thorstein Veblen, *The Theory of the Leisure Class (1899)*, in *The Portable Veblen*, ed. Max Lerner (New York: Viking, 1948), 53–214; cf. David Brooks, *Bobos in Paradise* (New York: Simon and Schuster, 2000).

2. Tastes of the upper middle class: for Bourdieu, these people were less the "affluent" than "intellectuals," or "the dominated part of the dominating class." See Pierre Bourdieu, *Distinction: A Social Critique of the Judgement of Taste*, trans. Richard Nice (Cambridge: Harvard University Press, 1984).

3. Status shopping: Veblen, *Theory of the Leisure Class*. "Keeping up with the Joneses": Vance Packard, *The Status Seekers* (New York: McKay, 1959).
4. Men became more interested in style: on how more frequent changes in men's fashions encouraged style consciousness, see Thomas Frank, *The Conquest of Cool: Business Culture, Counterculture, and the Rise of Hip Consumerism* (Chicago: University of Chicago Press, 1997); on how style consciousness played out in London, especially among gay men, see Frank Mort, *Cultures of Consumption: Masculinities and Social Space in Late Twentieth Century Britain* (London: Routledge, 1992); on how the social space of a store changed over time to attract male shoppers, see Gail Reekie, "Changes in the Adamless Eden: The Spatial and Sexual Transformation of a Brisbane Department Store 1930–90," *Lifestyle Shopping: The Subject of Consumption*, ed. Rob Shields (London and New York: Routledge, 1992), 170–94.
5. A woman in her late fifties: in this chapter, I draw on a small number of interviews with middle-class shoppers in New York City and Toronto conducted by my research assistant Jennifer Smith Maguire and on two focus groups that I conducted in Brooklyn with working-class black and Latino teenagers and mothers. I have provided all the respondents with pseudonyms and changed details by which they could be identified.
6. Unexpected geographical mobility: see Elizabeth Chin, *Purchasing Power: Black Kids and American Consumer Culture* (Minneapolis: University of Minnesota Press, 2001).
7. The "treat": in *A Theory of Shopping* (Cambridge, England: Polity Press, 1998), Daniel Miller says that working-class and lower-middle-class women in North London whom he interviewed about grocery shopping emphasize such treats as having lunch or a snack while shopping, or buying food that *they* like in addition to food for their loved ones. This leads him to conclude that the treat is an integral part of the shopping experience.
8. Having children as turning point: I suspect this is universally true, except among the rich. For North London examples, see Peter Jackson and Beverly Holbrook, "Multiple Meanings: Shopping and the Cultural Politics of Identity," *Environment and Planning A* 27 (1995): 1920–21.
9. Ability to make good choices: on the significance of the "choosing self" in consumer culture, see Don Slater, *Consumer Culture and Modernity* (Cambridge, England: Polity Press, 1997).

chapter 3: from woolworth's to wal-mart

1. Kmart is isolated: in the interests of full disclosure, I must point out that there is a lot of foot traffic as people cross from east to west along Eighth Street. A large liquor and wine store and a Barnes & Noble bookstore on the next block bring many shoppers to the immediate area. Moreover, since Kmart arrived, not one but two Starbucks coffee shops have opened at the same big intersection—where Astor Place meets Cooper Square—and a luxury residential condominium and new hotel are planned.
2. Importance of neighborhood shops: the classic statement is in Jane Jacobs, *The Death and Life of Great American Cities* (New York: Random House, 1961), chap. 2. Also see Tom Schachtman, *Around the Block: The Business of a Neighborhood* (New York: Harcourt Brace, 1997).
3. Largest supermarket: *New York Times*, September 19, 1999. In 1900, almost two decades before the first zoning laws were passed, Woolworth built a 12,000-

square-foot store on Sixth Avenue at Seventeenth Street, which was called at the time the "world's largest Five and Ten."

4. Borrowing a yarmulke: an Italian-American woman I know told me her brother borrows a yarmulke to go shopping on Thirteenth Avenue in Borough Park, Brooklyn, where there is a concentration of Hasidic-owned stores. Shoppers tell me that sales clerks in these stores treat customers who look Hasidic, or at least Orthodox, better than they treat other customers, and male sales clerks often tend to ignore female customers, perhaps because of religious strictures against close contact with women outside of the family.

5. Opposition to big box stores: there is both a mainstream and a grassroots nation-wide opposition, both dating to the early 1990s. See Constance Beaumont, *How Superstore Sprawl Can Harm Communities and What Citizens Can Do about It* (Washington D.C.: National Trust for Historic Preservation, 1994) and Al Norman, *Slam-Dunking Wal-Mart! How You Can Stop Superstore Sprawl in Your Hometown*, available on the Sprawlbusters website at www.sprawl-busters.com.

Failure of the plan to build an IKEA store in Brooklyn: Amy Waldman, "Plans to Build Ikea Store Are Scrapped in Brooklyn," *New York Times*, June 17, 2001; Ruth Ford, "Gowanus Ikea Dead," *Park Slope Paper*, June 18, 2001; and Trevor O'Driscoll, "Ikea Backs Away from Controversial Brooklyn Site," *Park Slope Courier*, June 18, 2001. On earlier opposition to IKEA in the suburb of New Rochelle, New York, see Debra West, "Ikea Wants to Move In, but Neighbors Fight Moving Out," *New York Times*, March 7, 2000, and Lisa W. Foderaro, "Suburbs Try to Limit Projects outside Their Borders," *New York Times*, March 11, 2000, and three reports by Amy Eddings on WNYC-FM: "There Goes the Neighborhood: IKEA vs. New Rochelle," June 28, 2000; "IKEA Go Home," November 17, 2000; and "IKEA Backs Out of New Rochelle," February 1, 2001, all at www.wnyc.org. In contrast to the opposition to superstores in these residential areas, the borough of the Bronx, where there is much unused industrial space, eagerly tried to interest IKEA in locating there. On attempts by the Bronx Overall Economic Development Corporation to bring IKEA to the Bronx, see www.riverdalereview.com/3_15_01news1.html.

Although mayors from New York to San Francisco have supported proposals to build superstores, newspapers usually side with local merchants who oppose them. See the column by Geneva Overholser, "The Box Stops Here," *Washington Post*, October 31, 1999, celebrating the decision by the City Council of Rockville, Maryland, to impose a six-month moratorium on the construction of "mega-stores" within their borders. For a "contrarian" column in favor of the economic efficiency of chain stores, see Daniel Akst, "Why Chain Stores Aren't the Big Bad Wolf," *New York Times*, June 3, 2001.

6. Business experts advise: Sandra S. Vance and Roy V. Scott, *Wal-Mart: A History of Sam Walton's Retail Phenomenon* (New York: Twayne Publishers, 1994). "Low prices, always": this is Wal-Mart's slogan.

7. If the shoppers are poor: Stephen Halebsky, "Retail Development and the Growth Machine," unpublished manuscript, Department of Sociology, University of Wisconsin-Madison, 2000.

8. Activist in East Texas: Bill Quinn, *How Wal-Mart Is Destroying America and What You Can Do about It* (Berkeley, Calif.: Ten Speed Press, 1998); also see Edward B. Shils, *The Shils Report: Measuring the Economic and Sociological Impact of the Mega-Retail Discount Chains on Small Enterprise in Urban, Suburban, and Rural Communities*, Wharton School, University of Pennsylvania, February 7, 1997,

http://www.ufcw.org/shils_report/cover.htmll, accessed September 16, 1997, and www.sprawl-busters.com.

9. Top ten retailers: according to a survey of the National Retail Federation, reported on *Marketplace: Morning Report*, National Public Radio, July 6, 2001. It is noteworthy that not a single department store chain made this list. Survey of suburban shopping, loss of $3 billion a year: New York City Department of City Planning, *Comprehensive Retail Strategy for New York City*, winter 1995.

10. Joseph B. Rose: "Industrial Strength Retail: Transcript of Conference on Superstores," Municipal Art Society, New York, May 2, 1995, 1–6.

11. Same for everyone: the Russian word for department store is *universalni magazin*, a term that suggests an ideal type of social space, connected historically with mass electoral democracy, especially as practiced in the United States, and with both public and private bureaucracies.

12. "Democratized desire": William Leach, *Land of Desire: Merchants, Power, and the Rise of a New American Culture* (New York: Pantheon, 1993).

13. Woolworth's five-and-dime: J. P. Nichols, *Skyline Queen and the Merchant Prince*; Peter Nulty, "National Business Hall of Fame," *Fortune*, April 3, 1995, 108–14; Karen Plunkett-Powell, *Remembering Woolworth's: A Nostalgic History of the World's Most Famous Five-and-Dime* (New York: St. Martin's Press, 1999).

14. "Nor does even the aristocratic shopper": "Woolworth's $250,000,000 Trick," *Fortune*, November 1933, 106–8. Emphasis added.

15. Development of self-service in American stores: James R. Beniger, *The Control Revolution: Technological and Economic Origins of the Information Society* (Cambridge: Harvard University Press, 1986); Susan Strasser, *Satisfaction Guaranteed: The Making of an American Mass Market* (New York: Pantheon, 1989); Richard S. Tedlow, *New and Improved: The Story of Mass Marketing in America* (New York: Basic Books, 1990). On self-service in supermarkets, see James M. Mayo, *The American Grocery Store: The Business Evolution of an Architectural Space* (Westport, Conn.: Greenwood Press, 1993); John P. Welsh, *Supermarkets Transformed: Understanding Organizational and Technological Innovations* (ASA Rose Monograph Series and New Brunswick, N.J.: Rutgers University Press, 1993); Lizabeth Cohen, *Making a New Deal: Industrial Workers in Chicago, 1919–1939* (Cambridge: Cambridge University Press, 1990). On sales clerks' role in department stores, see Susan Porter Benson, *Counter Cultures: Saleswomen, Managers, and Customers in American Department Stores, 1890–1940* (Urbana: University of Illinois Press, 1986).

16. Believed shoplifting would increase: Rachel Bowlby suggests that turnstiles were introduced in the Piggly Wiggly stores because, with self-service, "losses from pilfering [rose to] as much as six percent." *Carried Away: The Invention of Modern Shopping* (New York: Columbia University Press, 2000), 140.

17. Tin cans and milk: Waverley Root and Richard de Rochemont, *Eating in America: A History* (New York: Ecco Press, 1976), 190, 231. Made shoppers feel modern: by the 1920s, packaging was presented as a modern "revolution" in selling by the food industry and its advertising agencies (Bowlby, *Carried Away*, 80–90).

18. Becoming centralized: on meat, see William Cronon, *Nature's Metropolis: Chicago and the Great West* (New York: Norton, 1991), 230–47. Variations began to be phased out: of course, this is still not completely true. Chain stores have to cater to local and ethnic preferences, with more brands of baked beans carried in supermarkets in New England, and more Mexican beans in the Southwest.

19. Radio advertisements: Susan J. Douglas, *Listening In: Radio and the American Imagination* (New York: Times Books, 1999); billboards: Catherine Gudis,

Buyways: Billboards, Automobiles, and the American Landscape (New York: Routledge, forthcoming).

20. Young, female shoppers: Ada Louise Huxtable, "The Death of the Five-and-Ten," in *Architecture Anyone?* (New York: Random House, 1986), 311–17. Quality of writing paper: "Woolworth's $250,000,000 Trick," 66.

21. "The stores smelled": Huxtable, "The Death of the Five-and-Ten," 314.

22. Clerks in place: "Woolworth's $250,000,000 Trick." Racial integration at local discretion: Miles Wolff, *Lunch at the 5 & 10*, rev. ed. (Chicago: Ivan R. Dee, 1990 [1970]), 169–72. Prior to the 1960s, African Americans were permitted to shop at the five-and-dimes in the South, and to work there in menial jobs, but they were not permitted to eat at the lunch counters with white people.

23. Average weekly salary: "Woolworth's $250,000,000 Trick," 104.

24. "On these wages," "sent home": Therese Mitchell, *Consider the Woolworth Workers* (New York: League of Women Shoppers, n.d. [1940]), 8–17.

25. Mitchell, *Consider the Woolworth Workers*, 5.

26. Discounters' wage bill, self-service: James R. Lowry, *The Retailing Revolution Revisited*, Ball State Monograph no. 16 (Muncie, Ind., 1969), 12, 14.

27. Walgreen's innovations: Beniger, *Control Revolution*, 336.

28. "Autonomous presence": Kim Humphery, *Shelf Life: Supermarkets and Changing Patterns of Consumption* (Cambridge: Cambridge University Press, 1998), 180. Mobile public: on the "commodified visual mobility" that is common to both shopping and moviegoing, see Anne Friedberg, *Window Shopping: Cinema and the Postmodern* (Berkeley and Los Angeles: University of California Press, 1993).

29. Different experience of the city . . . Los Angeles: Richard Longstreth, *The Drive-In, The Supermarket, and the Transformation of Commercial Space in Los Angeles, 1914–1941* (Cambridge: MIT Press, 1999). Only 5 percent . . . half the total business: "Shopper's Delight," *Life* magazine, January 3, 1955, 38. Corner stores . . . disappeared: Ellen Beasley, *The Corner Store: An American Tradition, Galveston Style* (Washington, D.C.: National Building Museum, 1999).

30. "Mountains" of goods . . . "physically and visually": Bowlby, *Carried Away*, 146; "mountains" is quoted from a 1953 trade journal. "I drive my car": John Updike, "Superman," in *Collected Poems: 1953–1993* (New York: Knopf, 1993), 270.

31. "Mythical cycle of seasons": Rachel Bowlby, "Modes of Modern Shopping: Mallarmé at the Bon Marché," in *The Ideology of Conduct: Essays on Literature and the History of Sexuality*, ed. Nancy Armstrong and Leonard Tennenhouse (New York: Methuen, 1987), 191.

32. They bridged: the big discount stores were "heterotopic" spaces in the sense that they combined old elements of social life in new ways; they were antique as well as modern, and were organized for both freedom and control. On "heterotopia," see Kevin Hetherington, *The Badlands of Modernity: Heterotopia and Social Ordering* (London and New York: Routledge, 1997), 14.

33. "What had occurred": Huxtable, "The Death of the Five-and-Ten," 316–17.

34. "Repetition and banality": Keller Easterling, *Organization Space: Landscapes, Highways, and Houses in America* (Cambridge: MIT Press, 1999), 135.

35. Penney's credo: Vance H. Trimble, *Sam Walton: The Inside Story of America's Richest Man* (New York: Dutton, 1990), 33–34.

36. "Skinflint with wages": Nulty, "National Business Hall of Fame," 108. According to this profile, Woolworth's "early lieutenants" became rich from their stockholdings. Moreover, store managers—who were always males—received a share of the profits of their stores, and so, it seems, did the men who worked in the stockrooms ("Woolworth's $250,000,000 Trick").

37. Paternalism: in 2001, six current and past employees sued Wal-Mart, claiming the chain "discriminates against women in pay, compensation, and promotions" (Ann Zimmerman, "Six Current, Ex-Workers Sue Wal-Mart," *Wall Street Journal*, June 20, 2001).

38. Walton's strategies: Vance and Scott, *Wal-Mart: A History of Sam Walton's Retail Phenomenon*: Woolworth's visits to stores: Nichols, *Skyline Queen*, 35. In a curious polemic against Wal-Mart, a people greeter complains that since Walton's death, local managers no longer enforce the rules Walton devised; moreover, since managers no longer fear surprise visits by the CEO, their incompetence and arrogance have grown. See Avis—The Greeter (Devon Hammond Sr.), *What's Wrong at Wal-Mart? Is America's Greatest Success Story Going Down the Tubes?* (Las Vegas: Hamco Books, 1997). People greeters deter shoplifters: Paco Underhill, *Why We Buy: The Science of Shopping* (New York: Simon and Schuster, 1999), 49.

39. Middle-income shopper: according to H. Lee Scott Jr., president and CEO of Wal-Mart, the company focuses on households with an annual income of less than $60,000: "that is where the bulk of the people are, that is where we at Wal-Mart are going to continue to focus all of our efforts" (Keynote speech to Second Annual Fairchild Apparel CEO Summit, Carefree, Ariz., May 31–June 3, 1998, 64).

40. Upgrade their offerings: Lowry, *Retailing Revolution Revisited*, 11.

41. Demanded that manufacturers: manufacturers thanked Wal-Mart for this continuous stream of information, which helped both the store and the supplier to balance supply and demand. According to management gurus in the 1980s, the just-in-time delivery system, with its low inventories, also kept costs down.

42. "Giant melting-pot": "My Wal-Mart 'Tis of Thee," *The Economist*, November 23, 1996, 27.

43. Employees cannot afford: Barbara Ehrenreich, *Nickel and Dimed: On (Not) Getting By in America* (New York: Metropolitan Books, 2001), 181. Forced to work overtime: in December 2002, the company lost the first of these suits, in Oregon, but thirty-nine more had been filed nationwide. See http://www.cbsnews.com/stories/2002/12/20/national/main533818.shtml. China: Joseph Kahn, "Snapping Up Chinese Goods despite Qualms on Trade Bill," *New York Times*, May 17, 2000. Unfortunately, selling imports from low-wage countries spelled the end of Sam Walton's Buy American campaign. Announced in 1985, when U.S. factories were closing down in droves or shifting production overseas, this plan gradually disappeared and ended completely in 1998. Vance and Scott, *Wal-Mart*, 110–11; Leslie Kaufman, "As Biggest Business, Wal-Mart Propels Changes Elsewhere," *New York Times*, October 22, 2000.

44. "Humility," roll back, "full value": Scott, Keynote speech, Second Annual Fairchild Apparel CEO Summit. "We can all be middle class": the rise of outlet malls makes this point even more dramatically. See Marianne Conroy, "Discount Dreams: Factory Outlet Malls, Consumption, and the Performance of Middle-Class Identity," *Social Text* 16, no. 1 (spring 1998): 63–83. Thanks to Randal Doane for calling this article to my attention.

45. Bowling alleys: Andrew Hurley, *Diners, Bowling Alleys, and Trailer Parks: Chasing the American Dream in Postwar Consumer Culture* (New York: Basic Books, 2001).Chardonnay: www.walmartstores.com/newsstand/archive, September 29, 2000. Selling California wine in Wal-Mart stores outside the United States is also a part of the chain's global merchandising strategy.

46. Ivana Trump: "She Stoops to Spend," *New York Times Magazine*, October 15, 2000, 26.

47. "Consumption communities": Daniel J. Boorstin, *The Americans: The Democratic Experience* (New York: Random House, 1973), 90.
48. "This Woolworth's on Vermont": Steve Abee, "Woolworth's," in *King Planet* (San Diego: Incommunicado Press, 1997), 38, 41.
49. End of Woolworth's: Hoover's Company Profile Database, 2000. Lunch counter to Smithsonian: Plunkett-Powell, *Remembering Woolworth's*.
50. Loopholes in the zoning laws: Kirk Johnson, "As Zoning Debate Rages, Giant Stores Settle In," *New York Times*, October 15, 1996.
51. When the stock car racer: Rick Bragg, "Racer's Death Leaves Hole in Heart of His Hometown," *New York Times*, February 21, 2001. Sixteen years earlier, in *White Noise* (New York: Viking, 1985), the novelist Don DeLillo had already noted the supermarket's central place in a small-town community; one of the main characters rushes to the supermarket as soon as he hears about the death of his professional rival (168).

chapter 4: "the perfect pair of leather pants"

1. "Women born with the shopping gene": Mimi Avins, "Music Gives Shopping a Bum Rap," *Los Angeles Times*, August 24, 2001.
2. Daydreams, "imaginative hedonism": Colin Campbell, *The Romantic Ethic and the Spirit of Modern Consumerism* (Oxford and New York: Basil Blackwell, 1987), 77–95.
3. Most common complaints: the first is that women "just don't like the styles that are out there." The second is Cindy's complaint: that the styles they want are not in the stores. The third is that nothing fits. Adele Kirk, director of consumer research, Kurt Salmon Associates, Second Annual Fairchild Apparel CEO Summit, Carefree, Ariz., May 31-June 3, 1998, 18–19 (emphasis added).
4. "Two thirds of consumers": Adele Kirk, Second Annual Fairchild Apparel CEO Summit, 21.
5. Importance of "personal service": this is confirmed by retail executives at stores ranging from the mass-market Sears and J. C. Penney to the high-price Mitchell's in Westport, Conn. Second Annual Fairchild Apparel CEO Summit, 37, 38, 43.
6. Shopping for used cars: George Akerlof, "The Market for 'Lemons': Quality Uncertainty and the Market Mechanism" [1970], in *An Economic Theorist's Book of Tales* (Cambridge and New York: Cambridge University Press, 1984), 7–22.
7. "Solution providers": Second Annual Fairchild Apparel CEO Summit, 27. "87% of women": Adele Kirk, Second Annual Fairchild Apparel CEO Summit, 21. A good salesperson: Henri Peretz, "Le vendeur, la vendeuse et leur cliente: Ethnographie du prêt-à-porter de luxe," *Revue française de sociologie* 33 (1992): 49–72; Mimi Swartz, "Annals of Retail: Victoria's Secret," *The New Yorker*, March 30, 1998, 94–101.
8. Cover of a recent issue: November 2001. Average consumer is a size 12: Adele Kirk, Second Annual Fairchild Apparel CEO Summit, 20.
9. "Our dream of wholeness": Roland Barthes, *The Fashion System*, trans. Matthew Ward and Richard Howard (New York: Hill and Wang, 1983 [1967]), 254–55. Bodies divided into zones: while every woman may laugh with recognition on this point, the only research I have seen on the issue was reported by Rachel Colls, then a graduate student at the University of Sheffield, in "An Exploration of the Spatial and Embodied Experiences of Women's Clothes Shopping," Annual Meet-

ing of the Association of American Geographers, New York, February–March 2001.

10. Product designers . . . fashion press: Harvey Molotch, *Where Stuff Comes From* (New York and London: Routledge, 2003); Paul du Gay et al., *Doing Cultural Studies: The Story of the Sony Walkman* (London: Sage, 1997); Stuart Ewen, *Captains of Consciousness: Advertising and the Social Roots of the Consumer Culture* (New York: McGraw Hill, 1976); Marylin Bender, *The Beautiful People* (New York: Coward-McCann, 1967).

11. "So much junk": quoted by Steve Powell, managing director, Prudential Securities, Second Annual Fairchild Apparel CEO Summit, 29.

12. Success of discount stores: David Cole, chairman and CEO, Kurt Salmon Associates, Second Annual Fairchild Apparel CEO Summit, 26; Marvin Traub, former chairman of Bloomingdale's and current president, Marvin Traub Associates, Second Annual Fairchild Apparel CEO Summit, 71. Not a single department store: *Marketplace: Morning Report*, National Public Radio, July 6, 2001. As Dr. Carl Steidtmann, director of research and chief economist at Management Horizons, Price Waterhouse, says, "If you think about the success of Wal-Mart, if they were able to continue that success for the next eight years . . . they'll control all general merchandise in apparel and furniture retailing in the United States. They'll have 100% market share." Second Annual Fairchild Apparel CEO Summit, 51. I describe Wal-Mart's success in chapter 3 and The Gap's in chapter 8.

13. "Lifestyle brand[s] . . . channel captains": Robin Lewis, vice president and group executive editor, *Women's Wear Daily* and *Daily News Record*, opening remarks to Second Annual Fairchild Apparel CEO Summit, 14.

14. "Tough out there": David Cole, Second Annual Fairchild Apparel CEO Summit, 17; "unhappy . . . unloved": Adele Kirk, 18.

15. Advertising industry in the 1920s: Ewen, *Captains of Consciousness*. Other writers question whether a historic change from unwilling to willing consumers really occurred at this time, and whether capitalists knowingly used advertising to foment the change. See John Levi Martin, "The Myth of the Consumption-Oriented Economy and the Rise of the Desiring Subject," *Theory and Society* 28 (1999): 425–53. For a similar argument against a dramatic, ideologically induced shift from unwilling to willing consumers in an earlier period, see T. J. Jackson Lears, "Beyond Veblen," in *Consuming Visions: Accumulation and Display of Goods in America, 1880–1920* (New York: Norton, 1989). "What the public really wants": Lammot du Pont, quoted in Roland Marchand, *Creating the Corporate Soul* (Berkeley and Los Angeles: University of California Press, 1998), 230.

16. Until then, advertising: Roland Marchand, *Advertising the American Dream: Making the Way for Modernity, 1920–1940* (Berkeley and Los Angeles: University of California Press, 1985), 75; styling variations: Emma Rothschild, *Paradise Lost: The Decline of the Auto-Industrial Age* (New York: Random House, 1973). At the same time, you could say that GM undertook consumer research to foster the "organized creation of dissatisfaction." Mark Steele, "Attention Shoppers: Don't Look Now But You Are Being Tailed," *Smithsonian*, January 1993, 70–78.

17. GM's consumer research program: Marchand, *Creating the Corporate Soul*, 230–35.

18. Invented the audience: Susan J. Douglas, *Listening In: Radio and the American Imagination* (New York: Times Books, 1999), 124–60.

19. Strident criticism: Theodor Adorno, *The Culture Industry*, 2d ed. (London and New York: Routledge, 2001).

20. Herta Herzog: Douglas, *Listening In*, 139ff.

21. "Mobilized . . . forming connections," Tavistock: Peter Miller and Nikolas Rose, "Mobilizing the Consumer: Assembling the Subject of Consumption," *Theory, Culture and Society* 14 (1997): 2.

22. Fear that some brands were better: Miller and Rose, "Mobilizing the Consumer," 25–26.

23. "Brainwashing": Vance Packard, *The Hidden Persuaders* (New York: D. Mackay, 1957). "Psychographics": James Atlas, "Beyond Demographics," *The Atlantic,* October 1984: 49–59. Marketing concepts: George Kress, *Marketing Research* (Englewood Cliffs, N.J.: Prentice Hall, 1985).

24. "Life-style analyses": Atlas, "Beyond Demographics."

25. Replaced social classes: Lizabeth Cohen, *A Consumers' Republic: The Politics of Mass Consumption in Postwar America* (New York: Knopf, 2003), 292–313; VALS: Atlas, "Beyond Demographics"; also see Joseph Turow, *Breaking Up America: Advertisers and the New Media World* (Chicago: University of Chicago Press, 1998). According to Cohen (311–12), SRI stressed the importance of heterogeneous lifestyle choices within social classes as early as the fifties.

26. Organized diversity: Kalman Applbaum, *Marketing Observed: From Professional Practice to Global Provisioning* (New York and London: Routledge, 2003).

27. "Individuals rather than statistics"; Plummer defended it; "We spent a lot of time . . . 34 percent of the market": Atlas, "Beyond Demographics."

28. "More than a market research outfit": Atlas, "Beyond Demographics."

29. Headbands, hypnosis: Yumiko Ono, "Marketers Seek the 'Naked' Truth in Consumer Psyches," *Wall Street Journal,* May 30, 1997.

30. Could be "mobilized": Miller and Rose, "Mobilizing the Consumer." Watch shoppers as they moved: Paco Underhill, *Why We Buy: The Science of Shopping* (New York: Simon and Schuster, 1999).

31. "Own the aroma": Jack Hitt, "Does the Smell of Coffee Brewing Remind You of Your Mother?" *New York Times Magazine,* May 7, 2000, 71–74, at 73.

32. "Come up with products": Emily Nelson, "P&G Checks Out Real Life," *Wall Street Journal,* May 17, 2001. Crayons: Leslie Kaufman, "Enough Talk: Focus Groups Are Old News; Today's Marketers Prefer Crayolas, Collages and Surveillance," *Newsweek,* August 18, 1997, 48. On globalization as a self-fulfilling marketing strategy, see Applbaum, *Marketing Observed.*

33. Measuring the efficacy of "clickthroughs": Rob Walker, "New Economy," *New York Times,* August 27, 2001. The surprising willingness of thousands of subjects to interact online with political pollsters: Michael Lewis, "The Two-Bucks-a-Minute Democracy," *New York Times Magazine,* November 5, 2000, 64–67.

34. Cannot trace the sources: nonetheless, new market researchers are continually being born. A new paradigm, "relationship marketing," uses in-depth, life-history interviews to trace people's attachment to specific brands; a brand is then described as "an active relationship partner." Though this work addresses brand loyalty rather than the sources of desire in general, the interviews do go deeply into experiences and attitudes about all sorts of things, including the self. Susan Fournier, Susan Dobscha, and David Glen Mick, "Preventing the Premature Death of Relationship Marketing," *Harvard Business Review,* January–February 1998, 42–50, and Susan Fournier, "Consumers and Their Brands: Developing Relationship Theory in Consumer Research," *Journal of Consumer Research* 24 (1998): 343–74.

35. "An audience of consumers," "the basic commodity": Eileen R. Meehan, "Why We Don't Count: The Commodity Audience," in *Logics of Television,* ed. Patricia Mellencamp (Bloomington: Indiana University Press, 1990), 121, 124. "Audited

eyeballs": Michael Riego, senior vice president for advertising, Jordache Jeans, quoted in Bill Carter, "Some Sponsors Can't Accept Racy Reality," *New York Times*, January 29, 2001.

chapter 5: b. altman, ralph lauren, and the death of the leisure class

1. Ralph Lauren: Second Annual Fairchild Apparel CEO Summit, Carefree, Ariz., May 31–June 3, 1998, 119.
2. B. Altman history: information screens, New York Public Library, Science, Industry and Business Library, February 24, 1999; Christopher Gray, "B. Altman's; The Life and Death (?) of a Palace for the Chic," *New York Times*, January 28, 1990. Third Avenue and Bowery in mid-nineteenth century: Edwin G. Burrows and Mike Wallace, *Gotham: A History of New York City to 1898* (New York: Oxford University Press, 1999), 727, 740, 745, 782; "New York Trade Offs: Single Trade Districts; A Walk on the Bowery, "www.mcny.org, accessed April 15, 2003.
3. Macy's: M. Christine Boyer, *Manhattan Manners: Architecture and Style, 1850–1900* (New York: Rizzoli, 1985), 90.
4. "Dream worlds": Rosalind H. Williams, *Dream Worlds: Mass Consumption in Late Nineteenth-Century France* (Berkeley and Los Angeles: University of California Press, 1982).
5. Prostitutes, sweatshops, skyscrapers: Boyer, *Manhattan Manners*, 104–8, 119–29.
6. Moralists, kleptomania: Williams, *Dream Worlds*; Elaine S. Abelson, *When Ladies Go A-Thieving: Middle-Class Shoplifters in the Victorian Department Store* (New York: Oxford University Press, 1989); William Leach, *Land of Desire: Merchants, Power, and the Rise of a New American Culture* (New York: Pantheon, 1993), 71–72.
7. Marshall Field windows, Dreiser: Leach, *Land of Desire*, 70. "Window nights": Leonard S. Marcus, *The American Store Window* (New York: Whitney Library of Design and London: Architectural Press Ltd., 1978), 23.
8. Workshops on the higher floors: such an arrangement would be similar to that of Montgomery Ward, the late nineteenth-century mail-order house in Chicago, and to Saks Fifth Avenue, built in 1930. Altman's as palazzo: Gray, "B. Altman's: The Life and Death (?) of a Palace for the Chic"; Gray quotes O'Connor's article. "Overdecorated" mansion: Boyer, *Manhattan Manners*, 141.
9. Public street of the arcades: Walter Benjamin, *The Arcades Project*, trans. Howard Eiland and Kevin McLaughlin (Cambridge, Mass.: Belknap Press, 1999); Pierre Missac, "Perspectives on the Atrium," in *Walter Benjamin's Passages* (Cambridge: MIT Press, 1995), 173–98.
10. The crowded counters: Milton Mackaye, "On the Square (S. Klein)," *The New Yorker*, June 25, 1932, reprinted in *Profiles from The New Yorker* (New York: Knopf, 1938), 165–73.
11. Decor: Gray, "B. Altman's: The Life and Death (?) of a Palace for the Chic." "Shopping was to become a pleasure": Dennis Duggan, "A Fond Farewell to Altman's: It Was Worth Saving," *Newsday Magazine*, March 25, 1990, 6.
12. "First department store to provide bathrooms": Duggan, "A Fond Farewell to Altman's." On employee benefits at other department stores, see Leach, *Land of Desire*, 118–19. Charitable foundation: this was one of the problems that eventually led to the store's demise. The Federal Tax Reform Act of 1969 forced the foundation to sell its "excess" business holdings, which amounted to about half of the store's stock ownership, or incur heavy penalties. The foundation sold the

store in 1985, at the height of a wave of mergers and acquisitions of consumer goods and chain store companies. Although the sale price of these acquisitions may have been high, the buyers were often inexperienced in the retail field, and the sales were usually leveraged by untenable levels of debt. Kathleen Teltsch, "Store's Sale Is Bonanza for Altman Foundation," *New York Times*, October 20, 1985; also see John Rothchild, *Going for Broke: How Robert Campeau Bankrupted the Retail Industry, Jolted the Junk Bond Market, and Brought the Booming Eighties to a Crashing Halt* (New York: Simon and Schuster, 1991).

13. "I miss being able to browse": Duggan, "A Fond Farewell to Altman's."

14. "Superior fashion merchandise": *Women's Wear Daily*, January 12, 1965.

15. "The 60s was a time": Arthur Miller, "The Past and Its Power: Why I Wrote 'The Price,'" *New York Times*, November 14, 1999. "Unified audience . . . Shakespearean ideal": Arthur Miller, introduction to fiftieth-anniversary edition of *Death of a Salesman*, quoted in John Lahr, "Making Willy Loman," *The New Yorker*, January 25, 1999, 49.

16. Bloomingdale's: Lois Gould, "Confessions of a Bloomingdale's Addict," *New York* magazine, March 5, 1973, 56–57.

17. "Each store aimed for a certain style": Grace Mirabella with Judith Warner, *In and Out of Vogue* (New York: Doubleday, 1995), 44.

18. Vignettes of shoppers: Joni Evans and Carol Rinzler, "You Are Where You Shop," *New York* magazine, March 5, 1973: 56–60. Evans became an editor; Rinzler is an author.

19. Bermuda Shop: at the time, this was a store that carried preppy styles. Bigi: this was a department for teenage girls that Bergdorf's installed on its top floor in the midsixties, amid criticism from other retail merchants that Bergdorf's was cheapening its image by catering to teenage shoppers. Bonwit Teller: clearly signifies a transitional status.

20. Bloomingdale's in the 1950s: Marvin Traub and Tom Teicholz, *Like No Other Store . . . : The Bloomingdale's Legend and the Revolution in American Marketing* (New York: Times Books, 1993), 50–55. Emphasis added. The exclusivity that stores claimed at the time is underlined by the fact that certain brand-name manufacturers would not permit Bloomingdale's to sell products with their labels in them. In 1960, Andrew Goodman, the president of Bergdorf Goodman, complained that Bloomingdale's was showing fashions by the French house of Patou "on Lexington Avenue" (43).

21. "Artisanal" products: it is Veblen's idea that in the machine age, the irregularities of handcrafted goods confer social status on consumers who acquire them. "The visible imperfections of the hand-wrought goods, being honorific, are accounted marks of superiority, of serviceability, or both." Thorstein Veblen, *The Theory of the Leisure Class*, in *The Portable Veblen*, ed. Max Lerner (New York: Viking, 1948 [1899]), 192.

22. "Well made, reasonably priced, and unique": Traub, *Like No Other Store . . .* , 61.

23. Casa Bella: Traub, *Like No Other Store . . .* , 77–79. For a critical examination of Bloomingdale's cross-marketing in the 1980s, see Debora Silverman, *Selling Culture: Bloomingdale's, Diana Vreeland, and the New Aristocracy of Taste in Reagan's America* (New York: Pantheon, 1986).

24. Neiman Marcus: Stanley Marcus, *Minding the Store: A Memoir* (Boston: Little, Brown, 1974); Frank X. Tolbert, *Neiman-Marcus: The Story of the Proud Dallas Store* (New York: Henry Holt, 1953).

25. Democratic, sexy, working class: Marylin Bender, *The Beautiful People* (New York:

Coward-McCann, 1967), 30. On Mods and looking different, also see Dick Hebdige, *Subculture: The Meaning of Style* (London: Methuen, 1979).

26. "Kookiness" . . . "unintelligible": this is the complaint of Kenneth Collins, who wrote the column "Today and Yesterday in Retailing" in *Women's Wear Daily* during the early sixties. These words are from his column of January 6, 1961. In *The Conquest of Cool*, Thomas Frank makes a different argument about the acceleration of style change in men's fashions fomented by manufacturers and clothing stores from the late fifties—but I cannot confirm this from my examination of women's fashions in *Women's Wear Daily*. Thomas Frank, *The Conquest of Cool: Business Culture, Counterculture, and the Rise of Hip Consumerism* (Chicago: University of Chicago Press, 1997).

27. "Youth has become a class": Bender, *Beautiful People*, 27.

28. Young people identifying downward: probably the first market researcher to identify the initiation of fashion trends by "the disenfranchised—the Negro population and students in general" was William Capitman, who spoke to the convention of the National Retail Merchants Association in 1966 (*Women's Wear Daily*, January 11, 1966).

29. Fashion as pervasive: Bender, *Beautiful People*, 18.

30. "A symbolic language," "national goods . . . celebrities": David Farber, *The Age of Great Dreams: America in the 1960s* (New York: Hill and Wang, 1994), 49.

31. "Impossibly glamourous and young": Caryn James, "When TV Changed American Politics," *New York Times*, November 2, 1999. "Enthroned in the White House": Bender, *Beautiful People*, 35. An exhibition of Jacqueline Kennedy Onassis's wardrobe from the White House years, organized by the Metropolitan Museum of Art in 2001, took a much more adulatory tone.

32. Early twentieth-century magazines: Christopher P. Wilson, "The Rhetoric of Consumption: Mass-Market Magazines and the Demise of the Gentle Reader, 1880–1920," in *The Culture of Consumption*, ed. Richard Wightman Fox and T. J. Jackson Lears (New York: Pantheon, 1983), 39–64. *Good Housekeeping*: Susan Strasser, *Never Done: A History of American Housework* (New York: Pantheon, 1982), 265. Neiman Marcus: Marcus, *Minding the Store*, 74.

33. "Willing exhibitionists," "new idols of materialist America": Bender, *Beautiful People*, 35. Nan Kempner: Cathy Horyn, "Outdated, Trivial, Adored: The Best-Dressed List," *New York Times*, May 4, 1999. The "best-dresssed list" had been invented some years earlier as a publicity ploy for the fashion industry by Eleanor Lambert, a PR consultant. About a dozen women were named to the list each year, supposedly on the vote of two thousand international fashion observers, but probably on the informal decisions of Lambert and several of her friends. "The best-dressed list," and the women on it, had high visibility in newspapers and magazines, especially in the women's pages, during the sixties.

34. Traditional, sociological sense of status: Max Weber, "Class, Status, Party," in *Max Weber: Essays in Sociology*, ed. H. H. Gerth and C. Wright Mills (New York: University Press, 1946), 180–95. "Money helps" . . . "personal flair": *Women's Wear Daily*, January 6, 1961. For a history that demystifies the best-dressed mystique, see Bender, *Beautiful People*, and Horyn, "Outdated, Trivial, Adored."

35. "Yearned for social acceptability": Bender, *Beautiful People*, 35.

36. "Democratization of fashion": Gilles Lipovetsky, *The Empire of Fashion: Dressing Modern Democracy*, trans. Catherine Porter (Princeton: Princeton University Press, 1994 [1987]).

37. Buyers to Paris, Ohrbach's: Leach, *Land of Desire*, 95ff.; Bender, *Beautiful People*;

Marcus, *Minding the Store*; Tolbert, *Neiman-Marcus Texas*. Russek's: Walter R. Brooks, *New York: An Intimate Guide* (New York: Knopf, 1931), 154.

38. "Bearing blue jeans": Bender, *Beautiful People*, 20.

39. "Givenchy . . . arrogant": Bender, *Beautiful People*, 96. Cunningham wrote this in 1962 or 1963.

40. "Yves had created . . . ": Traub, *Like No Other Store . . .* , 96.

41. "Essential meaning of boutique": Bender, *Beautiful People*, 226.

42. First retail merchant: Stewart & Company, a store that opened at Fifth Avenue and Fifty-sixth Street in 1929, was the first to divide the store, by both designer and product, into "luxurious" boutiques, but Stewart's went bankrupt eight months later, during the Great Depression. The building was then occupied by Bonwit Teller, which, ironically, eliminated the boutiques. Robert A. M. Stern, Gregory Gilmartin, and Thomas Mellins, *New York 1930: Architecture and Urbanism between the Two World Wars* (New York: Rizzoli, 1987), 319.

43. Bendel: Bender, *Beautiful People*, 227–28.

44. In-store boutiques: Traub, *Like No Other Store . . .* , 93–94. Traub also traces the Americanization of the boutique to Bloomingdale's establishment of its first in-store shop for Christmas merchandise, in 1950, in a department it called Place Elegante.

45. Saks, Bonwit's, "total sell": *Women's Wear Daily*, December 6, 1968. "Showing people a look": *Women's Wear Daily*, November 8, 1968.

46. Yves Saint Laurent boutique: *Women's Wear Daily*, January 10, 1968.

47. Men's designer fashions: "Retailers Recall," *Daily News Record*, January 18, 1995, emphasis added. Barney's also claims to have introduced men's designer fashions and boutiques, although its merchandising of designers really took off with Giorgio Armani in the 1970s. Joshua Levine, *The Rise and Fall of the House of Barney's* (New York: William Morrow, 1999).

48. Postwar evolution of boutiques: Peter Copeland, "The Boutique in Store Design," *Stores*, December 1967, 23–27.

49. "Longed for the intimacy": Copeland, "The Boutique in Store Design."

50. Calvin Klein: Anne-Marie Schiro, "Mildred Custin, 91, Retailer; Made Bonwit's Fashion Force" (obituary), *New York Times*, April 1, 1997; Joyce Wadler, "Calvin Klein's Partner Defines a Long Shot," *New York Times*, April 21, 1999.

51. Traub trolling, Saint Laurent, Ralph Lauren: Traub, *Like No Other Store . . .* , 83–96. In contrast to the dominant style of narrow neckties, Lauren insisted on designing wide ties.

52. "Home-grown designer": Traub, *Like No Other Store . . .* , 212.

53. Licenses . . . "not unkindly": Traub, *Like No Other Store . . .* , 219

54. Dismissed Ralph Lauren: Marcus, *Minding the Store*, 309–10.

55. "Stores . . . must be hangouts": *Women's Wear Daily*, January 10, 1967. Sanger Harris: John J. Gerdel, "Department Stores: A Bright Future," in *Competitive Structure in Retail Markets: The Department Store Perspective*, ed. Ronald W. Stampfl and Elizabeth Hirschman (Chicago: American Marketing Association, 1980), 64. On the boutique as a swinging hangout, see Amy Larocca, "The House of Mod," *New York*, February 17, 2003, 118–27.

56. Acquisitions mania: Rothchild, *Going for Broke*; Traub, *Like No Other Store . . .*

57. Overcoming shoppers' boredom: Anthony Ramirez, "Department Stores Shape Up," *Fortune*, September 1, 1986: 50–52. Lost trust and civility: Marjorie Rosenberg, "A Sad Heart at the Department Store," *The American Scholar*, spring 1985, 183–93. The title of this article echoes the poet and author

Randall Jarrell's earlier lament about the lowering of standards in both mass consumption and mass culture, in his book of essays, *A Sad Heart at the Supermarket* (1962).

58. "Choice shapes the economy": Peter Baita, "A Happy Heart at Bloomingdale's," *American Heritage*, December 1986, 16–18.

59. The face: the historian Warren Susman discusses the growing importance of the face, in the early twentieth century, as an embodiment of theories of the self and a reflection of the development of motion pictures (" 'Personality' and the Making of Twentieth-Century Culture," in *Culture as History* [New York: Pantheon, 1984], 271–85). Following this argument, Daniel Harris also calls attention to the increasing prominence of the face in fashion photographs and cosmetic advertisements during the early 1960s (*Cute, Quaint, Hungry and Romantic* [New York: Basic Books, 2000], 209–32).

60. "What woman has time": Alex Kuczynski, "Old Formula for a Magazine on Fashion Is Out of Style," *New York Times*, June 21, 1999.

61. Immigrant workers: Robert Fitch, "Planning New York," in *The Fiscal Crisis of American Cities*, ed. Roger E. Alcaly and David Mermelstein (New York: Vintage, 1977), 256–57.

chapter 6: artemio goes to tiffany's

1. Black is hot: for confirmation by the business press, see Joshua Levine, "Badass Sells," *Forbes*, April 21, 1997, 142–49.

2. Cultural value of cool: see Thomas Frank, *The Conquest of Cool: Business Culture, Counterculture, and the Rise of Hip Consumerism* (Chicago: University of Chicago Press, 1997) and Naomi Klein, *No Logo* (New York: Picador, 1999), 63–85. Two volatile groups: to say that teenagers and racial groups are "volatile" doesn't need any scholarly justification, but I want to refer to Elizabeth Grosz's ideas in *Volatile Bodies* (Bloomington: Indiana University Press, 1994). Borrowing from Grosz's ideas about corporeality in general, we can say the bodies of teens and blacks are constantly changing as others—more powerful groups like manufacturers, marketers, and advertising image makers—move them to the center of our attention. The migration of urban wear from black teens to all teens gives eerily graphic confirmation of Grosz's concept of the body as a dynamic process of "becoming," and when we think about the big bucks involved in the consumer products and entertainment industries, we certainly see volatile bodies as important sites in creating, in her terms, an "event" of power.

3. White Negro: Norman Mailer, "The White Negro" (1957), *The Penguin Book of the Beats*, ed., Ann Charters (New York: Penguin, 1993), 581–605. Identified with the "disenfranchised": William Capitman, in a talk to the 1966 annual convention of the National Retail Merchants Association (Bernard Groger, "Paris, S.A. [Seventh Avenue] Follow Youth, Sociologist Tells NRMA," *Women's Wear Daily*, January 11, 1966). The literary critic Susan Gubar believes that Mailer and other whites had (or have) a barely suppressed envy of, and desire for, black people; see her discussion of Mailer and other whites who identify themselves with black hipness in *Racechanges: White Skin, Black Face in American Culture* (New York: Oxford University Press, 1997), 176–89.

4. Qualities "whiteness" lacked: David R. Roediger, *The Wages of Whiteness* (London and New York: Verso, 1991).

5. Marketing strategies: during the 1990s, the press was fascinated by the manipulation of teenagers by media conglomerates, advertising agencies, shoe manufacturers, and the marketers they employed; they focused mainly on the
manipulation of white teenagers because of their purchasing power. But why was
it self-explanatory that black teens wanted the latest Nikes? See *Merchants of Cool*,
documentary on *Frontline*, PBS, 2001; Malcolm Gladwell, *The Tipping Point*
(Boston: Little, Brown, 2000); Klein, *No Logo*; Janine Lopiano-Misdom and
Joanne De Luca, *Street Trends: How Today's Alternative Youth Cultures Are Creating
Tomorrow's Mainstream Markets* (New York: HarperCollins Business, 1997).

6. Basquiat and Koons: works reproduced in *Black Male: Representations of
Masculinity in Contemporary American Art,* ed. Thelma Golden (New York:
Whitney Museum of American Art, 1994), 66, 72. See the great discussion of
how superstars were used for the corporate branding of the NBA in Donald Katz,
"Triumph of the Swoosh," *Sports Illustrated*, August 16, 1993, 24–64.

7. Major characters of American literature: Toni Morrison, *Playing in the Dark:
Whiteness and the Literary Imagination* (Cambridge: Harvard University Press,
1992). Rumors: impossible either to trace or to kill, these rumors alleged that
such designers as Tommy Hilfiger and Calvin Klein appeared on television to
deny that African Americans bought their products in great numbers; other
rumors claimed that the chief executives of Timberland made the same denials.
Dual consciousness: W. E. B. Du Bois, "Of Our Spiritual Strivings," in *The Souls
of Black Folk* (New York: Signet, 1995 [1903]), 43–53.

8. The Lo-Lifes: Greg Donaldson, *The Ville* (New York: Ticknor and Fields, 1994);
cf. Neal Gabler, *Life: The Movie* (New York: Knopf, 1998).

9. "Round brown face": this is the experience described by the law professor Patricia
J. Williams, in *The Alchemy of Race and Rights* (Cambridge: Harvard University
Press, 1991), 44–46. To add to the insult, a law journal refused to publish this
story in an essay on "excluded voices" Williams had been invited to submit.

10. Violates shoppers' civil rights: when a salesperson recently filed a legal complaint
against A Children's Place, a retail clothing chain, claiming she was instructed to
follow dark-skinned shoppers around the store, the chain settled the case (Carey
Goldberg, "Accused of Discrimination, Clothing Chain Settles Case," *New York
Times*, December 22, 2000). Don't merchants assume?: Regina Austin, "A Nation
of Thieves," in Black Public Sphere Collective, *The Black Public Sphere* (Chicago:
University of Chicago Press, 1995), 229–52. For other experiences of dark-
skinned shoppers being followed around stores, see Elizabeth Chin's account of
teenage African American girls shopping at a Claire's Accessories store in a
suburban shopping mall in *Purchasing Power: Black Kids and American Consumer
Culture* (Minneapolis: University of Minnesota Press, 2001), 91, 101; also see
John Fiske, "Radical Shopping in Los Angeles: Race, Media and the Sphere of
Consumption," *Media, Culture, and Society* 16 (1994): 469–86, and British
researchers' interviews with minority-group teenagers in North London in Daniel
Miller et al., *Shopping, Place and Identity* (London and New York: Routledge,
1998), 107.

11. Shopping for tuxedos: "Police Procedure Investigated after Search of 10
Teenagers," *New York Times*, May 25, 2001. Half of the black men: Richard
Morin and Michael H. Cottman, "Discrimination's Lingering Story," *Washington
Post*, June 22, 2001. By contrast, one-fifth of the Latinos and Asians said they had
been stopped unfairly by the police.

12. Falsely arrested or killed: in a notorious 2000 case in New York City, a black security guard named Patrick Dorismond was shot and killed on the street by an

undercover police detective who tried to arrest him because he thought he was selling illegal drugs; the police officer was wrong (William K. Rashbaum, "Officer Denies Race Played Role in Killing of Unarmed Black Man," *New York Times,* July 30, 2000).

13. Believe they will be treated with disdain: all surveys and interview projects confirm this widespread belief. According to an ABC News poll, for example, two-thirds of blacks, but only one-quarter of whites, think clerks in expensive stores make blacks feel unwelcome. A smaller but still significant proportion— 47 percent—of blacks, compared with 34 percent of whites—say sales clerks have actually made them feel unwelcome. This sense of discrimination divides most blacks from most whites: "A plurality of whites feel that blacks exaggerate the amount of discrimination they experience, while a majority of blacks think that's not the case." "Perception vs. Experience: ABC News Poll on Racial Discrimination," www.abcnews.go.com/onair/2020, February 17, 2000, accessed February 2000. Thanks to John Goering for calling this survey to my attention.

14. Shortweighted: on the way blacks were treated in general stores in the rural South, and on racist stereotypes in packaging, see Grace Elizabeth Hale, *Making Whiteness: The Culture of Segregation in the South, 1890–1940* (New York: Pantheon, 1998), 173–78; on African American shoppers in Chicago, see Lizabeth Cohen, *Making a New Deal: Industrial Workers in Chicago, 1919–1939* (Cambridge: Cambridge University Press, 1990), 147–57. On racist stereotypes in British packaging, see Anne McClintock, *Imperial Leather: Race, Gender and Sexuality in the Colonial Context* (London and New York: Routledge, 1995).

15. Gold teeth, Cadillacs: These depictions have endured at least from George Jean Nathan and H. L. Mencken's *The American Credo* (1920), which states, "Negroes who have money head straight for the dentist to have their front teeth filled with gold." In our time, we replace gold teeth with diamond-capped teeth and gold chains. Maurice Berger, *White Lies: Race and the Myths of Whiteness* (New York: Farrar Straus & Giroux, 1999), 32–36; Chin, *Purchasing Power,* 46–57.

16. "A Cadillac has its point": "Selling the Negro Market," *Tide* 25 (July 20, 1951): 40, quoted in Marcus Alexis, "Racial Differences in Consumption and Automobile Ownership," unpublished Ph.D. dissertation, Department of Economics, University of Minnesota, 1959.

17. Even in the 1980s: Bart Landry, *The New Black Middle Class* (Berkeley and Los Angeles: University of California Press, 1986). Since legal disputes continue over whether black customers get deliberately bad treatment in stores and fast-food restaurants, this is not an unreasonable expectation.

18. Whether blacks shop differently: Alexis, "Racial Differences in Consumption and Automobile Ownership."

19. To keep up appearances: the sociologist Elijah Anderson describes a status competition among poor, young, undereducated black mothers today that compels them to buy their children expensive, brand-name clothing. Anderson explains this quest for status as a means of compensating for "the generalized notion that a teenage mother has 'messed up' her life, and in this sea of destitution nothing is more important than to show others you are doing all right." Elijah Anderson, *Streetwise: Race, Class, and Change in an Urban Community* (Chicago: University of Chicago Press, 1990), 126.

20. Postwar black consumers: Dwight Ernest Brooks, "Consumer Markets and Consumer Magazines: Black America and the Culture of Consumption, 1920–1960," unpublished Ph.D. dissertation, Department of Communication Studies, University of Iowa, 1991. Exhorted . . . to spend money: this moral

lesson is also related to the "Gospel of Prosperity" preached in many churches, regardless of race, during the economic expansion of the fifties and early sixties. *Ebony* urged its readers: throughout its history, some blacks have criticized *Ebony* for promoting too materialistic a lifestyle and failing to emphasize blacks' historical repression and deprivation. In a graduation speech at Howard University, the television host Bryant Gumbel warned students they could not change society if "all you're going to seek is a superficial *Ebony* magazine view of life—one that accentuates only your cars and your clothes" ("Gumbel and Ebony Argue over Recent Remarks," *New York Times*, June 11, 2001).

21. Spending power of black consumers: D. Parke Gibson, *The $30 Billion Negro* (London: Collier-Macmillan, 1969).

22. Not been docile consumers: for black consumers' activism throughout the twentieth century, see Lizabeth Cohen, *A Consumers' Republic: The Politics of Mass Consumption in Postwar America* (New York: Knopf, 2003).

23. Black shoppers in Birmingham: Louise Passey Maxwell, "Re-Making Jim Crow: Segregation and Urban Change in Birmingham, Alabama, 1938–1963," unpublished Ph.D. dissertation, Department of History, New York University, 1999.

24. "Percentage of Negro trade": Gibson, *$30 Billion Negro*, 88–89.

25. Black teens in malls: during the 1990s, when students in my introductory sociology course at Brooklyn College interviewed shoppers at Kings Plaza, the only suburban-style shopping mall in Brooklyn, both black and white shoppers indicated they were afraid the black teenage males they saw at the mall would commit crimes. Nevertheless, in contrast to white shoppers, black shoppers often said they were glad to shop in a racially and ethnically integrated place, "where all people shop together."

26. Consumption patterns of low-income African American families: Chin, *Purchasing Power.*

27. When other means of gainful employment dry up: Robin D. G. Kelley, "Playing for Keeps: Pleasure and Profit on the Postindustrial Playground," in *The House That Race Built,* ed. Wahneema Lubiano (New York: Pantheon, 1997), 195–231.

28. Lurid sexual and criminal stereotypes: see Golden, ed., *Black Male.*

29. Abandon lip service: on the racializing of the Democratic and Republican Parties during the seventies, see Thomas Byrne Edsall and Mary D. Edsall, *Chain Reaction: The Impact of Race, Rights, and Taxes on American Politics* (New York: Norton, 1991).

30. Label happened to be . . . hot: for quite a few years, JanSport backpacks were favored targets of muggers in Manhattan; for an example of muggings directed toward another label, see Arthur Santana, "Crooks Target Coats in Metro Holdups; Transit Police Plan More Patrols after Armed Robberies of Eddie Bauer Apparel," *Washington Post,* February 5, 2000.

31. "Sneaker wars": Tom Vanderbilt, *The Sneaker Book: Anatomy of an Industry and an Icon* (New York: New Press, 1998). "A hot new product": Keri Christenfeld, "Case Study: A One Time High Flyer, Nike Struggles to Hit Its Stride Again," *New York Times,* May 19, 1985.

32. "Make Michael Jordan a label": J. B. Strasser and Laurie Becklund, *Swoosh: The Unauthorized Story of Nike and the Men Who Played There* (New York: Harcourt Brace Jovanovich, 1991), 648, quoting a former Nike executive (Strasser's husband).

33. "We just expand on the image": Katz, "Triumph of the Swoosh." But on the business world's appreciation of Nike's R and D, see Michael Treacy and Fred

Wiersema, "Customer Intimacy and Other Value Disciplines," *Harvard Business Review*, January-February 1993, 84–94.

34. Reeboks as a "fad," Mick Jagger: Lois Therrien, "Reeboks: How Far Can a Fad Run?" *Business Week*, February 24, 1986, 89–90; Barbara Buell, "Nike Catches Up with the Trendy Front Runner," *Business Week*, October 24, 1988. 265 NBA players: Katz, "Triumph of the Swoosh."

chapter 7: consumer guides and the invention of lifestyle

1. "Finest Guigal has produced": quoted in Morrell & Company catalog, December 2001, 70.

2. So sincere: "sincerity" from Pierre Bourdieu's discussion of cultural critics, in *The Rules of Art*, trans. Susan Emanuel (Stanford, Calif.: Stanford University Press, 1996 [1992]), 164.

3. "Hidden persuaders": Vance Packard, *The Hidden Persuaders* (New York: D. MacKay, 1957). "Captains of consciousness": Stuart Ewen, *Captains of Consciousness: Advertising and the Social Roots of the Consumer Culture* (New York: McGraw-Hill, 1976).

4. What we like: the contrast between critics who write about mass cultural products (films, TV shows) in terms of what consumers will like, and critics who write about sophisticated cultural products (paintings, operas) by situating the product in a field but without necessarily judging it, comes from Richard E. Cave, *Creative Industries: Contracts between Art and Commerce* (Cambridge: Harvard University Press, 2000), 191–92.

5. "And our dispositions": Bourdieu, *The Rules of Art*, 165. Speaking of drama critics, Bourdieu says that for their sincerity to be effective, there must be "a perfect, immediate harmony between the expectations inscribed in the position occupied"—that of the writer, the reader or consumer, and the producer of the product under review—"and the dispositions"—the likes or dislikes—"of the occupant." The criticism must align each pair of positions: writer-reader and producer-consumer. "Critics cannot exercise 'influence' on their readers unless the readers grant them that power because they are structurally attuned in their vision of the social world, their tastes and their whole habitus."

6. "In the middle": I emphasize the honest brokers' position in the middle—mediating between commodities and humans, and between producers and consumers—despite their claim to speak as authorities. My interpretation thus differs from John Winward's interpretation of product reviewers as *experts*, in "The Organized Consumer and Consumer Information Cooperatives," in *The Authority of the Consumer*, ed. Russell Keat, Nigel Whiteley, and Nicholas Abercrombie, (London and New York: Routledge, 1994), 75–90, and William Leach's interpretation of advertising creatives and stylists as *brokers* who represent the interests of producers, or manufacturers and retailers, in *Land of Desire: Merchants, Power, and the Rise of a New American Culture* (New York: Pantheon, 1993). On the "middle" position of cultural critics, see Wesley Shrum Jr., *Fringe and Fortune: The Role of Critics in High and Popular Art* (Princeton: Princeton University Press, 1996).

7. "Smooth powertrain": *Consumer Reports*, August 1997, 47. "Growth as a director": Elvis Mitchell, "Film Review: A Security Guard. Then Kapow! A Sorrowful Superhero," *New York Times*, November 22, 2000. Instant cultural currency: Winward,

"The Organized Consumer," describes these authoritative judgments as cultural capital in consumers' hands.

8. Status consumption: ThorsteinVeblen, *The Theory of the Leisure Class* [1899], in *The Portable Veblen,* ed. Max Lerner (New York: Viking, 1948), 53–214.

9. New era of abundance: Simon Patten, *The New Basis of Civilization* (Cambridge: Harvard University Press, 1968 [1907]) and see Leach, *Land of Desire,* 231–44. "What intellectuals preferred": Daniel Horowitz, *The Morality of Spending: Attitudes toward the Consumer Society in America, 1875–1940* (Baltimore: Johns Hopkins University Press, 1985), 162.

10. "Practicality, 'inside dope'": Christopher P. Wilson, "The Rhetoric of Consumption: Mass-Market Magazines and the Demise of the Gentle Reader, 1880–1920," in *The Culture of Consumption,* ed. Richard Wightman Fox and T. J. Jackson Lears (New York: Pantheon, 1983), 61; also see Susan Strasser, *Never Done: A History of American Housework* (New York: Pantheon, 1982).

11. First consumer economics textbook: Leland J. Gordon, *Economics for Consumers* (New York: American Book Co., 1939), quotations from preface to the first edition; "buymanship": 352. On the making of sales techniques at the time—or salesmanship—see Olivier Zunz, *Making America Corporate, 1870–1920* (Chicago: University of Chicago Press, 1990), 175–98.

12. Good Housekeeping Institute: *Good Housekeeping,* January 1940, 104–7.

13. "With strict impartiality": *Good Housekeeping,* January 1940, 106, emphasis added.

14. Not an honest broker: Gordon, *Economics for Consumers* (1939), 545–47. Suspicions soon confirmed: Gordon, *Economics for Consumers,* 4th ed. (1961), 475–77. The FTC also charged that many advertisements in *Good Housekeeping* were false, deceptive, or misleading, and a "shopping service [operated by the magazine was] represented as free [of charge] when in fact respondents got a 5 to 7 per cent commission from the sellers."

15. Revised the seal: Gordon, *Economics for Consumers,* 4th ed. (1961), 476.

16. Before 1936: in contrast to the American experience, the British magazine *Gramophone,* founded in 1923, reviewed recordings of classical music, but those reviews followed the model of high-end cultural criticism rather than the model of comparison later developed by consumer guides. I am indebted to Kees van Rees for calling *Gramophone* to my attention.

17. "Wise selection increasingly difficult": American Home Economics Association, Committee on Standardization of Consumers' Goods, *Scientific Consumer Purchasing* (Washington, D.C.: AAUP, 1935 [1932]), quote at 7, emphasis added.

18. Activism around consumption: Lizabeth Cohen, *A Consumers' Republic: The Politics of Mass Consumption in Postwar America* (New York: Knopf, 2003), 18–61.

19. "In the future": FDR quoted in Cohen, *A Consumers' Republic,* 24. A Communist "front": M. C. Philips, "Half-Way to Communism with the League of Women Shoppers," *Consumers' Digest,* April 1940, 39–44; an editor's note states: "This is the third in a series of articles highlighting Communist activities in organizing and making use of consumers to further Communist Party ends." On the League of Women Shoppers, also see *Time,* April 27, 1936, 72, and *Consumers' Union Reports,* May 1936, 2.

20. Founding of Consumers Union: www.consumerreports.org/Home/About/history. html; also see Timothy Noah, "People's Choice Awards," *New York Times Magazine,* August 8, 1999, 44.

21. Grade A milk: "Milk: Grade A versus Grade B," *Consumers Union Reports,* May 1936, 12–13. Nevertheless, grading milk was not initially a marketing ploy. If it follows the example of grading grain, grading milk was begun to standardize

pricing of milk from various producers when their milk was collected by, and stored together in, large dairies. On grading of grain, see William Cronon, *Nature's Metropolis: Chicago and the Great West* (New York: Norton, 1991).

22. "167 . . . restaurants": Daniel Gross, "Face Value," *U S Airways Attaché*, May 2001, 17; *Cue, Gourmet* founded: personal interviews with staff members.

23. Schwann catalogue . . . "invaluable": William Schwann obituary, *New York Times*, June 18, 1998. Car magazines: Warren Weith, "Tales of a Misspent Youth," *Car and Driver*, July 1980, 97. Consumers Union, Consumer Reports: Gordon, *Economics for Consumers*, 4th ed. (1961). 329, 332.

24. "Rate a Ford or Chevvie": Bob Yount, "Buyer's Briefing," *Sports Cars Illustrated*, October 1955, 47.

25. "New sensibility": Susan Sontag, *Against Interpretation* (New York: Farrar Straus & Giroux, 1965), 298–99. No longer high-culture critics: Michael Kammen, "Cultural Criticism and the Transformation of Cultural Authority," in *American Culture, American Tastes* (New York: Knopf, 1999), 133–61; Morris Dickstein, *Gates of Eden: American Culture in the Sixties* (New York: Basic Books, 1977).

26. Aesthetics of everyday life: David Lehman, *The Last Avant-Garde* (New York: Doubleday, 1998).

27. "Big Four": Nora Ephron, "Critics in the World of the Rising Soufflé," *New York*, September 30, 1968; *Los Angeles Times* survey: December 28, 1980.

28. Negative reviews, professional standards: Claiborne attended hotel school in Switzerland after serving in the U.S. Army in Europe during World War II. See his autobiography, *A Feast Made for Laughter* (Garden City, N.Y.: Doubleday, 1982).

29. "Each of the dishes": quotes in this section from *New York Times*, April 5, 1963.

30. Began weekly publication: *New York* was first developed as the Sunday magazine of the *World-Journal-Tribune*; when that newspaper went out of business, Clay Felker and a number of journalists who had written for him transformed *New York* into an independent magazine. Felker expected her: information on Gael Greene's early career from a personal interview with Greene, 1994; also Gael Greene, *Bite: A New York Restaurant Strategy for Hedonists, Masochists, Selective Penny Pinchers, and the Upwardly Mobile* (New York: Norton, 1971).

31. Felker recalled: interview with Clay Felker, *New York Times*, April 9, 1995.

32. "Scarcely more than 10 years old": Craig Claiborne, "Café Chauveron," *The New York Times Guide to Dining Out in New York* (New York: Atheneum, 1968), 29. "With my . . . Puritan hangover": Gael Greene, "The Chauveron," *New York*, September 22, 1969. "Infanticide": *New York*, March 23, 1970.

33. Production knowledge, craft knowledge: adapted from William Leiss, *The Limits to Satisfaction* (Toronto: University of Toronto Press, 1976), 16. Dying port: since the late 1920s, people with big holdings in Manhattan real estate and the heads of banks had planned to replace the port's facilities with new office and apartment buildings that would confirm New York's preeminence as a headquarters city for national corporations. In the 1960s, the wholesale fruit and vegetable market was moved from the Lower West Side to the Bronx, and in its place, the World Trade Center was built. At the same time, new methods of container shipping abandoned New York for other ports and eliminated most dockworkers' jobs. Robert Fitch, *The Assassination of New York* (New York: Verso, 1993) and Eric Darton, *Divided We Stand: A Biography of New York's World Trade Center* (New York: Basic Books, 1999).

34. "How to eat with the rich": *New York*, January 6, 1969.

35. Bought by Rupert Murdoch: John Bradshaw and Richard Neville, "Killer Bee Reaches New York," *More*, February 1977, 13–23. Not lost on media critics: John

Peters, "New York's Evolutionary Design," *Folio*, June 1986, 121–22. On *New York's* evolution to an urban consumption manual, see Miriam Greenberg, "Branding Cities: A Social History of the Urban Lifestyle Magazine," *Urban Affairs Review* 36 (2000): 228–63.

36. "Endless lists": interview with Clay Felker, *New York Times*, April 9, 1995.

37. "Dominant lifestyle choices": Robert Gottlieb, *Forcing the Spring: The Transformation of the American Environmental Movement* (Washington, D.C., and Covelo, Calif.: Island Press, 1993), 95.

38. "False consciousness": Herbert Marcuse, *One-Dimensional Man: Studies in the Ideology of Advanced Industrial Society* (Boston: Beacon Press, 1966). "Big corporations": C. Wright Mills, *White Collar* (New York: Oxford University Press, 1953) and *The Power Elite* (New York: Oxford University Press, 1956). "Domestic imperialism": Dave Gilbert, Bob Gottlieb, and Susan Sutheim, "Consumption: Domestic Capitalism" (1968), cited in Todd Gitlin, *The Sixties* (New York: Bantam, 1987), 382. "Manipulated": Bob Gottlieb and Marge Piercy, "Movement for a Democratic Society: Beginning to Begin to Begin" (1968), cited by Gottlieb, *Forcing the Spring*, 95.

39. Optional features: buyers could request Regular Product Option 696, which provided heavier suspension springs and shock absorbers, a stabilizer bar, and rear-axle rebound straps. "From instrument panels to windshields": Ralph Nader, *Unsafe at Any Speed: The Designed-in Dangers of the American Automobile* (New York: Grossman, 1965), 60. "The industry left it": Nader, *Unsafe at Any Speed*, 164.

40. *Silent Spring*: this book began as a series of articles in *The New Yorker*. In the fifties, Carson, a scientist and nature writer, had published another best-selling book, also serialized in *The New Yorker*, about the environmental damage to oceans. She gave voice to a growing anxiety among Americans who were enjoying the suburban lifestyle of herbicide-induced green lawns and backyards, air conditioning and aerosol cans that released harmful fluorocarbons into the atmosphere, and pesticides that produced bumper farm crops and cheap groceries. Though a few writers had explored these issues as early as the 1930s, Carson was the first writer to gain widespread public attention and support—and also garner vicious criticism from both the chemical industry and male scientists. See Gottlieb, *Forcing the Spring*, 81–86, and Alexander Wilson, *The Culture of Nature* (Oxford and Cambridge, Mass.: Blackwell, 1992), 89–115.

41. Class action suits: Nader's success in battling GM was really due to the relatively narrow grounds of his winning a lawsuit against the corporation for invasion of privacy. General Motors had hired a private detective to investigate Nader and, presumably, discredit him.

42. "For the first time": Leland J. Gordon and Stewart M. Lee, *Economics for Consumers* (New York: American Book Co., 1967). Smoking to health: the first U.S. surgeon general's warning about the carcinogenic effects of cigarettes, *Smoking and Health: Report of the Advisory Committee to the Surgeon General of the Public Health Service*, was issued in 1964. Burial practices: Jessica Mitford, *The American Way of Death* (New York: Simon and Schuster, 1963). Also see Cohen, *Consumers' Republic*.

43. Credit policies of a major bank: David Leinsdorf, *Citibank: Ralph Nader's Study Group Report on First National City Bank* (New York: Grossman, 1973).

44. Black lung disease: see Gottlieb, *Forcing the Spring*, 280. Many of the labeling practices: the New York Public Interest Research Group, founded in 1973, claims to have lobbied successfully for at least one major regulatory reform a year in New York State. In the seventies, alone, these included a Freedom of Information Law,

a Hearing Aid Sales Practice Act, an Item Pricing Law, a Generic Drug Law, and a Truth in Testing Law (see www.nypirg.org).

45. "Another blow to the mystique": "Scotch Whiskies," *Consumer Reports,* November 1968, 622–25.

46. *Roe v. Wade*: the Supreme Court decided this landmark case in 1973. Counter-culture's "entrepreneurial energies": Michael Kammen, "Consumerism, Americanism, and the Phasing of Popular Culture," *American Culture, American Tastes*, 60. New stores and restaurants: after the 1967 "Summer of Love," the Bay Area around San Francisco provided fertile ground for these new entrepreneurial ventures. The Gap and Tower Records were founded there to sell clothing and music for young, counterculture tastes, and Chez Panisse, the famous restaurant that developed and publicized New American cuisine, was opened by Alice Waters in 1971, a few years after she had begun to write a food column in the *Berkeley Barb*, an alternative newspaper.

47. Self-help and consumers' performance: Evan Watkins, *Throwaways: Work Culture and Consumer Education* (Stanford, Calif.: Stanford University Press, 1993).

48. Designer jeans: Stuart Ewen and Elizabeth Ewen, *Channels of Desire*, rev. ed. (Minneapolis: University of Minnesota Press, 1992 [1982]).

49. Sadly reflects: Stanley Marcus, *Quest for the Best* (New York: Viking, 1978).

50. Investment bankers: though fictional, the best account of their lifestyle is Tom Wolfe, *Bonfire of the Vanities* (New York: Farrar, Straus & Giroux, 1987).

51. "Sales jumped": R. W. Apple Jr., "Zagat at 20: Populist, and Powerful," *New York Times*, November 11, 1998.

52. Consumer democracy, "*vox populi*": Apple, "Zagat at 20." Zagat's success parallels that of J. D. Power, a market research firm founded in the sixties, which conducts extensive surveys on consumer products for businesses; client companies buy the right to use the ratings in these surveys to promote their brands. See Timothy Noah, "People's Choice Awards," *New York Times Magazine*, August 8, 1999, 42–45, and the company's website, www.jdpa.com.

53. More than 18,000: Apple, "Zagat at 20"; 125,000: www.findarticles.com/m0EIN/2000August11/64053939/p1/article.jhtml, accessed November 24, 2000.

54. "Explain and regulate. . . . knowledges": Terry Eagleton, *The Function of Criticism* (London: Verso, 1984), 48–49.

chapter 8: how brooks brothers came to look like banana republic

1. "A national icon": www.brooksbrothers.com, accessed April 1999.

2. Thoroughly predictable: Mary McCarthy, "The Man in the Brooks Brothers Suit" (1942) in *The Company She Keeps* (San Diego: Harcourt Brace, 1970), 81–134. "Everybody wears": Gilbert Millstein, "Lament for New York's Night Life," *New York Times Magazine*, May 22, 1955, 19.

3. "Organization man": William H. Whyte, *The Organization Man* (New York: Simon and Schuster, 1956); C. Wright Mills, *White Collar* (New York: Oxford University Press, 1953). "Cheever camouflage": Rebecca Mead, "Brooks Brothers A-Go-Go," *The New Yorker*, March 22, 1999, 89. Cheever's novels and short stories often illuminate the repressed, inner turmoil of wealthy, suburban, corporate executives.

4. Campeau's financing, Marks & Spencer: John Rothchild, *Going for Broke: How Robert Campeau Bankrupted the Retail Industry, Jolted the Junk Bond Market, and Brought the Booming Eighties to a Crashing Halt* (New York: Simon and Schuster,

1991); Mark Maremont, "Marks & Spencer Pays a Premium for Pinstripes," *Business Week*, April 18, 1988, 67.

5. Earnings fell: Joshua Levine, "An Escalator? In Brooks Brothers?" *Forbes*, July 9, 1990, 76–77. "Hideous trendiness": Jeff Danziger, "A Catalog of Horrors," *Wall Street Journal*, November 8, 1996. Outlet stores: Sharon Moshavi, "Calling All Mall Rats," *Forbes*, April 25, 1994, 123.

6. Stores: Hoover's Company Capsule Database, Austin Tex., accessed April 15, 1999. Image consultants: Mead, "Brooks Brothers A-Go-Go," 91. "Authenticity, integrity . . .": "Brooks Brothers Trying to Shed Stuffy Image," *Marketing News*, March 18, 1991.

7. New CEO: Mead, "Brooks Brothers A-Go-Go." Increase in sales, Anne Faircloth, "Brooks Brothers Dresses Down," *Fortune*, September 7, 1998, 44–48.

8. "Two-tier marketing": cover story, *Business Week*, March 17, 1997. Prada: Mimi Swartz, "Annals of Retail: Victoria's Secret," *The New Yorker*, March 30, 1998, 94–101.

9. "Distinctive, Correct . . .": Mead, "Brooks Brothers A-Go-Go," 91.

10. An entire issue: "The Store Strikes Back," *New York Times Magazine*, April 6, 1997.

11. ". . . to bedazzle the customer": Paul Goldberger, "The Store Strikes Back," *New York Times Magazine*, April 6, 1997, 45.

12. "Part Disneyland": Michael Lev, "Store of Future, It Also Sells Shoes," *New York Times*, June 17, 1991. $28 million: Rachel Spevack, "Innovations Runneth over at Niketown NY," *DNR* (*Daily News Record*), October 31, 1996.

13. Statue of Michael Jordan: John F. Sherry Jr., "The Soul of the Company Store: Nike Town Chicago and the Emplaced Brandscape," in *Servicescapes*, ed. John F. Sherry Jr. (Lincolnwood Ill.: NTC Business Books, 1998), 109–46. "Extravagantly-paid . . . endorser": Donald Katz, "Triumph of the Swoosh," *Sports Illustrated*, August 16, 1993, 54–74.

14. The more time: this has been widely reported; see "Reinventing the Store," *Business Week*, November 27, 1995, 84–96; 80 percent of sales: Paco Underhill, *Why We Buy: The Science of Shopping* (New York: Simon and Schuster, 1999), 201.

15. Invest more money: "The Profit Wedge: Key to Successful Retailing," *Chain Store Age Executive*, January 1995, 46. According to this theory of the "wedge," costs to upgrade stores increase in absolute numbers, but, as sales increase, they decrease as a percentage of gross sales. $25 billion: Underhill, *Why We Buy*, 206. "Reenchantment": George Ritzer, *Enchanting a Disenchanted World* (Thousand Oaks, Calif.: Pine Forge Press, 1999).

16. "Competition is rampant": Charles V. Bagli, "As Retail Space Grows and Spending Wanes, Some Stores Feel Pinch," *New York Times*, October 15, 2000. "Too much selling space," "shopping is a pain": "Reinventing the Store." Actually, the point of this article is that despite the negative conditions, *some* stores are wildly successful. They may develop a new format for selling a single category of goods (e.g., Sunglass Hut), apply an existing format to a different category of merchandise (e.g., Carmax at Circuit City), conceive of synergistic formats (McDonald's and gas stations), or focus on specific kinds of merchandise in a general format (prepared foods in a supermarket, home furnishings in a department store). Significantly, in this 1995 article, "virtual shopping" on the Internet is mentioned only briefly.

17. Cut back . . . fewer stores: between 1980 and 1995, women "cut down from three mall visits a month to 1.6. And instead of stopping by seven stores at a clip, they're down to just three." "Reinventing the Store," 85. Women do major share

of shopping: generally reported, but see Underhill, *Why We Buy* and Michael Mondavi, president and CEO, Robert Mondavi Winery, Second Annual Apparel CEO Summit, Carefree, Ariz., May 31–June 3, 1998, 111. "Tightfisted . . . imperfections of retail": Mona Doyle, president of Consumer Network Inc., a market research firm that surveys shoppers, quoted in "Reinventing the Store," 85. Sales per square foot: "Reinventing the Store," 87.

18. Freestanding stores: Penny Gill, "The Disney Store Blends Retailing and Entertainment," *Store*, June 1991, 20–24. Produced in Haiti: for this reason, Disney stores have been targeted by the social movement against sweatshops. See National Labor Committee, "An Appeal to Walt Disney," in *No Sweat: Fashion, Free Trade, and the Rights of Garment Workers*, ed. Andrew Ross (New York: Verso, 1997), 95–112.

19. Sony stores: Sharon Zukin, *The Cultures of Cities* (Cambridge, Mass.: Blackwell, 1995), 3–4. Viacom store: "La Dolce Viacom," http://suck.com, June 27, 1997.

20. "Like an advertisement": Beth Greenwald quoted in Alexandra Zissu, "Tang's Glitzy Shanghai Megashop May Not Be Long for Madison Avenue," *New York Observer*, March 15, 1999. "Better than an Ad in *Vogue*": Tim Green quoted in Ann Landi, "Madison Avenue," *Metropolis*, May 1997, 59.

21. Lose their aura: Walter Benjamin, "The Work of Art in the Age of Mechanical Reproduction," in *Illuminations: Essays and Reflections* (New York: Harcourt Brace and World, 1968), 217–52. Rei Kawakubo's store interiors: Pilar Vilardas, "Up from SoHo," *New York Times Magazine*, March 14, 1999, and *The New Yorker*, March 8, August 23, August 30, 1999.

22. Into the modern business world: in ancient Greece and Rome, goods were identified with individual merchants by iconic pictures. Adrian Room, "The History of Branding," in *Brands: The New Wealth Creators*, ed. Susannah Hart and John Murphy (New York: New York University Press, 1998), 13. Federal laws: Susan Strasser, *Satisfaction Guaranteed: The Making of an American Mass Market* (New York: Pantheon, 1989).

23. Baked beans: Strasser, *Satisfaction Guaranteed*, 52.

24. Radio networks: Susan J. Douglas, *Listening In: Radio and the American Imagination* (New York: Times Books, 1999). "Supername": Richard S. Tedlow, *New and Improved: The Story of Mass Marketing in America* (Cambridge: Harvard Business School Press, 1990), 15.

25. "Protection against competition": Strasser, *Satisfaction Guaranteed*, 57.

26. Provoke a crisis: H. Lee Scott Jr., president and CEO, Wal-Mart Stores, keynote address to Second Annual Fairchild Apparel CEO Summit, Carefree Ariz., June 1, 1998, 65.

27. General Electric and General Motors: Roland Marchand, *Creating the Corporate Soul: The Rise of Public Relations and Corporate Imagery in American Big Business* (Berkeley and Los Angeles: University of California Press, 1998), 130–63.

28. Charisma, GE, GM: Marchand, *Creating the Corporate Soul*, 144, 159. Getting greater value: Susan Fournier, "Consumers and Their Brands: Developing Relationship Theory in Consumer Research," *Journal of Consumer Research* 24 (1998): 343–407.

29. Cream of Wheat, store brands: James M. Mayo, *The American Grocery Store: The Business Evolution of an Architectural Space* (Westport, Conn.: Greenwood Press, 1993), 101. Great Depression, FTC: Kevin Lane Keller, *Strategic Brand Management: Building, Measuring, and Managing Brand Equity* (Upper Saddle River, N.J.: Prentice Hall, 1998); George S. Low and Ronald A. Fullerton, "Brands, Brand

Management, and the Brand Manager System: A Critical-Historical Evaluation," *Journal of Marketing Research* 31 (1994): 173–90.

30. Brand management system: Keller, *Strategic Brand Management*; Low and Fullerton, "Brands, Brand Management, and the Brand Manager System."

31. "A business Esperanto": Jean-Noel Kapferer, *Strategic Brand Management: New Approaches to Creating and Evaluating Brand Equity* (New York: Free Press, 1992), 3.

32. Brands competing in stores: for interesting comments on cosmetics firms jockeying for prime positions in a department store, see Marvin Traub and Tim Teicholz, *Like No Other Store: The Bloomingdale's Legend and the Revolution in American Marketing* (New York: Times Books, 1993).

33. "Nontangibles" versus "real factors": John Murphy, "What Is Branding?" in *Brands*, ed. Hart and Murphy, *Brands*, 1–12. Pepsi generation: Thomas Frank, *The Conquest of Cool: Business Culture, Counterculture, and the Rise of Hip Consumerism* (Chicago: University of Chicago Press, 1997).

34. "Brand personality": Joseph T. Plummer, "How Personality Makes a Difference," *Journal of Advertising Research* 24 (December 1984–January 1985): 27–30; also see "Brand Image, Character Termed All-Important," *Advertising Age* 53 (August 30, 1982): 14, and Robert S. Duboff, "Brands, Like People, Have Personalities," *Marketing News* 20 (January 3, 1986): 8.

35. UEDs: John Hannigan, *Fantasy City: Pleasure and Profit in the Postmodern Metropolis* (London and New York: Routledge, 1998). Faneuil Hall: Bernard J. Frieden and Lynn Sagalynn, *Downtown Inc.* (Cambridge MA: MIT Press, 1989). South Street Seaport, in Lower Manhattan, seems to be one of the few unsuccessful UEDs on an urban waterfront, maybe because of the lack of a mall-like anchor store or a large fresh-food market.

36. Jerde on Italian hill towns: Frances Anderton, "At Home with Jon Jerde: The Global Village Goes Pop Baroque," *New York Times*, October 8, 1998.

37. Greatest profits: "New? Improved?: The Brand-Name Mergers," *Business Week*, October 21, 1985, 109.

38. Boards of directors, market segmentation: Bryan Burrough and John Helyar, *Barbarians at the Gate: The Fall of RJR Nabisco* (New York: Harper & Row, 1990). Near monopolies: Jonathan Franzen, Paul M. Hirsch, and Philip C. Zerrillo, "Consumption, Preferences, and Changing Lifestyles," in *Handbook of Economic Sociology*, ed. Neil Smelser and Richard Swedberg (Princeton: Princeton University Press, 1994), 413; this is just a more extreme version of Wendell Smith's argument when he initiated the discussion of market segmentation in the late fifties: "As 'many companies' are finding that 'their *core* markets have already been developed . . . to the point where additional advertising and selling expenditures [are] yielding diminishing returns, attention to smaller or *fringe* market segments, which may have small potentials individually . . . [will yield] a more secure market position." Wendell R. Smith, "Product Differentiation and Market Segmentation as Alternative Marketing Strategies," *Journal of Marketing* 21 (July 1956): 7, quoted in Lizabeth Cohen, *A Consumers' Republic: The Politics of Postwar Consumption in Postwar America* (New York: Knopf, 2003), 295. Or as the textbook *Consumer Behavior*, published in 1970, asks: "Will 80 percent of a small market segment produce more revenue than 10 percent of a mass market?" Quoted in Cohen, *A Consumers' Republic*, 296.

39. Baby boomers: David Brooks, *Bobos in Paradise* (New York: Simon and Schuster, 2000). Interest in cultural products: Sharon Zukin, *Landscapes of Power: From Detroit to Disney World* (Berkeley and Los Angeles: University of California Press,

1991); Scott Lash and John Urry, *Economies of Signs and Space* (London: Sage, 1994). "Sneaker revolution": Tom Vanderbilt, *The Sneaker Book: Anatomy of an Industry and an Icon* (New York: New Press, 1998). Designer jeans: Stuart Ewen and Elizabeth Ewen, *Channels of Desire* (New York: McGraw-Hill, 1982).

40. Personality of the store: Pierre Martineau, "The Personality of the Retail Store," *Harvard Business Review*, January–February 1958, 36–55.

41. "*Intangibles*" . . . "total environment": Martineau, "Personality of the Retail Store," my emphasis.

42. Status differences: Martineau, "The Personality of the Retail Store," 50. Reporting a few years earlier, however, on women shoppers' attachment to neighborhood stores in Chicago, the sociologist Gregory Stone describes "the personalizing consumer." "Strong personal attachments were formed with store personnel, and this personal relationship, often approaching intimacy, was crucial to her patronage of a store. . . . Her conception of a 'good' clerk was one who treated her in a personal, relatively intimate manner." Gregory Stone, "City Shoppers and Urban Identification: Observations on the Social Psychology of City Life," *American Journal of Sociology* 60, no. 1 (July 1954): 36–45, passage quoted on 40.

43. Labor costs: Arthur I. Cohen and Ana Loud Jones, "Brand Marketing in the New Retail Environment," *Harvard Business Review*, September–October 1978: 141–48. "Push-button shopping," "services, fashion, and prestige": Malcolm P. McNair and Eleanor G. May, "The Next Revolution of the Retailing Wheel," *Harvard Business Review*, September–October 1978: 81–91. "Push-button shopping": cited from Alton F. Doody and William R. Davidson, "Next Revolution in Retailing," *Harvard Business Review*, May–June 1967. The first writer to popularize the idea of push-button shopping done at the shopper's convenience was not a business professor, but the science fiction writer Isaac Asimov.

44. Sold same products: Cohen and Jones, "Brand Marketing in the New Retail Environment," 142.

45. One of the first American retailers: Benetton, the Italian designer and manufacturer of casual clothes, was surely a model for The Gap's branded stores, but for many years Benetton organized its multinational chain of stores as franchises, which allowed for more individual variability. See my *Landscapes of Power*, 43–44.

46. Gap history and Drexler's career: *Stores*, November 1985, 95–99, and December 1989, 21; "Millard S. Drexler," *1993 Current Biography Yearbook*, ed. Judith Graham (New York: H. W. Wilson, 1993), 167–71; and The Gap, financial disclosure statements, U.S. Securities and Exchange Commission, 1985–1998.

47. "$2.5 billion empire": "Millard S. Drexler," *1993 Current Biography Yearbook*, 167.

48. "World of meaning": writing just before the rise of branded stores, the anthropologist Grant McCracken says that fashion designers create a universe of meaning in each seasonal collection, but they are able to control the meaning of their designs *only in a few situations*, such as the "highly managed, rhetorical circumstances" of "meaning-giving context[s]" like trade shows and advertisements. *Culture and Consumption* (Bloomington: Indiana University Press, 1986), 82. "Only tangible experience": Andrew P. Mooney, president of Disney Consumer Products Worldwide, quoted in Bruce Orwall, "Disney's Magic Transformation?" *Wall Street Journal*, October 4, 2000. "Meanings" here refers to a meeting point of producers' and consumers' imaginations, not to the meanings consumers autonomously create.

49. The United States was first: Thomas J. Schlereth, "Country Stores, County Fairs,

and Mail Order Catalogues: Consumption in Rural America," in *Consuming Visions*, ed. Simon J. Bronner (New York: Norton, 1989), 363. The great department stores: "By 1915 it was *de rigeur* for theater owners, restaurateurs, and department store retailers to design adult fantasy environments" (William Leach, *Land of Desire: Merchants, Power, and the Rise of a New American Culture* (New York: Pantheon, 1993, 82). "Atmospherics": Philip Kotler, "Atmospherics as a Marketing Tool," *Journal of Retailing* 49, no. 4 (1974): 48–64.

50. Overcomes our resistance: according to the retail consultant Paco Underhill, in *Why We Buy*, most decisions to buy are made at the POP, the point of purchase, within a store.

51. "Consumes the consumer": Jody Patraka, "Foreword," in Martin M. Pegler, *Lifestyle Stores* (Glen Cove, N.Y.: PBC International, 1996), 9.

52. "Movie of life": Neil Gabler, *Life: The Movie; How Entertainment Conquered Reality* (New York: Vintage, 1998).

53. "In better malls": Pegler, *Lifestyle Stores*, see pages on Domain chain of furniture stores. "Faustian bargain": Goldberger, "The Store Strikes Back," 45.

54. "Memorable" experience: B. Joseph Pine II and James H. Gilmore, *The Experience Economy* (Cambridge: Harvard Business School Press, 1999). In their framework, "the progression of economic value" proceeds in historical stages from fungible commodities to tangible goods, intangible services, and "memorable experiences."

55. Club Monaco: "Can Ralph Turn a Tiny Monaco into His Own Republic?" *Women's Wear Daily*, March 3, 1999.

56. "If you're going to be public," "they want growth": "Can Ralph Turn a Tiny Monaco into His Own Republic?"

57. If you could buy them at Sears: an interesting case of these conflicts of values arose when the Calvin Klein Trademark Trust sued Linda Wachner, the CEO of Warnaco, for diluting the value of the Calvin Klein brand by selling Calvin Klein jeans, which Warnaco manufactured on license, in "price-conscious retailers like Sam's and BJ's Wholesale Club Inc." According to Calvin Klein, selling their jeans in these stores "cement[ed] the decline of the Klein brand from elite to mass market," and violated the terms of their contract (Leslie Kaufman, "Calvin Klein-Warnaco License Trial Finally Set to Begin," *New York Times*, January 19, 2001). The lawsuit was settled at the very last minute, on the morning the trial was to begin (*New York Times*, January 2, 2001). Within the year, Wachner was ousted by Warnaco's board. Of course, you can buy some brand names at discount stores, and Target has made a promotional strategy of selling designer names from Michael Graves's housewares to Massimo jeans.

58. "A perfected version": *Kansas City Star*, January 12, 2001.

59. Hickey-Freeman: *DNR* (*Daily News Record*), November 29, 2000.

60. Banana Republic: *Financial Times* (U.S. edition), October 6, 2000.

61. Begin to look déclassé: Bagli, "As Retail Space Grows." Neglect to develop new producers: Bruce Orwall, "Disney's Magic Transformation?" *Wall Street Journal*, October 4, 2000. Nike's: Gina Binole, "Nike Reinvents Brand with Outlet Strategy," *Business Journal-Portland [Oregon]*, March 27, 1998.

chapter 9: the zen of internet shopping

1. Shopping for electronics: according to market research, 30 percent of the PCs bought by American households are bought directly from the manufacturer, and many of these are bought online. Steve Lohr, "The Web Hasn't Replaced the

Storefront Quite Yet," *New York Times*, October 3, 1999. Recent surveys also show that the websites of computer manufacturers (Hewlett Packard, Apple, Dell) consistently appear among the top ten retail websites. "Top 10 Retail Sites March," Jupiter Research (http://www. jmm.com/xp/jmm/press/reports/featured-DataAndResearch_05142001.xml#4, accessed March 3, 2002).

2. Same number . . . share files: "The Holidays Online," http://www.pewinternet. org/reports, January 1, 2002, accessed March 28, 2002. According to this study, the twenty-six million who make a purchase or share files represent only 4 percent of the sixty-four million Americans who access the Internet each day.

3. GUI browsers: Robert X. Cringely, "Valley of the Nerds," http://www.pbs.org/cringely/pulpit/pulpit19981210.html, December 10, 1998, accessed May 17, 2002.

4. Twenty-six million people: according to "Holiday 2001online shopping: Results," at Jupiter Research (http://www.jmm.com/xp/jmmpress/2002/pr_010702.xml, accessed May 21, 2002). Jupiter Research estimates that this number rose to thirty-four million in 2000 and fifty-one million in 2001.

5. More logical to navigate: though many of us don't remember the early days, the reviews, including instructions, published in the "premiere issue" of *Internet Shopper* (spring 1997), an offline magazine I bought at a newsstand in La Guardia Airport several years ago, show how hard it was to navigate most retail sites during the Internet's first few years. Automation at the warehouse: see Malcolm Gladwell, "Annals of Retail: Clicks & Mortar," *The New Yorker*, December 6, 1999, 106–15.

6. The more we buy: Matt Hyde, vice president of online sales for Recreational Equipment Inc., quoted in Bob Tedeschi, "E-Commerce Report," *New York Times*, March 13, 2000, and Jupiter Research report, "File Sharing: To Preserve Market Value, Look beyond Easy Scapegoats," May 13, 2002, cited in "Congressman Rick Boucher to Challenge Music Industry on Digital Anti-Piracy Technologies at Seventh Annual Jupiter and Billboard Plug.In," http://www.jmm. com/xp/jmmpress/2002/pr_051302. xml, accessed May 23, 2002.

7. The closest match: Michelle Slatalla, "Online Shopper: Dream Car, Dream Colors? A Dream Indeed," *New York Times*, March 28, 2002.

8. Making the purchase: Robert LaRose, "On the Negative Effects of E-Commerce: A Sociocognitive Exploration of Unregulated On-Line Buying," http://www. ascusc.org/jcmc/vol6/issue3/larose.html, April 2001, accessed April 24, 2002.

9. "Flow experience": Joshua Quittner, "An Eye on the Future" (Jeff Bezos), *Time*, December 27, 1999, 59.

10. Bayesian statistics: Thomas Bayes was an eighteenth-century minister and mathematician who devised formulas for calculating probabilities.

11. "Ease of the shopping experience": Michelle Slatalla, "Online Shopper: Book Bargains to Warm a Mommy's Heart," *New York Times*, May 16, 2002. She was actually looking for used copies of mystery books at cheap prices, but, allowing herself to be led by the software, she wound up buying two used books and preordering a not-yet-published book by the same author at full price. Impulse buy: "On the Negative Effects of E-Commerce."

12. "Any reasonable girl": Kim France, quoted in Alex Kuczynski, "A New Magazine Celebrates the Rites of Shopping," *New York Times*, May 8, 2000, emphasis in original. "Actionable": Stacy Lastrina quoted in David Carr, "Magazine Imitates a Catalog and Has a Charmed Life, So Far," *New York Times*, September 16, 2002. "You can have it": Martha Nelson, quoted in David Carr, "In Style's World of Fashion," *New York Times*, February 15, 2002.

13. "Very egalitarian": also Kim France, speaking of Japanese, youth-oriented fashion magazines, in Guy TreBay, "Tokyo Street Fashion in New York Bows to No

Horizon," *New York Times*, May 23, 2000. Just us shoppers: In *The Social Life of Information* (Boston: Harvard Business School Press, 2000), John S. Brown and Paul Duguid argue that "disintermediation" on the Internet is a sham; behind the seemingly direct presentation of electronic data stand people and institutions that shape it. More dramatically, this is the message of the *Matrix* movies.

14. Negative reviews: LaRose, "On the Negative Effects of E-Commerce," makes the same point. Number one: Amazon recently got the highest score of any company on the University of Michigan's consumer satisfaction index, which I take to reflect not only the company's fast deliveries and excellent customer service but also the quality of the website (*Marketplace: Morning Report*, National Public Radio, February 19, 2002).

15. More than half: "Holiday Shopping Online."

16. Slow to start using bots: Erin White, "No Comparison," *Wall Street Journal*, October 23, 2000. Only 4 percent: according to the CEO of DealTime.com, quoted in Bob Tedeschi, "E-Commerce Report: Comparison-Shopping Sites Have Felt the Shakeout but Hope That a Diversified Source of Revenues May Serve as a Buffer," *New York Times*, February 5, 2001.

17. "More elaborate search," price-matching strategies: Hal R. Varian, "Market Structure in the Network Age," April 1999, http://www.sims.berkeley.edu/~hal/Papers/doc/doc.doc, accessed March 15, 2002.

18. A third: 32 percent of survey respondents said they did at least some of their online holiday shopping at work in 2001, compared with 26 percent a year earlier ("The Holidays Online"). "24/7 bazaar": Larry Downes, quoted in Denise Caruso, "Digital Commerce," *New York Times*, May 22, 1999.

19. Broadband users: "The Broadband Difference: How Online Americans' Behavior Changes With High-Speed Internet Connections at Home," http://www.pewinternet.org/ reports, June 23, 2002.

20. Ninety-four billion ads a year: according to a survey by Nielsen/Net Ratings, cited in Bob Tedeschi, "E-Commerce Report," *New York Times*, June 24, 2002.

21. Bezos: Quittner, "An Eye on the Future," 63–64.

22. "Internet is the future," "readable on the Internet": Ginia Bellafante, "Front Row," *New York Times*, April 24, 2001.

23. Style365.com: "The Link to Glamour," *New York Times*, February 8, 2000.

24. "Stately Tuareg and Songhay people": http://www.style365.com/lounge/feature.jhtml?featureID=124491, accessed February 9, 2000.

25. Visit fewer sites: Amy Harmon, "Exploration of World Wide Web Tilts from Eclectic to Mundane," *New York Times*, August 26, 2001. New users less affluent: "Holiday 2001 Online shopping: Results." Small number of "platforms": as Brown and Duguid (*The Social Life of Information*, 28) say, "Where it does occur, disintermediation doesn't necessarily do away with intermediaries but it just puts it into fewer hands with a larger grasp. Moreover this kind of limited disintermediation often tends to a centralization of control."

26. Richer and poorer: "Top 10 Retail Sites March."

27. "Typical programmer's view": Adam Cohen, "The Attic of e," *Time*, December 27, 1999, 79.

28. Most eBay managers, from "collectibles marketplace" to compete with Wal-Mart: Eryn Brown, "How Can a Dot-Com Be This Hot?" *Fortune*, January 21, 2002, 78–84. "Global garage sale": Cohen, "The Attic of e," 79.

29. Japanese blended yarn: Karen Kaplan, "Online Shopper: Oh, What a Tangled Web We Weave in Search of Rare Yarn," *Los Angeles Times*, January 3, 2002.

30. Souvenir, collector, producer: Susan Stewart, *On Longing: Narratives of the*

Miniature, the Gigantic, the Souvenir, the Collection (Baltimore: Johns Hopkins University Press, 1984). "It's about learning": Newell Turner, "EBay Addicts: Playing It Straight," *House & Garden,* October 1999, 34.

31. "The sweet honesty": Gregory Cerio, "EBay Addicts: The Miseducation of a Gentleman," *House & Garden,* October 1999, 34.

32. Authentic experience: similarly, in *The Tourist* (New York: Schocken, 1976), Dean MacCannell says of authentic tourist attractions: "A defining quality of a true attraction is its removal from the realm of the commercial where it is firmly anchored outside of historical time in the system of modern values" (157). But it's peculiar to the modern world to shift objects and experiences back and forth between the material and symbolic worlds (145).

33. Constantly trying out: but they know they can't confuse or annoy eBay subscribers by making too many changes too fast. Colin Berry, "Ebay under Construction," *Edesign,* March–April 2002, 82–85.

34. "Number of bids tripled": Jennifer S. Lee, "ABC's of EBay: Auction, Bid and Conquer," *New York Times,* June 14, 2001.

35. "24/7": Larry Downs, quoted in "Digital Commerce." "Perfect store": Adam Cohen, *The Perfect Store: Inside eBay* (Boston: Little, Brown, 2002). "Rapid retreat . . . truly global": James Gleick, "Stop Me Before I Shop Again!" *The New Yorker,* May 24, 1999.

36. eBabes: Brown, "How Can a Dot-Com Be This Hot?" "Take a look around your house": Marsha Collier, Roland Woerner, and Stephanie Becker, *eBay for Dummies,* 2d ed. (New York: Hungry Minds/John Wiley, 2000), 9.

37. Twin Towers: "EBay Is Asked to Remove Trade Center Items," *New York Times,* February 22, 2002. Malcolm X: Emily Eakin, "Malcolm X Family Fights Auction of Papers," *New York Times,* March 7, 2002. Argentina: *Marketplace: Morning Report,* National Public Radio, February 4, 2002. Also see "For Auction Online: Enron's Memos," *New York Times,* February 18, 2002 and Carey Goldberg, "On Web, Models Auction Their Eggs to Bidders for Beautiful Children," *New York Times,* October 23, 1999. Defeat: Tamar Lewin, "Online Bid Is Made, Briefly, to Save Dartmouth's Swim Team from Budget Cuts," *New York Times,* December 6, 2002; Bridgeville reported in *Marketplace: Morning Report,* National Public Radio, December 25, 2002. Bridgeville may be more complicated than it appears; the town was owned before this point by a woman who lived there.

38. "Nation of collectors": Andrew Ferguson, "Auction Nation," *Time,* December 27, 1999, 86.

39. "Monuments of stupidity": Christos Cotsakos, quoted in "E*Trade Considers Offering Advice," *Wall Street Journal,* June 12, 2002.

chapter 10: zagats "r" us

1. "Eating, drinking, procreating": Karl Marx, *Economic and Philosophical Manuscripts of 1844,* in *The Marx-Engels Reader,* ed. Robert C. Tucker (New York: Norton, 1972), 60. Than their European counterparts: Werner Sombart, *Why Is There No Socialism in the United States?,* ed. C. T. Husbands (White Plains, N.Y.: M. E. Sharpe, 1976 [1906]).

2. "Manufactured" on the job: Michael Burawoy, *Manufacturing Consent: Changes in the Labor Process under Monopoly Capitalism* (Chicago: University of Chicago Press, 1979).

3. Invoke a consensus: Lizabeth Cohen, *A Consumers' Republic: The Politics of Mass*

Consumption in Postwar America (New York: Knopf, 2003). Without really thinking about it: the ability of consumption not only to rationalize but to naturalize the "rules of the market" is nicely worked out by Bertell Ollman, "Market Mystification in Capitalist and Market Socialist Societies," *Socialism and Democracy*, fall 1997, 1–45.

4. Narrow our focus: dating the origins of consumer society in terms of public attitudes and culture has been the subject of much lively debate among social historians; it becomes a political question when economists and politicians question the public's willingness to save rather than consume. See John Levi Martin, "The Myth of the Consumption-Oriented Economy and the Rise of the Desiring Subject," *Theory and Society* 28 (1999): 425–53. Buy a suit: the brief but, to me, classic statement about the role of mass-produced goods in inspiring modern attitudes is John Berger's essay "The Suit and the Photograph," in *About Looking* (New York: Pantheon, 1980), 27–36.

5. "Gastronomic texts": Priscilla Parkhurst Ferguson, "A Cultural Field in the Making: Gastronomy in 19th-Century France," *American Journal of Sociology* 104 (1998): 597–641, quotation on 600. "Celestial": Burton Anderson, "Tartufi Bianchi d'Alba: Roving with the Spirits of the Night," in *Treasures of the Italian Table* (New York: William Morrow, 1994), 21.

6. "So many things": Daniel J. Boorstin, *The Americans: The Democratic Experience* (New York: Random House, 1973), 90.

7. Gave marketers a handle: for a workmanlike approach, see the articles in William D. Wells, ed., *Life Style and Psychographics* (Chicago: American Marketing Association, 1974).

8. "Creative consumers": Emanuel H. Demby, "Psychographics and from Whence It Came," in Wells, ed., *Life Style and Psychographics*, 11–30, at 14–15.

9. Arbiters of distinction: Pierre Bourdieu, *Distinction: A Social Critique of the Judgement of Taste*, trans. Richard Nice (Cambridge: Harvard University Press, 1984).

10. "Vehicles of community": Boorstin, *The Americans: The Democratic Experience*, 89.

11. Trading post: see the approaching end of the "Trading Post" feature on radio station KCLW, in Hamilton, Texas. ABC Evening News, May 18, 2003. "Total organization of everyday life": Jean Baudrillard, *The Consumer Society* (London and Thousand Oaks, Calif.: Sage, 1998 [1970]), 29. "Kind of guy": quoted in Shaila K. Dewan, "Who's 14, 'Kewl' and Flirty Online?" *New York Times*, April 7, 2003.

12. The arcades: Walter Benjamin, "Paris, Capital of the Nineteenth Century [1939]," in *The Arcades Project*, trans. Howard Eiland and Kevin McLaughlin (Cambridge, Mass.: Belknap Press, 1999), 14–26. On the collective dream, see Susan Buck-Morss, *The Dialectics of Seeing: Walter Benjamin and the Arcades Project* (Cambridge: MIT Press, 1989).

acknowledgments

This book began, like so many others, with the unanswered questions of the last one. Shopping figured prominently in *The Cultures of Cities*, which I published in 1995, though it was not the dominant theme. In that book, I looked back at the neighborhood shopping street in Philadelphia where I spent my childhood and thought about how it helped to shape my growing up as female, Jewish, and middle class. I compared it with other childhood experiences of shopping streets that appear all too rarely in the pages of memoirs and history books, and then I set these experiences alongside the history of shopping streets that had gone through serious racial change—125th Street in Harlem and Fulton Street in downtown Brooklyn. Shopping also figured in other chapters of the book, since the redevelopment of cities today is based in large part on culture and shopping—or, more precisely, on the culture of shopping.

When, shortly after *The Cultures of Cities* appeared, Roger Waldinger invited me to give the Irene Fleckner Ross lectures in the sociology department at UCLA, I decided to expand on these themes. Though the final version of this book differs markedly from those lectures, I am grateful to Roger and his colleagues for encouraging me to take the first, halting steps.

I am also grateful to the research assistants and institutions that provided me with material help. Above all, I thank Jennifer Smith Maguire, who carried out and transcribed most of the interviews with middle-class shoppers, as well as with Artemio, discussed them with me, and read my interpretations of them for accuracy and nuance. I also thank Alex Vitale, who ferreted out restaurant reviews; Miriam Greenberg, who read through the early years of *New York* magazine; and Michelle McBeth, who did a preliminary transcript of the interviews with mothers and teenagers in East New York. Their help in creating the content of this book was made more valuable by the luxury of time off from teaching to write early drafts of several chapters, and I am grateful to the Wolfe Institute for the Humanities at Brooklyn College, and its director, Robert Viscusi, for a one-year fellowship that provided me with this time. No less appreciated is a series of small PSC-CUNY faculty research grants, which enabled me to pay my research assistants.

Many thanks are due to my patient, knowledgeable, and entirely supportive editor, David McBride. A man of many parts, Dave brought to this project his intellectual sophistication, familiarity with some of the more arcane aspects of popular culture, and ability to read quickly on many levels at once. He has been totally committed to the book from the beginning.

I also want to thank the very small number of trusted friends and colleagues who read chapters of the manuscript at various stages and offered helpful advice: Naomi Schneider, whose support and encouragement were second only to Dave's, Priscilla Ferguson, Harvey Molotch, Ted Burrows, and George Ritzer. They truly deserve the author's usual, heartfelt disclaimer: this work is better for the criticism they offered and suffers to the degree that I didn't take it seriously enough.

Over the past six years, my pesky questions about shopping have driven to distraction an inordinate number of students, friends, interview respondents, and passing acquaintances. I am grateful for their willingness to tolerate and answer my questions, which must always have seemed to belabor the obvious and require them to speak aloud the unspoken assumption. I am especially grateful to the respondents who shared their shopping lives with me; though I cannot reveal their names, I hope they will see how useful their experiences are. I also want to thank my students Gina Neff, Betsy Wissinger, and Siddhartha Lokanandi, for discussing fine points of consumer culture with me (and also sharing shopping tips); my students in two seminars on cultures of consumption at the City University Graduate Center, for giving me the opportunity to try my thoughts aloud; and my friends Bertell Ollman, Paule Ollman, Daniel Miller, Katharine Moseley, James Dickinson, Marshall Berman, Michael Sorkin, Cynthia Fuchs Epstein, and Maggie Noach, for indulging me with newspaper clippings, suggestions, and conversations. Though my interpretation of shopping differs, I'm sure, from any of theirs, I have depended on their kindness in sharing their views.

I have also benefited from the opportunity to present parts of this book at conferences at the Center for Contemporary Culture in Barcelona,

University College London, and Princeton University, as well as in talks at Fordham, Northwestern, Yale, and Rutgers Universities; the University of Potsdam; and Amherst and Union Colleges. Thanks to all the folks who supported my work by listening, offering their own stories, and assuring me that studying shopping is both intellectually and politically worthwhile.

Finally, I continue to rely on the unquestioning, but not uncritical, support of Richard Rosen and Elisabeth Rosen. During the years that I worked on this book, my daughter has grown into a trenchant critic of consumer culture. As a writer, I hope that my work lives up to her critique— and as a mother, I hope that it contributes to her moral education.

New York City
April 2003

index